M000315663

Film and the
Anarchist Imagination

Film and the Anarchist Imagination

Expanded Second Edition

RICHARD PORTON

UNIVERSITY OF ILLINOIS PRESS
Urbana, Chicago, and Springfield

© 1999 by Richard Porton,
© 2020 by the Board of Trustees
of the University of Illinois.
Reprinted by arrangement with the author.
All rights reserved.
Manufactured in the United States of America
1 2 3 4 5 C P 5 4 3 2 1
∞ This book is printed on acid-free paper.

Library of Congress Cataloging-in-Publication Data
Names: Porton, Richard, author.
Title: Film and the anarchist imagination : expanded
    second edition / Richard Porton.
Description: Expanded second edition. | Urbana :
    University of Illinois Press, [2020] | Includes
    bibliographical references and index.
Identifiers: LCCN 2020006535 (print) | LCCN
    2020006536 (ebook) | ISBN 9780252043338
    (cloth) | ISBN 9780252085246 (paperback) | ISBN
    9780252052217 (ebook)
Subjects: LCSH: Anarchism in motion pictures.
Classification: LCC PN1995.9.A487 P67 2020 (print)
    | LCC PN1995.9.A487 (ebook) | DDC 791.43/658—
    dc23
LC record available at https://lccn.loc.gov/2020006535
LC ebook record available at https://lccn.loc.gov/
    2020006536

To the Memory of Jerome and Edith Porton

Contents

Acknowledgments
Second Edition

WHEN THIS PROJECT was still slated for publication by Verso, Colin Beckett agreed there was a need for a second, revised edition of *Film and the Anarchist Imagination* and provided invaluable editorial and moral support. I owe him a great debt, especially because it's unlikely that a new edition would have gotten off the ground without his input and enthusiasm. I am equally grateful that Daniel Nasset of the University of Illinois Press evinced an equal amount of enthusiasm and proved eager to publish this new edition when the need for a new publisher arose.

Without the participation of key filmmakers, an updated glimpse at twenty-first-century anarchist cinema would also have been impossible. I'm grateful for the willingness of the following individuals to share their insights, as well as links to films: Lizzie Borden, Abigail Child, the videographer known as "Heatscore," Diyar Hesso, Adam Khalil, Adam Kossoff, Bruce LaBruce, Jason Livingston, Nick Macdonald, Luis Miranda, Matt Peterson, Maple Razsa, Philip Rizk, Brett Story, Astra Taylor, Leslie Thornton, Travis Wilkerson, Amanda Rose Wilder, Pacho Velez, Huw Wahl, and Želimir Žilnik.

Pavle Levi, with his incomparable knowledge of the cinema of the former Yugoslavia, was particularly helpful in providing feedback to portions of the afterword and for arranging Skype conversations with Želimir Žilnik and Branimir Stojanovic. Stuart Christie, who has become an important advocate for anarchist cinema through his website, promptly answered queries and suggested pertinent films, especially titles addressing the legacy of the Spanish Revolution. Alexander Khost, the putative "star" of *Approaching the Elephant,* was an enthusiastic correspondent and passed on many helpful insights concerning the history of radical pedagogy in the United States.

Christopher Robé patiently answered queries concerning the state of contemporary anarchist video activism.

Several editors allowed me to try out some of my ideas at various publications—especially Gary Crowdus, my *Cineaste* colleague and the magazine's editor in chief; Mark Peranson of *Cinema Scope;* Dennis Lim, the former editor of *Moving Image Source;* and Adrian Martin of *Lola.*

Finally, the forbearance of friends, family, and colleagues, who proved invariably good-natured as I droned on about my snail-like progress on this revision, was greatly appreciated. I couldn't have done without the support of Shaista Husain, Gary Lucas, Bill and Toby Peterson, Tracy Quan, Ella Shohat, Caroline Sinclair, Leo Goldsmith, and Robert Stam, whose invitation to collaborate on *Keywords in Subversive Film/Media Aesthetics* allowed me to situate the elusive anarchist aesthetic within a broader theoretical framework.

Film and the
Anarchist Imagination

Introduction

Anarchism swept us away completely because
it both demanded everything of us and offered
everything to us. There was no remote corner of
life that it failed to illumine . . . or so it seemed
to us. . . . Shot through with contradictions,
fragmented into varieties and sub-varieties,
anarchism demanded, before anything else,
harmony between deeds and words.
—Victor Serge, *Memoirs of a Revolutionary*

IN ADDITION TO BEING the name of a political movement, "anarchism" is a time-honored epithet—a word often uttered with a derisive snort by conservatives, liberals, and mainstream leftists alike. Despite the continuing pertinence of the slogan "anarchy is not chaos," which was revived by anti-authoritarian socialists in the Soviet Union after the demise of Stalinism, the tendency to heap calumny on anarchists is at least partially the result of historical amnesia. It is all too easy to forget that anarchists have long shared the enthusiasm for working-class self-activity promoted by the First International—a movement torn famously asunder by protracted disagreement between Bakuninists and Marxists. Yet, in subsequent years, the anarchist emphasis on self-emancipation became refashioned to include far more than a promotion of proletarian consciousness; anarchists such as Emma Goldman and Francisco Ferrer extended the indivisibility of theory and practice to sexual politics, avant-garde art, and radical pedagogy—realms that the more rigid Marxist ideologues dismissed as mere frivolity or "superstructural" epiphenomena.

In the years before the first edition of this book was written, certain scholars seemed to believe that anarchism is a sub-variety of postmodernism,[1] thereby ignoring more than a hundred years of labor agitation and revolutionary struggles. *Film and the Anarchist Imagination* endeavors to demonstrate how these struggles have been both celebrated and derided by a diverse group of filmmakers. It should be noted, however, that this is not a clear-cut task; occasional references in the critical literature to a vague rubric called "anarchist cinema" only underline the nature of the definitional morass that confronts, and occasionally ensnares, critics and film historians.² Many anarchists would agree with Horkheimer and Adorno's contention that mainstream cinema—with its ludicrous caricatures of anarchism and anarchists—demonstrates the way in which the "industrial system lodges itself within men's minds." Nevertheless, while one section in this book's first chapter details the stereotypes of anarchists that permeate both Hollywood fluff and European art cinema, the bulk of this study is devoted to links between anarchist self-activity and films that not only reflect, but often actively promote, workplace resistance, anarchist pedagogy, and anti-statist insurrections. In addition, the definition of "anarchist cinema" is broadened to include discussion of films not made and produced by anarchists; well-intentioned films made by devoted anarchists are sometimes of less interest than non-anarchist works that, perhaps unwittingly, brilliantly encapsulate the anarchist amalgamation of antinomian individualism and collective direct action. This vantage point explains the rationale for including a discussion of *Tout va bien,* a film made by nominal Maoists—Jean-Luc Godard and Jean-Pierre Gorin—that possesses tangible affinities with the anarchist and libertarian Marxist promotion of self-emancipation and direct action. Similarly, the dissident Marxist Elio Petri's *The Working Class Goes to Heaven* is easily amenable to an interpretation inspired by contemporary "anti-work" proponents, while the liberal documentarian Frederick Wiseman's *High School* critiques authoritarian pedagogy with a verve that nearly equals the anti-authoritarian lyricism of Jean Vigo's *Zéro de conduite.*

Although it doubtless won't prevent the inevitable complaints about omissions, I should emphasize that this book, while attempting to be relatively comprehensive, is not meant to be encyclopedic. For those seeking a filmography, instead of an overview of selected films, I recommend one of CIRA's (Centre International de Recherches sur L'Anarchisme) useful publications: Marianne Enckell's *Les anarchistes à l'écran: Anarchists on Screen, 1901–2003* (Lausanne, 2004).

Since almost every introduction to anarchist thought begins with an admission that "because of its protean nature, it is notoriously difficult"³ to discuss systematically, a brief consideration of the most influential strands of left-libertarian thought is necessary to lay the groundwork for this study's assumption that the provocative legacy of Max Stirner, Pierre-Joseph Proudhon, Mikhail Bakunin, and Peter Kropotkin can be discerned in an important cinematic tradition.

Before anarchism became a bona fide political movement in the late nineteenth century, its theoretical birth pangs revealed a nascent chasm between an idea of freedom embedded in a concrete vision of a new society and extreme variants of what Isaiah Berlin called "negative liberty."[4] The state, whether extolled by Locke or Lenin, is therefore identified with modern bureaucratic domination.[5] Even though the protagonist of John Henry Mackay's novel *The Anarchists—A Picture of Civilization at the End of the Nineteenth Century* is an exemplar of individualist anarchism, collectivist anarchists and anarcho-communists would have few problems endorsing the hero's delineation of anarchism as "a system of society in which no one disturbs the action of his neighbor, where liberty is free from law, where there is no privilege, where force does not determine human actions."[6]

The competing varieties of anarchism endeavor to reconcile the seemingly conflicting claims of individual autonomy and collective struggle. Despite significant differences between the classical anarchists, Alan Ritter's superficially oxymoronic term "communal individuality" allows us to recognize affinities between the evolving connotations of anarchy embedded in the works—and deeds—of Proudhon, Bakunin, and Kropotkin.[7] In addition, a productive tension between individuality and communal solidarity fuels the fascinatingly contradictory work of two thinkers sometimes not considered part of mainstream anarchism—William Godwin and Max Stirner. Godwin's late-eighteenth-century magnum opus, *Enquiry Concerning Political Justice,* is a radical embellishment of the most fundamental components of Enlightenment rationalism. Despite Godwin's abhorrence of economic inequality, and his belief in the perfectibility of mankind, his individualist creed compelled him to proclaim that "everything that is usually understood by the term cooperation is in some degree an evil."[8] The contradictions embraced by Godwin manifest themselves in a more audacious theoretical stance in Stirner's radical egoism—an intriguingly eccentric offshoot of Young Hegelianism[9]—that still proves unsettling for anarchists today. George Woodcock, for example, claims that Stirner, the most radical of nineteenth-century Young Hegelians, wrote in a turgid style, and influenced "only a few small marginal groups of individualists,"[10] while Daniel Guérin praises Stirner for his lively, "aphoristic" prose and argues that Bakunin's belief in unfettered liberty retains a Stirnerian residue, despite the Bakuninist contempt for "bourgeois individualism."[11]

Stirner is an unavoidable irritant for many anarchists, since his eagerness to negate bourgeois morality appeals to many of them, while his contempt for communal endeavors smacks more of Ayn Rand–style right-wing liber-

tarianism than the mainstream anarchist tradition. Finding links between
Stirner's near-monadic conception of the individual and subsequent syndicalist and anarcho-communist tendencies that are contingent upon collective
struggle presents considerable, although not insurmountable, difficulties.
Stirner's paeans to undiluted individuality proved especially indigestible for
many socialists and anarcho-communists: maintaining an uneasy equilibrium between the often antithetical needs of the individual and the collective
has provided anarchism with some of its thorniest theoretical quandaries.
Emma Goldman's useful distinction between anarchist "individuality" and
reactionary "rugged individualism—. . . a masked attempt to repress and
defeat the individual and his individuality"[12] effectively preserved the radical core of Stirner's individualist hostility toward the state while simultaneously preventing his notoriously vague sentiments from congealing into a
conservative dithyramb to narcissistic insularity. It is difficult to deny that
the anticlericalism and disdain for conventional moral strictures evinced
by Stirner in his alternately fascinating and infuriating individualist tirade
Der Einzige und sein Eigentum (known in English as *The Ego and Its Own,*
although *The Unique One and His Property* would be a more accurate translation) has certain affinities with the polemical wrath of Bakunin's *God and
the State* or Goldman's assault on hidebound sexual morality. And Stirner's
diffuse, nonlinear argument, like the radical disdain for systematization
evinced by subsequent philosophers such as Nietzsche and Wittgenstein, can
be pilfered with creative abandon by both idealists and materialists, radicals
and conservatives.[13] Guerin argues cogently that *Der Einzige*'s individualist
creed in fact contains a prescient critique of authoritarian communism, even
if this left-libertarian interpretation of radical egoism is difficult to reconcile
with Stirner's assertion that he does "not want the liberty of men, nor their
equality, only . . . power over them."[14]

    In the work of subsequent activists and theorists, Stirner's anti-bourgeois
sentiments are channeled into a positive vision—"a strategy for change
involving immediate institution of non-coercive, non-authoritarian, and
de-centralist alternatives."[15] Like Stirner's daunting corpus, the work of
Pierre-Joseph Proudhon, usually credited as the first writer to use the word
"anarchy" in a positive sense, highlights the fact that the anarchist "classics"
must be creatively and, above all, selectively appropriated. Anarchist texts
have rarely been taken as gospel truth by adherents of anti-authoritarianism,
and it is emblematic of anarchist diversity that Proudhon's scattershot mode
of theorizing inspired some commentators to hail him as the progenitor of
the anarchist tradition of self-management, while many Marxists and some
anarchists dismiss "Proudhonism" as petty-bourgeois at best, and, at worst,

irredeemably sullied by misogyny and anti-Semitism. There is more than a grain of truth in both diagnoses, and the task of extracting what is still valid in Proudhon from the dross of his more crackpot formulations has been recognized as an arduous one by most commentators. George Woodcock, Richard Sonn, and Peter Marshall all describe Proudhonian anarchism as paradoxical, and E. H. Carr merely states the obvious when he observes that Proudhon's opinions, like those of Bakunin, were in a perpetual state of flux.[16]

Proudhonian anarchism champions multiple agents of historical trans-formation—small artisans and individual proprietors as well as industrial workers. His advocacy of gradualist mutualism (a doctrine linking anarchism with the activities of workers' and artisans' participation in decentralized co-operatives) stands in sharp contrast to the subsequent emphasis on anarchist insurrection promulgated by Bakunin, Elisée Reclus, and Errico Malatesta. Unlike later versions of collectivist anarchism and anarcho-communism, as well as, of course, Marxism, Proudhon's final writings on mutualism retain a version of the market economy and an ideology that consolidates the interests of the petty-bourgeoisie and the proletariat.

If Proudhon's anarchism seems occasionally limited by its French parochi-alism, Mikhail Bakunin's considerably more militant revolutionary passions are as deeply rooted in nineteenth-century Russian radical traditions. As Franco Venturi's magisterial *Roots of Revolution* makes clear, an understand-ing of Bakunin's great debt to nineteenth-century Russian populism is es-sential to comprehending what eventually becomes the Bakuninist version of anarchy. Like the great liberal Alexander Herzen (whose thought was tinged with more than a little anti-authoritarianism) and the authoritarian neo-Jacobin populist Peter Nikitich Tkachev, Bakunin had a great political and emotional investment in the Russian tradition of the *obshchina*—agrarian communities that, once "detach[ed] from the feudal society of which they formed a part," could "become the basis of a social order founded on the universal right of humanity to the necessities of life."[17] Bakunin's transmuta-tion of the Russian obshchina or *Mir* (agricultural community), purged of its Tsarist heritage and transformed into the ideal of the autonomous commune, accounts for his devout, un-Marxist faith in the peasantry's revolutionary potential. He was well aware, however, of the authoritarianism inherent in traditional agricultural communities, observing that "the power and the arbitrary bureaucratic will of the state is hated by the people and the revolt against this power and its arbitrary will is at the same time a revolt against the despotism of the rural community and of the *Mir*."[18]

Unlike Godwin or Proudhon, Bakunin's anarchism is difficult to extricate from his revolutionary activism. In the mid nineteenth century, Bakunin emerges as something like the Johnny Appleseed of European anarchist revolt, lending his support to uprisings in Prague in 1848, Dresden in 1849 (his participation in the insurrection earned him eight years in Austrian and Russian prisons), and spreading his doctrines to Italy, Switzerland, France, and, through his emissary, Giuseppe Fanelli, to Spain. Bakunin is often caricatured as an apostle of violence, and a sentiment from his pre-anarchist essay *The Reaction in Germany* (1842)—"the passion for destruction is a creative passion"—is too often cited as an anarchist tenet, rather than as a prolegomenon to a more constructive vision of decentralized federalism—"a free grouping of individuals into communities, of communities into provinces, provinces into nations, and lastly, nations into united States, first of Europe, then of the whole world."[19] The disparity between an anarchist concept of social revolution and supposedly more pragmatic varieties of radicalism became most acute during the Marx–Bakunin debates of the International Working Men's Association (usually referred to as the First International). Anarchist commentators view the widening schism between Marx and Bakunin during the 1870s as the first volley in the battle between "anarchist socialism and state socialism,"[20] while Bakunin's detractors insist that his warnings concerning the hierarchical potential of Marxist theory are sullied by "an overestimation of the potency of revolutionary will among society's lower depths and outcasts."[21] Marx thought that the future of socialism resided in the strength of an advanced industrial proletariat in countries, most notably England and Germany, that had weathered full-scale capitalist development. For several historians, however, the Bakuninist synthesis of the interests of the proletariat, the peasantry, and so-called déclassé elements despised by Marx looks forward to the works of Frantz Fanon.[22] The split within the First International laid the groundwork for a series of continuing polemics between anarchists who feared that Marxism was doomed to succumb to either the Scylla of tepid parliamentarianism or the Charybdis of totalitarian socialism, and Marxists who believed that the anarchist enthusiasm for social revolution was a foolishly voluntarist preoccupation that neglected economic realities.

Bakunin never met Peter Kropotkin, the last great representative of classical anarchism, but Bakuninist collectivism and Kropotkin's anarchist communism are intimately, even symbiotically, linked. A caricature of Bakunin as an anti-intellectual devotee of violence and Kropotkin as a saintly proponent of harmonious cooperation has gradually faded in the light of later scholarship. Even though Kropotkin's posthumous reputation is for an antipathy to violence, he pondered the efficacy of peasant revolts during his youthful membership in the Bakuninist Chaikovsky Circle and qualified his opposition to terrorism with the caveat that it might be useful in "exceptional instances when it provides a great stimulus for the revolutionary arousal of the masses."[23] Kropotkin's eventual critique of a "doctrinaire collectivism . . . which envisaged only the collectivization of the means of production" and subsequent embrace of a communal idea that promoted the "socialization of all wealth"[24] can be considered an enhancement, rather than an outright rejection, of the Bakuninist tradition.

Remembered today primarily for his contribution to anarchist theory and practice, Kropotkin was equally renowned during his life as a geographer and zoologist. His forays into anarchist theory were frequently augmented by auxiliary scientific inquiries, and the gist of what could be termed Kropotkin's philosophical anthropology is compressed in his erudite refutation of social Darwinism, *Mutual Aid*. *Mutual Aid*'s thesis is unquestionably out of step with contemporary political theory, since it ultimately implies that cooperation, the linchpin of Kropotkinite anarcho-communism, is rooted biologically in the human species, despite an equally vital strain of ruthless competitiveness that has, of course, often culminated in war. "Mutual aid" is located within the animal kingdom, extolled as the basis of harmony between members of preindustrial societies (labeled "savages," an appellation that was employed even by radicals in 1902), and hailed as the impetus for the medieval city's network of guilds and cooperative federations. It would be easy to deride Kropotkin's vision as a naively essentialist inversion of the Hobbesian tradition, and his adherence to an unyieldingly optimistic view of human nature deserves to be treated skeptically during an era when the concept of human nature itself is often assumed to be moribund.[25] But even if *Mutual Aid*'s synthesis of philosophy and historiography is found deficient, much of Kropotkin's social theory, particularly *The Conquest of Bread* and *Fields, Factories, and Workshops*, reflects an eminently practical approach to decentralized agricultural and industrial production.[26]

The splintering of the anarchist left, reminiscent in some respects of the balkanization of Marxism, has naturally led to a considerable amount of internecine dissension. Yet the tensions between individualist anarchism, anarcho-syndicalism, and anarchist communism bring to mind the "family resemblances" that Wittgenstein claims unite the disparate linguistic and social practices he labels language games—"a complicated network of similarities overlapping and crisscrossing."[27] Traces of all of these anarchist sub-varieties can be located in mainstream, documentary, and avant-garde films. Attempts have been made to isolate modernism or avant-gardism as intrinsically anarchist aesthetic choices,[28] but Ken Loach's *Land and Freedom*, despite its realistic aesthetic and its screenwriter's ties to Trotskyism, is as much a part of the anarchist cinematic tradition as an incendiary surrealist film such as Luis Buñuel's *L'Âge d'or*. *Film and the Anarchist Imagination* does not propose a Manichean division between "retrograde" and "progressive" styles of filmmaking. Even though the first chapter begins with a discussion of the ideological obfuscation that allows certain directors to reduce anarchism to a few stereotypical quirks, this study is chiefly concerned with films that explore and promote anarchist self-activity.

In the years since the first edition of this book was published in 1999, the so-called "post-anarchist" turn has posed a challenge, in both activist and academic circles, to the canonical anarchism of Proudhon, Bakunin, and Kropotkin. In its most hyperbolic form, "post-anarchism" is informed by Todd May's claim that post-structuralism is more "consistently anarchist than traditional anarchist theory has proved to be."[29] In a more restrained version of the post-anarchist creed, Saul Newman maintains that it "does not, in any sense, refer to a superseding or moving beyond of anarchism . . . yet it contends that this project is best formulated today through a different conceptualization of subjectivity and politics: one that is no longer founded on essentialist notions of human nature or the unfolding of an immanent social rationality."[30] In addition, post-anarchists such as May and Tadzio Mueller object to classical anarchism's emphasis on hopes for a transformative, "cataclysmic" concept of revolution and instead laud the potential for radical actions generated by "communities of resistance."[31]

A certain amount of gentle pushback is evident in a few commentators' efforts to puncture post-anarchist claims that classical anarchist thought, however defined, is hopelessly retrograde. Allan Antliff,[32] for example, argues that Emma Goldman's conception of liberation was not contingent upon a naive essentialism that implies a priori human goodness. Similarly, Ruth Kinna's defense of Kropotkin is sufficiently nuanced to account for the fact that, although the apostle of anarcho-communism believed that "revolution was necessary," he also insisted that it was a work in progress as much as a cataclysmic event; and its success depends centrally on the extent to which individuals" are "able to seize initiatives and act for themselves."[33]

In an afterword written especially for this edition, films are featured that illustrate how Kropotkin's injunction to "seize initiatives" is congruent with forms of direct action practiced by participants in contemporary social movements. The concept of mutual aid is of paramount importance to the Croatian anarchists chronicled in Maple Razsa and Pacho Velez's *Bastards of Utopia*. Kropotkin's prescient condemnation of the nineteenth-century prison system, moreover, is surprisingly pertinent to a cycle of films excoriating police violence and the ongoing prison-industrial complex. In many respects, the "micro-politics" advocated by twenty-first-century anarchists was foreseen by a classical anarchism that is too glibly dismissed as irredeemably mired in Enlightenment humanism.

1. Anarchism and Cinema

Representation and Self-Representation

Film and the "Anarchist Peril"

It is not at all surprising that anarchism has been marginalized by mainstream historians. The cliché "hidden from history" has rarely been more apt. Historians often reduce anarchist history to a series of sterile platitudes, and it would be foolish to expect filmmakers to depart from the stereotypes and half-truths that pepper seemingly reputable texts, whether by unabashedly conservative writers or the estimable Marxist historian Eric Hobsbawm.[1] Before proceeding to nuanced historical films that fulfill Robert Rosenstone's injunction to "interrogate the past for the sake of the present, creating a historical world complex enough so that it overflows with meaning; so that its meanings are always multiple,"[2] the task of dealing with films whose vision of anarchism is often laughably unsubtle becomes unavoidable.

From early cinema to the present, the demonization of anarchist protagonists is evident in films made by both commercial hacks and auteurs with more rarefied sensibilities. But, in a manner that parallels discussions of stereotypes of ethnic and racial groups in films, a "binarism" that thinks only in terms of positive and negative images fails to convey historical and aesthetic fluctuations that determine how stereotypes are formed.[3] In ways that are strikingly similar to Bryan Cheyette's mapping of "constructions of "the Jew" in English literature and society, the inept and often hilarious efforts to depict anarchists on screen "resulted in a bewildering variety of contradictory and over-determined representations."[4] And, echoing the racist typologies of African Americans detailed by Henry Louis Gates Jr.,[5] malicious portrayals of anarchists were often coterminous with, not discouraged by, the supposedly rational discourses of science and reason bequeathed to us by the Enlightenment. Like the so-called "atavistic races" stigmatized by eugenicists and criminologists—the Irish, Jews, the unemployed, criminals, and the insane"[6]—the vast majority of anarchists in commercial films are associated with irrationality and violence.

Since anarchism first became a tangible political philosophy, anarchists have voiced outrage at their foes' attempts to stereotype them as maniacal renegades. Marcus Graham's pained observation that "according to the picture painted by the intellectual hirelings of capitalism, the philosophy of anarchism" is reducible to "assassination, bomb throwing and violence"[7] typifies many of his comrades' oft-expressed anger, even if verbal fusillades have done little to counteract the popular image of anarchists as impetuous hotheads. Films have often invoked the bearded, usually foreign-born, anarchist terrorist as the quintessential agent of chaos. Yet the fascination of the many cinematic depictions of anarchist protagonists, as well as of films merely peppered with brief but suggestive allusions to anarchism, lies in their ability to offer a funhouse mirror image of common political and social anxieties. A bomb inadvertently lobbed into Buster Keaton's buggy in *Cops* (1922) by a black-clad, hirsute anarchist is paradoxically double edged—the film participates in the usual demonization of anarchist terrorism while allowing the resourceful Buster unwittingly to disturb the peace at a parade attended by throngs of policemen and stuffy dignitaries.[8] Similarly, the eponymous press magnate in *Citizen Kane* (1941) can think of no more heinous epithet with which to smear a man suspected of murder than "anarchist," even though the audience is simultaneously aware that Kane's own unscrupulousness nullifies his ability to make reasoned political judgments. As in many films, the odiousness of the accuser exceeds the sting of the accusation.

This sort of double vision is particularly observable in allegorical films that either deal with or were produced during periods of political repression. In Brazilian filmmaker Glauber Rocha's *Terra em Transe* (*Land in Anguish*, 1967), for example, the condemnation by his enemies of the protagonist, Paulo Martins, as an "anarchist" is more an indictment of the tortured hero's neo-fascist and reactionary populist adversaries—and former allies—than of anarchism itself. In a parallel vein, during the transitional Soviet cinema of the *glasnost* years, the authoritarianism of state socialism began to be undermined by some influential directors. This is especially true of Tengiz Abuladze's *Repentance* (1986), a film in which Varlam Aravidze, the dictatorial mayor and thinly disguised Stalin surrogate, attacks an artist named Baratoli as an "anarchist" whose work is a "shameful blot" on Soviet culture;

in this context, "anarchism" comes to epitomize the full range of aesthetic and political options that Stalinism sought to obliterate. In a much less focused manner, the decision of an impulsive elderly bank robber named Jose to style himself an anarchist in Marcelo Piñeyro's *Caballos Salvajes* (*Wild Horses,* 1995) is an implicit rebuke to the murderous repression suffered by many Argentinian citizens during the reign of the military junta. At times, what seems to be a flippant reference to anarchism has more far-reaching implications. The kindly father in Clarence Brown's adaptation of Eugene O'Neill's *Ah, Wilderness* (1935), who playfully taunts his mildly rebellious son with the label "anarchist," serves as a subtle reminder of the fact that the playwright was on intimate terms with prominent anarchists such as Emma Goldman and Hippolyte Havel. O'Neill's familiarity with anarchism, humorously submerged in *Ah, Wilderness,* is conspicuous in *The Iceman Cometh* (1940), and in John Frankenheimer's faithful cinematic adaptation (1973): the melancholy Larry Slade was closely modeled on the individualist anarchist Terry Carlin, and the agitated bohemian Hugo Kalmar is a rather nasty caricature of Hippolyte Havel.[9]

Unlike O'Neill, most filmmakers usually proffer de-historicized versions of anarchism, which nurture specific agendas that have little to do with historical reality. It is important to remember, nonetheless, that hyperbolic images of anarchist terrorists, conspicuous in both Hollywood and European cinema, from the early work of Edwin S. Porter and D. W. Griffith to the apparently more sophisticated films of European cineastes such as Claude Chabrol and Bertrand Tavernier, do not exist in a vacuum. For this reason, a brief historical excursus is necessary to explain the staying power of the wild-eyed, homicidal anarchist as a popular cinematic stereotype.

A series of inadequately understood events from the late nineteenth century continue to fuel distorted views of anarchism and anarchists. The most powerful sources of anti-anarchist literature and cinema probably lie in two interrelated traumas from the late nineteenth century that still reverberate in our own era: the brief, but spectacularly ill-fated, alliance of Bakunin and Sergei Nechaev in 1869–1870 and, some years later, the popular misinterpretation of Malatesta and Paul Brousse's doctrine of "propaganda by the deed"[10] as a justification for random acts of terror. To be sure, the recent stereotype of the anarchist activist encompasses a somewhat more subtle, if equally insidious, image of a comically "woke" middle-class white male. Still, there are precious few films that reflect this sea change.

Few incidents in the history of anarchism have done as much to besmirch its reputation as the aging Bakunin's dalliance with the youthful Nechaev's brand of revolutionary violence, an ideological fling that the elder revolutionary came to regret bitterly. Whether exponents of liberalism, Marxism, or anarchism, various scholars, such as Franco Venturi, Isaiah Berlin, Paul Avrich, and E. H. Carr,[11] agree that Nechaev combined the conspiratorial vigor of Russian Jacobinism and nihilism with a single-minded, even apocalyptic, devotion to his cause. To a great extent (and this fact has not gone unmentioned by conservative and radical scholars alike), this brand of ascetic politics resurfaced in the elite twentieth-century cadre formations of extra-parliamentary groups such as the Weather Underground and the Red Brigades.[12] The Nechaevan determination, moreover, to root out and if necessary exterminate real or imagined enemies smacks more of proto-Stalinism than of genuine anarchism. Nechaev's chillingly simple creed is encapsulated in his pamphlet "Catechism of a Revolutionary," and even his biographer, Philip Pomper, cannot decide on the extent of Bakunin's contribution to this document with its "bloodthirsty rhetoric" and odd oscillation between "anarchist-populist" and "Jacobin-conspiratorial" ideas.[13]

The controversy surrounding exhortations to direct action and "propaganda by the deed" is much more intricate and laden with far-ranging implications than the largely parochial issues raised by the Bakunin-Nechaev affair. Propaganda by the deed—the injunction to match incendiary rhetoric with concrete acts—was a contentious issue for anarchists during the era of the First International, and a strategic option that continued to be debated among anarchists during the twentieth century. For serious proponents such as Bakunin and Malatesta, propaganda by the deed did not entail arbitrary or isolated acts of terrorism but was linked to a programmatic belief in insurrection designed to inspire unabashed social revolution. Near the end of his life, Malatesta summarized propaganda by the deed as the belief that carefully orchestrated revolutionary acts could be catalysts for "the working masses to fling themselves against the bourgeoisie and take possession of the land, the factories, and all that they produced with their toil and that had been stolen from them."[14] Malatesta and his compatriot Carlo Cafiero's unsuccessful attempt in 1877 to launch an insurrection among peasants in Campania proved pivotal.[15] Although Malatesta would continue to believe that "anarchist violence is the only violence that can be justified . . . that is not criminal,"[16] he devoted the rest of his life to grassroots forms of working-class anarchist organization.

The abandonment of attempts to foment peasant insurrections through strategic violence is explored with rueful irony in Paolo and Vittorio Taviani's *San Michele aveva un gallo* (*St Michael Had a Rooster*, 1972). Released at a time when extra-parliamentary violence made the Italian extreme left a pariah to communists as well as conservatives and liberal parliamentarians, the Tavianis' film examines the literal—and psychological—isolation of a nineteenth-century "internationalist," Giulio Manieri, who gradually realizes that his endorsement of propaganda by the deed has not led to a large-scale peasant revolution. Much of the film details Manieri's ten years in prison, but the hapless altruist is even more alone when he finally emerges from his cell to learn that his former comrades now believe that a romantic faith in revolutionary violence is wrong-headed and self-defeating.

Daniel Guérin argues that the increasing emphasis on propaganda by the deed in the late nineteenth century was engendered by debilitating weaknesses within the working-class movement.[17] As the memory of the Paris Commune faded, isolated acts of terror committed by individuals with tenuous, or in many cases nonexistent, links to the anarchist movement began to be identified in the popular imagination with anarchism per se. The public became convinced that anarchism was nothing more than the details of the assassinations of Tsar Alexander II, French President Carnot, King Umberto I of Italy, and U.S. President McKinley, as well as the sporadic attacks on civilians by deranged pseudo-anarchists such as Émile Henry and Ravachol (*nom de guerre* of François-Claudius Koenigstein). Given this outpouring of defamation inspired by offbeat interpretations of propaganda by the deed, it is not surprising that Octave Mirbeau wrote that "a mortal enemy of anarchism could have not done better than Émile Henry when he hurled his inexplicable bomb in the midst of peaceful anonymous people"[18] at Paris's Café Terminus. André Breton lauded Henry's act, calling it "a magnificent expression of individual revolt." While this typically provocative statement is reminiscent of Buñuel's hope that *Un Chien andalou* (1929) would be received as a "passionate incitement to murder," it also exemplifies a common romantic tendency to associate anarchism with grandiloquent, if foolhardy, gestures.[19]

Despite the indigenous American anarchist tradition of, among others, Josiah Warren and Benjamin Tucker, the arrival of fiery European anarchists on U.S. shores initiated the first full-scale anarchist movement, which, predictably, inspired a vehement anti-anarchist backlash. Johann Most, the German anarchist who arrived in America in 1882, has been called "the most vilified social militant of his time,"[20] and his fire-and-brimstone advocacy of social conflagration made him one of the most conspicuous radical bogeymen of his era. Even though Most became the typical anarchist for Americans conditioned to quaver at his name, his melodramatic infatuation with destruction led Emma Goldman eventually to dismiss him as a putative authoritarian. Alexander Berkman, Goldman's long-time lover, urged that the assassination of tyrants was not only legitimate but necessary. He was also a sincere, if admittedly inept, practitioner of revolutionary violence: his bungled attempt to assassinate Henry Clay Frick, the chairman of Carnegie Steel whose hatred of labor radicalism resulted in the death of ten strikers at his Homestead, Pennsylvania plant, was one of the most ardent examples of propaganda by the deed. Richard Drinnon's conclusion that Goldman and Berkman "foolishly tried to apply Russian revolutionary tactics directly to American problems"[21] seems indisputable, although the sensitive, erudite Berkman had almost nothing in common with the lurid caricature of the anarchist bomber cherished by the yellow press.

Unsurprisingly, the commercial cinema's view of anarchist violence made no distinction between the pointless bombings of Henry and the principled *attentats* of anarchists like Berkman. Most directors at the turn of the century appear to subscribe intuitively to Félix Dubois's view that anarchists—"men whose object is the annihilation of all existing social institutions"—were literally suffering from brain damage.[22]

This laughably crude genetic reductionism is evident in Edwin S. Porter's straightforward dramatic reenactment, *Execution of Czolgosz, with Panorama of Auburn Prison* (1901). Leon Czolgosz, whose electrocution is commemorated in Porter's film, assassinated President McKinley in 1901 during the head of state's visit to Buffalo. Czolgosz is what journalists delight in calling a self-proclaimed anarchist; his knowledge of anarchism seemed limited and he was purported to have shot McKinley to prove to the anarchist community that he was not a police spy. Charles Musser notes that "executions, still considered a form of entertainment by some turn-of-the-century Americans, had been popular film subjects during the novelty phase of cinema."[23] Musser's plodding description of the film's narrative structure, however, fails to covey the fact that this reenactment of a hated anarchist's electrocution was tinged with a peculiarly cathartic value inasmuch as it reignited Americans' pleasure at one representative of the anarchist peril being extinguished. The film's last shot, with its graphic depiction of Czolgosz's death agonies, did not merely fulfill an eager public's communal sadism, as they witnessed Porter's restaging of a public execution. This early docudrama commemorates, with gruesome cinematic flair, the killing of a man who inspired mass hysteria—all "radicals were instantly considered guilty of an enormous and vicious crime."[24] Czolgosz's murder became the impetus for a wave of anti-anarchist vigilantism, which included the arrest of Emma Goldman, the tarring and feathering of a United Brethren Minister who criticized McKinley's demagoguery from the pulpit, and the near-lynching of one of the editors of *Freie Arbeiter Stimme*. Porter's film is a macabre entombment of this phase of America's ongoing anti-radical bloodlust.

Many subsequent films, most of them lost even though plot summaries in trade journals such as *Moving Picture World* remain,[25] took relish in depicting anarchists as bomb-tossing foreign renegades. One of the most famous extant films, Griffith's *The Voice of the Violin* (1909), exemplifies the unsavory mixture of political paranoia and cloying sentimentality that permeates most of these films. Released a year after what has been called "the anarchist scare of 1908,"[26] the film explores the plight of Herr von Schmitt, a gentle but impoverished German émigré who teaches the violin for a living but is duped into becoming an anarchist saboteur by his scruffy companions. The anarchists in Griffith's film are essentially more rabid and unkempt precursors of the liberal do-gooders that he will go on to deride in *Intolerance* (1916). When von Schmitt realizes that he has been dispatched to bomb the family of a beautiful and wealthy young woman who previously spurned his advances, he magically regrets the errors of his class resentment and saves the day with a typically Griffithian last-minute rescue. It is beside the point to insist that "the film seems commercially rather than politically motivated, capitalizing on the widespread fear of the bomb-throwing anarchist legions that the popular press conjured up at the time."[27] Even though it is obvious that Griffith plunders anarchist stereotypes for the sake of rousing melodrama, it is also true that the film reflects a common turn-of-the-century conception of anarchism as an odd form of depraved, and more often than not criminal, contagion. Most notoriously, Cesare Lombroso was convinced that "impulsiveness" and "love of orgies" were anarchist vices, especially since there were a greater number of "lunatics" and "indirect suicides . . . among anarchists than among ordinary criminals."[28]

Since Griffith's hierarchy of passions ordains that romantic love must always take sovereignty over politics, his gullible hero is able to extricate himself from anarchist dementia in the nick of time. It should come as no surprise that Griffith took little interest in disagreements between anarchists, Marxists, and social democrats. As Kevin Brownlow observes, "socialism and anarchism were confused, intentionally by the press, unintentionally by the public."[29] A 1909 review of the film claimed that von Schmitt becomes "imbued with the doctrines of Karl Marx, the promoter of the Communistic principles of socialism that . . . under the control of intemperate minds becomes absolute anarchy."[30] His fondness for the contrivances of melodrama nonetheless allowed him to grant secular redemption to individuals who were willing to renounce this virulent form of political insanity. Griffith's fear of anarchist rebellion was the pop culture counterpart of an intellectual horror of irrational mobs best exemplified by Gustave Le Bon's *The Crowd* (1895). This visceral hatred of *hoi polloi* is transformed into a more sophisticated theory of the "circulation of elites" in the work of Vilfredo Pareto, Gaetano Mosca, and Robert Michels.

Louis Feuillade's crime serials never specifically refer to French anarchist violence, although the conservative royalist director's fascination with the criminal *demi-monde* has been viewed as covertly anarchistic by several commentators; voice-over commentary in Noel Burch's documentary series *What Do Those Old Films Mean?* (part 2, 1986) straightforwardly states that "the spirit of anarchism lies at the heart of Feuillade's early serials." No doubt inspired by Marcel Allain and Pierre Souvestre's novel that was the source for Feuillade's *Fantômas* (1913–1914), the historian André Salmon invoked the eponymous master criminal of screen and literature to set the stage for his study of French "illegalist" anarchists such as the notorious "Bonnot Gang."[31] The Bonnot Gang, named after Jules Bonnot and noteworthy for attracting the young Victor Serge (then known as Victor Kibalchich) as an active supporter, was the first, and perhaps the last, convocation of Stirnerian bank robbers.[32] They were credited with pioneering the use of the getaway car, and were profoundly influenced by the political orientation identified with the journal *L'Anarchie*—an anti-authoritarian organ that did not adhere to the anarcho-communist view that "there were two opposed classes, bourgeois and proletarian," but believed that only rebellious *individuals,* who could "come from either category," were capable of a "revolt against existing society."[33] Well-known anarchists such as Jean Grave and Kropotkin denounced the illegalist ethos, but the Bonnot Gang's heady mixture of Stirner and audacious violence was certainly ripe for cinematic romanticization or demonization. *Fantômas,* a film whose anti-hero could be considered an avatar of a depoliticized illegalism, is distinctive for converting a stock paranoid revulsion against anarchy into a rousing thriller in which the huge police bureaucracy is continually undermined by the lone brilliant criminal. For the most part, however, the dashing and elusive Fantômas is much more appealing than the bland, seemingly incompetent detective, Juve.[34]

Rarely departing from a haughty iciness, Joseph Conrad's novel *The Secret Agent* showcases a motley group of anarchist protagonists who are far more repellent than appealing. Given the fact that *The Secret Agent* offers the most dazzling and sophisticated array of anarchist stereotypes yet assembled, comparing the disparities between Conrad's fictional account of London anarchists intoxicated with the revolutionary potential of dynamite and Alfred Hitchcock's extremely loose film adaptation, *Sabotage* (1936), can prove instructive. Conrad's anarchists, inspired by voluminous but selective research geared to confirm his antipathy to the tenets of Bakunin and Kropotkin, are a seedy collection of grotesques: Karl Yundt, a near-maniacal advocate of propaganda by the deed who nurtures a dream of "men absolute in their resolve to discard all scruples in the choice of means"; Michaelis, the altruistic anarchist whose enduring "optimism" seems like a vicious lampoon of the Kropotkinite cooperative ethic; and the crazed Professor, whose habit of carrying dynamite in his pocket appears to combine a desire to lay waste bourgeois society with a craving for self-immolation.[35] Hitchcock's adaptation entirely eliminates Conrad's gloomily conservative dissection of the London anarchist milieu; the word "anarchism" is never uttered by anyone in the film. What differentiates *The Secret Agent* from most vicious caricatures of anarchism is its belief that "the terrorist and policeman both come from the same basket." Conrad's equation of police bureaucrats and marginal outlaws—what one critic termed "the structural and moral kinship of the policeman and the criminal"[36]—is probably what most appealed to Hitchcock, although this updating of *The Secret Agent,* oblivious to an "anarchist peril" that had faded into distant memory since the turn of the century, implies that the shadowy terrorists could well be Nazi agents.

Irving Howe claimed that The *Secret Agent*'s rabidly anti-anarchist bias revealed the "desolation a modern ego fears to find beneath its domesticated surface."[37] *Sabotage* expresses similar fears, although it immerses the audience in the destructive urges that Conrad kept at arm's length. Conrad's snobbish detachment from the seediness, as well as the often-invigorating energy, of urban life is exemplified by the fact that his protagonist, Verloc, the duplicitous double agent who is the novel's cynosure, is a lowly proprietor of a pornography shop. Hitchcock's characteristically reflexive decision to make Verloc the owner of a movie theater radically alters our perception of this disreputable saboteur. As spectators of *Sabotage,* we cannot sneer, like Conrad, at Verloc's shabby-genteel home, a petit bourgeois domicile that conceals murderous rage. Point-of-view editing directly implicates us in Verloc's pathetic schemes. Hitchcock, the cinematic *magister ludi* who manipulates the film's action, treats his anti-hero with a modicum of pathos that is far removed from Conrad's characteristic hauteur. Hitchcock's total disregard for the ideological controversies that preoccupied Conrad, his oddly appealing agents of destruction, and bland, forgettable policeman (the nominal, and quite dismissible, hero) are closer to the combination of paranoia and absurdist humor perfected by modernist novelists such as Nabokov. Conrad's central tragic incident—the accidental death of a dim-witted child by an anarchist bomb—becomes tragicomic farce in *Sabotage.* A reactionary distortion of anarchist doctrine is no longer the narrative linchpin; instead Hitchcock's exclusively psychological focus conveys an inner chaos that is more the product of urban isolation than murderous intent. Unlike *Sabotage,*

Christopher Hampton's literal-minded adaptation (*The Secret Agent,* 1996) featured a studied re-creation of the nineteenth-century London anarchist milieu. But, at a time when the "Unabomber" was being denounced as our era's anarchist scourge, Conrad's anti-anarchist fury was defused by a prim concern with period detail.

Stan Douglas's *The Secret Agent* (2015), a multi-screen installation designed for gallery spaces, uses Conrad's cynical equanimity as a departure point to explore how radicalism was defused by the state during Portugal's "Hot Summer" of 1975, an interregnum following the "Carnation Revolution" of 1974 when land seizures and experiments in workers' self-management flourished despite the desire of social democrats and communists to control and defuse what were deemed militant excesses. If the efflorescence of workers' control and agrarian collectives during this brief interlude reflected the fervent hopes of anarchists and situationists, Portugal's subsequent government—headed by social democratic Prime Minister Mario Soares, the United States' preferred leader—marked a retreat from the radicalism from below that prevailed during the early days of revolutionary ardor.

Douglas's installation recasts Conrad, and moves the action to Lisbon, in order to reframe the collusion between Verloc, the duplicitous double agent who screens Bertolucci's *Last Tango in Paris* (1972) in his art house cinema, and agents of the state.

For Douglas, Bertolucci's erotic melodrama seems to reflect the inner life of his incarnation of Verloc. Verloc, supposedly an anarchist veteran of May '68, actually reports to a retrofitted version of Conrad's "Mr. Vladimir," a diplomat subservient to the United States and CIA. The counter-revolutionary conspiracy that Mr. Vladimir and Verloc hatch to "bomb modernity"—a plan to incinerate underground telephone cables connecting Portugal and South Africa—fails as miserably as the act of sabotage depicted in Conrad's novel. Yet as Jason E. Smith argues, the modernization of Portugal led to the dawn of the present "crisis . . . a future of no future, a directionless drift, a horizon of technocratically managed austerity, running up against little to no organized mass opposition."[38]

Robert Baker's *The Siege of Sidney Street* (1960) was inspired by a much more notorious event from British radical history than the minor incident that ignited Conrad's imagination, even though this workmanlike low-budget film eschews the psychological complexity of either *The Secret Agent* or *Sabotage.* Baker's film fictionalizes a famed 1911 battle between *émigré* bank robbers and policemen in the East End of London (the same incident that was the historical catalyst for the climactic shoot-out of Hitchcock's 1934 version of *The Man Who Knew Too Much*[39]), assuming, as many have over

the years, that this ragged gang were anarchists. John Quail's history of
the British anarchist movement clears away the dust by proving "the men
involved were either unpolitical" or affiliated with non-anarchist "Social
Democrat combat groups."[40] Mere facts rarely impede the recycling of the
standard clichés that constitute a rousing thriller, and *The Siege of Sidney
Street* revels in creating a portrait of "anarchists, atheists, and vegetarians,"
to borrow a line from a dyspeptic bartender who provides the film's comic
relief. Peter the Painter, the unofficial leader of the Sidney Street gang, played
with sinister relish by Peter Wyngarde, combines the dissolute bohemianism and impulsive violence that constitute the classic stereotype of the wild
anarchist. Peter's rhetoric seems like a malicious parody of the ethos of anarchist direct action; his claim that he steals so that the oppressed will not
be massacred is scripted as a mindless non sequitur designed to confirm
the moral bankruptcy of anarchist derring-do. The contention of this bogus
(and quite typically bearded) "anarchist" that he joined the movement after
learning of floggings and executions in Tsarist Russia provides a certain sympathetic "backstory," even though Peter's idealism is seen as inextricable from
his fanaticism. The appearance on the scene of Home Secretary Winston
Churchill (a historically accurate detail used to buttress the film's fanciful
misrepresentations of anarchist riff-raff) signals the generic restoration of
law and moral equilibrium. Tory order replaces "anarchist"-bohemian chaos;
in an ending that might have pleased Lombroso, these incorrigibly criminal
anarchists are efficiently exterminated.

The Siege of Sidney Street, with its nefarious anarchist villains, was a throwback to the melodramatic preoccupations of Griffith and Porter. After Bolshevism replaced anarchism as the cinema's favorite political *bête noire,* it
was more common for anarchists to be either ignored or lampooned as
nincompoops. Many of these films express an intriguing ambivalence toward
their anarchist protagonists: contempt is intermixed with covert admiration. Comedy often ends up interrogating, however unwittingly, many of
the stereotypes about anarchism that melodrama takes for granted.

Ben Hecht's lame satire *Soak the Rich* (1936) is an early example of this trend.
Most of the film is a strained attempt to derive humor from Hecht's cynical
view of campus communism. A peculiar subplot, however, skewers Muglia
(played with raspy exuberance by Lionel Stander), the head of the ludicrous
Society for the Preservation of Monsters and one of the cinema's few Stirnerian
anarchists. Unsurprisingly, Hecht's version of individualist anarchism bears
little resemblance to the reasoned discourse of a Benjamin Tucker or Ezra
Heywood. As critic Richard Watts Jr. wrote at the time of the film's release, the
narrative's only bona fide radical turns out to be "a bomb-throwing maniac."[41]

Oddly enough, the psychotic Muglia is more memorable—and in a perverse way more admirable—than any of the film's other characters.

In a very different vein, Fred Zinnemann's *Behold a Pale Horse* (1964) is exceptional for partially rehabilitating the image of an anarchist saboteur, even though this static melodrama eventually scolds its rebel hero. Loosely based on the exploits of Francisco Sabate,[42] an anarchist guerrilla who attempted to bring down Franco's regime through strategic violence during the 1960s, the film provides Gregory Peck—the incarnation of noble outlaw values—with his comeuppance when he (and the audience) finally endures a reprimand delivered by a philosophical priest.

Unlike Peck's dashing but stoical anarchist guerrilla, the turn-of-the-century anarchists in Peter Ustinov's adaptation of Romain Gary's novel *Lady L* (1966) are cuddly, bomb-toting anarchists. These Edwardian radicals, played with a disarming lack of conviction by Paul Newman and Sophia Loren, are fetchingly quaint. Their passion for explosives and the occasional robbery is meant to elicit knowing smirks from the audience.

Lady L trivializes anarchism by making it the subject of an inept sex farce, even if the audience is meant to enjoy, and at times even admire, its heroes' forays into larceny and murder. Paul Newman's Armand is a suave burglar who appears to lose his beloved to the bland but wealthy aristocrat Sir Percy Rodiner (David Niven). The film concludes, however, with the wealthy dowager capitulating to the charms of her old dynamite-obsessed flame. Blithely oblivious to history, the filmmakers are drawn to anarchism because it contains ready-made ingredients for a comic romp, even if the proceedings rarely inspire anything more substantial than a tepid chuckle. Both Ustinov's film and Gary's novel view anarchists as harmless denizens of a colorful past, although Gary at least distinguishes the fictitious Armand's silly exploits from the activities of Proudhon, Bakunin, and Reclus. *Lady L* merely uses Armand's fanciful illegalism as the pretext for a series of detonations designed as rollicking fun.

Ustinov's film, like later cinematic salvos aimed at anarchist terrorists, such as Lina Wertmüller's *Love and Anarchy* (*Film d'amore e d'anarchia*, 1973) and Claude Chabrol's *Nada* (1974), views the political underground as an extension, even an elaboration, of the sexual underground. All of these films juxtapose the brothel *demi-monde* with the realm of anarchist intrigue. In *Lady L,* the title character begins her career as a lowly but chaste laundress in a brothel; she has access to the illicit sexuality that the film leeringly relishes, but is spared pariah status since she is merely an innocent onlooker. The anarchist view of prostitution underwent a gradual sea change; for the misogynistic Proudhon, the prostitute became the decidedly negative "model of any *femme émancipé*,"[43] while Emma Goldman concluded that the "traffic in women" was not a moral aberration, but was instead emblematic of capitalist wage slavery.[44]

Wertmüller is a defter comic artist than Ustinov, but the vagueness of *Love and Anarchy*'s political stance—and its profoundly muddled view of both anarchist violence and prostitution—spawned a curious array of kudos and brickbats from critics representing various points on the ideological spectrum. Wertmüller's odd hybrid of historical fiction and *commedia all'italiana* takes the several attempts to assassinate Mussolini by committed anarchists as its departure point, but, since the film's fictional would-be assassin, Tunin (played with undeniable bravura by Giancarlo Giannini), is an unmitigated buffoon, contemporary anarchists perceived the film as an unwelcome affront to their Italian comrades' anti-fascist endeavors. The impulsive Tunin, with his utter ignorance of the anarchist tradition, bears no resemblance at all to the actual individuals, accused, rightly or in some cases completely erroneously, of attempting to kill Il Duce. Men such as Anteo Zamboni (the victim of a fascist mob in 1926 and the subject of a more earnest film by Gianfranco Mingozzi) or the erudite Michele Schirru,[45] whose unsuccessful attempt on the life of Mussolini inspired an Italian biographer to document his complex political and intellectual affinities, could never be reduced to a primal, but ultimately apolitical, embodiment of some fancifully "anarchist" life force. Ironically enough, Wertmüller's most vocal American champion, the conservative critic John Simon, defended the director against her detractors by claiming that the communist-dominated Italian left was unable to appreciate her "anarchic socialism"![46] From a less straightforwardly reactionary perspective, Millicent Marcus asked if "Tunin exemplifies not so much a committed member of a radical political movement as an embodiment of . . . the anarchist truth that natural man is innately just and good?"[47] Conveniently overlooking (perhaps owing to ignorance) the fact that anarchism's appeal often extended to urban and industrial areas as well as rural enclaves, Marcus constructs a facile homology between Tunin's peasant origins and anarchism's supposed faith in the purity of "natural man." This picture of anarchism's supposed valorization of humanity's innate goodness is also something of a straw target, since, as Kingsley Widmer observes, anarchists such as Emma Goldman and Colin Ward, among others, never assume the existence of a "universally benign social essence."[48]

The film damns anarchism with faint praise, especially since the protagonist's ill-fated *attentat* becomes the departure point for Wertmüller's evocation of ineffectual, if well-intentioned, anti-fascism. For Marcus, Wertmüller's sardonic vision of the Resistance has "none of the heroic illusions which

Rossellini had to promulgate in the name of the new society which his film was designed to inspire." While an attempt to deflate the pieties of classic neo-realism might have proved appealingly subversive, Wertmüller merely dresses up old-style humanism in the colors of superficial outrageousness. Like many examples of pseudo-radicalism, *Love and Anarchy's* desire to scandalize the bourgeoisie—particularly its maternal chiding of anarchists as mush-headed dreamers—is the product of general ideological befuddlement. More enthralled by the tepid pragmatism of the Italian Socialist Party,[49] she gushes that "Malatesta was a wonderful human being," but "the philosopher of an impossible utopia." An early sequence, which indulges in Italian comedy's traditional scatological zest while also offering a breezy *summa* of the film's didactic orientation, features Tunin's first childhood glimpses of anarchist idealism. As he eavesdrops on adult conversations while perched upon a chamber pot, the young Tunin listens with awe to the saintly anarchist Michele Sgaravento's Kropotkin-like faith in a future where "we will be at peace with one another, sharing, in harmony." Years later, Sgaravento's murder by fascists, an act that aborts his goal to kill Mussolini, triggers the mature Tunin's yearning to avenge his mentor's death by vowing to fulfill the unconsummated *attentat.* Unfortunately, this decision is more the product of an improperly assimilated trace memory than that of well-formulated political convictions. The doctrine of propaganda by the deed becomes narrativized as a farcical variant of repetition compulsion. The film is, above all, imbued with a vulgar, reductive Freudianism that implies anarchism is not acquired through concerted struggle or sustained reflection, but is "imprinted . . . upon the young."[50]

Wertmüller does not promote orthodox psychoanalysis as the antidote to this process of imprinting. *Love and Anarchy's* libidinal economy skirts the issue of the intimate relationship between sexuality and politics by promoting a conformist affirmation of sexual abandon as a salutary regression from anarchy. This evasion comes to the fore in sequences in the brothel run by Tunin's flamboyant comrade-in-arms, the lusty anarchist madam Salomé. Salomé's righteous indignation mirrors Tunin's; just as the male country bumpkin becomes embroiled in anarchism after the death of the fictional Sgaravento, her hatred of Mussolini is sparked by the lynching of Zamboni. Salomé delivers an earnest soliloquy decrying the "bastards" who attacked Zamboni, but Wertmüller's *mise-en-scène* neutralizes these earnest sentiments by panning across the lovers' reflections in some ostentatious oval mirrors. This showy visual flourish makes it clear that Wertmüller regards her characters' fondness for anarchist violence as fundamentally specular.

Of course, *Love and Anarchy's* caustic portrait of Spatoletti, a fascist bureaucrat whose absurd macho preening provides moments of inspired farce, is not incompatible with an anarchist critique of statist authoritarianism. Elephantine fascist architecture often dominates the sequences that feature Spatoletti's sputtering attempts to elucidate his creed, and Marcus makes a perfectly reasonable comparison between the bloated edifices associated with this unapologetically cardboard villain and the warm domesticity of the brothel. Yet depicting this prototypical fascist as a rapacious gargoyle does little to clarify the way in which anarchist agitation of the late nineteenth and early twentieth centuries was aborted by fascists who shrewdly, and tragically, co-opted important elements of anarchism's appeal for the working class. *Love and Anarchy*'s simplistic moral universe, with its sweet but clueless anarchist peasants, and fascists whose brutality is nothing more than a product of raging hormones, ignores the fact that Italian fascism exploited the terror that the middle class felt when confronted with working-class and peasant insurgency—the food riots, general strikes, and factory occupations that characterized the *biennio rosso* ("red two years") of 1919–1920. After all, Mussolini himself transmuted beyond recognition Georges Sorel's anti-statist conception of the syndicate into ultra-statist fascist corporatism—the ultimate "instrument of class domination by the method of the forced collaboration of economic classes?"[51]

Love and Anarchy concludes with some moments of finely honed black comedy. Tunin makes a half-hearted, ultimately suicidal, attempt to fulfill his *attentat* after Salomé and her cohorts fail to wake their guest in time for his rendezvous with destiny. Confronted with an overweening sense of failure, Tunin impulsively aims his revolver at a policeman making a routine examination of the brothel—*Love and Anarchy*'s final indulgent sneer at what it perceives as the delusions of anarchist cloud cuckoo land. Tunin's fateful decision to make himself the victim of his own misbegotten *attentat* met with predictable derision from anarchist commentators. A group of San Francisco anarchists who leafleted theaters screening the film during the 1970s decried Wertmuller's psychosexual equation of political revenge and suicide, her promotion of the belief that "it is really a death wish that motivates political assassination, and not an imperative to defeat tyranny, whatever the cost."[52] This equation, of course, was not formulated by Wertmüller; her film merely refined the cinematic tradition of reducing anarchism to hapless violence by making its anarchist assassin a lovably incompetent peasant instead of a demonized agent of chaos.

The anarchist peril resurfaces in Chabrol's thriller *Nada,* although the film's recasting of Conrad's mordant equation of terrorists and the police made it ripe for interpretations that conceive of both the state's surveillance and its supposed terrorist antinomy as (to use situationist phraseology) essentially *spectacular* activities. Based on Jean-Patrick Manchette's novel, published by Série Noire, the Gallimard crime fiction imprint, this departure from the usual Chabrolian territory of middle-class adultery and purely apolitical homicide focuses on a ragtag group of Paris-based anarchists' inept kidnapping of the American ambassador. Despite a brief interchange in which an anarchist accuses a comrade of harboring covert Marxist beliefs, Chabrol's anarchists appear to be comic-opera versions of Red Brigade or Baader–Meinhof Leninists rather than bona fide anarchists. Nevertheless, *Nada,* despite its pulp-novel origins, is an unabashedly Dostoyevskian account of anarchists' supposed passion for destruction. The feuding cadres—the Spanish ringleader, Buenaventure Diaz (Fabio Testi), the dilettante Professor Treuffais (Michel Duchaussoy), and the shamelessly mercenary Epaulard (Maurice Garrel)—are portrayed as ruthlessly conspiratorial and thoroughly humorless. Diaz's appearance—bearded, perpetually clad in black while sporting a spiffy sombrero—prompted Nora Sayre to ponder: "Why do anarchists in contemporary films always have to wear black broadbrimmed hats?"[53]

After the gang's badly timed plan to whisk the ambassador away from his favorite Paris brothel misfires, Chabrol's lurid sketch of modern Nechaevists is intriguingly supplemented with a few graphic sequences highlighting the police force's unblinkingly enthusiastic annihilation of the entire cadre. Diaz's final manifesto is eerily similar to the situationist Gianfranco Sanguinetti's trenchant analysis of the Red Brigades' fatal strategic flaws.[54] Sanguinetti's glum post-mortem concludes that the Italian leftists' 1977 kidnapping of Aldo Moro unwittingly reinforced the state's ideological agenda. In a theoretically acute interrogation of terrorist efficacy, he muses that "in the case of a small terrorist group spontaneously formed, there is nothing in the world easier for the detached corps of the state than to infiltrate it"; it is not absurd to assert that these groups often become nothing more than "a *defensive* appendage of the State."[55] Similarly, Diaz grimly concludes that: "the State hates terrorism, but prefers it to revolution. When each man realizes the desire to destroy the State, he tries to destroy all. . . . Thus the . . . assassin becomes a type consumable by society. . . . Terrorism is a trap for revolutionaries."

Nada's weakness for crazed, fanatical "anarchist" protagonists distorts the left-libertarian tradition with a clumsiness analogous to *The Voice of the Violin*; Chabrol's incoherent blurring of the distinctions between Bakuninists and Leninist apostles of terror mirrors Griffith's inability to distinguish between Marxists and anarchists. But Chabrol's more sophisticated, and infinitely more cynical, stance prevents him from granting redemption to the rebels he castigates with respectful contempt. *Nada* also looks forward to Rainer Werner Fassbinder's grimly satirical *Die dritte Generation* (*The Third Generation*, 1979), a film in which bumbling terrorists—who regard Bakunin's writings as sacred texts—become puppets of the West German state security apparatus.

Bertrand Tavernier's admittedly sober and thoughtful *Le Juge et l'assassin* (*The Judge and the Assassin*, 1976) was in many respects an even more dispiriting response to the years of radical exhaustion that followed the brief exhilaration of May '68 and the cul-de-sac of extra-parliamentary violence. Tavernier's fictionalized rumination on the last days of Joseph Vacher (called Bouvier in the film), a French mass murderer and rapist who preyed on women during the 1890s, has been hailed by Jill Forbes as an example of radical filmmaking—"a critique of the French penal and judicial systems which raised questions about the definitions of madness and sanity by suggesting that these are as much social as clinical."[56] Whatever the Foucauldian implications of Tavernier's amalgam of historical re-creation and tasteful gorefest, it is nevertheless more than a little alarming to listen to Bouvier's constant reiteration of his "anarchist" sentiments. Tavernier's most shameless addition of insult to injury is probably a sequence in which Bouvier mutters some lyrics written by Jules Vallès, the anarchist novelist and hero of the Paris Commune who continued to influence radicals during the events of May '68. Vallès's expansive vision of a decentralized "free association of citizens" is rendered unrecognizable in a film that equates hammy lunacy with the spirit of anarchism. We are apparently meant to find this "anarchist of God" (as he continually refers to himself) bracingly transgressive, especially since the bourgeois judge (Philippe Noiret masterfully captures the character's oily stodginess) who doggedly pursues him is less sympathetic than his homicidal quarry. But this quasi-affirmation of an amoral hero is, in the final analysis, more chic than insightful: another French intellectual's infatuation with "anarchistic" criminality and the glamour of pathology.

As urban political violence became a hazy memory, filmmakers mined the past to commemorate whimsically the heyday of propaganda by the deed. Dusan Makavejev's *Manifesto* (1988) is a case in point—a wan evocation of a Central European anarchist's zany flirtation with violence. Makavejev's early films tried to define an anti-Stalinist politics that was, at least by default, anarchist in spirit. Unlike the anti-Stalinist avant-gardism of *WR: Mysteries of the Organism* (1971) and *Sweet Movie* (1974), *Manifesto*'s political perspective is utterly conventional. The bomb-throwing hero, portrayed without conviction by Eric Stoltz, spends most of his time flailing around in bed with nubile women while uttering inanities like "those who eat cake while others starve deserve to be blown up."

If Griffith and Porter laid the groundwork for the stereotypes of fanatical anarchists who never left home without a detonator, Hal Hartley's *Simple Men* (1992) could be considered the postmodern apotheosis of these outmoded clichés. Hartley's film, with its trademark clipped dialogue and intricately plotted coincidences, is both an absurdist thriller and an equally ironized Oedipal drama—a road movie in which two brothers from the McCabe family finally locate their errant father, an aging radical who supposedly enjoyed a career as a mad bomber during the 1960s. The awkward reconciliation climaxes with the palpably dotty father reading a lengthy passage from Malatesta's *Anarchy* to his assembled sons and admiring girlfriend. Writing in *Freedom*, the London anarchist fortnightly whose press published the edition of *Anarchy* visible in Hartley's film, Colin Ward observed that the youthful contingent repeats Malatesta's words "phrase by phrase, like children of the cultural revolution in China learning the thoughts of Chairman Mao."[57] Taking Malatesta's words out of context, the passage from *Anarchy* intoned by the fanatical McCabe—with its promotion of "intransigence" and revolutionary "selflessness"—makes the Italian's eloquent manifesto seem like a shrill screed. Hartley, however, fails to quote Malatesta's advocacy of "the sentiment of solidarity" and the "community of comradeship."[58] For even an ostensibly hip director like Hartley, anarchists are robotic and, above all, fanatically violent doomsayers.

Jim Jarmusch's *Paterson* (2016) offers a more magnanimous glimpse of a doomed Italian anarchist. The lanky Adam Driver plays a bus driver named Paterson, who lives in the onetime anarchist stronghold of Paterson, New Jersey. On Paterson's bus route, two teenagers, played by Kara Hayward and Jared Gilman, the young stars of Wes Anderson's *Moonrise Kingdom*, discuss the career of Gaetano Bresci, an Italian American anarchist who once resided in Paterson and went on to assassinate King Umberto I of Italy. Both allusive and playful, the scene self-referentially reminds us of the city of Paterson's rich, if largely forgotten, radical past. Life in the United States of Amnesia being what it is, few schoolchildren, outside of perhaps a Jarmuschian dreamscape, are aware of, say, the Industrial Workers of the World participation in the Paterson Silk Strike of 1913—an event that resulted in the arrest of approximately 1,850 strikers. If the kids played by Hayward and Gilman seem incongruously precocious, the fact that they continually mispronounce Bresci's surname slightly tarnishes their veneer of sophistication.

If anarchists are depicted somewhat more sympathetically in the twenty-first century than they were in the twentieth, these portrayals are often tinged with barely concealed condescension. In Dani de la Torre's *La sombra de la ley* (*Gun City*, 2018), a quasi-gangster film that recapitulates the street battles between right-wing *pistoleros,* police, and anarchists during the 1920s, the anarcho-syndicalist Salvador Seguí, usually referred to as a gradualist, emerges as a noble figure. But in de la Torre's superficial thriller, anarchists like Seguí, who was assassinated in 1923, are little more than impractical dreamers destined to be devoured by more powerful and corrupt forces.[59]

Ambiguous Representations of Anarchism in the Twenty-First Century

During the 1960s and 1970s, many seasoned anarchists came to believe that the wave of student activism and antiwar activity during that period signaled the resurgence of an anti-authoritarian left. By 1999 the old Manichean divisions of the cold war had dissolved and Andrej Grubačić and David Graeber, in a 2004 pamphlet called "Anarchism, Or the Revolutionary Movement of the Twenty-First Century," proclaimed that "it is becoming increasingly clear that the age of revolutions is not over. It's becoming equally clear that the global revolutionary movement in the twenty-first century will be one that traces its origins less to the tradition of Marxism, or even of socialism narrowly defined, but of anarchism."[60]

James McTeigue's *V for Vendetta* (2006), while neglecting the explicitly anarchist content of its source material—Alan Moore's hugely popular graphic novel—nevertheless grappled with the quandaries posed by both anti-authoritarian direct action and terrorism in the post- 9/11 era. (Although McTeigue provides the lackluster direction, Lana and Lilly Wachowski, the screenwriters, are the film's true auteurs.) Moore himself found the Hollywood adaptation repellent—a version, while ostensibly quite "critical" for a commercial film, erased his own embrace of anarchism and transposed an allegory of Thatcher's Britain to the era of George W. Bush and the strictures of the Patriot Act.

Moore's graphic novel is something of a cult phenomenon. While far from the great work of narrative art its most fervent fans claim it is—and rife with its own contradictions—this epic dystopian fable is an ambitious polemic with a focused political agenda. Written shortly after Margaret Thatcher's ascendancy to power in the 1980s, Moore's comic imagines a grimly repressive Britain of the future where Tories have metamorphosed into full-blown fascists, homosexuality has been criminalized, and state-sanctioned torture is taken for granted. A shadowy figure calling himself V and donning a mask representing Guy Fawkes—the radical Catholic whose thwarted plan to blow up Parliament on November 5, 1605 (the so-called Gunpowder Plot) led to his speedy execution—is presented as the ultimate antidote to rampant authoritarianism. Two-thirds Zorro and one-third Zarathustra, V ambles out one night and rescues a would-be teenage prostitute named Evey during her first night on the job and recruits her as a revolutionary accomplice and multipurpose object of desire. While the film culminates in the destruction of the Houses of Parliament, masterminded by V and implemented by Evey, the demolition occurs in Moore's comic by the time six pages have elapsed! From a political vantage, the late years of the cold war in Europe prove crucial to Moore's didactic thrust. Much of the planet, with the exception of the United Kingdom, has been devastated by a nuclear holocaust spurred on by the last gasp of American tensions with the Soviet Union. British fascists offer to stem the chaos that already engulfs the United States by insisting that iron rule is preferable to unchecked pandemonium. Most commentators refer to Moore's V as an "anarchist." Nevertheless, while he is clearly determined to "smash the State," he seems more like a complacent individualist entranced with Rabelais's quasi-aristocratic Abbey of Thélème (a section of the comic, during which V encourages average citizens to foment rebellion, borrows the motto of Rabelais's freewheeling abbey—"Do What You Will"—and tweaks it into the "Land of Do What You Please") than a bona fide anarcho-syndicalist or anarcho-communist.

In a peculiar Hollywood compromise, the Wachowskis and McTeigue are more determined to combat the excesses of creeping authoritarianism in post-9/11 America while preserving the noirish London setting of Moore's cautionary tale. This engenders a disconcerting alienation effect; a studio-bound London is the home to a rabid, O'Reilly-like talk show host with close ties to the secret police. He pontificates on the fictional BTN (British Television Network)—a thinly veiled surrogate for Fox News. Anti-Muslim feeling of course now abounds in the U.K. as well as in this country, and it's arguable that the State's banning of the Koran in Warner Bros.' version of *V for Vendetta* is far from inapt or gratuitous, as Stephanie Zacharek claimed in her *Salon* review.[61] But the compulsion of secretly subversive citizens— such as V (portrayed by the Australian actor Hugo Weaving, who must still be bitching about the constrictions of wearing a Guy Fawkes mask for two hours) and Evey's boss at BTN, Gordon Deitrich (Stephen Fry) to hoard forbidden art—Hollywood movies, jazz, avant-garde paintings—smacks more of the ongoing American culture wars than a Britain blessedly lacking an equivalent to the U.S. Christian right. The movie's Evey (Natalie Portman, whose rather grotesque attempt at an English accent came off as vaguely South African to Peter Bradshaw in *The Guardian*[62]) is of course slightly sanitized; instead of a budding sixteen-year-old prostitute, she is merely a well-groomed young woman of indeterminate age who is saved by V from fascist thugs when she demurely violates curfew.

The critical controversy generated by the film version of *V for Vendetta* is more interesting than the film itself. It's especially astonishing that debates once confined to esoteric political sects and academic journals are now surfacing in more accessible form in the popular press. For example, whether consciously or not, critics who decry the hypocrisy of a multi-million-dollar film's seeming endorsement of terrorism and revolution recall the situationists' more convoluted assertions that superficially radical gestures within mainstream culture are usually little more than self-negating manifestations of the "society of the spectacle." Conversely, the unabashed fans of the film seem to unwittingly channel the ranting of academic pop culture cheerleaders who argue that knee-jerk condemnations of mainstream movies and television reek of self-defeating snobbism. An honest assessment of *V for Vendetta* probably requires us to eschew both of these polarities. Far from a revolutionary manifesto, this inevitably compromised film is still unusually audacious compared to the usual Hollywood product. Yes, the climactic destruction of Parliament is an example of "spectacular" politics— a fireworks display paying homage to the culminating hollow gesture of a hyper-individualist superhero (who defeats his foes with the same magically propelled knives that we know and love from Hong Kong films and the Wachowskis' own *Matrix* movies) and his devoted disciple. Nevertheless, this incoherent allegory was the most undiluted attack on the Bush administration launched by a largely complacent film industry in the wake of the War on Terror. It's also notable, moreover, that the hacker collective known as Anonymous appropriated *V for Vendetta*'s trademark Guy Fawkes mask for its own purposes. As Gabriella Coleman observed, Anonymous took "a symbol popularized by Hollywood and made it revolutionary. It is a prime example of counter-commodificaton—a rare occurrence."[63]

If *V for Vendetta* falls prey to the clichés of Hollywood dystopianism, Elie Wajeman's *The Anarchists* (2015) takes on a neglected chapter in the history of anarchism but fails to reinvigorate the tired tropes of the costume film. The plot revolves around the efforts of police informer Jean Albertini (Tahar Rahim) to obtain incriminating information on the activities of a Parisian anarchist cell at the end of the nineteenth century. Wajeman should be at least given grudging credit for making a group of French "illegalist" anarchists the film's cynosure. Like the slightly later and better known Bonnot Gang, the anarchists under surveillance desire the "expropriation of the expropriators" but, in Richard Parry's formulation, find themselves "reduced to individual acts—'re-appropriation' of bourgeois property."[64]

Despite glaring flaws, *V for Vendetta* and *The Anarchists* are at least earnest attempts to explore the contradictory legacy of propaganda by the deed. Jordan Susman's *The Anarchist Cookbook* (2002), despite its status as an "indie" film, proved as, if not more, blinkered in its conception of anarchism than many studio releases. An inept amalgam of political farce and screwball comedy, Susman's view of the anarchist project is thoroughly muddled. To a certain extent, the title, which is derived from William Powell's notorious manual for manufacturing homemade bombs and drugs, reflects the film's basic frivolousness. Anarchism is reduced to a "do your own thing" impetuousness, the ultimate form of countercultural "lifestyle" politics. This vulgarized anarchism, despite an early sequence that name checks anti-globalization battles in Seattle and Genoa, owes as much to some unholy marriage of the hippie ethos and right-wing individualism than it does to Bakunin and Kropotkin.

Puck, the hapless protagonist, is what commentators often term a "self-styled" anarchist. For him, the anarchist credo amounts to little more than "pure undiluted freedom." Joining an anarchist collective in Texas, he's ultimately torn between two antithetical role models: Johnny Red (John Savage), an aging hippie who comically invokes Sweden as a socialist paradise (in a film without any nuance at all, distinctions between social democracy and anarchism are completely effaced) and Johnny Black, an unsympathetic militant who favors direct action but whose eventual incongruous alliance with white supremacists smacks more of the tactics of the alt-right than the anti-authoritarian left. After Puck's run in with faux-anarchist Johnny Black—and an eventual jail term—he returns to the default position for Americans foolish enough to dabble with radicalism: apolitical quiescence aided by the ministrations of his Young Republican girlfriend.

While *The Anarchist Cookbook* was summarily dismissed by most critics, Christopher Nolan's characteristically self-important *The Dark Knight Rises* (2012), which included a grotesque caricature of an anarchist-inspired movement resembling elements of Occupy Wall Street, precipitated an orgy of critical commentary. In grandstanding op-ed pieces, commentators representing antithetical positions ranging from the *New York Times'* Ross Douthat on the right to Slavoj Žižek on the left,[65] attempted to unravel the incoherent strands of a minor film that emerged as a major pop culture phenomenon. Comic book movies proffer vulgar Nietzscheanism—a heroic Ubermensch like Batman is usually deployed to fight evil Untermenschen. Nolan's ponderous variation on this theme is no exception. The only twist is that Bane, the film's villain, despite his weakness for gratuitous bloodletting, might also be labeled a guerrilla leader who speaks on behalf of the oppressed and condemns capitalist decadence. In this cartoonish universe of discourse, the transgressions of the 1 percent embolden Bane—whose nemesis, Bruce

Wayne/Batman, is a billionaire dependent on wealth derived from specula-tion—to hold a city ransom by threatening to detonate a neutron bomb.

For the majority of critics on the left, Bane and his gang exemplified a ludicrous attack on anti-authoritarian movements and the contemporary disdain for income inequality. Douthat and Žižek begged to differ—primarily because the *The Dark Knight Rises'* stab at political analysis is, in true Holly-wood style, hopelessly vague and subject to infinitely pliable interpretations. For Douthat, co-screenwriters Christopher and Jonathan Nolan's claim that they derived inspiration from Dickens's *A Tale of Two Cities,* a novel known for its antipathy toward the Jacobin "reign of Terror," leads to a defense of a film he lauds as reflecting the tenets of a sedate conservatism that "owes more to Edmund Burke than Sean Hannity." A similar sort of ideological cherry-picking informs Žižek's backhanded tribute to *The Dark Knight Rises.* Although Žižek concedes that Bane's autocratic tactics are antithetical to the grassroots "self-organization" endorsed by the anarchist wing of Occupy Wall Street, he insists that violence can always accompany any project with "emancipatory" potential and is enamored of the film's perverse desire to imagine a People's Republic of Gotham City, "a dictatorship of the proletariat in Manhattan." For Žižek, even though the Nolans have nothing but scorn for a "dictatorship of the proletariat" (as do most anarchists, who view this terminology as implicitly encouraging a Leninist dictatorship "over" the proletariat), the fact that the film broaches this possibility makes it an "im-manent" component of its political impetus. *The Dark Knight Rises* becomes of interest inasmuch as it resembles a Rorschach test that reflects both conser-vative and leftist commentators' myopia. To believe that the Nolans' cynicism is "Burkean" confirms Corey Robin's contention that Edmund Burke was not an upstanding traditionalist who should be distinguished from contempo-rary, yahoo-like conservatives but was in fact a more refined variety of "the reactionary mind." Conversely, Žižek's propensity to elevate the film to the status of a presumed Leninist wish-fulfillment fantasy only reinforces the authoritarian elements of his preferred style of cultural critique.

Bertrand Bonello's *Nocturama* (2016) is noteworthy for eschewing the usual moralism that pervades most films determined to condemn terrorism. Despite a certain ideological opacity, Bonello subverts many of the standard clichés concerning violent direct action. The young Parisians of various eth-nicities and classes who assemble clandestinely to bomb outposts of capital such as HSBC and governmental edifices on the order of the Ministry of the Interior are neither religious zealots nor lunatics. Although it's rather difficult to locate these young insurrectionists within any tangible anti-authoritarian tradition, Bonello helpfully mentions the influence of Étienne de La Boétie's sixteenth-century manifesto, *Discourse on Voluntary Servitude*, in the press notes. Often termed a proto-anarchist document, La Boétie's succinct treatise tackles one of the knottiest questions in political philosophy: why do masses of individuals willingly relinquish their autonomy and become subservient to despots?

Saul Newman provides a post-Stirnerite gloss on La Boétie's denunciation of the tendency to meekly capitulate to tyranny: "La Boétie explores the subjective bond which ties us to the power that dominates us, which enthralls and seduces us, blinds us and mesmerizes us. The essential lesson here is that the power cannot rely on coercion, but in reality rests on our power. Our active acquiescence to power at the same time constitutes this power."[66] Newman terms this the quandary of "self-domination"; the implication is that what Stirner labeled "self-ownership" is crucial to resisting the structures of voluntary servitude. The teen protagonists of *Nocturama*, who, despite their hazy motivations for covert activism, bring to mind somewhat more alienated members of groups resembling Occupy Wall Street and the French equivalent, Nuit debout, appear to be as invested in personal autonomy as they are in urban sabotage. The film's climactic sequence takes place in a desolate department store as news of the *attentats* is being broadcast. The young militants prove besotted with hip clothing and, above all else, the electronic tools that enable them to transform their temporary digs into an ad hoc DJ station with an infinite number of dance tunes available for the comrades' delectation. This oscillation between militancy and seeming self-indulgence might seem perplexing. Nevertheless, this incongruous trajectory can be attributed to the Romantic roots of consumerism outlined by Colin Campbell in *The Romantic Ethic and the Spirit of Modern Consumerism*. For Campbell, hedonism or "pleasure-seeking" is "not . . . regarded as an end in itself, but as a means to moral and spiritual renewal."[67]

In fact, "moral and spiritual renewal" seem to be essential components of many of the films of the second decade of the twentieth century that tackle recent forms of direct action and contemporary permutations of propaganda by the deed. It's difficult to know if the young veterans of Montreal's "Maple Revolution" who go underground in Mathieu Denis and Simon Lavoie's *Ceux qui font les revolutions á moitié n'ont fait que se creuser un tombeau* (*Those Who Make Revolution Halfway Only Dig Their Own Graves*, 2016) are anarchists, Maoists, or anti-Leninist Marxists. The members of the cell engage in ruthless self-criticism that resembles old-style sixties Maoism while one militant constantly carries around a text by Rosa Luxemburg. As Denis and Lavoie insist, their protagonists are "disaffected youth" who question "postmodern cynicism . . . who refuse to resign themselves, who fight, who still believe in the greater good, in social change that will outlast them."[68] During an era where ideological confusion is commonplace, their befuddlement is not too different from the theoretical ecumenism embraced by one of the protagonists of Mia Hansen-Løve's *L'avenir* (*Things to Come,* 2016). Nathalie, an academic in late middle age played by Isabelle Huppert, enjoys a platonic relationship with a young anarchist named Fabien. Surprised that her young protégé stocks his library with both a tome by anti-Communist liberal Raymond Aron and *The Unabomber Manifesto,* we can only conclude that Fabien is one radical dedicated to keeping all of his options open. In our constricted neo-liberal world, Aron and the Unabomber represent the Scylla and Charybdis of unsavory antidotes to received wisdom. It is probably unassailable that many "left-millennials" are quite ecumenical in their political preferences, and pilfer ideas from neo-Stalinists such as Alain Badiou as well as from those with anarchist propensities like Chomsky and Graeber. This is also a matter of perspective: Mark Bray claims, for example, that at least 72 percent of the participants in Occupy Wall St. possessed anarchist proclivities.[69] Yet non-anarchist media and the mainstream press emphasized the presence of a wider ideological spectrum that was perhaps a significant minority, a contingent comprised of Ron Paul libertarians, liberals, and the occasional vanguardist Leninist.

Anarchism in America: Perils of Self-Representation

Joel Sucher and Steven Fischler's documentary *Anarchism in America* (1981) is replete with good intentions. The film is explicitly designed as a counterweight to the negative representations of anarchism and anarchists that have colonized the American unconscious—a clip from *The Voice of the Violin* drives home the puerility of such stereotypes. Unfortunately, Sucher and Fischler's (they were also known as the Pacific Street Film Collective) antidote to frequently malicious negative images of anarchists is too often constrained by a conservative documentary aesthetic and a refusal to subject its own assumptions to a process of critical interrogation.

Offering equal amounts of edification and obfuscation, Sucher and Fischler tackle the often-baffling ambiguities inherent in the American indebtedness to both reactionary and left-wing varieties of individualism. Perhaps because American anti-anarchist propaganda has often chastised individuals who "baited . . . their own country,"[70] this documentary elevates anarchism to the status of "twentieth-century Americanism," to employ the phrase that became identified with the patriotic communist Earl Browder. The filmmakers, consequently, devote a larger chunk of screen time to individualist, rather than collectivist or communist, anarchism. This orientation should not be dismissed as intrinsically reactionary. Contrary to popular misconceptions, it would be mistaken to caricature American nineteenth-century individualist anarchists as incipient right-wing libertarians, benighted precursors of Ayn Rand and Ludwig von Mises.[71] Although certain elements of Benjamin Tucker's New Englandized Proudhonism, for example, do seem to anticipate the worst excesses of American libertarianism, the nineteenth-century individualists still maintained a tangible, if frequently strained, relationship with the socialist movement and, unlike contemporary strains of American possessive individualism, had not entirely severed their ties to burgeoning workers' movements. As the biographer of the individualist anarchist Ezra Heywood is at pains to make clear, "the distinctions between the individualists and the social revolutionaries, and especially between socialism and anarchism, were not sharply defined in the nineteenth century.[72] Historians are certainly not remiss in speculating that the individualists' appeal was essentially "petty-bourgeois,"[73] but this eclectic agglutination of anti-slavery crusaders, free-love advocates, and early feminists anticipated many tendencies that flourish within today's American left. Unlike Tucker, Heywood's individualist convictions did not prevent him from making alliances with anarcho-communists such as Johann Most. The intermingling of libertarian socialism and various strands of anarchism during this period led the Haymarket martyrs—the Chicago "social revolutionaries" framed for the still-unsolved bombing of a police contingent during a workers' rally in 1886—to insist, without apparent self-contradiction, that they were anarchists in politics and Marxists in economics.[74]

Anarchism in America's preoccupation with the vicissitudes of American-ness is ultimately more troubling than its efforts to resuscitate the individualist tradition. It would be unfair, for example, not to acknowledge the fact that the anarchism embraced by Karl Hess late in life differed enormously from the Republican banalities he clung to during his days as a Goldwater fellow-traveler. Yet Hess's observation that Emma Goldman's anarcho-communist version of individualism reminded him of Ayn Rand without the "crazy solipsism" is all too congruent with the film's earnest attempt to domesticate anarchism for a mass audience.

Even if we accept one anarchist critic's jibe that Sucher and Fischler's film offers a gloss on anarchism that is perilously close to Public Broadcasting Service blandness,[75] the roots of their often-tame treatment of American anarchism is not primarily the result of the constrictions imposed by mainstream documentary practice. Sacvan Bercovitch presents a persuasive case that even the most admirable American dissidents usually redefine "injustice as un-American, revolution as the legacy of '76, and the inequities of class, race, and gender as disparities between the theory and practice of Americanness."[76] A desire to convince the audience that anarchism is as American as apple pie is apparent from the film's opening sequence—a busy montage sequence that integrates fatuous denunciations of anarchy by politicians such as Hubert Humphrey, Abraham Ribicoff, and George Wallace with a clip of the Sex Pistols' "Anarchy in the U.K." and footage of ordinary citizens being predictably dumbfounded when confronted with the task of defining anarchism in one minute or less. It is perfectly understandable that the filmmakers underline, with barely concealed gusto, the fact that anarchism has often been the victim of vicious, uninformed calumny. (It is difficult, however, to know whether the Sex Pistols' undeniably catchy punk ditty is meant as an example of common misconceptions concerning anarchism or a spirited antidote to these shibboleths.) Nevertheless, instead of presenting us with American anarchism's convoluted history—a legacy marked by intense feuds between individualists, syndicalists, and anarcho-communists—the directors collapse Proudhonian mutualism, anarcho-capitalism, and left-libertarianism into a nationalist mélange. This focus on anarchism as an adjunct of American exceptionalism can be at least partially ascribed to the influence of David De Leon's tract *The American as Anarchist*, a rather awkward attempt to reconcile anarchism's "red and black" fervor with the seemingly uncongenial interests of the "red, white and, blue."[77]

At times, calming potentially anxious viewers seems to be the documentary's main task. This timidity leads to banal juxtapositions: a cursory examination of the anarchist achievements of the Spanish Revolution of the 1930s is followed by a shot of a car careering down a highway. The invocation of the archetypal American "open road" is accompanied by narration that assures us that anarchism is nothing more than a reflection of the "American temperament," a sensibility that "idealizes distrust of government, suspicion of authority . . . and a belief in a do-it-yourself ethic." These tenets are obviously broad enough to encompass the ideals of Reagan as well as Goldman, right-wing militiamen as well as libertarian socialists. Apparently, an epochal rupture with the past that was fine for Spain is somehow alien to the spirit of American pragmatic reform. Keeping within this vein of frequently vacuous anarchist ecumenism, the filmmakers made the dubious decision to include the complaints of an independent trucker who resents government controls as a salient example of indigenous American anarchism. Poet Philip Levine's flip notion that the American penchant for jaywalking contrasts sharply with other cultures' lack of anarchistic verve is further evidence of the filmmakers' weakness for padding their hymn to anarchy with nationalist minutiae. Although *Anarchism in America* includes a fleeting reference to the martyrdom of immigrant anarchists such as Sacco and Vanzetti, David Wieck bemoaned the absence of even a brief reference to the nineteenth-century militancy of the Haymarket martyrs, and the glaring absence of the contributions of Mexican anarchists such as Ricardo Flores Magón, an omission that apparently implied that "anarchism in America" should not include anything except "the national territory of the U.S.A."[78] Like Walt Whitman, who was influenced by American individualist anarchists such as Stephen Pearl Andrews, the film condemns "ultraism, or any form of extreme social activism."[79] A similar cognitive dissonance is obvious in Karl Hess's commendable skepticism toward authority that is tempered by a near-pious reverence for "the glorious Bill of Rights of the U.S. Constitution."[80]

The film's often troublesome reluctance to offend is particularly noticeable in Sucher and Fischler's brief interview with Mildred Loomis, a proponent of agrarian homesteading who professes admiration for Benjamin Tucker's brand of nineteenth-century American anarchism. William Reichert attempts to establish parallels between Tucker's individualist anarchism and Bakunin and Kropotkin's more militant creeds by arguing that they were all united by a belief in libertarian socialism that eschewed the excesses of state socialism.[81] Yet when Loomis is asked by the filmmakers if she has any interest in anarchism, in addition to reviling the clichés of anarchist "bomb-throwing," she derides "collectivism," which she differentiates from indigenous American "do-it-yourself" anarchism. Loomis's "DIY" radicalism, with its sentimental Jeffersonian cadences, reflects the filmmakers' own yearning to make American anarchism an adjunct of the elusive and ill-defined American "temperament." Loomis's personalist "decentralist code," with its emphasis on self-sufficiency and living on the land, is merely an ecologically admirable, quasi-anarchist mutation of the Voltairean injunction to cultivate one's own garden. (It is also a little surprising that a documentary as attuned to the vicissitudes of 1960s counterculture as *Anarchism in America* almost totally ignores the pioneering sexual libertarianism of anarchists such as Heywood.[82]) The American fondness for untrammeled self-sufficiency also becomes the focus of a subsequent sequence that profiles Michael Carder, a hippyish denizen of Plainfield, Vermont. His version of anarchism, a post-1960s blend of Emersonian "self-reliance" and laid-back counterculturalism, is heart-warming but harmless: a toothless valentine to the voluntary cooperation that supposedly thrives in "New England town meetings or in volunteer fire departments." Carder's identification of potentially anarchist forms of organization beneath the conservative veneer of small-town America resembles Paul Goodman's fondness for discovering "ways by which—even without any recognizable revolution—constructive social tendencies can be liberated by piecemeal change, by what he often wryly called 'tinkering.'"[83] An emphasis on anti-authoritarian tinkering which could well make a difference in the "here and now" is an undeniably important component of anarchist thought and practice, but the fact that the screen time given to individuals like Loomis and Carder far exceeds the minimal emphasis on more insurrectionary tendencies within anarchism results in a well-behaved, defanged version of anarchist history.

Sucher and Fischler's compulsion to make anarchism an acceptable stance for the age of Reaganism reaches a farcical zenith in a sequence in which the Libertarian Party candidate for president, Ed Clark, is queried on his views on anarchism. The befuddled Clark has little to say on the matter, but the need to find traces of the American anarchist impulse in right-wing libertarianism seems like either ludicrous pandering or grossly misguided generosity. The word "libertarian" itself engenders a great deal of semantic confusion, since it was originally coined by Joseph Déjacque and Sébastien Faure during the nineteenth century "to stress the difference between anarchists and authoritarian socialists,"[84] but in the USA is routinely used to refer to undiluted anarcho-capitalism. In addition, since there is often an assumption that right-wing libertarianism is the twentieth-century counterpart of nineteenth-century anarchist individualism, the brief appearance of free-market guru Murray Rothbard in *Anarchism in America* disconcertingly muddies the conceptual waters. The film deliberately blurs the distinctions between anarchist polarities by featuring a brief clip of Rothbard and Bookchin genially sharing the same platform at a conference. Yet, despite the fact that Bookchin impishly remarks that he feels more comfortable with these free-marketeers than with authoritarian socialists, this bonhomie could prove misleading to uninformed viewers. Bookchin has often voiced his distaste for Stirnerian individualism and laissez-faire capitalism, but Sucher and Fischler place advocates of mutual aid and their natural antagonists, anarcho-capitalists, under the same ideological umbrella.

Occasionally, *Anarchism in America* pauses from its apparent mission to assure viewers that anarchism is an unthreatening precursor of yuppie individualism. A brief interview with the Jewish anarcho-communist Mollie Steimer,[85] conducted in Mexico City, provides a brief glimpse of an uncompromising brand of anarchism that fuses radical individualism and the rigors of working-class activism.

Oddly enough, Pacific Street's previous examination of anarchist history, *Freie Arbeiter Stimme* (*Free Voice of Labor*, 1980), avoided many of the political vagaries and structural inadequacies that marred *Anarchism in America*. The focus on the newspaper *Freie Arbeiter Stimme,* founded by immigrant Jewish anarchists, provides a supple structure, and the emphasis on labor activism—particularly the determination to alleviate the degrading conditions endured in industrial sweatshops during the early part of this century—ensures that the traditionally anti-capitalist bias of mainstream anarchism will not be mistaken for the faux-anarchism of what now passes for "libertarianism." The documentary is particularly vivid in its portrait of what interviewee Paul Avrich terms the political "counterculture"—anarchist dances, picnics, and alternative schools—of the Jewish immigrants. Yet the film does not regard this counterculture as merely the product of inchoate individualism. To quote a sign prominently displayed in one of the film's archival photographs, the Jewish anarchists viewed their comrades, who were frequently harassed by the government and local officials, as "victims of capital."

Nevertheless, like *Anarchism in America, Free Voice of Labor* manages to evade, and to a certain extent even suppress, matters of controversy that could threaten the image of anarchist harmony that the filmmakers are clearly striving to create. A brief interview with Charles Zimmermann, former vice president of ILGWU (International Ladies Garment Workers' Union), hints at the reformist path chosen by a certain segment of the Jewish anarchist community. But Sucher and Fischler fail to explore the critique of this reformism that was formulated by some of their anarcho-syndicalist colleagues such as Sam Dolgoff, despite the fact that Dolgoff himself is a fleeting presence in the film.[86] Perhaps more important, the debates surrounding Zionism and the formation of the state of Israel, which were certainly of crucial importance for many Jewish anarchists, are not broached at all. Perhaps references to a 1950 open letter that appeared in *Freie Arbeiter Stimme,* an anguished missive that expresses a Jewish anarchist's dismay that some of his comrades' Zionism incoherently paid homage to the "concept of Jewish-State-Anarchism"[87] would have tarnished the cheery images of lovable elderly anarchists. Nuance is sacrificed for the satisfaction of a warm nostalgic glow.[88]

Both *Anarchism in America* and *Free Voice of Labor* provide ample evidence of the rich American anarchist tradition, although the films are unfortunately marred by an unwillingness to chronicle these movements' contradictions, and the internal dissension that is an inevitable component of any radical movement. A self-reflexive orientation is well-suited to the purposes of auto-critique, anarchist or not, but even a conventional documentary such as *Anarchism in America* could have considered "its own processes rather than seal over every gap of a never-seamless discourse."[89] Perhaps documenting American anarchism requires filmmakers with the lyrical gift of a Chris Marker or the investigative drive of a Marcel Ophuls. Until these directors emerge, *Anarchism in America* and *Free Voice of Labor* can prove useful to audiences who view them with informed caution. Karl Korsch believed that it was important to critique Marxism's weaknesses from a Marxist vantage point; *Anarchism in America* would benefit from an anarchist critique of the flaws, as well as the virtues, of the American anarchist tradition.

A film that attempts to cover an even wider swath of history than *Anarchism in America,* Tancrède Ramonet's *No Gods, No Masters* (2017), an ambitious documentary on the history of anarchism from 1860 to 1945, is a curious artifact. A patchwork quilt of interviews featuring erudite historians sympathetic to anarchism such as Robert Graham, Marianne Enckell, and Kenyon Zimmer, among others, breathless voice-over narration, and only sparsely identified archival footage, the film offers a compendium of insights that at one time summed up a submerged anti-authoritarian history but now almost qualify as received wisdom, at least in the anarchist community. Unlike Sucher and Fischler's *Anarchism in America, No Gods, No Masters*'s first section, "The Passion for Destruction," does not shirk from the avatars of propaganda by the deed, most notably Ravachol—even though the episode culminates with more "respectable" anarchist achievements of the late nineteenth century, especially the formation of the *bourses de travail,* the French labor syndicates. Intricate historical arguments derived from obscure tomes pepper this frenetically paced tribute to anarchism's golden era. For example, the fact that many of the international protests against the execution of Sacco and Vanzetti were led by anti-anarchist communists, conveniently hijacking the doomed men's legacies for their own purposes, is duly noted. Similarly, baseless accusations of anti-Semitism lobbed at Nestor Makhno are dismissed in a few minutes of screen time. Goldman's *My Disillusionment With Russia* and Berkman's *The Bolshevik Myth* are the fodder for conveying how an early, naive anarchist faith in the promise of the Russian Revolution (after all, Lenin's *State and Revolution* occasionally appears to appropriate anarchist precepts) curdled with the betrayal of the factory committees and the Kronstadt massacre.

Excellent intentions notwithstanding, it's difficult to discern who constitutes the intended audience for *No Gods, No Masters.* The litany of anarchist triumphs and defeats might seem overly familiar to seasoned researchers, while novices are likely to find Ramonet's bite-sized summaries inadequately fleshed out. The film, moreover, raises the salient question of how to align the tradition of classical anarchism with evolving activist traditions that have surfaced in the last twenty years or so. While so-called "postmodernist anarchists" often seem to throw the baby out with the bathwater by reducing classical anarchism to Enlightenment bromides, it's a reasonable desire to assess the relationship of current social movements, some more explicitly anarchist than others, to older traditions. Richard J. F. Day's *Gramsci is Dead: Anarchist Currents in the Newest Social Movements* offers a strategy for cementing at least a partial reconciliation between current social movements and the revolutionary ethos of Bakunin and Kropotkin. Acknowledging that anarchists have traditionally been as invested in social revolution as consumed by purely economic demands, Day is skeptical of the "hegemonic" implications of Bakunin's notion of social revolution, suffused with a potentially authoritarian faith in "secret societies" and instead advocates a "logic of affinity," closely tied to Kropotkin's concept of mutual aid, that can facilitate radical, non-reformist demands in the "here and now." Of course, despite anarchism's rejection of Leninist vanguardism, the anti-authoritarian left has long been bound up in class-based agitation and Day, like other post-Marxists or even post-anarchists, confronts the conundrum of how to best address "a wide range of antagonisms that cannot be reduced to class struggle—racism, patriarchy, the domination of nature, heterosexism, colonialism, and so on."[90]

While rejecting the argument that the array of "antagonisms" usually associated with identity politics should not be dismissed perfunctorily as "individualistic," there's nevertheless a somewhat pessimistic veneer to his assertion that, following the German utopian socialist Gustav Landauer's lead, "we must free ourselves. . . . in an effort that cannot be expected to terminate in a final event of revolution." As one of Day's critics points out, anarchist theory and practice has often promoted both incremental demands in the here and now as well as revolutionary goals.

Of course, in tandem with contemporary Marxism, contemporary anarchism has frequently, by necessity, interrogated the Eurocentric assumptions of a nineteenth-century legacy. It's possible to view these two conflicting, if intersecting, motifs deployed in Raoul Peck's *The Young Karl Marx* (2017). Bruce Robbins[91] argues that, although Peck's biopic focuses on crucial events in European radical history that include Marx's intellectual jousts with Proudhon and Bakunin, the optimism imbued in a movie made during a reactionary time mirrors the Global South's continuing engagement with working-class immiseration that Marx and Engels initially located within Manchester's textile mills during the nineteenth century. Robbins might have added that Bakunin, whose unruly countenance is a marginal presence in *The Young Karl Marx,* presaged twentieth- and twenty-first-century eruptions in the Global South as much, or more, than Marx did. Peck, unsurprisingly, caricatures anarchists as myopic foils for Marx's genius. Proudhon, who Marx encounters as the French anarchist pontificates on his most famous, and often misunderstood admonition—"property is theft"—emerges as something of a caricature. Bakunin remains, alas, an even more shadowy figure.

Free Love and Anarchist Sexual Politics: WR: Mysteries of the Organism and Eros Plus Massacre

As scholars such as Hal Sears have demonstrated, nineteenth-century American advocates of "free love" included Fourierist socialists, individualist and communist anarchists—as well as an eclectic assortment of anti-censorship campaigners, feminists, and militant atheists. While Emma Goldman became famous for fusing anarchism with the dictates of "free love" embraced by urban bohemians and the British radical Edward Carpenter, the Whitmanic polemicist who proclaimed that "Eros is the great leveler," she also owed a debt to less well-known American "sex radicals" like Stephen Pearl Andrews and, especially, Moses Harman. Harman's defense of birth control and attacks on the sanctity of marriage in his magazine, *Lucifer the Lightbearer,* led to his imprisonment on obscenity charges under the notorious Comstock Act. Goldman's open relationship with Alexander Berkman became emblematic of how a woman could love without the encumbrances of Victorian morality and the shackles of marriage.

Even though the nineteenth-century apostles of free love appear strikingly modern and seem to share a kinship with left-leaning twentieth-century counterculturalists, Sears makes the point that "although the sex radicals took a more liberal view of sexual pleasure than did their opponents, both libertarians and restrictionists shared a fear of orgasmic sexuality."[92] Victorian-era sex radicals were preoccupied with "self-control," a marked contrast to the views espoused by Wilhelm Reich, the most renowned twentieth-century exponent of sexual radicalism.

Moving vertiginously between documentary and fiction while skewering the platitudes of both cold war American and Communist culture, Dušan Makavejev's *WR: Mysteries of the Organism* is a formative post-'68 film. The career of renegade psychoanalyst Wilhelm Reich, expelled from both the German Communist Party and the International Psychoanalytical Association, is the catalyst for a formally audacious assault on a variety of stale ideologies—American McCarthyism, inflexible Leninism, and moon-eyed New Ageism. The sad contours of Reich's tumultuous life—the heterodox doctor was as much a pariah in the United States as in Europe—is interwoven with elements that fuse pastiche and critique—a mock socialist realist melodrama set in Tito's Yugoslavia that recasts aspects of Milovan Djilas's *The New Class* as farce and interviews with slightly overzealous American Reichians are two of the most prominent tributaries. Makavejev's reinvention of Soviet montage introduces a playful antidote to hidebound varieties of political cinema that prefigures the meld of fiction and nonfiction—in the so-called hybrid film that would become ascendant in the early twenty-first century.

WR's slightly tongue-in-cheek treatment of the Reichian-influenced therapies of the 1960s, which many people believed degenerated into New Agey narcissism when the ostracized doctor's disciples transformed the master's work into disciplines like gestalt therapy and bioenergetics, reveal a creative tension between a Stirnerian "communist egoism" and an insular politics of the self. The chasm between the socialist Reich of the thirties, advocate of "worker democracy," and the New Reichians of the sixties becomes clear in a sequence that follows calm explanations of somatic therapies by Drs. Alexander Lowen and Myron Sharaf. A woman in the midst of a tension-releasing exercises grasps furiously at a towel while exclaiming, "Give it to me! It's mine." Raymond Durgnat postulates that this maniacal intensity might correspond to a "some mad, yet *deep,* fusion of *body, desire,* and *property,* in a word 'possessive individualism.'"[93] Alternately, there might be a modus operandi to align this woman's angry desires with the playful polemic published by an American situationist group For Ourselves during the seventies: *The Right to Be Greedy: Theses on the Practical Necessity of Demanding Everything*—a document that interweaves Stirnerian egoism and Debordian situationist tenets. This manifesto differentiates between "narrow greed"—"a holdover from times of natural scarcity . . . represented in the form of power commodities, sex (objects)" and "communist egoism . . . the egoism which wants nothing so much as other egos; of that greed which is greedy to love."[94] Of course, For Ourselves' anticipation of an imminent era of "post-scarcity" might appear antiquated during the ongoing Great Recession, as well as a betrayal of the working-class anarchism pioneered by Bakunin and his disciples during the nineteenth century. Peter Marin's fear that the more authoritarian offshoots of the New Age (for example, est) entailed a "denial of history and the larger community"[95] that ignored the fact that "human fulfillment hinges on much more than our usual notions of private pleasure or self-actualisation" expressed the wariness of many who feared that the path taken by neo-Reichians was more redolent of fascist than left-leaning tendencies.

WR's eastern European fictional narrative offers an equal number of multilayered paradoxes. Milena (who shares the name of the actress who plays her, Milena Dravić), is the driving libidinal force of the latter half of the film, a Yugoslav feminist activist and sexual revolutionary who makes clear that Reichian theory should be wedded to orgasmic practice. Yet when pontificating about "free love" in a vaguely Renoiresque courtyard, she comes off as a party hack spouting liberatory slogans: "Our road to the future must be life-positive. . . . Socialism must not exclude human pleasure from its program." Invoking the spirit of Alexandra Kollontai, the Soviet feminist whose reformist suggestions for implementing sexual equality were quickly jettisoned by the Leninist regime, she argues that the October Revolution failed when it abandoned the promotion of free love: what Marxist humanists used to label "the subjective factor." Her authoritarian paeans to sexual freedom pigeonhole her as a peculiarly repressed apostle of emancipatory desires. As Durgnat quips, she resembles "Germaine Greer and Margaret Thatcher rolled into one."[96]

Oddly enough, the phrase "free love," at least to certain ears, is more redolent of Victoriana—and Milena's theoretical enthusiasm for free love is not matched by an equally vigorous sexual athleticism. She seems to regard the concrete orgasmic pleasure experienced by her roommate Jagoda as slightly vulgar. Jagoda's noisy romps with her boyfriend, Ljuba the Cock, imbue the film with an earthy comic brio that remains unaffixed to any preordained ideological agenda.

In terms of *WR*'s extrinsic narrative concerns, Milena's sexual politics are compromised by her infatuation with a visiting Russian ice skater, the facetiously named V. I. (as in Vladimir Ilyich Lenin). From an allegorical perspective, Milena's oscillation between reformist zeal thinly disguised as a Yugoslav-style "revolution within a revolution" and a man who embodies Soviet rigidity mirrors the contradictions of Tito's rupture with Stalinism. For anarchists, the Yugoslav regime's rhetorical embrace of workers' control and self-management exemplified a statist co-optation of anarcho-syndicalist ideals. Appropriating the jargon of libertarian socialism, the Yugoslav Federal Assembly passed a legislative act in 1950 entitled "Basic Law on the Management of State Economic Enterprises and Higher Economic Associations by the Work Collectives." An ideal that once corresponded to workers' spontaneity "from below" congealed into a state-ordained legislative dictate. Like Milena, Yugoslavia was caught between a faux-libertarian veneer and Stalinist temptations (themes pursued in *Man is Not a Bird* [1965]—Makavejev's ribald portrait of a Serbian copper factory.).

In a characteristically paradoxical maneuver, the most wholeheartedly anarchist exhortations are mouthed by a drunken worker and sexist lout named Radmilović. Verbally assaulting Milena with impassioned rants against "Marx

Factor" and the "Red Bourgeoisie," it is no wonder that many critics invoke Djilas's concept of the "New Class." Expelled from the Yugoslav Communist Party in 1954, Djilas's assertion that cadres in Communist countries formed a bureaucratic elite that maintained power *over* the working class was, for true believers, the secular equivalent of blasphemy. However boorish, Radmilović is the film's anti-hierarchical dynamo, a straightforward champion of the Bakhtinian "lower bodily stratum" and advocate of a post-syndicalist "refusal of work" who interrupts the dour spectacle of V. I. and Milena's romantic interlude by crashing into their bedroom and nailing the clueless Russian into the wardrobe.

Unlike post-'68 films from western Europe such as Godard and Gorin's *Tout va bien* (1972)—a film that advocates a less reified mode of workers' control than the one that briefly thrived in Yugoslavia—there is not a smidgen of agitprop in *WR*. This is not only because Makavejev, intimately familiar with the doublespeak of "actually existing socialism," rejects political bromides in an open-ended manner. It is also because Makavejev's penchant for synthesizing ribaldry and melancholy belongs to a distinctly Balkan tradition that is more carnivalesque than hortatory. As the film's montage becomes more frenzied toward the end, it begins to resemble the most delirious film never made by Eisenstein; a manic feast of loopy "tonal" and "overtonal" thematic collisions. One case in point involves furious crosscutting between an artist constructing a plaster cast of *Screw* co-editor Jim Buckley's penis, footage culled from Mikhail Chiaureli's *The Vow* (1946) featuring an actor impersonating Stalin as benevolent patriarch, an anguished mental patient beating his head against a well, and the Beat generation anarchist Tuli Kupferberg, dressed in army regalia and fondling a rifle with masturbatory frenzy. Durgnat views this montage cluster as a "pre-text, a bare foundation for a quite complex integration by the spectator's mind."[97] More tangibly, this sequence's trajectory can be described as a dizzying dance of straightforward tumescence (Buckley), sublimation as ideologically warped tumescence (Stalin), and repressive detumescence and/or mock tumescence (the mental patient and Kupferberg). In other words, to recast the phallic motifs, with their implied correlations to the healthy sexuality promoted by Reich in *The Function of the Orgasm* and the critique of political cum sexual repression in *The Mass Psychology of Fascism,* utopian possibilities are incessantly disrupted (the motif Durgnat labels "Communismus Interruptus") by dystopian realities.

Kijû Yoshida's *Eros Plus Massacre* (1969) is an even more stylistically audacious exploration of the intersection of anti-authoritarian politics and "free love." The film provides a fascinating case study in how the conventions of the "historical film" prove infinitely pliable in the hands of a director entranced with non-linear narratives, disjunctive editing, and the deployment of a highly stylized *mise-en-scéne*. *Eros Plus Massacre* juxtaposes vignettes from two generations of Japanese leftists. A considerable chunk of screen time is devoted to the Taishō era (here covering the span from 1916 to 1923) and the coterie around the individualist anarchist Sakae Osugi, a theorist who, according to his biographer Thomas A. Stanley, espoused an odd mixture of collectivism, syndicalism, and anarcho-individualism.[98] Osugi also appropriated, with occasionally disastrous results, the Western doctrine of "free-love." The film continually blurs the boundaries between Osugi's brand of libidinal politics and the escapades of Eiko and Wada, late-twentieth-century fictional descendants of the Taisho anarchist milieu. Exemplifying the sexual experimentation associated with the Japanese New Left of the late sixties, Eiko, a student and part-time prostitute, and Wada, a young man scarred by childhood abuse, hold a funhouse mirror up to the foibles of their anti-authoritarian precursors.

In many respects, Osugi exemplifies the most extreme tendencies of what Murray Bookchin once denounced as "lifestyle anarchism." Although Osugi is usually considered the leading Japanese anarchist of his era—a dissident who served four terms in prison—Yoshida is primarily concerned with this charismatic nonconformist's desire to placate his wife while juggling romantic relationships with two mistresses—the journalist Kamichika Ichiko (renamed Masaoka Itsuko in the film) and the feminist firebrand Noe Ito, known for her association with the Bluestocking Society and for her role as one of the editors of *Bluestocking,* its feminist magazine devoted to discussion of the arts. Osugi's personal imbroglio is anchored in two historical incidents that define some of the contradictions of his radicalism. The first of these catalytic events is the so-called Hayama Incident, a benign name for Kamichika's failed attempt to murder her wayward lover. Curiously enough, this event is, for Yoshida, more crucial than the second incident—the eventual execution of Osugi, his nephew, and Ito by the military police in 1923.

Eros Plus Massacre's audacity resides in its resistance to depicting Osugi and his restive harem and the denizens of the modern framing story as autonomous individuals entrenched in two distinct historical epochs. A loosening of temporal boundaries allows the Taisho protagonists to enter the modern era and function as specters within a radical milieu influenced by their doctrines. Eiko hangs out with an aspiring filmmaker and is fascinated by the legacy of Osugi and Noe Ito. From this vantage point, it's arguable that all of the Taisho sequences are, as David Desser suggests, actually filtered through Eiko's tortured mindset. Yet, if one agrees with Vladimir Nabokov's assertion that, at least in an aesthetic context, the word "reality" should always be accompanied by quotation marks, this interpretation is nothing but a provisional, disposable hypothesis.

Despite his belief in the egalitarian potential of free love, Osugi is ultimately the personification of male hubris. The disparity between his idealism—what Desser terms a "60s motif . . . that equates monogamy and private property"[99]—and his obliviousness to the fact that he has, either intentionally or unintentionally, pitted his lovers against each other—becomes a key to his unbridled egotism. And the female protagonists, despite being staunch feminists, cannot equal the gutsy brio evinced by the heroine of a much pulpier film—Toshiya Fujita's *Lady Snowblood 2: Love Song of Vengeance* (1973). An assassin in the mode of Zatoichi, Yuki, also-known-as the eponymous Lady Snowblood, is, while allied with a male anarchist, driven to murder the bureaucrats who attempt to recruit her as a spy because of political fury that has nothing to do with romantic affinities or erotic zeal.

Charting the intersection of cinema, "free love," LGBTQ radicalism, and anarchism, poses a different set of challenges. For the historian Terence Kissack, turn-of-the-twentieth-century anarchist sex radicals such as John William Lloyd, John Henry Mackay, and Emma Goldman helped to transform the discourse concerning same-sex relations in an "unprecedented fashion." Kissack argues that "the anarchists were alone in successfully articulating a political critique of American social and legal norms" regarding homosexuality.[100]

Bruce LaBruce, the Canadian "queercore" provocateur, is one filmmaker who, despite an impish veneer, is well aware of the legacy of the sex radicals and has always resisted respectability politics. During a career that began in the 1980s, his films have—despite a frequently tongue-in-cheek facade—celebrated sex work (*Hustler White*, 1996) and the creative uses of pornography. LaBruce, moreover claims that "the inextricable link between the political and the sexual is really what my movies are all about, and that I owe to Reich and Makavejev."

As LaBruce himself admits, his films devoted to "queering" such as *WR* and *The Third Generation* are "tricky," primarily because they strive to produce what unsupportive critics termed "productive ambivalence"[101] and partially because they straddle the boundaries of earnest outrage toward sexual repression and satirical campiness. *The Raspberry Reich* (2004), as invested in a carnivalesque ideal of "pornotopia" as John Cameron Mitchell's *Shortbus* (2006), reimagines the Red Army Faction as a cult energized by a comically tinged libidinal leftism. Gudrun Ensslin becomes a Marcusean rebel against one-dimensionality and encourages shoplifting as a means to subvert consumer society. She encourages both public sex (in a sort of farcical enactment of a Bakhtinian desire to efface the difference between the public and private) and issues exhortations concerning the "homosexual intifada." "The Revolution is My Boyfriend" is her slogan of choice.

Far from shattering taboos in a purely frivolous fashion, *The Raspberry Reich* comically dissects the ultra-left in order to locate the authoritarian residue that still lurks within anti-authoritarian movements. Some of Gudrun's muscular disciples repeat passages from Raoul Vaneigem's *The Revolution of Everyday Life* in a rather robotic fashion. The commodification of authoritarian leftist heroes, in this case Che Guevara, is punctured in a scene highlighting a militant gay terrorist, also named Che, masturbating onto Alberto Korda's now "iconic" photo of the martyred revolutionary. Korda's estate sued LaBruce for his unauthorized use of the image. In recounting the absurdity of the lawsuit, LaBruce comments that "it was somewhat ironic, considering that the film, although a critique of the radical left, is obviously sympathetic to certain socialist and/or Communist beliefs. (Although I was also well aware of Che Guevera's toxic homophobia, and purposefully 'queered' him in the film as much as possible.)" In the hardcore version of the film, *The Revolution is My Boyfriend,* the photograph of Che was replaced by slogans such as "Fuck Copyright" and "Intellectual Property is Counter-Revolutionary."

Released more than a decade later, LaBruce's *The Misandrists* is something of a follow-up to *The Raspberry Reich*. Demonstrating the same ambivalent affection for, and skepticism toward, sectarian leftism that was evinced in *The Raspberry Reich, The Misandrists* both pays homage to radical lesbian separatism and gently skewers it.

A riff on the premise of Don Siegel's *The Beguiled* (1971), *The Misandrists* opens with the chance encounter of two German schoolgirls—Isolde (Kita Updike) and Hilde (Olivia Kundisch)—with a wounded political dissident named Volker (Til Schindler). In an impulsive act of derring-do, they clandestinely house him, a hated male, in the basement of an all-female enclave, an outpost of the lesbian separatist Female Liberation Army that doubles as a Catholic boarding school.

Big Mother (Susanne Sachsse, who also portrayed Gudrun in *The Raspberry Reich*), as imperious as Rosalind Russell's Mother Superior in Ida Lupino's *The Trouble With Angels* (1966), enforces the mock-convent's ideological agenda with inflexible ferocity. At the beginning of each meal, she leads a prayer that proclaims: "Blessed is the goddess of all worlds that has not made me a man." She also has a weakness for deliberately inelegant bons mots on the order of "Wake Up and Smell the Estrogen." Her partner Dagmar (Viva

Ruiz) shares her belief that pornography and prostitution are effective tools for subverting the established order—a credo that also reflects tenets that LaBruce has adhered to throughout his career.

If LaBruce is ambivalent about his zany separatists' antics, it's mostly attributable to the unfortunate propensity of many radical sects, even those who term themselves "anarchist," to preach anti-authoritarianism while internally imposing authoritarian strictures. Big Mother, the personification of lesbian libertinism, is a rigid feminist essentialist and has no room in the Female Liberation Army for a transgender member such as Isolde, who is forced to conceal her identity until the end of the film. A schism between dogmatism and true libidinal energy is underlined in the film by crosscutting between Dagmar and Big Mother's boudoir, adorned with the famous mug shot of Emma Goldman after she was falsely accused of conspiring with Leon Czolgosz to assassinate President McKinley, and an ecstatic pillow fight between the girls that pays homage to Jean Vigo's *Zéro de conduite*. Although the implication is that the girls possess the genuine sexual frisson that the older women lack, LaBruce's observations on the appeal of Goldman's legacy to Big Mother are nuanced and underline the salient contradictions of both Goldman and Big Mother: "No doubt Big Mother would have no problem with assassinating patriarchs! However, if you dig a little deeper, Goldman's political beliefs in terms of feminism have been deemed as problematic by some feminists, mostly because she was skeptical about women's suffrage, fearing that it would merely encourage women to participate in a corrupt, capitalist patriarchal system and thereby perpetuate their oppression. She hated liberal reformers, and Big Mother would definitely agree. Some critics have accused Goldman of supporting heteronormativity, when in reality she made supportive statements about homosexuals and gender outcasts, and reputedly was, herself, bisexual."

The Misandrists' satirical thrust is frequently a product of LaBruce's (who terms himself a "recovering academic") own intimate familiarity with anarcho-Marxist terminology. In an early scene, Ute, one of the most precocious students, suggests to her classmate Editha that they "posit themselves as 'self-conscious subjects.'" La Bruce, who admits that the "sexual often trumps the academic" in his films, then has Editha moving in for a kiss with Ute and suggesting that this is the way they can "authentically" affirm the subjective factor of radical praxis.

La Bruce mirrors contemporary controversies within feminism and anarchism by depicting Big Mother as an intolerant "TERF." The pivotal character of Isolde unravels the authoritarian core residing in certain segments of feminist essentialism. Boldly initiating an affair with Volker, the hated male sequestered in Big Mother's lair, this transgender woman urges her lover to "reconcile his 'revolutionary' beliefs with his sexual politics." In the final analysis, Isolde, labeled by LaBruce a "separatist among separatists" is the film's true heroine because of her willingness to challenge the hierarchical and authoritarian assumptions of so-called anti-authoritarians.[102]

Anarcho-Feminism, Cinema, and the Question of Violence

Ever since Bakunin urged in his *Revolutionary Catechism* (1866) that women be granted equal political and economic rights, the international anarchist movement has included militant feminism on its agenda. Influential anarchists such as Louise Michel, Voltairine de Cleyre, and Emma Goldman helped to fulfill the promise of Bakunin's manifesto, and introduced the concrete sexual politics only hinted at in the abstractions of that document. Foes of anarchism have always been especially enraged by female anarchists: since anarchism was thought to be incompatible with femininity, women anarchists were often singled out as "crazy" or "bloodthirsty."[103]

During the late 1960s, a number of women, inspired by the rebirth of feminism, rediscovered the anarchist tradition. Several films, most notably Yvonne Rainer's *Journeys from Berlin/1971* (1980) and Lizzie Borden's *Born in Flames* (1983), infused their explorations of feminist self-identity with anarchist leitmotifs. Inasmuch as these films are tentative efforts to suggest the relationship of anarchism to feminism, they are not full-fledged examples of anarchist self-representation. But their open-ended search for "alternative notions of subjectivity"[104] reflects the influence of the anti-authoritarian left. Before examining the cinematic manifestations of this search, the roots of what has become known as anarcho-feminism must be detailed.

The term "anarcho-feminism" came into the language with the publication in 1971 of a manifesto in which radical feminists proclaimed that "we believe that a Women's Revolutionary Movement must not mimic, but destroy, all vestiges of the male-dominated power structure—the State itself." Anarcho-feminism was proposed as "the ultimate and necessary radical stance at this time in world history, far more radical than any form of Marxism."[105] Even though the formal union of anarchism and feminism was not declared until the 1970s, the struggle of nineteenth- and early twentieth-century women anarchists against what Margaret Marsh labeled the "ideology of domesticity"[106]—the critique of repressive sexual mores and bourgeois marriage as well as the promotion of easy access to contraception—should be considered an early form of anarcho-feminism.

Anarchists have long been more receptive to feminist concerns than the orthodox left, but, like Marxists and liberals, anti-authoritarian feminists have often been startled by their male comrades' sexism. Soon after Proudhon published his reactionary, anti-feminist tract *La Justice dans la révolution et dans l'église* (1858), women began to challenge the misogynistic sentiments of this anarchist patriarch. Jenny d'Héricourt warned her nineteenth-century readers in 1860 that "all your struggles are in vain, if women do not march with you."[107] A little more than ten years later, the outspokenly anarchist heroine of the Paris Commune, Louise Michel, served as "soldier, ambulance, nurse, orator,"[108] and yearned to assassinate the ultra-royalist leader of the Second Republic, Adolphe Thiers. Bakunin, known for his support of women's emancipation, "astounded his female followers by announcing that he could not bear to see women drink or smoke,"[109] while even the magnanimous Kropotkin urged women to realize "what a noble career is that of a husband who devotes his life to the great cause of social emancipation."[110]

By the late nineteenth century, women, particularly Russian populists (*narodniki*), whose celebration of the peasantry was closely aligned to the place of pride given to the free agrarian commune in anarchist doctrine, became some of the most impassioned supporters of propaganda by the deed. Although the ideology of nihilists and populists shared components of both Bakunin's anarchism and Peter Tkachev's more authoritarian, proto-Bolshevik Jacobinism,[111] Emma Goldman often expressed her debt to the legacy of the Russian female incendiaries. Even historians sympathetic to the efflorescence of feminism and radicalism among late-nineteenth-century Russian women tend to treat this phenomenon as a vexing psychological conundrum. Richard Stites hypothesizes that these radical women, wealthy daughters of privilege, suffered from an "otherness" that could have been engendered by a "relative absence of contact between daughter and parents."[112] In any case, there is little doubt that despite or perhaps because of the suffocating repression suffered by women of all classes, the Russian radical movements produced an astonishing number of female practitioners of propaganda by the deed. Vera Zasulich, not the most important but perhaps the most notorious—and beloved—of these women, won surprising public acclaim for her 1878 attempt on the life of Fyodor Trepov, the hated, brutal governor of St Petersburg and former head of the Warsaw police. The idealistic desire of Zasulich and members of the radical populist group Zemlia i Volia (Land and Freedom) to live among "the people" assumed that "constant ties between women of the intelligentsia and the working masses would gradually eradicate among male and female workers the prevailing prejudice about the lesser worth of women."[113] Vera Figner, a sometime associate of Nechaev in the "People's Will" and best-known for her work on the bomb that eventually killed Tsar Alexander II, might be considered the nineteenth century's prototypical female insurgent. A compassionate nature initially drew her to study medicine, but she was ultimately convinced that "the only way the existing order could be changed was by violence."[114] Neither of these women could be considered feminists by contemporary standards. Both Zasulich and Figner believed that the social and economic emancipation of all was a greater priority than what was then known as the "woman question"—a belief echoed in the twentieth-century radical (and friend of Emma Goldman's) Ethel Mannin's conviction that "the need is not for a new feminist movement, but for the co-operation of women in the general struggle for workers' power against capitalism."[115]

Despite the prescient fusion of feminist and anarchist demands exemplified by the careers of such women as Emma Goldman and Voltairine de Cleyre, surprisingly few films have even offered a cursory look at the anarcho-feminist heritage. Louis Malle's *Viva Maria!* (1965) spun a fanciful tale of a few carefree female anarchists' penchant for bomb-throwing during the Mexican Revolution—a thinly veiled rationale for an extended soft-core frolic starring Jeanne Moreau and Brigitte Bardot. Penelope Wehrli's *Alice Dropped Her Mirror and it Broke . . .* (1988) viewed the entire anti-authoritarian movement through the prism of an obnoxious male anarchist whose macho narcissism made him a whipping-boy for the filmmaker's apparent displeasure with arrogant male radicals. Hungarian director Ildikó Enyedi's *My Twentieth Century* (1990), on the other hand, recycled the cliché of the carefree bomb-throwing anarchist by bifurcating her emancipated heroine into identical twins: a dynamite-smitten anarchist whose radicalism is merely a symptom of her charming insouciance and a foil to her sister's apolitical, rather vapid femininity.

Rainer's *Journeys from Berlin/1971,* unlike these politically—and aesthetically—vacuous films, is a cinematic meditation on diverse radical women from various epochs, and a rumination on the overlapping, although not always intersecting, realms of the personal and the political. The agitated interior monologue of a female psychoanalytic patient (played by film theorist Annette Michelson) is interspersed with recitations from the letters and journals of Zasulich, Figner, and Goldman, as well as fragments from Rainer's own adolescent diary. This constellation of issues, derived from twin streams of personal and political rage that never quite converge, is inevitably subsumed by Rainer's primary concern with the activities of the Red Army Faction (known popularly as the Baader–Meinhof group),[116] and the German state's repressive response—the *Berufsverbot* (roughly translatable as blacklist). Although the women that Rainer foregrounds were not consistent advocates of classical anarchism (and Ulrike Meinhof's peculiar amalgam of Leninist vanguardism and semi-anarchist direct action made her less conversant with tangible political realities than the nineteenth-century women), each of them drew moral sustenance from the belief that direct action could serve as a possible spur for revolutionary transformation.

Rainer's cinematic modus operandi is often compared to collage, and her filmic "heteroglossia" ("overlapping and intertwining"[117] the personal and political)—a meticulously orchestrated penchant for "horizontally juxtaposing or vertically superimposing a variety of voices and discourses"[118]—differentiates *Journeys from Berlin* from disingenuous films like *Nada,* which purport to unmask anarchist pathology. The daughter of anarchists, Rainer is unquestionably sympathetic to the anti-authoritarian tradition. Yet the film's dispassionate tone occasionally veers toward parodic self-negation. But the reluctance to assume an *engagé* stance (ambivalently reiterated by recurring shots of Stonehenge that seemingly drive home the point that history is often shrouded in mystery and resists definitive interpretations) is also refreshingly honest, since *Journey from Berlin*'s predilection for filtering reflections on political activism through the jaded sensibilities of contemporary SoHo loft dwellers makes room for an autocritique that verges on self-flagellation. The experiences of Zasulich, Figner, Goldman, and Meinhof are recounted by two disembodied voices—one male and one female—who quote large chunks of memoirs and essays by radical women. Paralyzed by doubts and as stymied by skepticism as Zasulich and Figner were energized by revolutionary self-assurance, the couple's banter conveys the exhaustion of the post-1968 generation, while providing a foretaste of the 1980s' smug complacency.

It seems fair to inquire how Rainer's quasi-aleatory avant-gardist aesthetic, which favors Cage and Duchamp's playful self-referentiality rather than confrontational didacticism, illuminates the quandaries of anarchist violence. Given her reluctance to mimic a cine-Brechtianism that (despite an earlier vibrancy) had become stale and clichéd by the 1980s, she abjures explicit "consciousness-raising" and chooses to imply subtly how female radicalism differs from its male counterpart. The film is in fact preoccupied with sometimes nebulous historical linkages that adumbrate the incommensurability, instead of the similarities, of disparate eras' radicalism.

To a certain extent, *Journeys from Berlin,* neither unequivocally denouncing nor affirming terrorist violence, partakes of what David Wieck labels the "negativity of anarchism," its need to clear ideological ground by revealing "significant barriers to the realization of potentialities of human beings."[119]

Rainer's specific political aporia, however, is the dual threat to male power from anti-authoritarian women's resistance to both statist autocracy and sexist conventions. Nonetheless, the distinctiveness of female—although not always feminist—radicalism does at least tenuously unite the radical tributaries represented by Zasulich and Figner's populism, Goldman's anarchism, and Meinhof's vague synthesis of Mao, Lenin, and Che. Even more important, all of these women, despite enormous historical and ideological differences, consistently resisted the strictures of authoritarian socialism, as well as the frequent condescension of their radical male comrades.[120]

However bizarre it may initially appear, it is ultimately appropriate that a therapy session provides the circumambient device that links the radical derring-do of the nineteenth-century Russian female "Amazons," a bickering couples badinage, and Baader–Meinhof's politics of despair. Since the Lacanian tradition that ineluctably influenced feminist theory (implicitly undermined and parodied in the film—the dictum that the historical "Real" is perpetually inaccessible becomes the material of intellectualized farce in the context of Michelson's bravura comic performance) has itself been labeled "theoretical terrorism,"[121] the patient's seemingly interminable analysis only appears to prolong her political despondency and suicidal despair. The psychiatric profession's misogyny, the hubris of the therapeutic inclination, and suicidal tendencies are also overlapping themes that surface in recitations from the works of Alexander Berkman and Ulrike Meinhof that punctuate the therapy session toward the end of the film.

The reading of passages from Berkman's *Prison Memoirs of an Anarchist* by the disembodied male voice (in fact artist and video-maker Vito Acconci, whose sardonic Brooklyn twang provides apt ironic distance) may seem initially jarring in a film devoted to probing the connections between anarcho-feminist *attentats,* contemporary feminism, and Meinhof's problematic martyrdom. But Berkman's eventual suicide in 1936 provides a submerged thematic rhyme with the patient's death-infected rants and Meinhof's apparent prison suicide. In addition, if taken out of context, the fragment from Berkman's memoir is not unlike the intensely emotional snippets from Figner and Zasulich's letters quoted in Rainer's film. The anarchist women's forthright acknowledgment of emotional anguish encourages conservative historians such as James Billington to sneer that "the distinctive role of women in the Russian movement was to purify and intensify terror, not to articulate ideas." Berkman's close collaboration with Goldman, his lover and more celebrated comrade, is implicitly mirrored in accompanying footage of a couple, played by Cynthia Beatt and Antonio Skarmeta, who are planning an unspecified *attentat.* The couple's spasmodic movements, conveyed with deliberately inept jump cuts and barely audible bickering, approximate a strangely whimsical visual and aural dance around the grave prospect of political assassination. Goldman and Berkman's own often uneasy anarchist alliance was characterized by an analogously strenuous effort to defend the occasional necessity of political violence and an equally earnest queasiness concerning the inherent weaknesses of violent strategies. Berkman's early years were marked by an unswerving devotion to the anarchist cause; his assertion that he believed himself to "be a revolutionist first and human afterwards"[122] is emblematic of the single-mindedness shared by all nineteenth-century practitioners of propaganda by the deed. Goldman's ultimate conviction that revolutionist fervor and the personal realm were "intertwined, although occasionally at war"[123] is more pertinent to Rainer's determination to explore the profound, and ultimately unresolvable, disequilibrium between the personal and the political. The chasm between anarcho-communism's moral earnestness and Reagan-era radical chic is foregrounded in a sequence in which the feuding couple interrupt their domestic regime with a reading from Goldman's essay "The Psychology of Political Violence." After the concluding paragraphs of this essay have been read by the unnamed woman (the voice of critic and filmmaker Amy Taubin), Goldman's comparison of sensitive individuals who are compelled to commit acts of political violence to "high-strung" violin strings breaking under pressure is dismissed as "purple" prose. Rainer's version of what Pasolini called "free indirect subjectivity"[124] (an attempt to find a filmic equivalent of "free indirect discourse"[125]—the suffusion or, if you will, imbrication—of a character's voice with the author's) is adroit enough that viewers are not quite sure if *Journeys from Berlin* actually sanctions this judgment of Goldman's measured reflections on political violence as kitsch or merely presents it as symptomatic of left-wing yuppie angst. In any case, despite its early twentieth-century pedigree, "The Psychology of Political Violence" is as riddled with ambiguity and self-doubt as any postmodern artifact: Goldman simultaneously empathizes with anguished individuals such as Czolgosz who resort to violence and concludes that a strategy of propaganda by the deed will have only limited efficacy in the American milieu. The inevitable inconclusiveness of Goldman's essay expresses the mixed feelings of many anarchists toward political violence: *individual* acts of bloodshed, especially if severed from the wider goals of social revolution, are not fetishized, but are occasionally tolerated as necessary contingencies. This spirit of radical doubt coincides with the film's reluctance to either glamorize or patronize the Russian "Amazons" and their twentieth-century descendants.

In some respects, the film's conclusion is a nuanced rejoinder to the notorious observation of Gunther Nollau (former head of the West German security police) that female terrorism was engendered by the "excessive" emancipation of women.[126] Dissecting Meinhof's rage was an admittedly delicate maneuver, since her precarious psychological state was intimately bound up with her political perspective. Acknowledging her critics' harshest accusations, Rainer admits that she somewhat "psychologized" Ulrike Meinhof.[127] The film's integration of a letter written by Meinhof in prison into its complex web of ambiguities does not, however, mechanistically reduce radicalism to apolitical psychological anguish. Meinhof's missive outlines her rage at the German state's efforts to subdue her with coercive "psychiatrification." The realization that a therapeutic technique, which no longer even genuflects to the tradition of the Enlightenment, can be distorted into an authoritarian form of social control justifies the pairing of Meinhof, a woman whose inchoate political orientation was far removed from genuine anarchism, with iconic anarchists such as Goldman and Berkman. The shift from Zasulich and Figner's nineteenth-century populism, which always retained at least tenuous links to the people it purported to serve, to the insular, doomed strategies of the Red Army Faction transcends the parochialism of mere doctrinal disputes. Ironically enough, a left-libertarian radicalism enjoyed surprising success in the indisputably repressive climate of nineteenth-century Russia, while the post–Second World War "liberal" West German state's paranoid mania for surveillance almost ordained that the latter-day emulators of Zasulich and Figner would simply contribute to a "spectacle of terrorism"; a confused, frequently farcical, emulation of the Bonnot Gang's antics. But the film's final citation of H. Herold's (head of the Federal Criminal Investigation Bureau) claim that "the aim of all enemies of the State is the deliberate creation of an opposing power over and against this State, or the denial of *the State's monopoly of force*" proves that the West German bureaucracy perceived the Red Army Faction as an anti-statist threat, even if Baader and Meinhof were more the children of Nechaev than of Bakunin or Kropotkin.

Lizzie Borden's less ruminative *Born in Flames* is, despite its dystopian scenario, a more optimistic evocation of contemporary currents within anarcho-feminism. Set in a not too distant future that eerily resembles the mid-1980s, Borden's film, in addition to its still topical consideration of the often strained relationships between white and African American, and lesbian and heterosexual women, assimilates into its narrative one of radicalism's perennial internal controversies: the critique of supposedly benign social democracy from an "ultra-left" anarchist perspective that does not hesitate to ponder the efficacy of armed violence. Since Reaganism considered liberal social democracy to be as heretical as anarcho-communism, Borden's vision of a future "ten years after" a social-democratic "revolution"—in which the inadequate reforms of a government headed by the fictional equivalent of Democratic Socialists of America are attacked by a militant feminist left— was viewed by many as naively preposterous or even irresponsible. Amy Taubin, for example, asked, with evident impatience, if Borden "seriously believe[d] that the future of the feminist movement is to repeat (and not as farce) the militant positions of the black and white underground during the sixties and seventies."[128] But Borden's cheerfully exorbitant desire to imagine a future where even European-style parliamentary socialism would seem reactionary to some Americans need not be relegated to the realm of wistful 1960s nostalgia. From a broader historical vantage point, her fantasia on anarchist themes recapitulates debates between anarchists and social-democratic antagonists such as George Bernard Shaw. Shaw famously looked askance at anarchist anti-statism and anti-parliamentarianism, arguing that the state, currently "used against the people," retained the potential to be "used by the people" for the beneficial ends that parliamentary reformism can provide.[129]

Born in Flames revives Bakunin's disdain for social democracy by suggesting that disenfranchised black women are now the primary agents of historical transformation, not impoverished peasants and members of the traditional proletariat. The film's staccato editing frantically juxtaposes personalities who espouse competing versions of anarcho-feminism: Isabel, the punk DJ of Radio Ragazza, who personifies incantatory rage against liberal complacency; Honey, the African American spokeswoman of the soul- and gospel-based Phoenix Radio, who rails against the false promises of the social democratic regime in cool and measured tones; the predominantly black and lesbian Women's Army and its ad hoc, radically decentralized anti-rape bicycle brigades. This uneasy alliance between racial minorities and sexual dissidents who share a skeptical view of liberal promises weds the anarchist counterculture to the agenda of radical feminism. The emphasis on alternative media as a locus of insurrectionary discontent corresponds to the recent anarchist fondness for pirate radio.[130]

The implication that anarchist spontaneity can be triggered, as well as repressed, by the media is in the spirit of Mark Poster's observation that "electronically mediated communication" can "challenge" as well as reinforce "systems of domination that are emerging in a postmodern society and culture."[131] The endearingly improvisatory bicycle brigades, moreover, suggest a feminist reinvention of the Dutch Provos' scheme to make bicycles freely available as alternative modes of transport for the Amsterdam counterculture during the 1960s.[132] Just as the Dutch anarchists' whimsical substitution of the "Provotariat"—a loose aggregation of rebels of disparate classes—for the classical ideal of the proletariat angered traditional socialists and anarchists in the Netherlands, the incremental alliances between marginalized white and black lesbians in *Born in Flames* incurs the wrath of mainstream socialists of both sexes. Borden believed that any "absolute position"—even if impeccably anti-authoritarian—could be vulnerable to the same revolutionary hubris that the film was critiquing. Consequently, Borden's anarchist heroines are not plaster saints, but fallible, sometimes misguided, individuals. Radio Ragazza, although virulently anti-authoritarian, represents a somewhat confused and pre-political orientation, while Phoenix Radio adheres to a more "rationalist" stance, "listening to other points of view but maintaining its autonomy."[133] The Women's Army anti-rape bicycle battalion, which could either be hailed as anarcho-feminist "mutual aid," or indicted as vigilantism, does not conceal Borden's awareness that this low-tech exercise in female solidarity is both "wonderful and ridiculous"; the film never remains solemn enough not to pause and parody its own pretensions. To a large extent, *Born in Flames'* self-conscious splintering or "refracting" of possible political positions into a multi-voiced critique of mainstream feminism and socialism accounts for Teresa de Lauretis' admiring characterization of the film as a "representation of women as a social subject and a site of differences; differences which are not purely sexual or merely racial, economic or (sub)cultural, but all of these together and often enough in conflict with one another."[134]

The film's defiant portrait of the female subject's "heterogeneity" is, argu-ably, inseparable from its formal strategies. Borden ingeniously blurs bound-aries between her sci-fi alternative universe and contemporary reality by mingling her own scripted sequences (often shot on grainy stock with a hand-held camera) with found footage culled from television broadcasts. The destruction of Radio Ragazza and Phoenix Radio, for example, is depicted with found footage chronicling the destruction of an Italian pirate radio sta-tion. Staged demonstrations foregrounding the enraged protagonists merge almost imperceptibly into newsreel footage of actual protest rallies. The film's tolerance, in fact its preference, for hybrid ideologies—evidence of subjects "in process"[135] rather than stable identities—is rooted in its penchant for exploratory aesthetic foraging.

Borden's inventive cinematic style is matched by her resourceful appro-priation of important anti-authoritarian currents. The Women's Army anti-hierarchical structure, for example, unmistakably resembles one of the most influential modes of anarchist organization—the affinity group. Borrowed from a term—*grupo de afinidad*—coined by Spanish anarchists, the affinity group is described by Murray Bookchin as a "collective of intimate friends who are no less concerned with their human relationships than with their social goals."[136] The anti-hierarchical structure of the affinity group, with its emphasis on both the "rational, as well as the joyous, sensuous, and the aesthetic side of the revolution,"[137] aptly encapsulates Borden's undogmatic feminism while also confounding the efforts of the film's authority figures to understand the Women's Army's instinctive knack for what Colin Ward called "spontaneous order."[138] The authorities are incredulous when confronted with an organization that spurns the regimentation and centralized leadership preferred by Leninists as well as the established middle-class parties. This bewilderment is amusingly illustrated in a sequence in which an FBI agent (played with comic sang-froid by Ron Vawter) attempts to explain the baffling transiency of affinity groups by drawing three concentric circles on a blackboard and droning on about "small cells" that frustrated concerted endeavors to "determine at any one time who is in charge." His exasperation with an all-female group whose decentralized structure makes effective infiltration virtually impossible helps to underline the fact that the anti-bureaucratic orientation of the affinity group corresponded to influential currents within the early women's movement that were intuitively anarchistic. Anarcho-feminist Peggy Kornegger maintained that "in many unconnected areas of the U.S., CR [consciousness-raising groups] developed as a spontaneous, direct reaction to patriarchal forms," bearing a "striking resemblance to . . . anarchist affinity groups in Spain, France, and many other countries."[139] *Born in Flames* does not portray the members of the Women's Army as unblemished heroines, implicitly affirming Jo Freeman's contention that feminist affinity groups often fell prey to the "tyranny of structurelessness"—a political malaise supposedly characterized by occasional elitism, the star system,' and political impotence.[140]

Ultimately, *Born in Flames* proved most scandalous, both within the feminist movement and outside it, by resisting the temptation to condemn definitively the use of revolutionary violence. This decision was partially a strategic provocation by Borden, since the encomiums given to the pacifistic anti-nuclear activists of Greenham Common in England (adherents of one variety of anarchist passive resistance) by many radical women during the early 1980s "ascribed to women a state of natural non-violence"[141] that she found dubiously essentialist. The Women's Army climactic bombing of a transmitter atop the World Trade Center made the film vulnerable to accusations that its anarcho-feminist reinterpretation of propaganda by the deed was not only adventurist, but also unabashedly silly. Yet the exhilaration that Borden's women experience as they perform an impromptu *attentat* that targets a behemoth of mass communications instead of an individual tyrant provides them with a brief moment of empowerment that can be both valued and found wanting. The ambivalence concerning anarchist violence in *Born in Flames* recasts the nuanced debates on the strengths and limitations of acts of terror that peppers Emma Goldman and Alexander Berkman's correspondence. In the space of one furiously argued letter to Berkman, Goldman asserted that "in the light of our experience we know that acts of violence are inevitable," but also denounced most of them as "pathetically inadequate."[142]

Journeys from Berlin/1971 and *Born in Flames* not only shed light on the particularistic concerns of anarchist women. These films' refusal to simplistically advocate either absolute pacifism or a program of universal armed struggle mirrors the complex historical debates within the anarchist movement between Tolstoyan pacifists and militant proponents of forms of direct action that do not preclude the use of tactical violence. Another strain of contemporary anarchism, best represented by the legacy of Britain's "Angry Brigade" and the Thatcher-era polemics of the London-based newspaper *Class War*,[143] associates passive resistance with crypto-religious, reactionary tendencies and obstinately maintains that armed struggle is an essential component of working-class anarchism. The tradition of anarcho-feminism, and the often confused but resolutely idealistic protagonists of Rainer and Borden's films, suggest that anarchist women are often uneasily wedged between unsavory polarities—they refuse to endorse wholeheartedly the often macho tradition of propaganda by the deed, but are equally alienated by a reflexive nonviolence that coincides with clichéd preconceptions of feminine radicalism.

Although some militant feminists were outraged that Borden's subsequent film, *Working Girls* (1986), shifted gears from insurrectionary concerns to the more mundane milieu of a middle-class bordello, an awareness of trends within contemporary feminism confirms that these two concerns are actually intertwined. As early as the 1970s, strains within Autonomist Marxism and anarchism, exemplified by Mariarosa Dalla Costa's participation in the Wages for Housework movement, campaigned for the rights of sex workers within a sphere in which capitalist production is intimately allied with questions of domestic "reproduction."[144]

2. Cinema, Anarchism, and Revolution

Heroes, Martyrs,
and Utopian Moments

Anarchism and the Specter of State Socialism

The hegemony enjoyed by mainstream socialists in the years following the Russian Revolution relegated anarchism to a relatively marginal status. (Spain, as we shall see, was a notable exception.) Filmmakers implicitly accepted Max Nomad's conclusion that anarchism was a "dying creed"[1] and moved on to trendier objects of opprobrium. Occasionally, however, a reference to Bakunin proved sufficient to establish a protagonist's rebellious credentials. In Sergio Leone's tongue-in-cheek tribute to the romance of explosives during the Mexican Revolution, *A Fistful of Dynamite* (a.k.a. *Duck You Sucker*, 1972),[2] an anarchist peasant named Juan (played with slapstick relish by Rod Steiger) embodies a comic-book version of Eric Hobsbawm's "social banditry."[3] He proudly carries a Spanish edition of Bakunin's writings with him during his trek through the countryside, but his sidekick, an ex-IRA explosives expert named Sean (James Coburn), displays his populist scorn for intellectualized anarchism by throwing the book into the mud. Mario Monicelli's antiwar comedy *La grande guerra* (*The Great War,* 1959) features a speech by a recalcitrant soldier, played by Vittorio Gassman, who needs only to shout his approval of Bakunin's injunction to "fight privilege" for the audience to realize that he will never be reconciled to the yoke of authority.

Even when Peter Lilienthal made Malatesta the center of his narrative in a respectful film of the same name (*Malatesta*, 1971), the Italian theorist and activist's noteworthy achievements in his native Italy were ignored in favor of a glum chronicle of a relatively insignificant period in the famous anarchist's life: his dispiriting visit to London during the time of the Sidney

Street siege. Eddie Constantine's sullen portrayal of Malatesta gives little indication that this aging radical was known for his passion and oratory; despite good intentions, Lilienthal appears merely to endorse the common view that the anarchists were doomed to suffer the consequences of being history's losers. Robin Blackburn protests that "bourgeois sociology only begins to understand modern revolutions in so far as they fail."[4] But the discussion that follows assumes that we can often learn more from this century's revolutionary defeats than from its ostensible revolutionary victories; the cinema's representation of anarchist heroes, martyrs, and fleeting revolutionary moments will enable us to formulate a critique of mainstream socialism that is far indeed from the banalities of bourgeois sociology.

After the Bolshevik Revolution of 1917, anarchism was fated to be judged by the standards of what eventually became known as "actually existing socialism." When Bertrand Russell wrote an insightful critique of the Soviet Union's "Bonapartist military autocracy," in 1920, Floyd Dell, who was once decidedly sympathetic to anarchism, condemned Russell as a reactionary. The philosopher's objections to state socialism were faulted for their resemblance to the grumblings of non-Bolsheviks, namely Mensheviks, Social Revolutionaries, and Anarchists, who had "been cluttering up the progress of Russian history for the past three years."[5] Anarchism was derided as "petty bourgeois" by Lenin and consigned to the past by so-called progressives, whether devout communists or mere liberals. The Spanish Revolution of the 1930s, and to a lesser extent the revived interest in anti-authoritarian thought during the 1960s, would ultimately breathe new life into a left-libertarianism that mainstream leftists loved to dismiss smugly as a throwback to the nineteenth century. But the aftermath of the Russian Revolution determined anarchism's ongoing two-pronged critique: a sustained interest in social revolution coupled with the belief that "it is impossible to use authoritarian means to realize libertarian ends,"[6] a conclusion strengthened by the disillusionment bred by the Soviet experience.

Two films, Bo Widerberg's *Joe Hill* (1971) and Giuliano Montaldo's *Sacco and Vanzetti* (1971), deal with a transitional historical period before the final polarization of Bolshevism and anarchism. These films are reverential tributes to radical martyrs, and reflect the fact that these members of the Old Left pantheon have long been heralded as all-purpose leftists whose legacies provide useful object-lessons for socialists, liberals, and communists, as well as anarchists. After their executions, Hill, the Swedish Wobbly whose life is still enveloped in mystery, and Nicola Sacco and Bartolomeo Vanzetti, the fiery Italian American workers who never relinquished their anarchist creed, were anointed secular saints. Hill faced the firing squad in Utah two years before the Russian Revolution; Sacco's and Vanzetti's deaths came in 1927, at a time when the young Soviet state had long abandoned its early efforts to woo anarchists into the party fold. By contrast, Travis Wilkerson's essay film, *An Injury to One,* is less invested in romantic hagiography and focuses on the systemic causes that triggered the murder of Frank Little, an IWW activist. Widerberg and Montaldo's films, their earnestness notwithstanding, demonstrate the limitations of the biopic while Wilkerson's digressive anti-biopic affirms the virtues of deploying a more stripped-down aesthetic to convey the consequences of radical martyrdom.

Joe Hill tackles the life of perhaps the most cryptic figure in the history of American radicalism. Hill was accused by the Utah authorities of robbing and murdering a grocer. Liberals, socialists, and anarchists have long been preoccupied with confirming the state's complicity in a frame-up that has turned the unassuming Swedish immigrant into a hallowed American leftist. It is even difficult to determine whether Hill, the famed "labor martyr,"[7] considered himself an anarchist. The Industrial Workers of the World—the organization with which he was linked during the best-documented phase of his career as a trade unionist—has been variously considered anarcho-syndicalist, an almost unprecedented amalgam of Marxism and anarchism, and, most commonly, if simplistically, a distinctively American variety of frontier leftism that could not conceivably be compared to European traditions of syndicalism or Marxism.[8]

As numerous reviewers noted at the time of the film's release,[9] Widerberg's film avoids addressing these political niceties by creating a sentimentalized Joe Hill, who is more archetypal folk hero than anarchist or libertarian Marxist. This strategy will not surprise anyone familiar with mainstream Hollywood biopics; what is interesting, for our purposes, is how the film, consciously or not, avoids the more anarchistic components of Hill's life while emphasizing his status as a folksy balladeer. Widerberg's film, moreover, must be understood partly as a Swedish director's attempt to make sense of the impact of American social and political mores on the Swedish immigrant Joseph Hilstrom (born Joel Emmanuel Hägglund), the man who would eventually reemerge as the legendary Joe Hill. Just as Jan Troell's *The Emigrants* (1971) and *The New Land* (1972) provide painstaking depictions of the rural hardships experienced by Swedish immigrants in the new world, Widerberg offers brief glimpses of the travails suffered by his forebears once their dreams were shattered by American urban squalor.

Even if the director of the famously saccharine *Elvira Madigan* cannot always control his weakness for soft-focus landscapes, these opening sequences benefit from Widerberg's gift for often effective, if crudely honed, lyricism. As is often the case with films that psychologize political protest, the protagonist's later revolutionary stance is depicted as primarily an outgrowth of personal despondency. According to Widerberg's impressionistic schema, Hill's future radicalism is rooted in a failure to find gainful employment in New York and the personal alienation he suffers when estranged from his Swedish siblings in the New World. The film's curiously unworldly Hill is primed for radicalism by a small boy whose colloquial patter is accompanied by rather standard visual contrasts—a close-up, for example, of the opera house followed by a panning shot of homeless men. The romantic subplot that often provides narrative ballast to biographical films in fact commingles the bloated privilege represented by the opera house and the economic exploitation encapsulated in shots of New York's slum dwellers. Disregarding the fact that next to nothing is known about Hill's love life, *Joe Hill*'s script provides its hero with a working-class Beatrice: a fellow Swedish immigrant named Lucia whom he meets while furtively listening to a Metropolitan Opera performance astride the theater's fire escape. Fusing working-class solidarity and the pleasures of high culture, the unemployed Hill finds temporary bliss with this fish-shop employee. Before long, the film dispatches Hill from the teeming streets of New York to the even more chaotic West and makes a far less seamless transition to the greenhorn's fondness for boxcar-hopping.

The ensuing sequences—which highlight shots of hoboes making their escape from cramped train cars, and include an extended analysis of the "tricks of the employing class" by a Wobbly named Mackie—are truer to the spirit of turn-of-the-century radicalism than a film like Martin Scorsese's *Boxcar Bertha* (1972).[10] (In time-honored B movie fashion, the IWW milieu is only the pretext for Scorsese's Cormanesque emphasis on sex and crime.) But, despite Widerberg's attentiveness to the romance of the rails, his film gives few indications that he is aware of the extent of Hill's anarchist affinities. For example, the virtual certainty that Hill supported Ricardo and Enrique Flores Magón's efforts to topple the regime of Mexican dictator Porfirio Díaz is not even broached.[11] Less well-known than Emiliano Zapata's peasant radicalism, the thinly veiled anarchism of the brothers' Junta Organizadora del Partido Liberal Mexicano (PLM) "anticipated the Zapatista agrarian revolution in more than just its slogan of 'Land and Liberty.'"[12] It is true that Hill's apparent alliance with the Magonists provides a filmmaker with little anecdotal information to draw upon. Yet, although there is no tangible evidence that Hill participated in the IWW free speech campaigns, *Joe Hill* suggests that his oratory was an instrumental component of their fight for civil liberties. The film's Hill remains a Christ-like cipher, committed to social change as long as it is not excessively violent or inflammatory.

Widerberg, whose work redefines the notion of a "lyrical left," prefers Hill, the "guerrilla minstrel"[13] with a knack for ingenious ditties, who might be considered a Swedish precursor of Woody Guthrie or Pete Seeger, to Hill the insurrectionist. *Joe Hill* ignores its hero's fondness for industrial sabotage, preferring to focus on his composition of such beloved ballads as "The Preacher and the Slave" and "The Rebel Girl." Hill's death in 1915, on the cusp of the radical movement's utter transformation, paved the way for his enshrinement as a folk poet whose sentiments were congenial to communists and liberal trade unionists as well as anarchists. As Robert Cantwell notes with subtle astringency, "when the culture of the Wobbly met the ideological left in the thirties, it discovered a kind of resurrection of itself in the . . . austere personal discipline of Leninism, as well as in the . . . projects and worker legions of the New Deal."[14] The odd conversion of Joe Hill into a Popular Front hero can probably be attributed to the fact that his brand of IWW militancy, although implicitly anarchistic, was vague enough to encourage hagiographers to mold him into a peculiar hybrid of Paul Bunyan and Earl Browder. Remaining true to this muddled ideological heritage, *Joe Hill* features Joan Baez singing Earl Robinson and Alfred Hayes's Popular Front anthem "The Ballad of Joe Hill" on the soundtrack. Eric Scholl's documentary *The Return of Joe Hill* (1990) hints that this "organic intellectual" carried the torch for an indigenous popular culture that has never been fully recognized by elite arbiters of taste. The aging Wobbly Carlos Cortez and the labor historian Joyce Kornbluh laud Hill as an exemplary representative of "workers' culture"; Cortez argues that Hill's lyrics and cartoons went a long way to define culture as an entity that could be claimed by the workers as well as by the wealthy. But both Widerberg's fictional labor idyll and Scholl's modest documentary, while offering occasional evidence of Hill's ties to anarcho-syndicalism, are testimonials to his goodness and martyrdom instead of full-bodied political portraits.

While Widerberg's portrait of Joe Hill is emblematic of well-intentioned liberal nostalgia, Travis Wilkerson's *An Injury to One* (2002), a documentary essay exploring the 1917 lynching of IWW activist Frank Little, known for his impassioned rhetoric while organizing copper miners in Butte, Montana, is an intriguing hybrid that synthesizes disparate cinematic currents—agitprop, Brechtian interludes, and self-reflexive narration. *An Injury to One* is noteworthy for upending a mainstream documentary tradition (exemplified by films such as *The Wobblies* and *The Good Fight*) that relies on interviews, archival footage, and an omniscient, depersonalized strain of voiceover.

Instead of taking his cues from traditional historians or documentarians, Wilkerson concedes that he was more influenced by the tradition of Third

Cinema. Although Wilkerson acknowledges that he viewed *The Wobblies* and consulted mainstream academic accounts of radical American syndicalism, his film's thematic and stylistic impetus is, in the final analysis, more indebted to having grown up in Butte, as well as his discovery of Cuban documentarian Santiago Álvarez's extraordinarily cost-effective form of agitprop.[15] Wilkerson's ability to function as a "one-man-band"[16]—a filmmaker operating as director, writer, and editor—is doubtless a legacy of Alvarez's cinematic credo—"Give me two photos, music, and a moviola, and I'll give you a movie."

In the spirit of anti-platitudinous agitprop, even the historical record becomes a site of contention, as Wilkerson recounts known facts concerning Little, occasionally referred to as merely "the agitator." An account of Little's second speech to the miners during the 1917 strike synthesizes factoids assembled from company spies from the Anaconda corporation—for example, assertions that the government views the Constitution as a piece of paper that could easily be torn up if found an impediment to corporate control, as well as credible disdain for Woodrow Wilson and his warmongering. For Wilkerson, this demonstrates how "company history" becomes indistinguishable from "official history," a quandary that mirrors the methodological dilemmas faced by radical labor historians in the tradition of Herbert Gutman and David Montgomery who attempt to practice history from "the bottom up." Even though Little's life and death is well-documented, biographical accounts such as Arnold Stead's *Always on Strike: Frank Little and the Western Wobblies*, demonstrate the fact that many of Little's pronouncements, particularly his more "seditious" statements, are culled from company organs like the *Daily Post* and the *Anaconda Standard*.[17] Wilkerson, however, is able to invoke some of Little's own words preserved in a pamphlet—an exhortation to "abolish the wage system . . . and establish a socialist commonwealth" that corresponds to the credo of militant anarcho-syndicalism.

Early in the film, affinities between Butte, where copper mining led to eventual environmental devastation, and "Poisonville," the fictional setting of Dashiell Hammett's *Red Harvest,* inspire a noirish ambiance. The historian Peter Rachleff speculates that *An Injury to One* might be characterized as the "first 'postmodern' labor film"[18] and the film's open-endedness, fueled by an inability of the filmmaker to tie up historical loose ends, is a seamless match with the hardboiled ambiguities of Hammett's prose. As in *Red Harvest,* Wilkerson depicts a milieu where it's difficult to distinguish criminals from capitalists and anything resembling a moral compass is nonexistent. Wilkerson reminds us that Lillian Hellman's memoir *Scoundrel Time* intimates that Hammett, during his sojourn working as a Pinkerton agent in Butte, was offered $5,000 to kill Frank Little. Nevertheless, because Anaconda destroyed the records that might implicate Frank Little's killer or killers, the identity of the culprit is unknowable. Yet Hammett becomes an essential component of the associative chain of digressions that Wilkerson constructs in his film essay. Hammett's refusal to name names, which led to his imprisonment during the Blacklist era, enables his McCarthy-era travails to be linked with the equally rabid campaign against anarchists, Wobblies, and foreign radicals during the early years of the twentieth century. Wilkerson's playful modus operandi depends on a certain radical serendipity. To wit, a man named "Joseph McCarthy," listed among Wobblies accused of "sedition" during the 1917 strike, generates an excursus on the leitmotif of "McCarthyism" in American political culture. A 1995 incident, in which a flock of geese perish in a polluted Butte lake, succinctly affirms that the twenty-first century's global environmental crisis is merely a massive extension of the toxic ethos exemplified by Hammett's "Poisonville." The remnants of the radical labor movement realize that the ravages of pollution are inextricably tied to economic exploitation. As Naomi Klein makes clear, "(R)esistance to high-risk extreme extraction is building a global grassroots, and broad-based network the likes of which the environmental movement has rarely seen."[19]

The value of Wilkerson's documentary essay resides in its ability to maintain a salutary aesthetic distance without aestheticizing its subject matter. Flashing nearly the entire preamble to the IWW constitution on the screen at the beginning of the film might seem like nothing but an outré Godardian gesture. But the unadulterated emphasis on class struggle embedded in the preamble possesses a surprising potency when read in this context, especially since even the most earnest radicals of our era rarely express themselves with such bluntness. Take, for example, the first paragraph: "The working class and the employing class have nothing in common. There can be no peace so long as hunger and want are found among millions of the working people and the few, who make up the employing class, have all the good things of life." The words of the preamble almost take on the tenor of silent incantations. Similarly, a subsequent sequence in the film documenting the IWW's "free speech" campaigns features a pithy onscreen query: "If we can't discuss, how can we invent?" Invoking the allure of free speech, coupled with "invention," summons up certain aesthetic priorities that were always part of the IWW's agenda. As the authors of *Solidarity Forever: An Oral History of the IWW* assert: "A distinguishing feature of the IWW approach was that rather than trying to win the allegiance of artists already recognized by the dominant culture, the IWW had the audacity to believe workers could create their own art. The aim was to liberate the imagination as well as the flesh."[20]

To an even greater extent than the Hill affair or Little's murder, the Sacco and Vanzetti case became a *cause célèbre* that inspired feuding leftists to join forces. Montaldo's film cannot ignore its protagonists' anarchism, but a tendency to veer from political thriller to lukewarm humanist uplift (Joan Baez again sings the theme song—"The Ballad of Sacco and Vanzetti") gives little indication of Sacco and Vanzetti's anarcho-communist fervor. *Sacco and Vanzetti* is essentially a simplified version of Herbert Ehrmann's meticulously documented argument that the robbery and murder of a paymaster in South Braintree, Massachusetts, which the prosecution pinned on the Italian anarchists, was actually the work of a network of criminals known as the Morelli gang.[21] Grappling, rather ineptly, with the class tensions peculiar to Boston that pitted a vindictive, Harvard-educated prosecutor, Frederick Katzmann, against impoverished Italian immigrants, Montaldo avoids the nuances of Sacco and Vanzetti's anarchism. *Sacco and Vanzetti* suffers from an ill-conceived effort to find parallels between the frenzied anti-radicalism that plagued the United States in the 1920s and analogous examples of contemporary Italian malfeasance. For example, there is a clear rhetorical inspiration for Montaldo's decision to detail the death of Sacco and Vanzetti's comrade, Andrea Salsedo, in an early sequence. The death of Salsedo, an advocate of anarchist direct action whose detention by the police can only be understood within the context of the government's vendetta against immigrant radicalism, was reported as a suicide despite the fact that anarchists viewed the official story with skepticism. While there is apparently little doubt that Salsedo actually killed himself, Montaldo is undoubtedly trying to link Salsedo's death with the genuinely murky "suicide" of Giuseppe Pinelli, a militant Italian anarchist whose death in 1969 "inspired Dario Fo's play *Accidental Death of an Anarchist.*"[22]

Sacco and Vanzetti's earnest attempt to emulate the thrillers of Francesco Rosi and Costa-Gavras sometimes backfires, but Montaldo does his best to place his heroes within a precise historical framework. An opening montage outlining the virulence of the anti-red Palmer raids (named after the notoriously reactionary attorney general) elucidates the tendency, still vibrant in the 1920s, to lump anarchists, socialists, and communists into a monolithic subversive threat. But just as Palmer himself could not distinguish between ideological factions, the film sidesteps Sacco and Vanzetti's specific anarchist beliefs (their indebtedness to the work of Luigi Galleani is delineated by Paul Avrich in a ground-breaking study[23]) for the narrative pyrotechnics of courtroom drama. Sacco and Vanzetti emerge as near-angelic anarchist lambs reluctantly led to the slaughter. In perhaps the film's pivotal sequence, Katzmann, directly confronting Sacco and Vanzetti, fumes that they "can never understand American ideals" because they "can't even speak our language." Katzmann's tirade prompts Sacco to reiterate his faith in anarchism and Vanzetti to testify that he "wants to live, but in a better world." This rather innocuous avowal seems cribbed from a letter Vanzetti wrote to Elizabeth Evans, which eloquently expresses (despite his limited command of English) his belief that the "anarchist looks for his liberty in the liberty of all, for his happiness in the happiness of all, for his welfare in the universal welfare."[24] The film captures Vanzetti's slightly platitudinous altruism, but fails to capture his (and Sacco's) ardent belief in propaganda by the deed.

This failure of nerve becomes even more pronounced as the film progresses. The contretemps between the two anarchists and Katzmann is followed by footage of demonstrators urging freedom for "Bart and Nick." Montaldo, like a barrage of writers with liberal, Marxist, and even anarchist sympathies, is primarily preoccupied with Bart and Nick's presumed innocence, despite the film's unavoidable acknowledgment of their anarchism. *Sacco and Vanzetti*'s urge to vindicate its heroes ends up (despite the compensation of Gian Maria Volonté's moving portrayal of Vanzetti) diluting their political convictions. Oddly enough, before the publication of Avrich's comprehensive study, the conservative journalist Francis Russell was one of the few writers to convey, albeit from a hostile perspective, the true nature of Sacco and Vanzetti's revolutionary anarchism.[25] Russell, making use of information culled from historians sympathetic to anarchism such as Avrich and Nunzio Pernicone, briefly details the immigrants' gradual progress from apolitical workers to disciples of Galleani, an unashamed advocate of revolutionary violence. Sacco and Vanzetti's apparent devotion to the Galleanist belief that "individual acts of rebellion . . . ineffable, inexorable, like air and like destiny,"[26] are necessary to crystallize revolutionary ferment leads Russell to excoriate these radicals as victims of a flickering "flame of paranoia": adherents of an irrational "cult of anarchism."

The Sacco and Vanzetti case marked the last time for many years after the Russian Revolution that U.S. communists felt compelled to come to the aid of beleaguered anarchists. In the light of the stinging indictments of the Soviet Union eventually published by Emma Goldman and Alexander Berkman,[27] it is important to remember that the blurring of anarchism and communism in the popular mind reached its apogee after the Bolshevik revolution. Christopher Lasch summarized the American government, press, and public's initial stupefied reaction to the revolution by drily observing that it was assumed that "the Bolsheviks, like all radicals since Robespierre, were at bottom opposed to 'order'"; Secretary of State Lansing's contention that "Bolshevism was the worst form of anarchism" typified this kind of befuddlement.[28] Of course, Berkman and Goldman's disillusionment with the Soviet experiment was not an overnight development. Their rejection of "the Bolshevik myth" was preceded by a brief period of euphoria in which they hailed the revolution as a historic milestone. As early as 1918, hopes that the Bolsheviks would at least pay some credence to a left-libertarian path dwindled when they fired their cannons upon the homes of Moscow anarchists.

The decision of the young Soviet state to centralize production and end their once enthusiastic support for workers' control generated a heated debate within the international left. For the council communist Otto Rühle, Bolshevism "remained fundamentally within the class frame of the bourgeois order," a bureaucratic formation uninterested in abolishing "the wage system" or promoting "proletarian self-determination over the products of labor."[29] From an antithetical perspective, Victor Serge, the anarchist-turned-Bolshevik, insisted that this reorientation of priorities was a provisional necessity that preserved socialist goals during the years of so-called "War Communism."[30]

Given the familiar constrictions of the commercial cinema, these historical fine points are rarely even alluded to in most Hollywood films. Occasionally, the propensity of filmmakers to foreground romance against a blurry background of revolution is interrupted with an interlude that briefly illuminates the tensions between Bolsheviks and anarchists. In David Lean's kitschy adaptation of Boris Pasternak's *Doctor Zhivago* (1965), screenwriter Robert Bolt expands on the novel's sympathetic portrait of "Kostoied-Amursky, a gray-haired revolutionary co-operativist, who had been in all the forced-labor camps of the old regime and was now discovering those of the new."[31] "Co-operativism" is a synonym for Kropotkinite communalism, and the Bolt–Lean version of Zhivago's encounter with the unrepentant anarchist on a congested train as they both leave Moscow for the Urals makes it clear that the filmmakers are determined to treat radical "co-operativism" with gingerly detachment. Pasternak's vaguely defined character (who nevertheless clearly elicits Zhivago's empathy) is treated ambiguously in the opulent film version. His unkempt, wild-haired presence is in sharp contrast to Omar Sharif's matinee-idol demeanor as Zhivago. The truculent co-operativist's reply to a poker-faced Bolshevik who declares "I want no anarchy" is in the form of a defiant declaration: "Long live anarchy!—I am the only free man on this train, the rest of you are cattle." This sentiment is not explicitly mocked by Lean, but the character's eccentric appearance and spontaneous outburst makes this relic of the Russian past as comically earnest as he is patently honest.

Kropotkin himself makes a brief appearance in Herman Axelbank's 1937 documentary *From Tsar to Lenin*. This assemblage of newsreel footage and stentorian narration is mainly of interest for offering an anti-Stalinist, essentially Trotskyist, version of Lenin's ascent during a decade when the Comintern had written both Trotskyists and anarchists out of history. The noted American leftist Max Eastman (who would become a curmudgeonly right-winger by the 1950s) intones his own narration in a high-pitched squeak; at one crucial point he portentously informs us that "Prince Peter Kropotkin, famous anarchist, foretold the storms to come" as the aging anarchist communist tips his hat to the camera. During the decades that preceded the preparation of *From Tsar to Lenin,* Eastman's skewed view of anarchism was typical of individuals who did their best to cope with the rapid transition from the era of the anarchist peril to the ravages of the red scare. Eastman's biographer recounts how "nothing upset him more than the deportation . . . of Emma Goldman, Alexander Berkman and 247 other aliens" in 1919, despite the fact that he dismissed his friend Robert Minor's criticisms of the Soviet Union as the whining of an anarchist.[32] Axelbank's film is also noteworthy for illustrating (perhaps inadvertently) the enormous chasm that separates pre-1917 American radicalism from the post-Leninist variant. Big Bill Haywood, the embodiment of the IWW's intransigent American syndicalism, is shown silently looking on as Soviet apparatchiks pontificate at a rally. The conversion of the fiery Haywood into a docile servant of the Soviet state is poignantly conveyed in a 1923 letter of Emma Goldman in which she laments that the "worst crime they [the Soviets] have committed against Bill . . . was that they induced him to . . . run away from the responsibilities of the IWW movement."[33] Unlike Haywood, Kropotkin, divining the authoritarian "storms" that Eastman speaks of in his voice-over, differentiated between "state communism" and "anarchist communism." He expressed his misgivings concerning Bolshevism to Lenin, warning him that "even if a party dictatorship were the proper means to strike a blow at the capitalist system (which I seriously doubt), *it is positively harmful for the building of a new socialist system.*"[34] This intriguing, if ultimately unsatisfying, documentary provoked a typically seriocomic feud between Trotskyists and Stalinists. (By this time, American anarchists were too marginalized to have any of their objections surface in the mainstream press.) The *Daily Worker* attacked the film for overlooking the role of Stalin in the revolution, while Eastman replied with mock innocence that he couldn't find any archival footage of Stalin sharing the spotlight with Lenin and Trotsky during the early days of revolutionary upheaval.

Years later, when Old Left debates were only hazily understood, Warren Beatty's *Reds* introduced Emma Goldman, as well as her friend and some-time antagonist, journalist John Reed, to a generation scarred by memories of Vietnam. *Reds* was intriguingly, if disappointingly, schizoid: screenwriter

Trevor Griffiths' politically savvy dialogue co-existed uneasily with a florid romantic subplot that made *Doctor Zhivago* seem surprisingly restrained. Goldman (stripped of her Russian-inflected English in Maureen Stapleton's otherwise admirable performance) is treated respectfully, even if the film's fuzzy view of both anarchism and Bolshevism often makes her seem more like a petulant liberal than a full-blooded revolutionary. Andrew Sarris, for example, whose review indicated that he had barely heard of Goldman before seeing *Reds,* informed his readers that "Emma Goldman . . . became disillusioned with life in the Soviet Union as early as 1919"; he confessed that he had "been told by scholars in the field that her disillusionment is well-documented!"[35] As the title of her memoir indicates, Goldman was indeed "disillusioned" with Russia. Unfortunately, a prototypical "God that failed" despondency—not Goldman's anarchist communism—became the dominant interpretive trope for Sarris and his critical cohorts.

Whatever this epic's shortcomings, Beatty and Griffiths's depiction of the left's internal warfare is generally incisive, although their emphasis on self-contained dramatic confrontations occasionally loses sight of the larger historical context.[36] A dramatization of a famous confrontation between Reed and a distraught Goldman near the end of *Reds* is a case in point. Some of the heated debates between these former allies (as recounted by Goldman in *Living My Life*) are cleverly interspersed with believably fabricated dialogue. As in her autobiography, Goldman's objection to the Cheka's arrest and the state's eventual execution of five hundred supposed "counter-revolutionaries" is followed by Reed's patronizing reprimand that his comrade seems "a little confused by the Revolution in action" because she has "dealt with it only in theory."[37] Beatty also replicates Reed's suggestion that Goldman brew "a cup of the good old American coffee," which acts as a soothing elixir in this film's universe of discourse. But the explanatory framework that precedes this poignant moment—Goldman's pained realization that the Bolsheviks themselves had assumed a counter-revolutionary role by their repressive treatment of non-Bolshevik radicals (primarily anarchists and Social Revolutionaries) is absent. By the time of Goldman's *cri de coeur* in 1919, Lenin had abandoned the pseudo-anarchism of *State and Revolution* for an unmitigated assault on the "ultra-left" in *Left-Wing Communism—An Infantile Disorder.* For this increasingly conservative firebrand, genuine workers' control was expendable, and "state capitalism wasn't a danger . . . it was, on the contrary, something to be aimed for."[38]

Despite growing repression, anarchism remained aboveground in the Soviet Union until 1921. As Leonard Schapiro observes, many Communist Party members were willing to tolerate repressive measures taken against socialists more than against anarchists, since they had fought alongside the anarchists during the early days of the revolution.[39] After the massacre of the rebellious Kronstadt sailors in winter 1921, formerly loyal Bolsheviks, whom Trotsky himself had referred to as the "pride of the Revolution," as well as anarchists and other dissidents who supported the sailors' short-lived commune, were no longer treated with even grudging tolerance. As historians of various ideological stripes make clear,[40] the sailors did not seek to dismantle communism but merely took literally the slogan "all power to the Soviets," which war communism and the subsequent quasi-capitalist NEP blithely ignored.

It is one of the many peculiarities of film history that the Kronstadt events, which proved traumatic for many partisans of the international left, have never been depicted with even a modicum of honesty on screen. Samson Samsonov's ingloriously didactic *Optimistic Tragedy* (1963) is typical of Soviet attempts to rationalize the brutal assault on the Kronstadt communards, even if this production understandably avoided references to Trotsky, the man most responsible for implementing the massacre. This faithful adaptation of a play by Vsevolod Vishnevsky collapsed the still-controversial events of 1921 into a protracted feud between a nameless female commissar and a bloodthirsty sailor named Vozhak, who bears no apparent resemblance to any of the actual participants in the Kronstadt uprising. Even many who viewed the Kronstadt rebellion as ill-advised admitted that the sailors were guided by deeply held principles, but Samsonov's leaden film depicts them as thieving, lascivious boors.

The Ukrainian anarchist Nestor Makhno was possibly even more maligned than the Kronstadt communards by official Soviet historians. Makhno began his guerrilla campaign during the Russian Civil War with daring raids against the White forces and, despite an initially congenial relationship with Lenin and the Soviet regime, was forced to fight the Reds, owing to unremitting Bolshevik hostility to the libertarian communism that many of the region's radicalized peasants embraced. Makhno's colleague Peter Arshinov provides a fairly comprehensive account of the movement's conception of anarchist social revolution and analyzes the strengths and sometimes fatal weaknesses of the strategies formulated by its Revolutionary Military Council. Yet the wartime destruction of crucial documentation has frustrated contemporary historians' efforts to embellish the incomplete biographical and political portrait of Makhno painted by comrades such as Arshinov and Voline (*nom de plume* of Vsevolod Mikhailovitch Eichenbaum).[41] An essay by Paul Avrich lays to rest unwarranted claims that Makhno was an illiterate bandit or a rabid anti-Semite. For Avrich, this "cossack of anarchy"[42] cannot be easily pigeon-holed; he emerges as both a self-consciously anti-authoritarian activist and a peasant leader whose anti-statism derived its potency from "the cossack–peasant rebellions of the seventeenth and eighteenth centuries."[43] He acknowledges, however, that there are aspects of Makhno's life and career that are still frustratingly inaccessible to even the most assiduous historians.

It would be surprising indeed if the Soviet cinema treated Makhno with anything but derision. What is surprising is that an early silent comedy, Ivan Perestiani's *Krasniye diavolyata* (*Little Red Imps*, 1923) treats the Makhnovist challenge to Bolshevik hegemony with a light touch that is more reminiscent of American slapstick humor than the lugubrious didacticism that would reign supreme in the subsequent Stalinist cinema. Despite the fact that Trotsky thought Makhno more dangerous than the reactionary White general Denikin, Perestiani's film, as light-hearted as Lev Kuleshov's better-known *The Extraordinary Adventures of Mr. West in the Land of the Bolsheviks* (1924), treats its Makhno surrogate as a relatively benign figure of fun, not a malevolent counterrevolutionary. Richard Stites notes that "the cultural fate of Makhno was ironic, since if any epic deserved romanticized and sympathetic treatment in fiction and cinema, it was that of his Ukrainian Insurgent Horse Army . . . [a] story closer to the legends of Stenka Razin and other folk rebels than anything in the Bolshevik hagiography."[44]

Since Makhno was summarily dismissed by both Soviet and conservative historians as little more than an anarchist bandit, it should not come as much of a shock that Alexander Berkman's film scenario *Batko Voilno* (c.1924),[45] a highly romanticized (if not inaccurate) version of the Cossack leader's early life, was never produced. Berkman names his hero Ivan instead of Nestor, but does not even bother to change the name of Makhno's birthplace, a village named Gulay-Pole. The affinities between anarchism and a colorful peasant past are accentuated in the scenario's first paragraph, in which the Ukraine countryside is described as an "old home of the Cossacks, whose love of fight and dare-devilry are celebrated in the heroic annals of Russia." Berkman dramatizes Makhno's youthful anarchist activities and his condemnation to death as an anti-government conspirator in 1908 (a sentence later "commuted to life"[46] because of the prisoner's age); in Berkman's somewhat sentimentalized narrative "the tireless efforts of his mother save his life." But Berkman's fondness for embellishing his scenario with treacly details does not prevent him from detailing the Makhnovist movement's experiments in agrarian self-management, although the ultra-heroic figure of Ivan is somewhat at odds with the Ukrainian collectives' communal spirit:

> By the inspiration of Ivan, the peasantry deprives the landed gentry of their too-great holdings in land and property. Everybody is given an equal

share and necessary machinery and tools become common property. The advice of Ivan is sought by the village folk in every knotty problem, and his influence considerably spreads . . . he becomes the acknowledged leader of the whole province.

Although an oft-repeated rumor that Makhno once worked as a village schoolteacher has been definitively disproved, Berkman's scenario provides the idealized peasant leader with a schoolteacher sweetheart named Tanya whose "sweet and appealing nature" makes her in all respects the perfect paramour. Ivan's "terrible prison life, his fearful experiences in the solitary dungeons, chained hand and feet," profoundly impress the young peasant woman, and this idyllic romance becomes the aspiring screenwriter's ruse for combining the anarchist spirit with a romantic intensity that brings to mind Hollywood "swashbucklers." Tanya eventually marries Ivan and is at his side during the long struggle against the Whites as well as "the life-and-death struggle with the strong and fresh armies of the Bolsheviki." While Berkman was as capable as anyone who ever lived to contextualize the rebellion against both White and Red authoritarianism within the history of anarchism, his efforts to transform Makhno's life into a series of nail-biting cinematic adventures has much in common with the unreflective grandiosity of historical epics such as *Doctor Zhivago*.

The commercial aspirations of this unfilmed scenario are not at all accidental. After enduring deportation to Russia and the disappointment engendered by the Russian Revolution's failed promise, Berkman's exile as a wandering anarchist made a hand-to-mouth existence almost unavoidable. The emotionally fragile revolutionary did everything possible to earn some meager income from translations (he was fluent in both English and Russian as well as several other languages) and adaptations. Several other unfilmed scenarios testify to the unlucrative European sojourn endured by this sometimes gloomy, but never embittered, anarchist. Emma Goldman's correspondence recounts in heart-breaking detail the false hopes aroused in Berkman after doggedly pitching his film synopsis to uninterested Hollywood bigwigs such as Jesse Lasky, Lionel Barrymore, and Carl Laemmle.[47]

The massacre of the Kronstadt rebels and Trotsky and Lenin's zealous war against the Makhnovists decisively shattered any anarchist hopes that the Soviet regime might prove receptive to a left-libertarian path. The Leninist appropriation of Marxism, too often assumed to be indistinguishable from Marxism itself, effectively prevented the dialogue between Marxists and anarchists that Daniel Guérin yearned for. The identification of Leninist autocracy with the Marxist tradition intensified (with predictably Manichean results) during the Cold War. Elia Kazan's *Viva Zapata!* (1952) was one of the most curious products of this legacy—a film condemned by the mainstream left at the time of its release as a reactionary distortion, and hailed by anarchists such as Albert Meltzer as "a very graphic picture of [Zapata's] romantic anarchism, which was more realistic than anything the political parties could offer."[48] The debates surrounding *Viva Zapata!*'s biographical tribute to the Mexican guerrilla leader make a good case for scrupulously anti-intentionalist criticism, since its creators' unsavory personal histories stymied an honest appreciation of the film's virtues. Although the Mexican Revolution obviously preceded the Russian Revolution and was driven by divergent socioeconomic issues, the liberal and communist left could not see beyond Kazan's eagerness to "name names" during the blacklist era and screenwriter John Steinbeck's cold war liberalism. On the other hand, anarchists such as Meltzer ignored—or perhaps were not fully aware of—the filmmakers' extrinsic alliances, and viewed the film as an implicit endorsement of Zapata's (and the more explicitly anarchist Ricardo Flores Magón's) conception of anti-hierarchical agrarian revolution. John Britton asserts that *Viva Zapata!* "stimulated criticism from the Marxist–Leninist left *and* the McCarthyite right—a predicament familiar to independent leftists for several decades."[49] Yet the film offers a peculiar mixture of conscious anti-communism and a sketchy but often stirring tribute to indigenous Mexican peasant traditions that renders the film almost unwittingly anarchist. Steinbeck and Kazan even depict President Francisco Madero, with whom Zapata was tenuously allied, as a well-meaning but vacillating social democrat. But, as Dan Georgakas points out, Steinbeck hoped that the film would be distributed internationally by "the State Department, the USIA and President Kennedy . . . as a 'public service.'"[50] The contradictory ideological motifs of *Viva Zapata!* make the film amenable to what Edward Said calls a "contrapuntal reading"—an interpretive strategy that views films or literary works as "vision(s) of a moment" that can be congenially "juxtapos[ed] . . . with the various revisions" that "a particular cultural artifact . . . subsequently generates."[51] Assessing Kazan's film from an anarchist perspective cannot obliterate its Cold War aura, but can illuminate a left-libertarian impulse that lies beneath the surface of its Hollywood contrivances.

During the Cold War era, few distinguished Leninism from Marxism, and many anarchists who reflexively condemn Marxist authoritarianism overlook, or were never familiar with, the anti-authoritarian components of Marx's own work. As Ulli Diemer demonstrates, despite widespread anarchist assumptions, Marx never advocated that the creation of an autocratic "workers" state was not an economic determinist, and never championed the implementation of a Leninist-style vanguard party.[52] On the other hand, Simone Weil's incisive critique of Marxism is still pertinent, and contains insights that Marxists should consider with care. She believed that so-called "scientific socialism" (with its peculiarly metaphysical "failure to explain why productive forces should tend to increase"[53]) degenerated into stale dogma. This pinpoints the hubris of the Marxism-Leninism of the Third International.

Films such as *Reds, Doctor Zhivago*, and *Viva Zapata!*, however crude or naive, offer vivid evidence of the fact that Marxism-Leninism's bureaucratized socialism (as distinct from Marxism *per se*) effaced all differences between civil society and the state and crushed the dreams of the libertarian left. The flip side of right-wing fears of an anarchist peril was the post-Soviet assumption that anarchism represented an impediment to true socialism. As recently as 1993, Claude Berri's adaptation of Zola's *Germinal*—a film warmly received by the French Communist Party—replicated the novel's pre-Bolshevik vilification of Souvarine, the anarchist saboteur.

In many respects, the Spanish Revolution of the 1930s continued the tradition initiated by Makhno and the Kronstadt commune, and in the next section we will examine the documentary and fiction films inspired by this brief, if fondly remembered and well-documented, historical moment when anarchism briefly flourished in the heart of Western Europe.

Cinema and the Spanish Revolution

Spanish anarchism became known to the world during the bloody years of the civil war, although the ferment of the 1930s was preceded by more than sixty years of labor agitation, anti-clerical provocations, and agrarian revolts. While the Bakuninist Giuseppe Fanelli introduced his mentor's teachings to Spaniards in 1869 and the Spanish section of the International was founded in 1870, many commentators believe that a rich tradition of pre-industrial communalism made Spain especially ripe for the cultivation of anti-authoritarian socialism.[54] To a certain extent, the history of Spanish anarchism is inextricable from anti-colonialist currents. Profound working-class resentment towards the government's call in 1909 for reservists to fight in Morocco precipitated a general strike. By 1910, the small anarchist organization Solidaridad Obrera was eclipsed by the establishment of the CNT (Confederación Nacional del Trabajo—the anarcho-syndicalist trade union), which amassed more than a million members by 1936. In addition, the Falange's counter-revolutionary *putsch* against the Republican government was launched in Morocco; conversely, radical anarchists hoped to encourage "revolt in the Arab world" during the 1936–37 period. The blunt voice-over of Richard Prost's documentary exploration of Spanish libertarian communism, *Un Autre Futur: L'Espagne rouge et noir* (1995), sums up the crisis by concluding that "Morocco, the last stronghold of the Empire, was the meeting place of frustrated ambitions . . . with a body of officers attached to out-of date values . . . the future civil war was forged."

Even if fascism eventually proved victorious, the war of words and images appeared to have been won by the left. The cliché that history is written by the victors not the vanquished seemed, for once, inapplicable. After all, many Americans learned of the Spanish crisis through novels such as *For Whom the Bell Tolls* and *Man's Hope*, as well as crusading documentaries such as Joris Ivens's *The Spanish Earth* (1937). The struggle to preserve the endangered Republic and defeat Franco was depicted as a clear-cut struggle between liberal democracy and malevolent fascism. Hemingway and Malraux's pro-republican novels, and Ivens's similarly stirring film, are fondly remembered; only a few desultory remarks by Evelyn Waugh and Ezra Pound in support of Franco can be cited as memorable examples of pro-fascist sentiment among distinguished members of the intelligentsia.

But although the Spanish Civil War is memorialized in film and literature, anarchists and libertarian Marxists believe that the concurrent Spanish Revolution and counter-revolution have been scandalously overlooked. In recent years, however, a wealth of scholarship conducted by historians with no axe to grind, as well as by committed anarchists and independent Marxists, has punctured the popular assumption, still shared by most well-intentioned liberals and leftists, that the defense of the Spanish Republic was merely a conflict between evil fascists and noble standard-bearers of the Popular Front. Even many historians who do not share Murray Bookchin's anarchist convictions would, none the less, now agree with his assertion that "it is not a myth but a sheer lie—the cretinous perversion of history by its makers in the academy—to depict the 'Spanish Civil War' as a mere prelude to World War II, an alleged conflict between 'democracy and fascism.'"[55] Anarchists such as Bookchin, the Marxist writers Pierre Broué and Émile Témime, and the non-aligned historian Burnett Bolloten,[56] who devoted fifty years of his life to debunking received ideas concerning the Spanish Civil War, came to essentially the same conclusion: the upheaval of 1936–39 was distinguished by both Western Europe's only noteworthy political *and* social revolution led by workers and peasants and a bloody period of repression in which the Communist Party, aided and abetted by the NKVD, sought to smear the left opposition as objective allies of the fascists, and finally succeeded in crushing the dramatic urban and agrarian collectivization spearheaded by the CNT and the Federación Anarquista Ibérica (FAI), its more militant political adjunct.

The systematic effacement of the anarchists' role in the Civil War (and an analogous neglect of the CNT–FAI's call for social revolution) is also reflected in the historical fiction films and documentaries of the post-war era. Among the more prominent examples are Alain Resnais's stream-of-consciousness memory film *La Guerre est finie* (1966) and documentaries such as Frederic Rossif's *Mourir à Madrid* (*To Die in Madrid*, 1963) and Sam Sills, Noel Buckner, and Mary Dore's *The Good Fight* (1984). *The Good Fight*'s distorted view of the war is particularly egregious; the film duplicitously reduces the struggle against fascism to *only* the contributions of the non-anarchist International Brigades. As Noam Chomsky observes in his essay detailing the flaws of Gabriel Jackson's staunchly anti-anarchist "liberal" history of the civil war, "the left-wing critique of Leninist elitism can be applied, under very different conditions, to the liberal ideology of the intellectual elite."[57] A film like *The Good Fight*, with its portrayal of the unquestionably admirable Lincoln Brigade members as noble American patriots and its avoidance of tangible schisms within the Spanish left, confirms, however unwittingly, the liberal pieties that Chomsky dissects with such élan.

While certain uninformed leftists still take for granted Hemingway's—and the Popular Front's—denunciation of the Spanish anarchists as "dirty, foul, and undisciplined,"[58] a sizable number of neglected films made during the war years under the aegis of the CNT–FAI, as well as a growing number of contemporary documentary and fiction films, can help to rectify such malicious stereotypes. *Un Autre Futur* is particularly interesting for uniting these two groups of films, since interviews with surviving anarchist militants are augmented with clips from several little-known narrative films made by anarchists during the 1930s, and excerpts from CNT documentaries.

The CNT's collectivization of the film industry and, primarily in Barcelona, control of exhibition and distribution was only a small part of the massive anarcho-syndicalist redistribution of social wealth, which included "the collectivization of at least 2,000 industrial and commercial firms."[59] A 1936 CNT proclamation pledges that the collectivization of the cinemas will benefit "the people, the revolution," and the development of "popular culture" in general.[60] Workers' control extended to the production process itself, since the trade union endeavored to reformulate the traditional role of the *auteur* by encouraging the film workers' syndicates, not the director, to choose much of the crew and personnel. As Julio Pérez Perucha demonstrates, the CNT's ambitious film productions are especially significant since their newsreels were the first to document the political and military milestones of the early years of the war.[61]

Film historian Román Gubern's claim that the CNT's documentaries and newsreels were far more innovative than their frequently clunky fictional efforts[62] is difficult to dispute. Yet these fiction films' idiosyncratic synthesis of anarcho-syndicalist agit-prop and recycled genre conventions is often fascinating. Several of the CNT–FAI's most significant fictional efforts are essentially political conversion narratives. Antonio Sau's *Aurora de Esperanza* (*Dawn of Hope*, 1937) resembles a more radical version of a Warner Brothers social conscience film. Sau's episodic protest film charts the political development of an unemployed worker named Juan. The hero's painful realization that he cannot feed his family leads inexorably to a climactic epiphany—his decision to join the CNT. Sau's blend of melodrama and consciousness-raising is often mawkish, but the film is nonetheless peppered with striking moments; a beautifully composed shot of unemployed women lining up for jobs advertised in the newspaper, and a sequence featuring a desolate Juan's reluctant visit to a soup kitchen are especially memorable. In a lighter but ultimately no less didactic vein, Valentín R. González's *¡Nosotros somos así!* (*That's the Way We Are*, 1937), an anarcho-syndicalist musical comedy, deals with a wealthy child's transformation from idle bourgeois to CNT supporter. This cinematic curio highlights debates on workers' and women's rights among precocious children who are the anarchist equivalents of Freddie Bartholomew and Shirley Temple. Sadly, this lighthearted film's happy resolution did not correspond to contemporary realities, since 1937 marked the decline of the CNT's influence in revolutionary Spain.[63]

If the CNT's fiction films grew out of an earnest, if sometimes inept, attempt to fuse radical politics with mass entertainment, their documentary shorts—particularly those focusing on the iconographic role of the anarchist militia leader Buenaventura Durruti—more accurately reflect the anarchist movement's strengths and internal contradictions. Since Durruti is an important presence in both the propaganda newsreels of the 1930s and the post-Franco non-fictional assessments of the Civil War years, the paradoxical fate of a military strategist who came close to becoming the object of a personality cult can prove edifying.

Brecht's frequently invoked aphorism "unhappy is the land that needs a hero" would seem tailor-made for anarchists. Yet at times even anarchists succumb to the lure of myth-making, and Durruti's tragic early death during a crucial phase of the war no doubt made possible his cinematic anointment as a beloved martyr. Durruti's brief life (1896–1936), chock-full of skirmishes with the law and remarkable flirtations with danger, would seem to be prime material for an exciting fictional film. His forty-year life span encapsulates in miniature much of Spanish anarchism's progress from an underground subculture to a mass movement that won the loyalty of millions of Spaniards. During the 1920s, when government terrorism sanctioned the cold-blooded murder of anarchist agitators by *pistoleros* paid by the state (the notorious *ley del fuga*—law of flight—implemented by Primo de Rivera's conservative government), Durruti's well-known talent for organizing workers' rebellions forced him to flee Spain for Latin America. During his sojourn in Cuba, Argentina, and Mexico, he funneled money to the CNT with the proceeds of a series of bank robberies. Durruti's biographer, Abel Paz, relates an incident that typifies the young anarchist's impetuous courage. After Durruti and his friend Francisco Ascaso found work cutting sugar cane on a Cuban plantation in the 1920s, they became allies of the impoverished workers, who decided to strike. After three of the strike leaders were mercilessly tortured, "Durruti and Ascaso . . . decided they must execute the boss . . . the next day [his] body was found in the office with this warning, '*La Justicia de los Errantes*'—Justice of the Wanderers."[64] In characteristically picaresque fashion, Durruti and Ascaso skillfully eluded the authorities' wrath.

Of course, it was Durruti's role as the leader of the anarchist militia (the famous Durruti Column) on the Aragon front in 1936 that led to his mythic status—the impetus for a series of cinematic tributes that range from the CNT-FAI's eleven-minute record of his funeral (attended by half a million mourners) in Barcelona, *Entierro de Durruti* (American title: *Homage to Durutti*, director unknown, 1936), to Hans Magnus Enzensberger's documentary portrait, *Durruti—Biographic einer Legende* (1972). It would be an exaggeration to claim that Durruti's image and reputation are fetishized; he never becomes "the kinetic icon" that Annette Michelson discerns in Vertov's cinematic embalmment of Lenin.[65] Yet paying homage to his antiauthoritarian fervor highlights certain unavoidable contradictions, since anarchists are obviously not known for being fond of wars or military pomp and have always been wary of creating cults of personality.

With a mixture of irritation and sadness, Vernon Richards regrets that, once in power, the CNT's leaders were often surrounded by a "religious aura," and decries their propaganda's references to "our immortal Durruti who rises from his tomb and cries, 'Forward'" as "mystical demagogy."[66] Durruti himself once remarked that "we anarchists don't give homage to a personality . . . or practice the cult of a leader."[67] But when he and his comrades formed the CNT defense committee, a group composed of the anarchists' leading military commanders, some of his admirers none the less feared that "anarcho-Bolshevism" was imminent.[68] *Homage to Durruti* handles with exceptional delicacy the challenge of conveying the Barcelona crowd's reverence for the dead anarchist without transforming him into a deity. The film's voice-over (spoken in the U.S. release print by Emma Goldman[69]) hails Durruti as the militant who, when "fighting for liberty, has often escaped the bullets of enemy assassins," but goes on to assure the audience that "he spent his early years like any proletarian child." The emphasis on the fact that all of the left-wing "political organizations participated" in the funeral could be interpreted as a subtle affirmation of the CNT's collaboration with liberals and communists in the Madrid central government—a decision bitterly denounced by many anti-parliamentarian anarchists who considered this policy tantamount to a betrayal of anarchist principles. (In his analysis of films devoted to Durruti, Marcel Oms rightly points out that the funeral of the slain leader allowed "the Catalan proletariat to forget ideological divisions."[70]) Shots of Durruti's friends carrying his coffin on their shoulders, a long shot of his grief-stricken wife, and the strains of Chopin's funeral march on the sound track could well be examples of the "mystical demagogy" lambasted by Richards, a man determined to ferret out hypocrisy among his anarchist comrades. Yet it seems likely that the throngs were as much in mourning for the fact that Durruti's death became emblematic of the death of a pure anarcho-communism, which the supposed anarchist leaders in Madrid, for reasons of pragmatism, continued to dilute. In addition, Durruti's military prowess involved rather ingenious ideological sleight of hand: while Gaston Leval argued that "war and anarchism" were antithetical concerns,[71] Durruti convinced his volunteers that their participation in the militia should be based on rigorous self-discipline, not authoritarian compulsion.

American director Louis Frank's *The Will of a People* (1939) also evokes Durruti's heroism, although this extremely conventional documentary is the product of contradictory political circumstances that give it a compromised, and at times close to indecipherable, ideological orientation. Frank was sympathetic to the anarchist agenda; *The Will of a People* is a re-edited version of *Fury over Spain* (1937), which the CNT used to promote its message among English-speaking audiences. In fact, Emma Goldman was instrumental in arranging screenings of the film for London audiences during her association with the CNT's propaganda section.[72] But despite the fact that Frank's documentary reassembles found footage primarily culled from the CNT–FAI's film archives, the end result is so denuded of specifically anarchist content that all of the sympathetic American critics who reviewed the film (including the staff writers of the Communist *Daily Worker* and *New Masses!*)[73] referred to it merely as a brief for "loyalist Spain."

There can be little doubt that *The Will of a People*'s squeamishness concerning its anarchist origins was engendered by a desire to appeal to non-anarchist

Popular Front sympathizers. The documentary's political vagueness is especially evident in a sequence devoted to the Durruti column and its leader's eventual death. Frank introduces Durruti with a shot included in the CNT film *Los Aguiluchos de la FAI (Young Eagles of the FAI,* 1936), which features the militia commander consulting his comrades at the front. Durruti's anarchist affiliations, however, are never mentioned. Moments later, the voice-of-God narration informs us that "Buenaventura Durruti, courageous leader, died of wounds he received leading his men into action," a capsule obituary that is followed by shots of the mass burial included in *Homage to Durruti.* The found footage is accompanied by narration that reiterates the fact that "the tribute to the fallen hero by 500,000 people . . . is the most spontaneous demonstration of grief in the history of the city," but there is not even a fleeting allusion to Durruti's vociferous support of libertarian communism.

Enzensberger's documentary, released in the early 1970s when the New Left was running out of steam, also highlights the footage of Durruti's funeral. Unlike Frank's film, however, Enzensberger takes this solemn occasion as a departure point for an exploration of anarchism's broader implications. The film treats Durruti with enormous respect, but he is more a catalyst for a quasi-Brechtian investigation of anarcho-communism than a static icon subjected to passive veneration. Enzensberger alternates between a straightforward biographical account of Durruti's political journey (his political trajectory from his days of exile during Primo de Rivera's repressive regime to his final achievements as an organizer of the anarchist militias is dutifully chronicled) and a more diffuse, essayistic account of the anti-authoritarian movement, which includes some musings on the Marx–Bakunin split as the camera tracks past the vast holdings of the archives of Amsterdam's International Institute of Social History. The punctuation of an unadorned explanation of the creation of the Spanish Republic in 1931 is followed by an intertitle—*Mort au Capital*—which seems positively Godardian, even though the film lacks Godard's (or Chris Marker's) lyrical verve. The film's value lies in its distinctive combination of commitment and dispassionate historical analysis, even if the obviously inexperienced filmmaker seems unable to decide whether he wants to make a traditional documentary or a modernist nonfiction essay.

Only a relatively small number of film historians and archivists are familiar with the CNT films. Enzensberger's film on Durruti has not received wide distribution outside Germany and Spain. Given the inaccessibility of these films and the fact that Hugh Thomas's *The Spanish Civil War* (a work that cavalierly dismisses the Spanish anti-authoritarian legacy)[74] is the best-known survey of this tumultuous period, it makes perfect sense that the anarchist component of the civil war is, by and large, forgotten by the general public. In fact, if George Orwell's lucid account of his experience as a soldier on the Aragon front, *Homage to Catalonia,* had not attained the status of a minor classic, the vantage point of the anti-Stalinist left might have been doomed to even greater obscurity. Although Franz Borkenau's roughly contemporaneous, and more comprehensive, *The Spanish Cockpit*[75] offered a strikingly similar perspective, the allure of *Homage to Catalonia* was its ability to encapsulate the fervor of a non-communist, but unassailably radical, left within the form of a compelling narrative. Although Orwell's book is a fine example of autobiographical journalism, it is also a deceptively straightforward work of literature which resembles an eighteenth-century *Bildungsroman*—a narrative of self-education and moral edification. In fact, *Homage to Catalonia's* literary achievement is multi-faceted enough for its paradoxical resemblance to both a picaresque novel and a secular conversion narrative to take nothing away from its moral and political astuteness. In almost classically comic picaresque fashion, Orwell finds himself fighting for the POUM (Partido Obrero de Unificación Marxista, the anti-Stalinist Marxist party, allied in a marriage of convenience, but not of ideology, with the CNT), despite the fact that he came to Spain convinced of the soundness of the Communist Party line. In addition, Orwell, who, despite his veneer of self-deprecation, is undeniably the "hero" of this work of non-fiction, emerged from his *crise de conscience* to become the twentieth century's archetypal version of an intellectual liberated from the chains of cant—the writer who, according to Lionel Trilling, defines "our sense of the man who tells the truth."[76]

Ken Loach's *Land and Freedom* (1995) shares much of *Homage to Catalonia's* moral earnestness, even if screenwriter Jim Allen's (Loach's long-time collaborator) frequently creaky narrative structure has little in common with the lucid compression of Orwell's reportage. Loach and Allen attempt to find a fictional equivalent for Orwell's saga of Stalinist betrayal, but their story is tethered to a thesis that much too often holds an admirable political stance hostage to wooden dramaturgy. *Land and Freedom* will undoubtedly prove revelatory for many viewers unfamiliar with the convoluted internecine warfare of the 1930s. Loach and Allen's film is often extremely moving in spite of itself. This eminently well-intentioned film merely demonstrates that it is extremely difficult to transform an event as intricate and riven with contradictions as the Spanish Revolution into a populist epic.

Throughout the film, a tenuous attempt can be discerned to contrast the current climate of political despair with the 1930s' arduous, if more optimistic, ideological battles. An opening shot of a Liverpool council estate's bleak stairwell, in which circled anarchist "A"s are clearly visible, sets the tone for the film, while a brief militant poem by the British socialist William Morris, read by the hero's granddaughter at the end of the film, cements Loach and Allen's insistence that the radicalism of the past cannot be reduced to mere nostalgia. This implicit rejection of contemporary cynicism is nothing if not admirable, but the filmmakers devise an exceptionally unwieldy narrative ruse to convey, and to a certain extent simplify, the complexities of the past. After the death of POUM veteran David Carr (Ian Hart), his young granddaughter, Kim, discovers a cache of letters—stored with a mound of Spanish earth and a healthy supply of communist and Trotskyist newspaper clippings—written by Carr to his fiancée Kitty, which will soon coalesce into the film's voice-over narration. Carr's sojourn in Spain is also inseparable from this intellectual journey—a circuitous trek from the platitudes of communism to the equally intransigent militancy of the anti-Stalinist left.

The interwoven flashbacks that follow form a kind of pilgrim's progress that stolidly mirrors Orwell's intellectual trajectory in *Homage to Catalonia*, although *Land and Freedom*'s substitution of a working-class hero for a middle-class intellectual is certainly not coincidental. Before long, David, whose grasp of internal Spanish politics is less than rudimentary, signs on with a POUM militia after failing to locate the indigenous communists. Loach provides an excellent sense of the camaraderie and egalitarianism that flourished among the international recruits, and his decision to include a considerable amount of subtitled Spanish dialogue, while casting French, German, Spanish, Italian, and American actors, serves as a useful reprimand to the ironing out of linguistic and national differences usually encountered in the commercial cinema. The film rightly recognizes that the democratic structure of the POUM and the CNT militias differed radically from the communist-controlled "Popular Army." As an anarcho-syndicalist newspaper observed in 1936, "a CNT member will never be a disciplined militiaman togged up in a braided uniform, strutting with martial gait through the streets of Madrid . . . rhythmically swinging his arms and legs,"[77] and the international assortment of militants encountered by David in the militia—a defiantly upbeat young Spanish woman named Maite; Bernard, an ardent French defender of the radical faith; and the passionate anarchist Blanca—remind us that anti-authoritarianism can sometimes be reconciled with the travails of war. Nonetheless, in his eagerness to replace the mainstream left's saga of heroic unity with an equally heroic narrative of ultra-left unity, Loach, perhaps understandably, overlooks many of the ideological quarrels that separated the Marxist POUM from the anarchist CNT. Relations between the CNT and the POUM were often chilly, even if due to subsequent tragic events, the destinies of anti-Stalinist Marxists and anarchists eventually became intertwined. Although it is certainly true that CNT members occasionally joined POUM militias, the naive viewer would have no way of knowing that in December 1936 the CNT, to the dismay of its more radical members, reluctantly supported the communist move to expel the POUM from the Catalan government.[78] Of course, the anarchist movement itself was split by the rank and file's outraged response to its leaders' decision to accept ministerial positions within the central Popular Front government. It may seem pedantic to chide *Land and Freedom* for sins of omission; after all, a fiction film of less than two hours which strives to fuse historical exegesis with adventure and romance will inevitably lack the leisurely scope of a lengthy documentary. But the film is flawed not by lack of detail or outright historical distortion, but by a yearning to render a messy past seamless and comforting.

The perils of sentimentality are especially evident in the cinematic treatment of Blanca, a character who must carry the cumbersome double burden of representing both the anarchists, in a film which devotes far more screen time to the POUM (a rather lopsided strategy, since the CNT–FAI membership was far larger than that enjoyed by the relatively tiny Marxist party), and the contributions of Spanish women to the war effort. After her lover, a POUM member and ex-IRA partisan named Coogan, is killed in battle, Blanca functions as both David's transient love interest and an ideological guide who must introduce the fairly dense Liverpudlian to the culture of the anti-authoritarian left. The Spanish Revolution certainly mobilized the energies of scores of impassioned anarchist women; in addition to fighting with men during the early phase of the war, their advocacy of abortion rights and denunciation of the economic exploitation of prostitutes was truly groundbreaking in the light of Spain's rigid Catholic tradition. Blanca, however, is less a flesh-and-blood female militant than a symbol who almost seems designed as an anarchist equivalent of La Pasionaria, the communists' most famous female activist. Her prominent red and black scarf provides visual evidence of her anarchist affinities, but the audience is never made aware of the nuances that might differentiate her from her Marxist comrades. Blanca is also the catalyst who sets David on his irrevocable path to anti-Stalinism. After their romantic interlude in Barcelona, she admonishes him for his decision to abandon the militia for the communist line and the Popular Army. Soon after, David witnesses the communist siege of the city's telephone exchange, a stronghold of the CNT. This pivotal incident in May 1937 became one of the war's most mulled-over events, part of an explicit "counter-revolution within the revolution" (commonly known as the Barcelona May Days) marked by street fighting between communists and anarchists. The May Days are only sketchily alluded to in *Land and*

Freedom, but, in any case, David acquires a fuzzy knowledge of Stalinism in action. His eventual decision to tear up his CP membership card appears, perhaps inevitably, more a result of his love for a beautiful anarchist than the end-product of genuine political sophistication. There is nothing especially · wrong with this admixture of love and war, but it is painful to admit that Loach's punctuation of lovemaking with anti-Stalinist polemicizing infuses the film with an inadvertent tenor of high-flown kitsch.

Yet it is possible temporarily to suspend any doubts concerning Loach's compromised synthesis of radicalism and Hollywood-style bathos during an extensive recreation of a Spanish village's decision to debate the merits of agrarian collectivization. Andrés Nin, the murdered (reportedly on orders from Moscow) leader of the POUM, maintained that the Spanish experiment in self-management was a "proletarian revolution more profound than the Russian Revolution itself,"[79] and the grass-roots, participatory ethos of the Spanish collectives stands in stark contrast to the bureaucratic morass created by the Soviet Union's disastrous effort to impose collectivization on an unwilling peasantry. *Land and Freedom*'s fictional village eventually votes in favor of collectivization, but the film is noteworthy for giving equal weight to opponents of the CNT line, particularly a seemingly reasonable American named Gene Lawrence. Although Lawrence is nominally a member of the POUM militia, he is essentially an articulate exponent of the standard communist argument that the war must be won before revolutionary goals can even be pondered. His warning that the anarchists "must moderate their slogans" sums up the cautiousness, occasionally sincerely pragmatic but often the product of unadorned cynicism, promoted by the Popular Front. This sequence, mixing the contributions of professional and non-professional actors, is the film's best example of Loach's earnest debt to the social realist tradition. Lisa Berger, a filmmaker and researcher who helped plan the sequence, observed that she was responsible for finding

> people who could argue for collectivization, without looking like city intellectuals, others who could be opposed, and others who could see the point, but weren't really convinced, based on real lived experience working in the countryside. The first group was comprised of young people who are currently active in the CNT in Castellón, Valencia and Sagunto, some of whom are studying the issues of war vs. revolution in the university and are well-versed in the arguments used in 1936. The men who were opposed to collectivization were the real mayor of the village where these scenes were shot . . . and a local farmer who Ken and I had lots of conversations with to know what he would say.[80]

Barry Ackroyd's fluid cinematography accurately captures the debate's vigorous fluctuations, and it is regrettable that this extremely engaging meld of fiction and documentary could not have been sustained for the entire film. To Loach's credit, the final sequences of his film give audiences an accurate idea of the Stalinists' accelerated repression of their left-wing rivals, which led by 1937 to the imprisonment of thousands of CNT and POUM partisans. None the less, *Land and Freedom*'s tragic denouement—which features Lawrence's flamboyant re-emergence as a communist apparatchik as well as the point-blank shooting of its anarchist heroine and her subsequent martyr's burial—must be deemed more a string of dubious contrivances than a satisfying thematic resolution. It is difficult not to be at least somewhat moved by these final sequences, but it is equally difficult not to feel that they are crassly manipulative.

The release of the film in Spain revived a certain amount of the sniping within the left that had been silenced after Franco came to power. Santiago Carrillo, the former head of the Spanish Communist Party, attacked the film's POUMists as "irresponsible adventurists."[81] On American shores, the bulletin of the Abraham Lincoln Brigade published several negative reviews of the film which caviled that "you would think it was Stalin, and not the appeasing democracies, who killed the Spanish Republic," and snorted that Loach "had blown up a minor sideshow of the war."[82] But POUM veteran Joan Rocabert, whose experiences inspired the film's climactic sequences, remained convinced that "if the Communists had won the civil war, not one Poumist would have been left alive."[83] While at times it seems like aging leftists do little else but re-fight the Spanish Civil War from their armchairs, it is instructive to learn that *Land and Freedom* has struck a responsive chord with Spain's young people, many of whom know little of their own turbulent history. Loach himself professed that the film, as well as rectifying the malign neglect of the so-called ultra-left, remains pertinent to the ongoing frustrated desire for "democratic control of resources, democratic resources of capital."[84] This intermingling of hidden left-wing history with the struggles of the present coincides with Gérard Noiriel's belief that "we are . . . living in the midst of dead history produced by past battles that today lie buried in the apparent neutrality of the material forms to which they have given rise."[85]

The cinematic mining of "past battles" for new, or at least slightly revised, interpretations of the Spanish Civil War and Revolution did not begin with *Land and Freedom*. Less heralded films such as *Un Autre Futur,* Jaime Camino's *La vieja memoria* (*The Old Memory,* 1977), and the Granada television series *The Spanish Civil War* all subtly challenged entrenched historical preconceptions. The romantic figure of Durruti, who died at forty, dominates many of the anarchist films made during the 1930s. The more pragmatic figure of Federica Montseny, the CNT leader who died at the age of eighty-eight and is still resented by many anarchists for joining the Madrid government and violating the tradition of libertarian anti-parliamentarism, takes precedence in the more introspective documentaries made in the 1970s, 1980s, and 1990s. For contemporary historians, the inevitable process of sifting through the archives has produced a complex view of Montseny's significance for contemporary radical movements. Feminist scholars have lauded her advocacy of women's emancipation, a motif evident even in her youthful novels and articles, written considerably before her participation in the Mujeres Libres (Free Women), an organization affiliated to the CNT.[86] She has also been praised for achieving 'broad changes in social roles and welfare benefits' during her brief tenure as Minister of Health and Public Assistance in the Popular Front government (November 1936 to May 1937) and assuming Durruti's role as spiritual leader of the revolution.[87] Yet many anarchists have still not forgiven her for briefly collaborating with Prime Minister Largo Caballero's Madrid government; her stance is still condemned as a betrayal of anarchist principles.

Despite the compromises Montseny accepted in 1936, she reiterates her unadulterated anarchist faith in the interviews she granted to documentarists in the 1970s and 1980s. The fact that the anarchists adhered to doctrinal purity by refusing to seize power in 1936, and were denied *matériel* by both the so-called liberal democracies and the Soviet Union, resulted in an unsavory political bind for the anti-authoritarian left. Montseny seems fully to acknowledge these political constrictions in the reminiscences included in *La vieja memoria;* she happily accepts the refusal of most anarchists to welcome the Republic's liberal reformism (which she disdains as "a chicken in every pot") and cannot muster up much enthusiasm for "bourgeois elections." Román Gubern describes Camino's film as "a great fresco in the film interview genre with figures from both sides and from all the political tendencies, who present[ed] in . . . their commentaries the problematic of the Civil War in all of its polyhedric complexity." Camino's fresco, however, hailed by Gubern as an "interactive montage . . . in which people seem to be listening to and contradicting each other,"[88] does not merely pit Trotskyists and anarchists against communists and the left in general against Carlists and Francoists. The film's ideological tapestry even manages to chronicle (in a fashion analogous to Ronald Fraser's "oral history of the Spanish Civil War," *Blood of Spain*) the anarchists' internal dissension. After Montseny's reaffirmation of her anarchist faith, Camino cuts to the testimony of the well-known anarchist writer and trade-unionist Diego Abad de Santillán, whose assertion that "boycotting elections would have meant turning the country over to the fascists" provides a capsule summary of the CNT's rationale for tentatively supporting "bourgeois" measures.

In *Un Autre Futur* and "Inside the Revolution," part five of the Granada series *The Spanish Civil War,* Montseny also assumes responsibility for introducing a new generation to anarchist ideas. Inasmuch as various anarchists considered her willingness to accept a ministerial post either naive or opportunist, her eagerness to explain her stance seems refreshingly frank.[89] In Prost's film, she insists that joining the government "wasn't an ideological choice . . . it was necessary to give an impression to the world that there was true unity in Spain and that the veritable revolutionaries, we anarchists, were not excluded from this unity." Although some of her comrades no doubt still find fault with her "possibilism," she is doubtless right in maintaining that "everything was circumstantial and provoked by the situation created by the Communists in the first place." Her remarks in "Inside the Revolution," on the other hand, can be appreciated as an adjunct of her concerted self-scrutiny, since instead of defending the CNT's ill-fated alliance with the Popular Front, she veers back to the contours of her youthful ideals by arguing that an anarchist seizure of power would have betrayed anarchism itself with a putschist mentality reminiscent of "Lenin and Trotsky." The French anarchist Sebastien Faure was appalled by the anarchist decision to join the government; he believed that the libertarian "impulse no longer came from the base but from the top; direction of the movement did not start with the masses but with their leaders."[90] Montseny grapples with this dilemma during her ruminations in these films; she alternates between mild defensiveness and self-effacement. Her reluctant dalliance with the state apparatus eloquently illustrates the moral agonies experienced by anarchists when faced with the tangible realities of power.

These films all strive for scrupulous accuracy, but it is still startling to observe the gaps and disparities that are obvious in their efforts to combat historical amnesia. For example, the Neal Ascherson script that accompanies the carefully assembled images in the Granada series offhandedly mentions the pervasive anarchist anti-clericalism of the war years, most famously exemplified by a number of churches and monasteries that were burned and looted. David Mitchell's companion book to the series, however, subtly alters Ascherson's disapproving tone by contextualizing anarchist violence within the temper of the times. Mitchell unflinchingly describes the admittedly regrettable massacre of monks, nuns, and priests that was defended by some as anarchist "social hygiene," but calls attention to the fact that the fascist "counter-revolutionary terror . . . claimed more victims than the more limited and spontaneous assassinations in the Republican zone."[91] George Esenwein and Adrian Shubert supplement this explanation of anarchist "revolutionary excesses" by pointing out that "in Barcelona, for example, some churches or religious buildings were destroyed because the people truly believed that rightists were seeking refuge there or even using the churches as fortifications in their attempt to crush the local populace."[92]

While these documentaries deserve praise for initiating a vital process of historical excavation, the famously irreverent post-Franco cinema has approached the anarchist and anarcho-syndicalist heritage with a certain amount of trepidation. Manolo Matji's *La guerra de los locos* (*The War of the Madmen,* 1987) is a characteristically oblique treatment of the revolutionary fervor of 1936. Matji's tale of a group of mental patients who become fond of an anarchist guerrilla unit at the outset of the war is more tough-minded than other films (particularly Philippe De Broca's superficially similar *King of Hearts*) in which the mentally ill are portrayed as lovable heroes. But despite Matji's compassion for society's outcasts, his anarchist characters, although sympathetically etched, are one-dimensional zealots. Vicente Aranda's *Aventis* (1992) reinvents the dubious tradition of *Love and Anarchy* and *Lady L* by focusing on a furtive romance between a prostitute and an anarchist terrorist during the early years of Francoist repression. Like the films of his more famous compatriot Pedro Almodóvar, Aranda's work derives its appeal from a commercially savvy sexual frankness that would have been taboo during Franco's regime. Yet their films often deflect social and political issues by defusing them with camp irony.

As *Land and Freedom* made clear, the left-libertarian revolution of 1936 remains particularly intriguing to activists for its emphasis on feminist as well as proletarian self-emancipation. Contemporary feminists have rediscovered the activities of the Mujeres Libres, although the CNT leadership was both alarmed and baffled by the female militants' "simultaneous insistence on inclusion and autonomy."[93] Women anarchists soon discovered that even their fiercely anti-capitalist male comrades were not cognizant of the indignities that Spanish women had long endured.

Lisa Berger and Carol Mazer's documentary . . . *de toda la vida* (. . . *All Our Lives,* 1987) rekindles the revolutionary passion of this period through an examination of the lives of these women anarchists. Their struggles against both a reactionary Catholic tradition and their own comrades' mixture of indifference and irritation soon found expression in a form of self-activity linked to educational pursuits "essential to releasing women's potential and enabling them to become fully contributing members of the movement and the new society."[94] Berger and Mazer, for example, emphasize the testimony of Lola Iturbe, a women who recalls her participation in Catalonia's general strike of 1919, an insurrection that planted the seeds for the subsequent factory collectives and experiments in self-management that flourished after 1936. Iturbe also maintains that the Mujeres Libres' agitational work often had an almost comically immediate impact; she tells an anecdote about a woman who exultantly celebrated the "sexual freedom of our time" after briefly browsing through anarchist literature at an open-air book fair. The Mujeres Libres viewed their role as both educational and interventionist, and . . . *All Our Lives* documents these activists' participation in Ferrer's Modern School movement. Their insistence on abortion on demand and the rights of prostitutes have a decidedly topical resonance sixty years later. This fusion of political conviction and personal integrity reminds us that anarchist women combined particularistic struggles with the broader goals of a mass social movement.

Aranda's *Libertarias* (*Libertarians*, 1996) is a considerably more backhanded tribute to the Mujeres Libres' legacy. This heavily fictionalized tale of feminist martyrdom during the heady days of 1936 is a curious amalgam of historical epic and mildly risqué sex farce. When Pilar Sanchez (Victoria Abril), the film's central anarchist firebrand, "liberates" a brothel[95] with the help of her comrades from Mujeres Libres, the anarchists' ideological browbeating makes it easy for the audience to dismiss them as humorless ideologues. Eventually, the film takes a salacious pleasure in highlighting the comic incongruousness of former nuns and prostitutes fighting alongside Bakunin-spouting women at the front (the contemporary sex workers' movement would probably look askance at the Mujeres Libres' desire to establish *atorios de prostitución,* "retraining centers for prostitutes" that Martha Ackelsberg speculated would include "medical-psychiatric research and treatment" as well as "psychological and ethical programs to develop in the students a sense of responsibility"). In the final analysis, *Land and Freedom*'s occasionally strained earnestness is preferable to Aranda's facetious evocation of the past.

The saga of anarchists fighting fascism in the years following the Republic's defeat represents something of a missed opportunity for filmmakers. Yet, in addition to the sanitized and fictionalized portrait of Francesc Sabaté Llopart in Zinnemann's *Behold a Pale Horse,* several films tackle the resistance of anarchists in exile from various perspectives. The post–Civil War malaise is succinctly summed up by a shot in Fernando Arrabal's *The*

Guernica Tree (1976): a soldier slumped over a precipice adorned with a "Vive CNT" poster represents the last gasp of the Republic's radicalism as fascist forces overrun Spain.

Pere Portabella's 1974 documentary—*El Sopar*—is perhaps the most distinguished example of a director wrangling with the complexities of revolutionaries determined to resist the encroachments of an authoritarian state. Portabella's nonfiction ruse—a dinner conversation between Communist and anarchist militants as they await the grim news of the execution of the anarchist militant Salvador Puig Antich—is a subtle commentary on, and tribute to, the efforts of anti-fascists to stay true to the revolutionary spirit of 1936–1939 and engage in frontline fights designed to overthrow the Franco regime.

El Sopar's dinner guests endured an aggregate total of more than fifty years in Franco's prisons and their conversations are animated by the desire to retain the fervor of what they consistently term "frontline fighters" within a hostile environment. The testimonies of the assembled militants speak to the difficulties of sustaining a movement within a state that seeks to eradicate all traces of resistance and brand them as terrorism. As Albert Meltzer recounts, Puig Antich's execution inspired a wave of militancy: it "led to an enormous clash between protestors and police in Saragossa, as well as fighting in Valencia and Madrid. In Paris, Spanish banks were attacked, and similar activities occurred in Dublin, Toulouse, Perpignan, Lyon, Pau, Bologna, Rome Milan, Genoa, Brussels, Liege, Luxembourg, Geneva, Liverpool, and London."[96] This type of revolutionary ardor no doubt undergirds some of *El Sopar*'s impassioned debates concerning the efficacy of hunger strikes, the possibility of fighting fascism while remaining underground, and the particularly lonely plight of revolutionary female prisoners. *El Sopar* has suffered from critical neglect—primarily because it lacks the conspicuous formal audacity of Portabella's other work. Jonathan Rosenbaum, on the other hand, discerns a formal prowess embedded in Portabella's austere modus operandi and views it as a political film with "its own formal concerns, most of them related to camera movements and sound recording, as well as the pregnant silences that eventually overtake the conversation." Of course, this clandestinely shot documentary's "pregnant silences" are also profoundly political, engendered by the scars of repression and thwarted hopes.[97]

A more conventional narrative film that amalgamates aspects of romantic melodrama and political thriller, Marie Noelle and Peter Sehr's *The Anarchist's Wife* (2008), is notable for leavening a soapy scenario with an account of a little-known incident involving the anti-Franco resistance in exile. After her husband Justo leaves home to fight the Nationalist forces, Manuela spends years waiting anxiously for his return from battle. When they finally reunite and emigrate to France to escape Franco's clutches, family problems—the rebelliousness of the couple's teenage daughter and the marital fallout from Justo's affair with a German woman—vie with a sketchy account of guerrilla resistance against the Spanish state. True to his anarchist ideals, Justo aids a failed attempt to bomb Franco's yacht, a subplot inspired by the derring-do of Laureano Cerrada, an anarchist whose escapades alienated the leadership-in-exile of the CNT in Toulouse.

Despite the setbacks of the post-Franco era, most anarchists maintained a defiantly optimistic tone. Some elements of this intransigence are captured in Valentí Figueres's compelling documentary, *Vivir de pie* (*Living on Your Feet: The Struggles of Cipriano Mera,* 2009). Mera (born Cipriano Mera Sanz) gained renown during the Spanish Civil War as, along with Durruti, one of the oxymoronic "anarchist generals" whose courage and fealty to the left-libertarian cause made him legendary. A bricklayer by profession, Mera, a devotee of the FAI's radical brand of anarcho-syndicalism, gained a reputation as a successful and pragmatic military strategist. Mera was instrumental in winning the battle of Guadalajara, a key victory that prevented Madrid from being besieged by the Nationalists. As the subsequent commander of the Fourth Army Corps, Mera became one of the most influential military figures in the Republican effort and is mentioned prominently in mainstream accounts of the war such as Antony Beevor's *The Battle Over Spain,* a revisionist history that shares the anarchist skepticism toward the intentions of the Communist Party and its Stalinist apologists.[98]

Figueres's documentary, although occasionally marred by a gimmicky propensity for split-screen compositions, deftly demonstrates how Mera functioned as a bridge between generations of anti-authoritarian radicals. Finding asylum, like the refugees highlighted in Michael Curtiz's *Casablanca* (1942), in North Africa, Mera is eventually extradited to Spain and sentenced to death. But Mera languished in prison until 1946, when he was unexpectedly released and joined his comrades in France. Mera's dogged attempts to overthrow the Franco regime also end up revealing the disappointingly conservative orientation of the postwar CNT. As Stuart Christie observes, the "Toulouse leadership expelled Cipriano Mera claiming, totally falsely, he had misappropriated funds intended for Defensa Interior"[99]—a militant anti-Franco organization founded in 1961 committed to direct action that ran afoul of the Toulouse faction's desire to curry favor with the French government at a time when it was intent on normalizing relations with Franco's

Spain. The stirring denouement of Mera's life arrives when, in the anarchist version of a storybook ending, he joins up with the insurgents of May '68 and is revered for his status as an anti-authoritarian elder statesman.

It's difficult to identify a precise contemporary equivalent of the fervor—and sense of urgency—within the international left generated by the Spanish Revolution during the thirties. The passionate interest, however, of many anti-authoritarian leftists in the plight of the ongoing communal experiments in Syria's Rojava region comes close. As with any revolutionary upsurge, there are conflicting narratives. One of the most prominent is encapsulated in the arguments of David Graeber and Janet Biehl, which are synopsized in the anthology *Revolution in Rojava: Democratic Autonomy and Women's Liberation in Syrian Kurdistan.*[100] Within this framework, the transformation of Abdullah Öcalan's Kurdistan Workers Party (PKK) from a traditionally rigid Marxist–Leninist entity into an anti-hierarchical formation influenced by Murray Bookchin's "libertarian municipalism" spawned a remarkable focus on "democratic autonomy" and "democratic confederalism." Not only has Öcalan attempted to revise the idea of "councilist democracy," but Rojava's promotion of the idea that "women would be the spearhead of the revolution" has galvanized many feminist radicals. The principle of "dual leadership" (where power is "vested in two people . . . one must be a woman"), and an anti-patriarchal impetus that aspires to subvert the ideology of Islamic fundamentalism, are key tenets of this decentralized movement. A more skeptical view of the Rojava experiment is proffered by the anti-Leninist Marxists Gilles Dauvé and T.L, who maintain that Öcalan has not shed Marxism–Leninism by embracing the radical strategies of Makhno or Pannekoek but has instead incorporated Bookchin's gradualist "democratic confederalism" into the PKK's overall agenda. For Dauvé and T.L., the supposed anti-hierarchical bias of the Rojava Revolution is merely a somewhat cynical ruse for a national liberation struggle that facilely touts anti-authoritarianism while retaining aspirations to continue its entrenchment as a party apparatus, a holdover from its Leninist incarnation.[101]

Western film culture, for better or worse, has not caught up with these events or produced even passably convincing documentaries or fictional treatments that offer a reasonably adequate analysis of these contradictions. As a necessary corrective, the Rojava Film Commune has made a concerted effort to train filmmakers and technicians and produced a feature film, Şêro Hindê's *Stories from Destroyed Cities,* that has not yet been widely screened outside Syria and Turkey but attests to the efforts of committed filmmakers in the region to produce work that is as lyrical as it is didactic. A documentary/fiction hybrid, *Stories* is a three-part lamentation recounting the devastation wrought in the fight against ISIS's fascistic ideology in the cities of Sinjar, Kobani, and Jazza. Scripted vignettes nevertheless reflect the experience of many of the professional actors; for example, in the final segment detailing a couple's efforts to pay final respects to their martyred son, the mother is played by a woman who in fact lost a son during the conflict.

Diyar Hesso, the film's co-editor, explains the Rojava Film Commune's desire to overcome the "alienation" engendered by the hierarchical division of labor, usually deemed a necessary evil in filmmaking. In this film made among ruins, he describes a collective effort in which aesthetics and social transformation are intimately linked:

> Art has always constituted a mass effort to obtain a better, more beautiful life. The elementary forms of art all emanated from one source; the rhythmic movements of dance, were intended to harmonize collective work . . . the music to build up mutual feelings; the poems to construct ideas shared mutually. . . . So art is always about the life of the collectivity, explaining its reality, exploring the problems and overcoming them. . . . Ideology = Form. Democratic autonomy, in one of its aspects, means every one and every institution has its own independence while simultaneously being interdependent . . . that's how we think we should approach cinema and art in general.[102]

The struggle for democratic autonomy fares less well in Eva Husson's *Girls of the Sun* (2018). A fictionalized portrait of women fighting in a YPJ (Women's Protection Unit) that premiered in competition at Cannes, the much-ballyhooed epic is a pathetic farrago of war movie clichés. The political convictions of the protagonists' battle against ISIS is deemphasized, the women's struggles are filtered through the perspective of a French journalist, and a scene in which the leader of the women's battalion gives birth becomes a treacly homage to the virtues of motherhood. With Husson's film as an unfortunate precedent, one shudders to think of the aesthetic and political compromises that might well coalesce in Jake Gyllenhaal's (as of this writing, yet-to-be-released) turn as an anarchist combatting ISIS.[103]

If contemporary arthouse cinema is not up to the task of evaluating Rojava's importance, it's perversely true that Hito Steyerl's 2004 *November,* made years before anarchists evinced any interest in Kurdish radicalism, offers a more illuminating gloss on subsequent history than woebegone attempts at naturalism like *Girls of the Sun.* Steyerl in fact is hostile to a "mimetic clinging to the conditions that are to be critiqued" in conventional political cinema.[104] Her route to understanding the significance of a childhood friend's emotional investment in Kurdish radicalism is filtered through glimpses of pop-culture artifacts celebrating female rebellion and resilience. Steyerl's voiceover invokes the memory of Andrea Wolf, a PKK militant raised in Germany but eventually killed by the Turkish military as a "terrorist." Footage of a martial arts film the two women collaborated on when teenagers, a slightly whimsical pastiche modeled on Russ Meyer's *Faster, Pussycat! Kill! Kill!* (1965) and kung fu movies, is juxtaposed with Wolf's martyrdom, during an epoch Steyerl terms a period of retrenchment and "peripheral" struggles. Even though Wolf died when Kurdistan was still a "white spot on a map," her idealism and intransigence underlines the difficulty subsequent filmmakers such as Husson experienced when trying to transfer the YPG's anti-patriarchal orientation to the screen. If Husson could only recycle generic clichés, Steyerl demonstrates how Kurdish feminism was the product of both ideological choices and a sensibility not that far divorced from the ideals of heroism enshrined in pop culture. This sort of multilayered approach, despite being conceived long before the events of 2011, avoids the pitfalls of either uncritically celebrating the Rojava experiment or dismissing it entirely—two positions that frequently brush up against each other in online anarchist media.

Cinema, Anarchism, and the "Free Commune": Gazing Backward toward the Future

> Only the gaze that is turned backward
> can bring us forward, for the gaze that
> is turned forward leads us backward.
> —Novalis

A prototypical sequence in Gregori Kozintsev and Leonid Trauberg's Soviet avant-garde epic *New Babylon* (1929) sums up the grassroots anti-authoritarianism of the seventy-two-day Paris Commune of 1871, while prefiguring the Spanish libertarian communism of the 1930s and the anti-statist radicalism that erupted during the events of May 1968 in France. Toward the end of Kosintzev and Trauberg's adaptation of Zola's *Au Bonheur des dames* (a film whose delirious montage and anarchic spirit make it one of the most anomalous Soviet films ever made), the young heroine, Louise, expresses her solidarity with the communards by constructing a makeshift barricade with a piano pilfered from the gigantic department store where she works as a clerk. Walter Benjamin observed in the unfinished Arcades Project, a mammoth investigation of the origins of consumer culture, that "a hell rages in the soul of the commodity!"[105] Louise's joyous improvisatory gesture transforms the reified soul of a commodity into a tool for social transformation.

While members of the authoritarian left—Maoists and Trotskyists—took credit for May '68's rupture with Gaullism, anti-Leninist anarchists and situationists yearned to revive the communal impetus embedded in Louise's spontaneous act of defiance. The media tried to create "'leaders" such as Daniel Cohn-Bendit, even if Cohn-Bendit himself had nothing but contempt for traditional concepts of leadership. Many of the participants in the '68 events envisaged a social order similar to the ideal invoked in Bakunin's retrospective assessment of the Paris Commune—a "society organized from the bottom upwards, by the free association and federation of workers: in associations first of all, then in the communes, then regions, nations, and finally in a great international and universal federation."[106] Anthony Masters has in fact termed May '68 "a revolution after . . . Bakunin's own heart, because of its direct action, its meeting of force by force and its policy of collectivity."[107]

The complexity of the May events eluded most of the directors who attempted to formulate a response to unprecedented social and political upheavals. Jacques Doillon's *L'An 01* (with the collaboration of Alain Resnais and Jean Rouch, 1973), for example, is essentially a series of neo-situationist black-out sketches—serio-comic vignettes suffused with the playful disrespect for authority that permeated the student rebellion. A quirky synthesis of science fiction and gentle provocation (a sequence in which a group of pranksters merrily disobey an order to keep off the grass is one of the film's most famous moments), *L'An 01* is somewhat stymied by a rather nebulous utopianism. A well-intentioned historical myopia is evident in one of the film's key fanciful sequences, a celebration of the cessation of production in Europe. Despite the charming gloss on 1968's spirit of negation, there is no trace of the period's reinvention of the "mass strike"—a huge wildcat action that engaged the energies of fifteen million workers and was met with hostile indifference by the French Communist Party. More recently, Hervé Le Roux's *Reprise* (1997), a sober documentary that painstakingly explores the intricacies of a strike at a provincial factory during the May Days, illuminates the internecine squabbles between communist and Maoist workers but gives short shrift to the influence of the anti-authoritarian left.

Even if one questions embittered ex-leftists' penchant for denouncing May '68 as a pseudo-revolution, the failure to build on this 1960s revival of the anarchist tradition of direct action plunged the international left into a slough of prolonged despondency. Conservative skeptics dismissed the May events as "chiliastic utopian[ism] . . . a form of irrationalism . . . based on 'absolute presentness.'"[108] Many of the political films that were made in the wake of the 1968 events reflected the international left's despair. Filmmakers took refuge in the past and encased their musings on recent events within tragicomic allegorical narratives. Walter Benjamin's rehabilitation of allegory, suffused with a world-weariness that does not, however, foreclose the possibility of utopian reconciliation, is supple enough to be applicable to films as disparate as Kevin Brownlow and Andrew Mollo's *Winstanley* (1975), Theo Angelopoulos's *O Megalexandros* (*Alexander the Great*, 1983), and Jean-Louis Comolli's *La Cecilia* (1975). Benjamin acknowledged that allegory was usually denigrated as a product of periods of decay, but his anti-classicist, radically modernist sensibility elevates what were termed (specifically with reference to the *Trauerspiel* of the German baroque) artifacts of societal fragmentation into an aesthetic virtue. Benjamin labeled allegory a "natural history" of the past's ravages, or what one commentator has called "shards of memory that frustrate the oscillations of organic closure."[109] In other words, allegory resists narrative closure but does not, unlike the more rarefied examples of modernism, operate within an ahistorical void. Benjamin's preoccupation with the "transience of human history" and the instability of meaning in *The Origin of German Tragic Drama* might seem irrevocably melancholy, but his superficially pessimistic emphasis on "the brokenness" of the world is always tempered by a radical optimism—"a visionary glance" granted to the historian who, armed with the capabilities of a "prophet turned backwards," can "perceive his own time through the medium of past fatalities."[110]

Winstanley is a salient example of this kind of radical backward glance, satisfying David Gross's desire to promote "a non-nostalgic" remembrance of things past that allows us to "think about tradition *within* modernity, and tradition *against* modernity."[111] Brownlow and Mollo's film examines the aftermath of the short-lived Puritan revolution from the vantage point of Gerrard Winstanley's Diggers, one of the most radical sects to emerge (and virtually vanish from the historical record until its twentieth-century rediscovery) from the radical ferment of the 1640s. The relatively little critical attention given to this film can probably be attributed to the fact that its alternately loving and slavish devotion to an aesthetic derived from the silent cinema did not sit well with radical critics weaned on the supposedly more rigorous Brechtianism of Godard and Straub-Huillet, as well as the fact that Brownlow's impatience with contemporary film theory led some commentators to dismiss him unfairly as a full-blown reactionary. Richard Philpott, for example, alleges that *Winstanley*'s focus on the failure of a proto-anarchist commune sadly confirms Brownlow's alleged belief that a concern with politics is only "acceptable if ineffectual."[112] It seems apparent, though, that mere "failure" should not be a justification for ignoring Winstanley's desire to establish libertarian socialism in one county.

The implicitly anarchist impetus of *Winstanley* comes to the fore in what Jonathan Rosenbaum termed its felicitously "crotchety"[113] prologue, a montage sequence that brilliantly compresses the failure of Cromwell's English Revolution to deliver genuine economic justice to English peasants and artisans. A rhythmic succession of images—close-ups of horses' hooves, swords colliding with shields, rifles being brandished and fired—are accompanied by Prokofiev's score to *Alexander Nevsky*. Explanatory intertitles inform viewers of the conflicts of King Charles I and Parliament, but finally underline the inadequacies of Cromwellian reform with the stark declaration that in "Autumn 1647—No Reforms have Resulted From the War." Cromwell's son-in-law, Commissary-General Henry Ireton, a representative of the Puritan grandees despised by his opponents for his "imperious carriage," quashes the demands of the Levellers for economic reform by proclaiming that he "would not let the world believe that we are for anarchy." He defends his view that only the propertied classes should be allowed to vote by insisting that "no one has a right to the kingdom" who lacks a "fixed interest" in the kingdom's sustenance. The prologue's mesh of pseudo-Eisensteinian montage and clipped rhetorical interchanges selectively culled from the historical record succinctly delineates the ideological antinomies that are such an intricate part of the Puritan Revolution's complex legacy. Ireton's fear of "anarchy" and reverence for property is a plainspoken version of Thomas Hobbes's conviction that "Covetousnesses of great Riches, and ambition of great Honours, are Honourable; . . . Riches are Honourable; for they are power." As *Winstanley*'s prologue implies, the revolution and eventual overthrow of the monarchy merely made possible the consummation of what C. B. Macpherson terms "possessive individualism"—the belief that "political society is a human contrivance for the protection of the individual's property in his person and goods."[114] According to Macpherson, even the disgruntled Levellers subscribed to a modified version of "possessive individualism" since they did not favor extending manhood suffrage to beggars and servants, a fact that Brownlow and Mollo dutifully underscore in a helpful intertitle.

After this brisk survey of revolutionary ferment, which proves how radical political realignment can, in actuality, reinforce the status quo, the film moves on to explore Winstanley and the Diggers' decidedly un-Hobbesian voluntary poverty. Kenneth Rexroth points out that "socialists, modern Communists, anarchists, all claim Winstanley as an ancestor."[115] Of course, Winstanley's writings never invoke any authority other than the Bible, and the ambiguity of his ideological provenance led critics, inconclusively if accurately, to describe the film's protagonist as both a communist and an anarchist. Brownlow himself observed that Winstanley is acclaimed as a founding father by the "communists in Russia, the Quakers (wrongly I think), and the anarchists,"[116] although the film steadfastly refuses to align itself with these fratricidal debates.

Despite Brownlow's ideologically neutral pose, the film's initial juxtaposition of a long shot of Winstanley's cottage with voice-over recitation of the Digger's early tract *The New Law of Righteousness* (large swathes of Winstanley's writings are intoned in voice-over throughout the film) confirms anarchist assumptions that the communal experiment on St George's Hill in Surrey was a precursor of what was later known as libertarian communism. Christopher Hill ascribes Winstanley's determination to dig up and collectively manure St George's Hill to a rage against the pervasive practice of royal enclosure that had robbed the English poor of their common land.[117] Mingling a Protestant version of liberation theology[118] with a communal vision that anticipates Kropotkin's secular, co-operative "conquest of bread," Winstanley's ideology is a curiously potent blend of materialism and mysticism. Nominally based on David Caute's novel *Comrade Jacob,* Brownlow and Mollo's film ignores Caute's often grating tendency to create narrative tension with clumsy, glaringly anachronistic, simulations of Winstanley's mystical visions. Instead, the film's integrity lies with its rejection of melodrama and mysticism; the strategically placed quotations from *The New Law of Righteousness,* thunderously exhorting that "the earth shall be made a common property for all" (the demand for "common property" and references to the land as a "common treasury" recur in many of Winstanley's subsequent writings), are accompanied by austere shots of the Surrey countryside. Winstanley's appeal to an anarchistic ideal of freedom, celebrating "the man who will turn things upside down," is followed by a transition to a shot of the mansion inhabited by Winstanley's chief antagonist, the wealthy Parson Platt. Platt becomes the most implacable enemy of the Digger commune, and the sequences featuring polemical exchanges between Platt and Winstanley vividly, and often humorously, amplify R. H. Tawney's insight that "the events which seemed to aristocratic Parliamentarians to close the Revolution seemed to the left-wing of the victorious army only to begin it."[119]

Since Winstanley is far to the left of the reformist Levellers alluded to by Tawney, the initial bout of verbal jousting between Platt and the obstinately antinomian Digger underscores the disparity between representatives of the Puritan gentry and a "primitive communism" that, while inspired by the principles of the Reformation, desires much more than piecemeal reform. This battle of wits between the sullen Platt and the unwaveringly earnest Winstanley directly follows several shots of Diggers collectively—and joyously—cultivating their "common treasury." Platt in close-up piously murmurs that "God is merciful because the poor people could not stand another poor harvest." A bemused Winstanley inquires whether the poor actually loom "so large" in Platt's thoughts. Visibly angered, Platt accuses Winstanley of being "enslaved by poverty and ignorance." In a nimble retort, Winstanley concludes that the "fault lies with poverty and ignorance." The antagonists' bickering effortlessly demonstrates that Winstanley's doctrines, couched in the language of eschatology and the mystical realm of the "kingdom within," actually have a greater pertinence to the rank injustices of the "kingdom without." Winstanley's radical Christianity assumed that redemption could and should be achieved in this world, a fact that has led some historians to consider his mystical pantheism paradoxically rational. Like a later mystic, William Blake, Winstanley uses the Bible as raw material for allegorical assaults on the established order. Yet, unlike the self-conscious, essentially modern Blake, Winstanley is flustered by questions of sexuality and gender—his approval of monogamy and the value of procreation is the most conventional aspect of his generally heterodox cosmology. Brownlow and Mollo unobtrusively comment on their protagonist's prudishness by showing us Winstanley's discomfort with the brief sojourn of Platt's wife among the Diggers, a woman whose husband views her with undisguised contempt.

By the end of her Digger hiatus, however, Mrs. Platt flees St George's Hill, disgusted with the visit of some obstreperous Ranters (who, she claims, live "like animals") to the Surrey commune. The Ranters, whose sexual libertarianism and enthusiastic blasphemy anticipated modern counter-cultural attitudes as presciently as the Diggers prefigured socialist and anarchist ideals, clearly tried the patience of the circumspect Winstanley, who wrote an impassioned tract in 1649, *A Vindication of those . . . Called Diggers,* to differentiate his followers from the libertinism and blasphemy sanctioned by the Ranters. Brownlow and Mollo's film emphasizes the tension between the prudish anarcho-communists and the Ranters, whose inversion of Puritan mores might have pleased Buñuel, by including a tête-à-tête between an exasperated Winstanley and a raucous Ranter representative—apparently based on Lawrence Clarkson, who attempted to convert the Diggers to his brand of antinomianism.[120] As the spokesman for inveterate provocateurs, the Ranter leader speaks of unconditional love and excoriates the Virgin Mary as "nothing but a whore." The final clash of wills between Winstanley and his unwelcome guest illuminates a millenarian factionalism that is not unlike internal divisions that later plagued the secular descendants of the Diggers and Ranters. After a long shot depicting the local authorities' seizure of the Diggers' commonly owned property, the camera lingers on a vengeful Ranter advising the communards that "the righteousness of Gerrard Winstanley will not feed you . . . he loves himself above others."

The Ranter–Digger contretemps foreshadows recent debates between traditional Marxist–anarcho-syndicalist productivism and a more recent anti-work ethos. Like the Marxists and syndicalists who condemn anti-work stalwarts, Winstanley accused the Ranters of merely mirroring middle-class mores and taunted them for remaining on the level of personal, rather than truly social, dissent. The Ranters' disdain for theological propriety and monogamy superficially resembles modern critiques of sexual repression, but, as Hill points out, their conception of sexual freedom "tended to be freedom for men only, so long as there was no effective birth control."[121] From this perspective, Mrs. Platt's horror of Ranter sexual licentiousness can be viewed as either clichéd "Puritanism" or understandable self-interest. Her husband's plutocratic theology is anathema to both radical history's agenda and Winstanley's left-libertarian orientation, but Brownlow and Mollo decided to transform the "unhinged" harridan of David Caute's novel into a more sympathetic and complex character.

In the final analysis, the film confirms D. W. Petegorsky's assertion that "if the theological heresies of the sects shocked the pious churchmen, the social implications of their teachings frightened the men of property."[122] The local gentry makes a vigorous effort to accelerate the Diggers' demise, but Brownlow and Mollo's lyrical re-creation of proletarian militancy's early stirrings highlights discrepancies in style and ideology among Winstanley's major upper-class foes.

The film ends grimly: the Diggers' communal experiment is reduced to ashes by Platt and his emissaries. The last shot's snowy, inescapably melancholy landscape is somewhat offset by Winstanley's voice-over—a defiant valediction expressing the conviction that truth shall eventually "sit down in triumph." His continued steadfastness, however, did not prevent him from revising his proto-anarchist agenda. Peter Marshall contends that the memory of the fratricidal sniping that occasionally marred the foray into utopia on St George's Hill inspired Winstanley to take refuge in the less anarchistic version of communalism outlined in *The Law of Freedom in a Platform, or True Magistracy Restored*.[123] The fact that this seminal tract, which Christopher Hill labeled "a draft constitution for a Communist commonwealth,"[124] is dedicated to Oliver Cromwell indicates that an intuitive anarchism is being replaced by a wily Machiavellianism. *The Law of Freedom*'s hierarchy of paternalistic "overseers" and monotonous codification of laws is a near-precursor of Leninist "democratic centralism." The contempt for "idleness" evident in Winstanley's late work is derived from mainstream Puritanism and resembles the authoritarian left's fondness for a secular variant of Puritanism. But Winstanley's regression from anti-authoritarianism does not justify the social-democratic bromides of Michael Walzer, who implies, in his study of seventeenth-century radical currents, that the revolutionary spirit is almost always besmirched by "repression and collective discipline."[125] The innumerable ambiguities of the English Revolution tend to make sweeping judgments of this sort untenable; instead of anachronistically concluding that the seventeenth century's brief anti-royalist zeal forecasts the horrors of the gulag, it might be more prudent to conclude that moments of revolutionary transition often contain the seeds of both genuine anti-authoritarian radicalism and statist repression. Brownlow and Mollo's moving but utterly unsentimental film features a stripped-down portrait of Winstanley during his most genuinely anarchist incarnation. The fact that *Winstanley*'s narrative ends before both its hero's revisionist change of heart and his post-Digger career as a prosperous landowner means that we are left with the remnants of radical aspiration, not the shards of radical disillusion. More an example of meticulous historical excavation than anarchist self-representation, the film nonetheless suggests how a near-forgotten chapter of left-libertarian history is pertinent to contemporary anti-authoritarian struggles.

Like *Winstanley*, Angelopoulos's convoluted epic *O Megalexandros* imagines a utopian sensibility capable of undoing the political injuries inflicted by "past fatalities." In their discussion of the major allegorical strands within Brazilian film history, Ismail Xavier and Robert Stam discern two dominant motifs: the "teleological Marxist-inflected meliorist allegories of early Cinema Novo" and a second phase in which allegory "is deployed as a privileged instance of language-consciousness in the context of the felt loss of a larger historical purpose."[126] *O Megalexandros*'s intricate account of a failed communal experiment, on the other hand, betrays a Benjaminian skepticism toward progress and vulgar-Marxist teleology, but refuses to snub its nose at the prospect of a "larger historical purpose." Angelopoulos's highly stylized film posits an alternative historical topography, a version of Greek history that lyrically interpenetrates mythic and historical concerns from various centuries. The film's allegorical impetus pulverizes chronological time and the ideology of progress, preferring what Ernst Bloch termed *non-synchronicity*—the belief that "not all people exist in the same Now . . . they do so only externally."[127]

In a famous essay on *The Iliad*, Simone Weil insists that "the key to history is not the idea of class, as Marx believed, but the idea of force."[128] Although *O Megalexandros*'s modern sensibility bears little relationship to Homer's ancient conception of heroism, Angelopoulos's more schematic and ironized exploration of national identity investigates questions of power and hierarchy in a manner that corresponds to the open-ended, fragmentary style of what Franco Moretti labels the "modern epic" or "world text." Moretti contends that "*pace* Bakhtin . . . the polyphonic form of the modern West is not the novel, but if anything precisely the epic: which specializes in the heterogeneous space of the world-system, and must learn to provide a stage for its many different voices."[129]

Angelopoulos's film is nothing if not a "stage for . . . many different voices"; it is distinctive in weaving nationalist-heroic themes and anti-authoritarian concerns into a synchronic narrative tapestry. Nominally set in 1900, *O Megalexandros* is loosely based on an actual incident in which British diplomats were kidnapped and held for ransom by radical brigands. The languidly paced film's protagonist (who is as much its anti-hero as its hero), Alexander the Great, evokes memories of a medieval bandit of the same name,[130] while the actor who plays him bears a close resemblance to Aris Velouchiotis, one of the most notable guerrilla chiefs to emerge during the Greek Civil War of 1943–1949. Unlike the superficially similar Nestor Makhno, Velouchiotis, "a wild, bearded figure who owed something to Chapayev and prefigured Castro,"[131] was a freedom fighter who renounced anti-authoritarianism and decided to follow a more orthodox political orientation. Dominique Eudes notes that "some Communists regarded him as a fanatical anarchist," although he eventually succumbed to the demands of the "Party machine."[132]

An anarchist commune in which Greek peasants celebrate their newfound freedom with Italian militants provides the film's anti-authoritarian focus. Unfortunately, the fact that the communal enterprise is located in Alexander's home village virtually assures its eventual demise. In addition, this joyous convocation at the beginning of the twentieth century has no grounding in historical reality; the imaginary bonhomie between militant Italian workers and rural peasants is a cinematic analogue of Bloch's "Not Yet"—a utopian hope "which men have envisaged in different forms through the centuries" but has "not yet" been concretely achieved. An Italian anarchist actually remarks that the commune is "like a dream." His grateful astonishment that "there is no private ownership . . . men and women have equal rights" has much in common with a collective dream, since Angelopoulos's sometimes agonizingly long takes distend chronology with distinctly oneiric results.[133] The film's disregard for chronological time is literalized when the communards chant the slogan "Down with the clocks," a sentiment that indicts the industrial order which the communards resist, as well as the time-governed culture of modernity itself.

The lyrics of a song heard during a communal dance—"the world is my country/ freedom of thought is my region"—merges questions of nationhood with specifically anarchist concerns. This dream of harmony proves evanescent. *O Megalexandros* eventually short-circuits the spirit of utopian wish-fulfillment when Alexander and his associates destroy the agricultural commune with brutal relish. An anarchist schoolteacher explicitly condemns Alexander's "policy" as typifying "the danger . . . of the charismatic leader." The teacher appears to be Angelopoulos's mouthpiece, since the director himself compared Alexander to contemporary authoritarian, if unquestionably charismatic, leaders such as "Hitler, Stalin, and Khomeini."[134]

Unlike *O Megalexandros*, Comolli's *La Cecilia* took an actual nineteenth-century anarchist commune as its departure point. Comolli's assessment of the free commune's liberatory potential is, however, equally nuanced. Conservative commentators such as E. M. Cioran and Leszek Kolakowski see the idea of utopia as at best a comforting self-delusion, and at worst a one-way ticket to totalitarianism and the gulag. But for many years, "utopianism" was also anathematized by the orthodox left. Given the fact that Comolli was an editor at *Cahiers du Cinéma* during its most rabidly Althusserian incarnation, his intellectual trajectory is particularly intriguing. There is a strongly Althusserian tinge to much of Comolli's writing for *Cahiers,* especially in the sporadically useful dissection of film's capitulation to the "dominant ideology," "Cinema/Ideology/Criticism," which he wrote in collaboration with Jean Narboni.[135] Yet when Comolli became a filmmaker, his interest in the liberatory potential of anarchism began to animate his work, particularly in films such as *La Cecilia* and *L'Ombre rouge* (1981).

There is not necessarily an egregious conflict between Comolli's ostensibly Leninist theoretical work and the anti-authoritarian bias of his films. In retrospect, the *Cahiers* appropriation of Althusser can be regarded as a primarily formalist maneuver that was meant to focus attention on how texts convey frequently contradictory ideological messages. Initially, Althusser's delineation of what has been termed "decentered totality" seemed more amenable to a modernist aesthetics than older components of the Marxist aesthetic arsenal such as Lukácsian idealism, with its contingent embrace of "expressive totality."[136] Yet both Lukács and Althusser offered an inadequate version of the relationship of actual individuals to historical experience by hypostatizing, respectively, the Party and science.

The *Cahiers* embellishment of Althusser's Marxism was linked to a romantic avant-gardism. *La Cecilia* recapitulates many of the paradoxes endemic to the post-1968 era, although the cinematic form and content chosen by Comolli for his initial stab at political cinema baffled many members of the small but ever contentious audience that debated its merits. The film eschewed the constipated rhetoric of Jean-Luc Godard's "Dziga Vertov Group" films for a more straightforward variety of political cinema that many thought too conventional. While the leisurely pace and avoidance of didactic clichés differentiated the film from Costa-Gavras-style thrillers, *La Cecilia,* despite some obligatory nods in the direction of Brecht, differs enormously from the radical variant of modernism favored by *Cahiers* during the 1970s. Consequently, Comolli's critical but essentially sympathetic examination of the travails of the Cecilia Colony, a short-lived nineteenth-century commune founded by Italian anarchists near Palmeira in Brazil, engendered some bewildering critical responses. One American critic referred to the film as "a species of self-criticism, a reflection on *Cahiers* utopianism which called for an end to the division of labor."[137] Several editors of *Cahiers du Cinema* itself found it difficult to evaluate the songs and slogans of the Italian anarchists without viewing them through the prism of a Maoism that was already growing moldy by the mid-1970s.[138] It seems fairly irrefutable, nevertheless, that Comolli's interest in a failed experiment in left-libertarian self-activity moved him away from the odd blend of Mao and Mallarmé that journals such as *Cahiers* and *Tel Quel* promoted during the 1970s. The film's cogent critique of the commune's frequently pedantic founder, Giovanni Rossi, could also be viewed as a veiled critique of the rather arid form of cine-Brechtianism that Comolli subscribed to during his *Cahiers* sojourn—an aesthetic stance that posited, with facile assurance, that a cinematic avant-garde could single-handedly promote an oppositional "theoretical practice."[139]

It is important to realize the Cecilia that gives Comolli's film its title refers both to a woman—the young heroine of Giovanni Rossi's 1878 utopian romance, *A Socialist Commune*[140]—and to the actual commune founded by Rossi and nine adherents in 1890. The idealized female figure and the parcel of land that becomes La Cecilia are not unrelated. The Italians' naive belief that they can establish a liberated zone in a country making the delicate transition from feudalism to capitalism masks a paternalism that is an outgrowth of the unstated conviction that the Brazilian colony is located in an ahistorical void. Yet, as we learn in the film's initial sequence, the land that makes Cecilia possible is bequeathed to Rossi by the emperor of Brazil, Dom Pedro II. The emperor, who is eventually overthrown by a republican coup toward the end of the film, wants to be known as a benevolent aristocrat, and a commitment to "utopian socialism" would surely neutralize any accusations of despotism. Significantly, this encounter between Rossi and

Dom Pedro takes place in a Milan theater. When Rossi later confronts his colleagues during a series of internecine squabbles in Brazil, their stylized interchanges create a polemical *Theatrum mundi*. As several commentators have remarked, the emperor mangles the title of Rossi's book when he refers to the treatise as "A Socialist Communion." Comolli orchestrates the subtle shifts between reaction shots and two-shots of the protagonists, in a manner that emphasizes these strange bedfellows' tentative communion. It is also pertinent that Dom Pedro refers to Brazil as "a new country" that is eager to embrace the efforts of "pioneers with land who can do things." This peroration indicates that the anarchists have inadvertently become settler colonialists. Unlike the twentieth-century Zionists, however, they have no sentimental or nationalist attachment to the land, and eventually return to Italy in 1894. Despite the claims of orthodox leftist polemicists, this sort of myopia is not endemic to anarchism *tout court,* and under other circumstances, the settlers might well have been Marxists, Fabians, or vegetarians. *La Cecilia* does, nonetheless, give an incisive account of class conflict within Rossi's ill-fated "free commune." In fact, much of the film highlights tensions between Rossi, an essentially bourgeois radical, and his cohorts from both peasant and proletarian backgrounds.

Early in the film, these conflicts dominate two crucial sequences. The first of these conveys the quasi-metaphysical jubilation of the Italian émigrés as they peruse Brazilian "virgin land." As the settlers arrive in Brazil, the camera pans to reveal a pleasantly verdant landscape. "How beautiful it is!" proclaims an anarchist, an aside that might have been uttered by a pioneer in a western. In addition, we learn that the indigenous Brazilians refer to the anarchists as "colonialists," and that the Cecilians must depend upon local peasants to find the route to Palmeira. Utopian hopes are quickly replaced by more mundane concerns. The second sequence provides a contrapuntal demonstration of the disparity between Rossi's Bakuninist musings and the middle-class milieu from which he draws sustenance. Medium close-ups of Rossi denouncing those he terms "impostors of religion" and proclaiming that the "family is the greatest source of criminality" alternate with the camera's revelation of the family portraits and Catholic statuary that decorate the Italian bourgeois parlor where Rossi is delivering his impassioned jeremiad.

Luigi, a working-class anarchist who often feuds with Rossi, performs the role of hard-headed skeptic, a man who must point out to the dreamy theorist the errors of his idealistic ways. Ultimately, Rossi cannot refute the criticisms of his Malatestan colleagues who have remained in Italy, and reprimands his fellow settlers for abandoning working-class struggle in their homeland. The colony embodies the utopic in only the most literal sense of being a no-man's land (or "no place"), a European enclave in the midst of Latin America.

Even more pronounced contradictions come to the surface in later sequences, since the putative "leader" of La Cecilia is an intellectual botanist whose cerebral temperament is far removed from the revolutionary activism promoted by Bakunin. It is perhaps from this perspective that the fusion of Comolli's critique of Rossi and an adjacent auto-critique of *Cahiers'* aesthetic imperatives becomes most obvious. Rossi's hubris brings to mind Bakunin's scathing attack on the "savants"—the intellectual class that reinforces hierarchical distinctions in the name of scientific truth. In *Statism and Anarchy*, Bakunin sums up the case against bureaucratic savants and the fetishization of science by proclaiming that "we must respect the scientists for their merits and achievements, but in order to prevent them from corrupting their own high moral and intellectual standards, they should be granted no special privileges."[141]

Interestingly, Comolli's film presents Rossi as a man imbued with a finely tuned self-awareness, a somewhat tragic figure who is perfectly cognizant of his own distance from the people he presumes to serve. Comolli occasionally includes close-ups of Rossi peering distractedly into his microscope, but at one point the supposedly disinterested scientist seems to paraphrase Bakunin when he proclaims that "scientists are prone to moral and intellectual perversion . . . their chief vice is to exaggerate their knowledge . . . give them power and they would become the worst tyrants."

This legacy of non-coercive education, which extends from Fourier to Paul Goodman, is highlighted in *La Cecilia* through the positioning of Olimpia, Rossi's occasional companion and the commune's principal teacher, as well as the film's paradigmatic female militant. Comolli appears to view her as the true embodiment of the anarchist conscience. In an interview, he held Olimpia up as an exemplary figure, since she opposes Rossi as a "bearer of knowledge." This stance is concretized in the film during a sequence in which her lesson with a supposed anarchist militant, Tullio, ends with this pupil's reiteration of patriarchal values. Olimpia chides him and urges her recalcitrant student to remember his principles as well as the alphabet.

For some viewers, however, Comolli's veneration of Olimpia was problematic. Jacqueline Rose claimed that *La Cecilia*'s foregrounding of a woman and her image was tantamount to a form of bad faith that equaled Rossi's own self-deception. She maintains that Olimpia is represented as "plenitude, as spectacle from the terms of her first appearance to the men, or else as disturbance."[142] If one can cut through the Lacanian fog inherent in the use of the word "plenitude," it seems reasonable enough to conclude that Comolli's use of Olimpia as a feminine antidote to Rossi's masculine over-cerebration essentializes, and to a certain extent trivializes, the legacy of anarcho-feminism and anarchist pedagogy. Of course, the only truly satisfactory solution would be the production of films by anarcho-feminists.

La Cecilia ends on an ambivalent note as the colonists perform a scene from Georg Büchner's great play *Danton's Death*. Although Büchner's play deals with a revolutionary crisis, no artist was more stoically fatalistic than this playwright, who caustically reflects on Robespierre's ability to transform revolutionary zeal into the petrified artifice of revolutionary law. The members of La Cecilia did not have the ill fortune of the victims of the Thermidor. They merely abandoned a failed utopian experiment, one ultimately not too dissimilar to the Transcendentalists' Brook Farm or Cabet's Icaria.[143] Yet Comolli's generation has had to deal with its own political quandaries: the failure of the left-libertarian hopes of May 1968 as well as the recent replacement of Stalinist state socialism by free-market cynicism. It remains to be seen whether La Cecilia will be remembered as merely an eccentric historical footnote or a harbinger of other social experiments that will avoid the mistakes of the hapless Italian colonists.

The relatively detached and reflexive films of Comolli and Angelopoulos not only examine historical crises from a generally anti-authoritarian perspective, but also function, with varying degrees of success, as critical self-interrogations. All of these films illuminate, either implicitly or explicitly, the materialist eschatology outlined in Walter Benjamin's "Theses on the Philosophy of History," the opposition postulated between a "social democratic concept of progress," which perceives history as a "progression through a homogeneous, empty time" and "fulfilled time," which attempts "to wrest tradition away from a conformism that is about to overpower it."[144] The Spanish anarchists found themselves oscillating between hesitant compromises with "a social democratic concept of progress" and their traditional desire to, in Benjamin's words, "make the continuum of history explode."[145] Films like *La Cecilia* and *O Megalexandros* demonstrate that the historical continuum can be temporarily disrupted, even though the status quo is often, to say the least, dismayingly resilient. At best, the work of filmmakers like Loach, Angelopoulos, and Comolli charts the disparity between conformist leftism and the anarchist injunction to demand the impossible.

3. Anarcho-Syndicalism versus the "Revolt against Work"

Anarchism and the "Degradation of Work"

If any proof is needed that anarchism is far from a monolithic creed, the continuing conflict between anarcho-syndicalists and proponents of the "refusal of work" provides evidence of the animating tensions within contemporary anarchism. To a certain extent, debates between the inheritors of an anarcho-syndicalist tradition, pioneered by Rudolf Rocker and Diego Abad de Santillán, and contemporary anarchists and neo-Luddites represent a schism between nineteenth-century "workerism" and a late-twentieth-century skepticism concerning the advisability of promoting the workplace as the only possible locus for direct action and social change. Yet the tensions between syndicalists and advocates of a militant "anti-work" position, which have intensified since the late 1960s, can be traced back to what the historian Paul Avrich calls the "classical phase" of the anarchist movement—the period "bounded by the Paris Commune of 1871 and the Spanish Revolution of the 1930s."[1] The First International's exhortation—the "emancipation of the workers must be achieved by the workers themselves"—has an indisputably anarchist resonance, but anarchists have always questioned whether the possibility of emancipation could be promised only to skilled workers. In many respects, the Industrial Workers of the World (IWW), the most radical trade union that has ever flourished on American soil, encapsulates these contradictory currents. The IWW's goal of "one big union" could be considered hyper-syndicalist, while its concurrent amenability to strategies of sabotage ("the conscious withdrawal of efficiency") and hospitable attitude to marginal individuals (itinerant workers, hobos, and so on) who were rarely unionized has many affinities with a recent resurgence of anti-work ideology.[2]

Hostile Leninist critics of anarchism, such as Eric Hobsbawm, have described the anarchist creed as mere "millenarianism"—a peasant religion masquerading as a political creed.[3] Several less-doctrinaire historians, however, have refrained from damning anti-authoritarian socialism with patronizing praise. Rather than labeling anarchism a "secular religion," historians such as Temma Kaplan and Jerome Mintz[4] insist that the anarchist belief in spontaneity and abhorrence of coercive authority was not uncongenial to, and in fact promoted, a specifically anarchist form of organization, which manifested itself in both regional insurrections and general strikes. In addition, the post–World War I resurgence of anarcho-syndicalism, exemplified by increased militancy in Spain and Latin America, proved that anarchism was not merely an agrarian movement with apocalyptic overtones. Yet anarcho-syndicalism's brief success was fraught with inevitable contradictions. For Michael Seidman, these contradictions are personified in the abrupt ideological shifts that punctuated the career of Diego Abad de Santillán, one of the Spanish CNT's chief theoreticians. Santillán went from an ardent condemnation of "industrialism, in the manner of Ford"[5] in 1931 to an equally enthusiastic embrace of industry and even Taylorization in 1933. As we have seen, the Spanish anarcho-syndicalists who briefly swallowed their pride and hesitantly modified their anti-parliamentarianism were accused of betraying anarchist ideals. Conversely, purists who remained faithful to Bakunin's ideal of the autonomous anarchist commune were often accused of feckless utopianism.

By the post–World War II era, many champions of "post-industrialist" theory claimed that the era of heroic labor struggles was over. Despite obvious ideological disparities, the neo-Marxist Herbert Marcuse, and Daniel Bell, who has been described as a liberal, a democratic socialist, or, more commonly, a neoconservative, both believed that workers were "no longer agents of historical transformation."[6] Bell welcomed the passage from smokestack industrialism to a service economy. His liberal corporatism assumed that the post-industrialist era would be blessed with a new sense of communalism—people would "now talk to other individuals rather than interact with a machine,"[7] but his later sociological jeremiads assume that the state will join hands with science to eradicate any vestige of alienated labor. The anarcho-syndicalist Sam Dolgoff was not impressed with this form of corporate communalism. With considerable bemusement, he observed that "bourgeois economists, sociologists, and administrators like Peter Drucker,

Gunnar Myrdal, John Kenneth Galbraith, and Daniel Bell now favor a large measure of decentralization not because they suddenly have become anarchists, but primarily because technology has rendered anarchistic forms of organization "operational necessities."[8]

Marcuse's prognosis was generally gloomy (he concluded that monopoly capitalism was "capable of containing qualitative change for the foreseeable future"[9]), although he asserted that technological developments under capitalism could possibly hasten the fulfillment of Marx's desire for an "abolition of labor." From a libertarian—and more orthodox—Marxist perspective, Paul Mattick assailed Marcuse, claiming that "the utopian 'abolition of labor' implies the abolition of capitalism, or of any other successive form of class exploitation."[10]

Harry Braverman's groundbreaking *Labor and Monopoly Capital* (1974)[11] threw down the ideological gauntlet by challenging many of the post-industrialists' rosier prognostications. Braverman's methodology is scrupulously Marxist, but many anarchists welcomed his probing critique of the ongoing "degradation of work." He had little patience for the post-industrialist assumption that the "service economy" could liberate workers "from the tyranny of industry"; only for a blinkered post-industrialist could the work of a chambermaid or a service-station attendant appear less onerous than assembly-line toil.[12] Braverman refocused attention on the labor process, which, peculiarly enough, Marxists had long ignored. And, unlike Marx, Braverman maintained that "it was Taylorism and associated changes in the industrial application of scientific knowledge that completed the transition to real subordination."[13] Yet, despite a difference in emphasis, Braverman's forecast did not substantially differ from the pessimistic view of the labor process articulated by Weber and Marcuse.[14] He did not envisage an easy way out of the "iron cage" of capitalist bureaucracy and rationalization—a system "which methodically undermined labor's autonomy . . . by eliminating society's dependence on the rich panoply of craft skills heretofore distributed among the working classes."[15] Many commentators who were otherwise sympathetic to Braverman's work regretted his unwillingness to consider the possibility of workers' resistance.

In recent years, many anarchists' energies have shifted from traditional workers' struggles to a preoccupation with the critique of what Lewis Mumford labeled the "Pentagon of Power"—the "replacement of traditional polytechnics" with a system that initially gave "primacy to the machine" and has now reached its zenith with the "electronic simulation of work."[16] Anarchists such as Murray Bookchin modified Marx's belief that technology could be harnessed to benefit workers by calling for a "post-scarcity anarchism." In the late twentieth century, however, another strain of anarchism, best represented by journals such as *Fifth Estate* and *Anarchy: A Journal of Desire Armed,* has refashioned the arguments popularized by neo-Marxist anthropologists such as Pierre Clastres and Stanley Diamond.[17] Clastres's celebration of "society against the state" and Diamond's rehabilitation of the term "primitive" have been appropriated—and pushed to a frequently absurd limit—by self-styled "future primitives" such as John Zerzan, an anti-work advocate whose contempt for modernity encompasses such disparate targets as agriculture, tonality, postmodernist theory, and even speech.[18]

Cinematic representation does not follow linear patterns of development. It is important to realize that anti-work motifs surface in films from the 1930s, while documentary and fiction films that attempt to recapture the repressed historical memory of anarcho-syndicalism were released during the 1970s and 1980s. Whether ardently syndicalist or determined to revile the labor process, all of the films discussed in this chapter demonstrate that workers' resistance has not been subsumed by late capitalist inertia.

Anarcho-Syndicalism in Fiction and Documentary Cinema

Hector Olivera's *Rebellion in Patagonia* (*La Patagonia rebelde,* 1974), a dramatization of one of the most tragic incidents in the history of Argentinian anarcho-syndicalism, and Stewart Bird and Deborah Shaffer's *The Wobblies* (1979), a documentary tribute to the legacy of the IWW, share a similar ideological impetus. Both films display a nostalgic affection for a militant solidarity that appears to have eroded in a contemporary milieu where trade-unionism is identified with the ossified bureaucracies of organizations such as the AFL–CIO and the International Brotherhood of Teamsters.

Rebellion in Patagonia straightforwardly acknowledges the Argentinian labor movement's debt to anarcho-syndicalism. Olivera's film synthesizes the tradition of the political thriller, pioneered by, among others, Francesco Rosi, with genre elements largely derived from westerns and "*gaucho* films." The result is a narrative in which the ideological agenda appears intriguingly skewed. Produced at a time immediately before Argentina reverted to severe state repression, the film could be viewed as an allegorical exhortation to return to the glory days of the 1920s. Conversely, Olivera's pessimistic conclusion, accurately chronicling the military's brutal murder of fifteen hundred strikers and anarcho-syndicalist leaders during the Patagonian strike of 1921, offered little hope for rejuvenated anarcho-syndicalism during the 1970s. The period from 1973, when *Rebellion in Patagonia* was shot under the auspices of Olivera's production company, to 1974, when the film was suppressed by a less-tolerant government after becoming a considerable box-office success, parallels in certain respects the movement from hypocritical liberalism to naked authoritarianism recounted in the film itself. For example, the Confederación General del Trabajo de la República Argentina (CGT), formed during the 1930s, was a vaguely social-democratic trade union that retained at least traces of the militant syndicalism that flourished during the 1920s. But by the time Isabel Peron's right-wing regime replaced her husband's slightly more lenient one in 1974, the state had decided to stamp out all vestiges of leftist opposition. Dennis West observes that, "in the heyday of Brazilian Cinema Novo, the government permitted showings of subversive but allegorical films, presumably because they could only be understood by or appeal to, a handful of intellectuals."[19] Nevertheless, West concludes that Olivera's re-creation of past struggles was too much of a provocation for the reactionary Argentinian Peronists, who wielded an equal amount of power. This film's importance derives from its distinctive meld of populist and radical elements. As an example of third-world cinema, it does not conform to the rather rigid "deconstructive" formulae proposed by some critics. Nevertheless, its accessibility entails no capitulation to the dominant ideology.

Rebellion in Patagonia opens with a flash-forward to an anarchist hurling a bomb at Lieutenant Colonel Zavala, the government emissary who masterminded the crackdown against the anarcho-syndicalist leadership as well as the Patagonian massacre. The film subtly employs composite figures to represent actual historical personages, and this opening sequence recasts the historical murder by Kurt Wilckens (a German anarchist who had originally been, ironically enough, a Tolstoyan pacifist; his complex political lineage is not mentioned in the film) of the actual, and comparably ruthless, colonel, Varela, into a thinly fictionalized portrayal of despondent vengeance. As Osvaldo Bayer demonstrates in his lively biography of Severino di Giovanni,[20] the Argentinian elite's near-eradication of the anarcho-syndicalist movement compelled despairing anarchists to adopt increasingly violent tactics.

Anarcho-syndicalism has often proved to be a controversial tendency within anarchism itself, since many anarcho-communists, most notably Peter Kropotkin, frequently maintained that the syndicalist orientation was susceptible to reformist strategies that could actually impede genuine social transformation. Principled anarcho-syndicalists such as Rudolf Rocker responded to these caveats by maintaining that the decentralized structure of the individual syndicates foreshadowed the contours of a post-revolutionary society.[21]

From the opening of *Rebellion in Patagonia* to its bitter conclusion, Olivera emphasizes the obvious division within the anarcho-syndicalists' ranks between intellectuals who cerebrally promote what Rocker termed the "social strike"—an intervention concerned with "the protection of the community against the most pernicious outgrowths of the present system"[22]—and organizers who actively attempt to bring about a catalytic event of this sort. Olivera illustrates this opposition between thinkers and doers by means of the fraternal antagonism of old-time anarchist idealists; the Spaniard Graña and the gnarled, eventually martyred German Bakuninist Schultz spar energetically with their equally altruistic but more pragmatic comrades— particularly the young Spaniard Antonio Soto. Although Schultz and Soto become inseparable colleagues, one of the film's few comic moments is a union meeting in which Graña is reprimanded for babbling on about the anarchist classics and told to save his exegesis for the gathering devoted to theoretical matters. Despite these lighthearted jibes at loquacious ideologues, *Rebellion in Patagonia* shares Schultz's wistful hope for an "earthly paradise," which appears like an increasingly elusive goal as the film progresses.

The film is one of the few examples of anarchist cinema to examine an alliance between urban and rural workers, and, as Olivera moves his narrative from Buenos Aires to Rio Gallegos, the cinematic style takes on a frenzied pace that rivals Leone's spaghetti westerns; the staccato editing style is in fact somewhat reminiscent of Arthur Penn's *Bonnie and Clyde* (1967). While the early part of the film employs a constrained classical style (primarily close-ups and two-shots) to reinforce the precarious alliance between the "black flag of anarchy and the red flag of syndicalism," the sequences devoted to the confrontation between the military and the Patagonian "Free Workers Association" feature zooms, swift tracking movements, and an adept use of montage. Long-shots of the army brandishing their guns lay the groundwork for our conception of the doomed anarchists as helpless victims. The film is limited by a somewhat mechanistic narrative trajectory in which the status of the oppressed as victims is unalterable; in the final analysis the government and the military are more wily than the strikers, despite, or perhaps because of, their evil motives. Rather surprisingly, the odious Zavala is one of the film's more psychologically complex characters. His transformation from pragmatic conciliator to ruthless autocrat is more lucidly presented than the occasionally muddled thinking of the syndicalist leaders. To a great extent, Zavala's descent into sanctioning bloodshed mirrors the policies of the supposedly "liberal" regime of Argentinian President Yrigoyen during the 1920s (this "reform" leader sanctioned several massacres of workers during an ignominious presidency), and looks forward to the equally inconsistent psuedo-reformism of the Peronists.

Ideological waters are further muddied in several sequences featuring common criminals—the self-styled "Red Council," which attempts to infiltrate the anarcho-syndicalist movement. Its presence in Patagonia provides the government in Buenos Aires a convenient excuse for a policy of brutal repression. These meddlesome *agents provocateurs* are not unlike the *pistoleros*, whose disruptive tactics proved continually debilitating during the history of the Spanish anarchist movement. Nevertheless, the rowdy Red Council members are perhaps justifiably perturbed by anarcho-syndicalists' ingrained puritanism. When Schultz rails against the deleterious effects of alcohol, a rowdy Red Councilist remarks that the anarchists "sound like priests." Like their Spanish comrades, the Argentinian syndicalists combined militancy with an ascetic personal regime. It is uncertain whether Olivera is affirming their secular creed or obliquely commenting upon the statist repression that would mar Argentinian history for the next sixty years. Soto survives the imminent massacres by escaping on horseback, while Schultz is one of the regime's many victims.

Although syndicalist goals have not always been identical with the overall anarchist agenda, most anarchists, at least until recently, would have agreed with the French syndicalist Fernand Pelloutier's conviction that "emancipation of the working class must be self-emancipation" and that this emancipation was to be attained through the "creation of institutions which the workers themselves were to control and organize."[23] Proceeding from *Rebellion in Patagonia* to an American documentary on the IWW might seem like a considerable spatio-temporal leap, but there has always been a fair amount of international cross-fertilization within the ranks of anarcho-syndicalists. Benjamin Martin, for example, postulates that the IWW's term "one big union" may have been the source for Spanish syndicalists' adoption of the term "*sindicato unico*."[24]

The IWW, one of the few American trade unions to strive, despite many difficulties, for workers' self-emancipation, made a concerted effort to create a "new society within the shell of the old." John Dos Passos's *U.S.A.* helped disseminate the image of the Wobbly as a fusion of radicalism and prototypical American individualism. After the union's demise, Hollywood often paid a backhanded tribute to its legacy by alluding to Wobblies with patronizing bemusement. When it became evident that the once-feared union would not rise again, even the Hollywood cinema could not resist disinterring memories of lovable Wobblies. Lewis Milestone's *Hallelujah, I'm A Bum* (1933), for example, took its title from a Wobbly song, while simultaneously stripping this IWW anthem of its radical implications. Many years later, Wim Wenders's *Hammett* (1982), a fanciful account of the hard-boiled mystery writer's early years, portrayed an aging Wobbly as harmlessly endearing. Eli (Elisha Cook Jr), a crusty but amiable cab driver, is hailed by the title character—former Pinkerton agent and future Communist Party member—as "the last of the IWW organizers." Eli replies, in a manner that must have baffled Wenders's largely apolitical fans, that he's "actually an anarchist with syndicalist tendencies."

Stewart Bird and Deborah Shaffer's *The Wobblies* (1979) is a far more earnest film, a documentary that attempts to revive historical memories of a time when trade-unionism co-existed with at least the possibility of work-ers' insurrection. (Bird and Shaffer's film wastes little time in recounting the apocryphal story of the Wobbly nickname—supposedly derived from a Chinese American restaurant owner's mispronunciation of the organization's acronym.) Although *The Wobblies* is considerably more radical than anything imagined by Hollywood, it is problematic in its failure to acknowledge the primarily anarcho-syndicalist inspiration that has guided the IWW since its inception in 1905. (Although the union is now a tiny sect, the film neglects to mention that the IWW still exists in an admittedly less visible form.) Bird and Shaffer merely claimed that "it was one of the topics that people found extremely difficult to talk about. . . . A blanket would fall down whenever that kind of subject came up, which caused us a lot of frustration."[25]

While it was undoubtedly true that aging Wobblies found it difficult to talk about internecine debates—and the filmmakers' reluctance to relate these debates in their voice-over certainly cannot be attributed to bad faith—the failure to emphasize anarchist and anarcho-syndicalist components that have been an extremely vital aspect of the IWW's legacy results in a number of odd lacunae throughout this documentary. The fact that leading Wobblies such as Big Bill Haywood, Lucy Parsons, and Elizabeth Gurley Flynn traveled a perilous and, in the minds of many, tragic road from de facto anarcho-syndicalism to the apple-pie Stalinism of the American Communist Party is completely ignored by Bird and Shaffer. This neglect of unfortunate politi-cal realities is not duplicitous; it is, however, inextricably tied to narrative strategies that become increasingly popular in American documentaries that attempted, during the late 1970s and early 1980s, to emulate the techniques of oral history. Films such as *The Wobblies, Seeing Red* (1984) and *The Good Fight* interweave interviews with aging participants in radical movements, archival footage, and restrained voice-over narration. This near-formulaic style has numerous advantages: elderly radicals are often appealing, and a synthetic approach allows for an informative overview of topics that have rarely, if ever, been tackled in mainstream cinema. A public unaware of how, during the last hundred years, insurgent workers consistently discovered radical alternatives to conventional trade-unionism can learn of America's hidden history in an unusually accessible form. Yet the very accessibility—or consumability, to use a more pejorative word—of these films indicates the weakness inherent in Bird and Shaffer's polite refusal to upset the apple cart and provide a historical account of the IWW that encompasses its complexity. The fact that an aging New Left did not want to open old wounds and expose the fact that the Old Left was torn asunder by internal quarrels as vicious as anything that occurred during the 1960s speaks to the fact that the depletion of radical energy by the late 1970s engendered a yearning for an untroubled, monolithic past. The refusal of self-reflexivity in films like *The Wobblies* is not merely the product of a stylistic conservatism that some critics have found deficient: it enabled nostalgic filmmakers to construct their own version of the Popular Front in which vital differences between anarchism, liberalism, Stalinism, and Trotskyism fade away as audience members remain reassured by an enveloping warm glow. One need not endorse Noel King's aesthetic preferences to concede that the fetishization of personal authenticity and nostalgic ethical humanism that he locates in a film such as *Union Maids* (1977) is also conspicuous in *The Wobblies*.[26]

It is true that *The Wobblies* includes one reference by lumberjack Tom Scribner to furious quarrels between anarchists and Bolsheviks in the Pacific Northwest as news of the Russian Revolution reached the IWW membership. Yet this is merely anecdotal reference to a split with far-reaching consequences. Bird and Shaffer's decision, moreover, to confine their overview of the IWW to the pre-1917 period avoids the organization's shifting relationship to the Communist Party and overlooks the participation of bona fide anarcho-syndicalists.[27] Admittedly, *The Wobblies* performs a service by informing its audience that the IWW was perhaps the only radical sect in the early part of the twentieth century to welcome African Americans into its ranks with open arms, and the film highlights the memories of a black Wobbly, James Fair. Yet the film entirely neglects to mention that a black woman, Lucy Parsons, was one of the founding members of the IWW and was reportedly as powerful an orator as Big Bill Haywood or Elizabeth Gurley Flynn. Could it be that the filmmakers were reluctant to highlight Parsons's contributions because her eventual Stalinism made her a less than exemplary paradigm of twentieth-century black militancy?

A sequence devoted to the Lawrence, Massachusetts textile strike of 1912 illustrates both the strengths and weaknesses of *The Wobblies'* popularized historiography. Bird and Shaffer feature interviews with Angelo Rocco, one of the surviving Wobblies—a now elderly man who was nineteen at the time of the strike. His memories of the bloody strike succeed in providing stirring testimony from a less cynical, more militant age. The interviews are interspersed with shots of Ralph Fasanella's murals commemorating the strike; the earnestness of his folk art shields it from kitsch. Reference is also made to Joseph Ettor and Arturo Giovannitti, the IWW leaders falsely accused, in a notorious travesty of justice, of a conspiracy to wreak havoc in the mills and incite unspecified persons to commit murder. Yet Bird and Shaffer, who introduce this sequence with stock footage of immigrants weathering the rigors of steerage, regard the Lawrence strike as important primarily for its emblematic role—a case study illustrating the burgeoning participation in the radical labor movement of these newly arrived workers. While these Italian Americans' contribution of syndicalist ardor to the American scene is undeniably important, the film avoids dealing with the crucial strategic questions that preoccupied the rank and file after the relatively successful conclusion of the strike. Local industrial demands are important for promoting reforms, but can they ever trigger a social revolution that will abolish wage labor? Should the structure of a trade union be decentralized in order to encourage spontaneous direct action, or can a more rigid organizational structure better determine when agitation is appropriate?[28] These polemics were apparently considered too abstract for a general audience, and perhaps would have detracted from the filmmakers' efforts to construct the Wobblies as uncomplicated, indigenous American heroes. Despite the IWW's tolerance for inventive direct action, the progress of the Lawrence strike was determined by the workers themselves, not the leadership—however decentralized it might have been. Yet, *The Wobblies* pays homage to a trade union, thus ignoring the relationship between the rank and file's needs and the organization's dictates.

The filmmakers' decision to employ Roger Baldwin (who headed the American Civil Liberties Union but uncivilly agreed to strip Elizabeth Gurley Flynn of her ACLU membership because of her communist affiliations) as the film's narrator becomes an essential component of this documentary's cautious folksiness. Like the historian Shelby Foote, raconteur-star of Ken Burns's *The Civil War*, Baldwin narrates with crusty charm. Yet *The Wobblies'* decision to opt for charm instead of complexity makes it a well-intentioned but far from definitive film. Bird and Shaffer thoroughly neglect, for example, the fascinating alliance between Greenwich Village intellectuals, most notably John Reed and Mabel Dodge, and Paterson silk workers during their

1913 strike. During a time when the avant-garde seems to have severed its ties with political activism, the implications of the pageant staged by the silk workers at Madison Square Garden (with the assistance of many artists and intellectuals) would seem an obvious subject to explore.[29]

Assessing the strengths and weaknesses of *The Wobblies* forces us to consider the paradox that some factions of the anarchist movement want to recapture the IWW's zealous promotion of "one big union" (espoused by journals such as *Libertarian Labor Review* and *Ideas and Action*) while other, equally influential anarchist voices regard the union's preoccupation with purely industrial organizing as hopelessly retrograde. Yet in the early 1990s, the "neo-individualist" anarchist Hakim Bey, known for his lyrical manifestos promoting the establishment of "temporary autonomous zones," vigorously defended his decision to join the New York City Artists and Writers' branch of the IWW. Bey claimed that "although we oppose the idea of the social construct 'work' . . . we are far from opposing the workers." Bey challenged "the IWW to broaden its horizons beyond class consciousness, just as we challenge the punks (or the environmentalists) to become more aware of class, of labor, and of anarchist history."[30] If a bridge can be built between these disparate streams within anarchism, perhaps Bird and Shaffer's film will no longer be regarded as merely an exercise in left nostalgia.

Just as the IWW could paradoxically embody both syndicalist and "antiwork" strivings, many films, most of them made by non-anarchist leftists, celebrate radical labor movements while questioning the sanctity of work. Mauro Bolognini's *Metello* (1970),[31] for example, charts an Italian worker's conversion from anarchism to militant socialism during the 1880s. Although the eponymous protagonist becomes more enamored of Marx than Bakunin, his fondness for wildcat strikes strongly resembles the aspirations of late-nineteenth-century syndicalists. Yet during the film's climactic strike, a colleague of Metello's remarks that he'd rather not fight for the dubious "right to work." This offhand remark questions the sanctity of work embedded in the productivist agenda of both socialism and anarcho-syndicalism, although *Metello* evokes a moment in Italian history when socialism and the demands of reformist trade unionism were supplanting an earlier anarchist mass movement. Betto Lambretti, an aging anarchist militant, is the film's craggy embodiment of unadulterated altruism. Yet Bolognini and screenwriter Suzo Cecchi D'Amico portray him as a noble if eccentric relic of the past. Metello tips his "hat to the anarchists," but views them as purists whose idealism has been submerged by the tide of history—exemplified by trade-unionist realpolitik.

Aporias of René Clair

René Clair's *À Nous la liberté* (1931) does not concern itself with tangible labor struggles: it seeks to will a world without work into existence through the sheer force of its own whimsy. Beneath its musical comedy veneer, however, lies a prophetic vision of our own consumer society. Clair stumbled upon one of modern life's central paradoxes: within a consumerist context, even Friedrich Schiller's Romantic, and completely non-utilitarian, "play drive" (*Spieltrieb*) can become vulnerable to the reified strictures of standardization. A contemporary commentator observes that for Schiller "'moral beauty' is the transformation of duty into inclination."[32] Unfortunately, industrial society's (and, without doubt, "post-industrial" society's) unwieldy conflation of work and leisure makes leisure merely an untenable adjunct of work itself. As Adorno and Horkheimer write in *Dialectic of Enlightenment*, "the paradise offered by the culture industry is the same old drudgery . . . pleasure promotes the resignation which it ought to help to forget."[33]

À Nous la liberté, itself greatly indebted to popular forms that the Frankfurtians regarded with jaundiced skepticism, outlines a light-hearted version of the forces of domination unleashed by the Enlightenment. Clair's film remains one of the cinema's most appealingly playful indictments of assembly-line travail, even if Clair's own political affiliations remain murky and contradictory. In his memoirs, Clair takes obvious pleasure in the scorn heaped upon *À Nous la liberté* by the French Communist Party, and embraces the derisive label of "anarchist" with a certain glee. He observed that the film demonstrates that "the end product of real revolution is anarchy," and wryly concludes that this is "ironically . . . what those self-styled Communists hated so much."[34] Yet, despite Clair's embrace of a playful, "anarchistic" style in films such as *Entr'acte* and *À Nous la liberté*, his subsequent films are apolitical dreamscapes. In addition, Clair, while at odds with official Leninism, also contributed to *Plans*, a magazine that subscribed to Henri de Man's meliorist ideal of a planned, mixed economy—a political tendency that merged certain strains of right-wing syndicalism (Mussolini's friend Hubert Lagardelle was also a contributor to the journal) with a decidedly non-anarchist strain of social democracy that offered a foretaste of post–World War II Europe.[35]

Notwithstanding Clair's contradictory aesthetic and political allegiances, *À Nous la liberté* offers an intuitive, rather than a programmatic, endorsement of Paul Lafargue's late-nineteenth-century assertion of "the right to be lazy." Lafargue's own work and career is distinguished by contradictory impulses. Although Lafargue, Marx's son-in-law, attempted to crush the Bakuninist faction in the First International and establish his father-in-law's centralized version of socialism as the dominant current within the international left, he has also been termed "a true ancestor of Tristan Tzara,"[36] and the first left-wing theorist to challenge the productivist ethos that permeates socialist dogma. In recent years, even some anarchists have used Fourier's essentially pre-industrial utopian schemes as a stick with which to beat anarcho-syndicalists, supposedly still under the sway of the ideology of work.

À Nous la liberté anticipates these debates between adherents of a radical work ethic and incendiary loafers, even though the film itself seems utterly oblivious to sectarian niceties of any variety. Indeed, Clair's decision to couch his critique of industrialism in the form of an operetta enables him adroitly to sidestep overt class conflicts and render his recalcitrant protagonists relatively innocuous. The roguish Émile prefers to luxuriate in Clair's seriously impoverished vision of nature, while his companion Louis's rebelliousness is defused by his success in respectable society.

The film opens with an equation of the factory assembly line with prison that wittily compresses the argument of Lafargue's tract The Right to be Lazy. A prison workshop is the backdrop for the film's initial sequences, although, for a few seconds at least, the impression is given that we are merely catching glimpses of a commercial toy factory. Before Émile is identified as "worker-prisoner no. 135," a tracking shot of a line of identical wooden horses underlines À Nous la liberté's depiction of a consumer society immersed in the arduous mass production of accoutrements of leisure. Seconds before Émile and Louis succeed in their escape from the carceral toyshop, they sing that "freedom is everything in life, but men have made prisons, rules, laws, convention, work, offices, houses." Shortly after Louis's near-miraculous escape, he fortuitously finds himself installed as the president of a gramophone factory. The labor-intensive artisanship needed to manufacture wooden horses gives way to a more streamlined, leisure-oriented culture industry.

Clair's critique of industrialism eventually becomes co-opted by his need to end the narrative with a saccharine flourish. Notwithstanding certain narrative compromises, À Nous la liberté clearly identifies the factory, school, and family as focal points of ideological domination. A seamless juxtaposition of the ideology of work and conformist pedagogy is achieved with one of the most celebrated shock cuts in early sound cinema. As Émile languishes in a grassy field within sight of factory chimneys, a disapproving policeman reproves him with the words, "Not working. Don't you know that . . ."—a sentence fragment that is finished by a schoolmaster dictating the words "work is compulsory" to his captive class. After the camera tracks back to reveal a row of bored prepubescent children, the teacher continues his deadpan dictation with the words, "because work is freedom." Clair's unwittingly prescient invocation of the Nazi motto emblazoned above Auschwitz—*Arbeit Macht Frei*—to condemn compulsory drudgery also looks forward to the situationist Raoul Vaneigem's more politicized tirade against work in *The Revolution of Everyday Life:*

> Nowadays ambition and the love of a job well done are the indelible mark of defeat and of the most mindless submission. Which is why, wherever submission is demanded, the stale fart of ideology makes headway, from the *Arbeit Macht Frei* of the concentration camps to the homilies of Henry Ford and Mao Tse-tung.[37]

À Nous la liberté's less than sanguine view of work is augmented by a problematic schism between "nature" and modernity, a thorny dichotomy that also surfaces in contemporary anarchist debates. Émile, Clair's unrepentant tramp, is consistently linked to the natural realm, although the film's clichéd view of nature—a fleeting close-up of Émile sniffing an unidentifiable flower typifies Clair's approach—seems culled from the picture postcard. More importantly, however, *À Nous la liberté* underlines the inescapable fact that modernity often seeks to emulate or masquerade as nature. A semi-parodic blurring of technology and the visible world comes to the fore in a sequence in which the hapless Émile attempts to attract the attention of Jeanne, an attractive young woman. Part of Jeanne's allure is, undoubtedly, the plangent love ballad she is, at least presumably, singing. Before long, however, a high-angle shot informs us that her hymn to love actually emanates from a gramophone, an "L" model manufactured by Louis, Émile's former comrade. A mass-produced siren's song playfully implodes the distinction between a spontaneous expression of love and its mass-mediated counterpart.

The critic Allen Thiher complains that undue attention to Clair's sociopolitical preoccupations prevents an awareness of his cinematic strategies. Thiher claims that Clair's emphasis on "two forms of order . . . the order demanded by work and the antiorder of play"[38] is not engendered by a fullfledged ideological critique, but is instead a product of a desire for a symmetrical, nearly "geometrically perfect" narrative. Thiher's argument illuminates some of the more conventional aspects of Clair's superficially experimental film. For example, Louis (Henri Marchand), the upwardly mobile ex-con, and Émile (Raymond Cordy), the carefree idler, possess the requisite equilibrium of id and superego needed to constitute an archetypal comedy duo. The film's idyllic resolution, moreover, can be viewed as a mode of closure that overlooks concrete questions of class conflict and state violence that would have undoubtedly manifested themselves in a film made by a director more attuned to radicalism than to the quirks of musical comedy. Yet, despite these generic concessions, *À Nous la liberté* successfully indicts the facile assumption, shared by some anarchists as well as most Marxists, that a radiant, technocratic future embodies a "progressive" ideal.

Clair's gentle indictment of progress is subtly reinforced with visual, aural, and narrative panache. The gleaming facade of Louis's gramophone factory, with its glass panels and streamlined simplicity, for instance, captured in a bravura low-angle shot, resembles the more ostentatious examples of Bauhaus-style architecture. Many of the original Bauhaus architects—Walter Gropius comes to mind—initially extolled a quasi-socialist idealism; the stripped-down minimalism of the edifices was suggested as the exemplary style for workers' housing. Their quasi-socialistic aspirations quickly evaporated when this ultra-functionalist style became *de rigueur* corporate style. Within *À Nous la liberté*'s version of the "world turned upside down," the glass and steel fortress becomes as oppressive as the prison factory featured in the film's opening shots. Similarly, when Émile is finally dragooned into finding work at this massive adjunct of the entertainment industry, a disembodied voice imperiously informing the stream of applicants that "we will give you work. . . . Turn 'round and straight ahead" is contrapuntally juxtaposed with Émile's blithe lack of interest—he is still distracted by his quixotic pursuit of Jeanne—in the hiring process. The clash between officious, monologic speech and impulsive spontaneity is more than merely a component, however playfully wrought, of a textual system. The opposing forces of bureaucratic efficiency and potentially rebellious lassitude are highlighted in a subsequent assembly-line sequence that almost certainly inspired analogous comic interludes in Chaplin's *Modern Times*. Émile, more concerned with amorous daydreaming than with work, continually fails to affix the required screws to a procession of newly minted gramophones.

Unsurprisingly, Émile's indifference to the task at hand enrages his fellow workers, and he eventually becomes embroiled in a brief skirmish with an elderly worker. Although mainstream opinion condemns workers like Émile as "lazy," most anarchists would agree with Kropotkin that most so-called lazy individuals are "people gone astray in a direction that does not answer to their temperament nor to their capacities."[39] Like a more obstreperous cinematic idler, Renoir's Boudu, Émile prefers merging with the flotsam and jetsam of urban life—and re-creating a pastoral alternative world within the city—to the conformist demands of work.[40] His former boon companion Louis, however, is an upwardly mobile go-getter, supremely eager to repress memories of penury as he relishes his newfound status as industrial magnate.

Ironically enough, Louis's factory is devoted to manufacturing a product that sanctions—even encourages—the cultivation of daydreams. *À Nous la liberté* rails against useless toil in a factory devoted to churning out a product that has become a staple of the consumer society. Marx's productivist model assumes that a post-socialist society will produce individuals who "stand outside of the process of production instead of being the principal agent in the process of production." This supposed transformation of alienated labor into meaningful work implies that "man . . . will achieve . . . mastery of nature through his societal existence."[41] Yet more recent qualms raised by both anarchists and libertarian Marxists have concerned the advisability of the domination of nature that is such an enormous contingency of the Enlightenment project, and have also mercilessly attacked the "technological rationality" that made this project and the "false needs" endemic to consumer society possible.

The elitism, however unwitting, that may lurk behind concepts such as "false needs" has not gone unnoted; Wolfgang Haug's demurral—"manipulation could only be effective if it 'somehow' latched on to the 'objective interests' of those being manipulated"—is a subtler critique of "commodity aesthetics?"[42] On a concrete level, the gramophone, alternately celebrated and derided in *À Nous la liberté,* both charts how routinized patterns of consumption came into existence and points to the very marriage of artistry and technology that animates—and made possible—Clair's film. One of the film's most intricate shots features Louis, photographed from a high angle, examining a new gramophone as assistants hover around him awaiting orders. A subsequent sequence demonstrates the effectiveness of the factory's elaborate surveillance system, a primitive if effective precursor of computerized databases. It is not at all coincidental that Clair chose to represent the display of power that accompanies the manufacture of record players, instead of constructing his narrative around the mass production of cars or toilets. As Jacques Attali observes, "with the introduction of the record, the classical space of discourse collapses."[43]

The mass consumption of recording devices parodied in *À Nous la liberté* undoubtedly led to changes, both positive and negative, in the public reception and appreciation of music. Although access to important classics and popular music has been enhanced by recording, we can identify the twentieth century with a privatized musical sphere, whose downward spiral, or inverted teleology, can be traced from the invention of the phonograph to the recent development of the digital music streaming. As Michael Chanan observed of the Walkman, music streamed from a smartphone through earbuds "induces a sense of solipsism . . . by isolating the listener from the world through music."[44] In many respects, *À Nous la liberté* is a plea for the restoration of communal pleasures, since modernity, and industrialism in particular, has not only had an adverse effect upon individual autonomy, but has also had negative consequences for communities that must deal with the encroachments of an insensitive state.

The musical, a genre that requires a minimum of expository dialogue and frequently summons up utopian longings, proved the perfect vehicle for Clair's gentle rebuke to industrialization. Even if Clair's political orientation was obscure, a children's chorus, sweetly intoning the sardonic lyrics, "Work is compulsory/Because Work is Freedom," demonstrates the antiauthoritarian potential of seemingly frivolous musicals. Nevertheless, the film's true contradictions become apparent in one of the final sequences highlighting Louis's decision to bequeath his newly built, even more streamlined factory to his colleagues, while hailing the advent of a thoroughly automated era in which ultra-sophisticated machines will render human labor obsolete. Exemplifying both narrative sleight of hand and muddled ideology, Louis's seemingly magnanimous gesture can be viewed as either technocratic downsizing, a harbinger of "post-scarcity" anarchism in which an egalitarian future is made possible by technological progress, or merely an authoritarian maneuver to displace workers but not truly abolish labor. Clair's frantic hedge-betting was recognized years ago by Harry Alan Potamkin, who mused that if "Clair kids rationalization . . . does he mean to kid Capitalism or Communism or both; the factory is handed to the workers—is he joshing social democratic fancy, the boss, the worker, the factory?"[45] Although Potamkin identifies some of the film's irreconcilable paradoxes, his own mainstream leftism blinded him to the fact that both capitalists and communists share startlingly similar views of rationalization. "Only the machine will work," proclaims Louis—a sentiment that was shared by P. M. Kerzhentsev[46] (considered the Soviet equivalent of F. W. Taylor) as well as American industrial magnates. Given Clair's own flirtation with authoritarian, if nominally "socialist," adherents of centralized planning, his endorsement of unmitigated "Organization, progress" should perhaps be feared instead of admired.

Whatever our verdict, Louis's proclamation of technological utopia inspires Clair's vision of a static workers' utopia in which shots of gleaming new gramophones untouched by human hands are juxtaposed with a montage of carefree workers dancing and playing skittles and cards. Murray Bookchin, known for his vigorous hostility to much of modernity's heritage, casts a fairly cold eye over Clair's vision of the future. He grouses that "the workers in *À Nous la liberté* . . . achieve their freedom in a highly industrialized land of Cockaigne: their functions are taken over completely by machines while they do nothing but frolic in nearby fields and fish *en masse* along river banks that have an uncanny resemblance to their assembly lines."[47]

The aridity of Clair's conclusion also troubled Dudley Andrew, who maintains that "Clair must surely have been aware that his own aesthetic conspires with the cold rational modernism he pretends to satirize."[48] For both Andrew and Gilles Deleuze, one of Clair's fiercest critics, *À Nous la liberté* reduces characters to interchangeable components within a mechanized landscape. While there is more than a grain of truth to this harsh conclusion, the aporias of this film reflect the quandary of critiquing industrialism and rationalization from within the context of a medium that was made possible by rationalization itself—the creation of films depends upon the "piecework" of innumerable participants. For this reason, a critique of *À Nous la liberté's* failings should be less of an auteurist enterprise than an interrogation of cinema's own productivist ethic and aesthetic.

Tout va bien: May '68 and Workers' Control

When asked, in 1994, to comment on his brief foray into the realm of political cinema during the late 1960s and early 1970s, Jean-Luc Godard reflected upon his past radicalism with seeming disingenuousness:

> I have memories of recreation—it was like school break. You pretend, and I was younger. I came to politics at a rather late age. I didn't come from a political family, my parents weren't militants, and I wasn't raised with a political consciousness. I learned more about history through novels than I learned about history directly. History for me was like the biggest novel of all time. While it was serious in some ways, it was still like a holiday.[49]

This infuriating, superficially uninformative response contains some clues to the process by which Godard, in collaboration with Jean-Pierre Gorin, made a film that exemplifies the revival of interest in anarcho-communist ideals of workers' control, despite the filmmakers' explicitly Maoist (anti-CP, but also neo-Stalinist) ideological convictions. What are we to make of the fact that supposed Maoists could make a film in 1972 that, in many respects, crystallizes many of the most vital left-libertarian currents that influenced the insurrectionary fervor of May '68? This paradox reminds us of the fact that ideological confusion can sometimes engender surprisingly insightful works.[50]

An empathy, however unwitting, with anarchist spontaneism was not always evident in the frequently turgid films of Godard and Gorin's "Dziga

Vertov Group." *Wind from the East* (1969), a film whose political incoherence is exceeded only by its tediousness, condemns council communists and anarchists with Olympian pseudo-rigor. Unlike the rather sterile, pseudo-Brechtian didacticism of *Wind from the East* (despite the nominal participation of the onetime left-libertarian Daniel Cohn-Bendit), however, *Tout va bien* can be viewed as a genuinely Brechtian synthesis of pleasure *and* instruction. The Maoists whom Godard and Gorin sympathized with, moreover, particularly the youthful members of the Gauche Prolétarienne (GP),[51] combined a thoroughgoing devotion to Mao's authoritarian "cultural revolution" (a thoroughly hierarchical social revolution) with a taste for militant direct action on French shores that shared a certain kinship with anarchism, however ill-digested and misbegotten. Robert Stam observes that *Tout va bien* "is structured around a tripartite play of ideological languages: that of capital, that of the Communist Party, and that of the Maoists."[52] For Stam, these juxtapositions point to the film's penchant for what Mikhail Bakhtin termed "heteroglossia" and provide evidence that Godard and Gorin's hostility to an illusionistic aesthetic reaps real political benefits. A Bakhtinian perspective aptly sums up *Tout va bien*'s irreducibility to monologic platitudes. An anarchist perspective, however, complicates matters slightly more, since the Maoists' rhetoric was considerably more monologic (it could be deemed neo-Stalinism masquerading as ultra-leftism) than the savants of *Cahiers du Cinéma* assumed during the 1970s. The film's polyphonic structure includes an interplay between its ostensible Maoism and an inchoate anti-authoritarianism, slouching toward Beijing, but struggling to be born. This may help to illuminate Godard's rather frivolous characterization of his political films as playful excursions during an aimless "school break." Wittgenstein termed art "language gone on holiday," and the Godard/Gorin concept of film as something of a provisional aesthetic experiment, not a closed system, does not preclude fortuitous political insights that clash with these directors' stated ideological convictions. This contradiction can be ascribed to the fact that *Tout va bien* does not depict political militancy as the heroic triumph of autonomous egos, but presents a heteroglot collection of voices that reflect the *unresolved* ferment of the post-1968 period in France.

Not surprisingly, *Tout va bien*'s covert, perhaps even unconscious, anarchism was noticed by numerous guardians of leftist orthodoxy. Irwin Silber chided Godard and Gorin for their failure to endorse a vanguard party, and discerned dire petty bourgeois attitudes in the film's climactic supermarket hiatus.[53] Similarly, a Maoist collective that attacked the film in the pages of *Cahiers du Cinéma* found fault with what was considered "petty bourgeois anarcho-syndicalism."[54] Perhaps most tellingly, Sylvia Harvey complained that "*Tout va bien* . . . operates as a sustained defence of the leftist position, offering finally an unproblematic endorsement of the politics of spontaneity, and thus reproducing an ideology which, it might be argued, constituted one of the chief weaknesses of the May movement."[55] Harvey, who fails to provide evidence of how the orthodox left could have avoided the transgressions of *gauchistes,* falls prey to the same bureaucratic logic of a Communist Party that never grasped the potential importance of May '68's brief worker–student alliance—a bureaucratic impotence attacked in Godard and Gorin's film. The apparent chasm between what ideologues considered odious anarcho-syndicalism and the Dziga Vertov group's presumed Maoist aversion to the anarchist legacy can be at least partly explained by Gorin's contention that *Tout va bien*'s collaborative approach represents an attempt to undermine, and perhaps supersede, the concept of authorial supremacy—to "reach the point where you are not speaking as an ego, where something is speaking through you."[56] This deeply Bakhtinian realization of the way in which a work of art's "cacophony of voices" can illuminate complex social realities also explains the contradiction of an anti-authoritarian film made by individuals with at least tentative links to an authoritarian ideology In addition, artists such as Godard and Gorin, as well as philosophers such as Jean-Paul Sartre and Ernst Bloch, have often masochistically suppressed anarchist impulses. Bloch's left-libertarian impulses, for example, were tempered by what his own son termed "steadfast political and philosophical loyalty to the East German Republic in the late Stalinist plague years after 1945."[57]

Film critics have tended to view *Tout va bien*'s political radicalism as an appendage of its formal radicalism. While the film's reinvention of Brechtianism and reflexivity are certainly part of its political gestalt, the specific historical roots of its unwittingly anarchistic leftism have been consistently ignored. Since, as Harvey asserts, *Tout va bien* is an elaboration of '68 *gauchisme,* it is important to delineate specifically the political currents that constitute the film's "leftism." Notwithstanding Godard and Gorin's fairly perfunctory allegiance to Maoism, the film is an oblique tribute to council communist currents, best exemplified in the work of Karl Korsch, Anton Pannekoek, and Paul Mattick, which were rediscovered by militants during the late 1960s and played a large part in the debates concerning workers' control that reached their apogee during the May events. The council communists differed from the anarcho-syndicalist in their acceptance of Marx, but agreed with anarchism's anti-bureaucratic orientation by rejecting Lenin's concept of "democratic centralism" as inherently undemocratic. Moreover, anarchists and council communists have often formed alliances; the anarchist editor Dwight Macdonald, for example, published articles by Korsch and Mattick in his short-lived journal *politics*. Pannekoek, the Dutch theorist and activist, is often the most representative figure to emerge from the councilist ferment, fusing "a materialist view of history" with the unapologetically idealist view that workers' revolts are actually "struggles of consciousness."[58]

There are many affinities, as well as certain differences, between anarcho-syndicalism and Pannekoek's vision of council communism. Although anarcho-syndicalists had little patience with Pannekoek's elaborate Marxist epistemology, they shared much of his ultra-productivist bias.[59] In addition, the council communists were in total agreement with the anarcho-syndicalists' anti-parliamentarianism and belief in direct action—the wildcat strike became the paradigm of the so-called "ultra-left" assault on bureaucratic socialism condemned explicitly by Lenin in his *Left-wing Communism: An Infantile Disorder*. The council communists, therefore, belong to a current Mattick christened "anti-Bolshevik Communism"; they believe that the Bolsheviks had no interest in abolishing wage labor and convincingly argued "that there is nothing in the arsenal of Stalinism that cannot also be found in that of Lenin and Trotsky."[60] Many of these ideas were assimilated into the French left—as well as subtly modified—by the activist and philosopher Cornelius Castoriadis, a theorist whose tortuous political progression catapulted him from orthodox communism to Trotskyism and finally on to an idiosyncratic meld of anarchism and council communism.[61] With an ingratitude that was as typical as it was occasionally endearing, the situationists borrowed heavily from Castoriadis's work and subjected it to merciless, and sometimes scurrilous, condemnation. Despite Godard and Gorin's professed "Maoism," *Tout va bien* is a film often graphically posing the unpalatable choices between an inflexible capitalist state and the pretensions of official communism that sound surprisingly like the status quo it supposedly opposed.

Tout va bien's often anguished reflexivity enables the film to avoid facile sloganizing and achieve the status of a historical meditation that is still pertinent. If *Wind from the East* was stymied by strained didacticism, much of *Tout va bien*'s effectiveness stems from the fact that the actors' dialogue is composed primarily of quotations from disparate political sources. Godard and Gorin chronicle the turbulent progress of a wildcat strike at the "Salumi" sausage factory, and the factory manager's animated recitation of passages from the economist Jean Saint-Geours's *Long Live the Consumer Society* illustrates how a dialogic strategy—"a relativizing of linguistic consciousness"—reinforces this cinematic endorsement of workers' self-management. Instead of the usual psychological portrait of the tyrannical boss familiar from many left-wing films, Godard and Gorin feature a monologue delivered by a slick, "progressive" manager. His verbatim regurgitation of Saint-Geours's platitudes—a vapid, but surprisingly "liberal" précis of ideas culled from Marx, Weber, and Galbraith—illustrates the fact that, in an era of de-industrialization, even the bosses had to mouth liberal rhetoric and shun the more strident anti-worker sentiments of nineteenth-century moguls such as Henry Clay Frick. This sly appropriation of Saint-Geours's banalities demonstrates, in a thoroughly de-psychologized fashion, the reified nature of what often passes for sociological observation. *Tout va bien's* cacophony of discourses is, as we would expect from Godard, also exemplified by a carefully choreographed collision of sounds and images. A particularly complex shot, for example, juxtaposes a CGT delegate's conformist spiel—culled from a manifesto entitled *La Vie ouvrière*—with a *gauchiste's* conversation with his comrades and a throng of seemingly unaligned workers. The CGT functionary's claim that the "task of establishing democracy must be made by a people's coalition government" that is, a bureaucratic regime that "speaks for" the people—is subtly, but effectively, refuted by the indifference of actual workers.

Tout va bien's mock-autobiographical preoccupations enable Godard and Gorin to avoid the disingenuousness that sometimes afflicts middle-class leftists who attempt to compress working-class discontent into seamless narratives. It is obviously too simplistic to accept Yves Montand, the film-maker torn by desire for commercial success and political commitment, and Jane Fonda, the idealistic if self-absorbed journalist, as surrogates for Godard and Gorin. It is not so much that these glamorous representatives of the media—whose cash value is referred to in the film's opening voice-over, which accompanies a montage of checks—function as parodic, or even quasi-confessional, self-indictments of liberal guilt. The film's insistent self-interrogation is more concerned with critiquing the unadorned naturalism of films such as Marin Karmitz's *Coup pour coup* (1972). Karmitz's political stance on workers' control was quite similar to Godard and Gorin's and his film was severely, and quite unfairly, attacked by some of the more militant *gauchiste* critics.[62] Reflexivity should certainly not be regarded as the only viable aesthetic option for politically engaged filmmakers.

Nevertheless, a reflexive strategy works brilliantly for Godard and Gorin. They invariably find novel visual metaphors to pinpoint their own complicity in the system they seek to indict, without engaging in unproductive self-flagellation. For example, as a worker's voice-over explains the exhaustion and tedium that accompany life on the assembly line, the image track features shots of Montand wheeling slabs of meat on to the factory floor and Fonda industriously stuffing sausages. In addition to chronicling the nuances of the "struggle of consciousness" (or *geistige*) that Pannekoek isolated as the necessary catalyst for social transformation, these shots pithily convey both the necessity and absurdity of middle-class intellectuals' efforts to empathize with the working class. Although the superficial glamor of stars is difficult to eradicate, in some respects the quotidian tasks performed by Montand and Fonda are part of a process of de-individuation that can never be entirely successful. On another level, Fonda and Montand's reenactment of some snippets of erotic dialogue originally spoken by Brigitte Bardot and Michel Piccoli in Godard's *Le Mépris* (*Contempt*, 1962) both de-aestheticizes the hyper-lyricism of the earlier film and posits an alternative to the constrictions imposed by the traditional constitution of the bourgeois couple. *Tout va bien*'s deployment of its stars verges on textual narcissism; the mélange of politics and self-reflection resembles the genre Bakhtin christened "polemically colored autobiography." Montand's offhand references to perfunctory support for trade unions and victims of Spanish fascism allude to the actor's association with mainstream communist ideology; the film's rejection of the CP's bureaucratic strategy, and embrace of a quasi-anarchistic agenda, implies that even the star of the film can benefit from a "struggle in consciousness." Even the two-tiered, cutaway set that serves as the locus for much of the film's action, providing us with simultaneous glimpses of both the shop floor and the management's offices—embodies the schism between our sympathies with the workers' demands and the filmmakers' preoccupation with the politics of representation. *Tout va bien*'s revamped version of Erwin Piscator's aesthetics, particularly his efforts to "put an end to the peep-show world of the bourgeois theater,"[63] helps to replicate the inevitable polyphony of political struggle as well as the often-ineffectual attempts of detached intellectuals to understand that struggle.

Tout va bien combines a backward glance at the events of May '68 with a forecast of the resurgent interest in workers' self-management that would sweep across France in 1973 (the occupation and brief workers' collective at the LIP factory is usually cited as the archetypal example)[64] after the release of the film. Godard and Gorin's commingling of media personalities' neuroses and workers' preoccupations corresponds to the hesitant, and not always successful, desire of students and intellectuals to collaborate with workers during the May events. Roger Gregoire and Fredy Perlman's account of worker–student coalitions during this period, particularly the occupation of Citroen and Renault factories, emphasizes the fact that "even though the committees were composed of workers as well as "intellectuals," and even though committee members ceased to separate each other into these two categories, they developed a 'specialist' attitude which separated committee militants from both workers as well as 'intellectuals.'"[65]

The media stars in *Tout va bien* experience a more radical "social separation" (it should be recalled that one of the key situationist texts is called "critique of separation"), since they are primarily passive bystanders who witness the workers' transformation into self-conscious subjects. Fonda's character expresses her anguish with particular alacrity; she believes that the futility of her work is akin to "a mountain giving birth to a mouse" and laments the fact that she is an American correspondent in France who "corresponds to nothing." In Fredy Perlman's neo-situationist formulation, the average worker "does not exist in the world as an active agent who transforms it . . . he consumes and admires the products of human activity passively."[66] *Tout va bien* follows the lead of May '68 in demonstrating that workers do not need institutions or leaders in order to emerge from this debilitating passivity. The representatives of the "society of the spectacle"—Fonda, for example, dejectedly realizes that her copy on the strike is "full of crap"—are much more passive than workers who lucidly voice their complaints, analyzing the physical and mental ravages of production quotas as they usurp the authority of their boss with carnivalesque glee. A sequence in which a young worker covers a portrait of the Salumi factory with blue paint exemplifies the workers' active negation, a stance that has little in common with Fonda and Montand's self-lacerating introspection.

The film's climactic melee at a French "hypermarket" illustrates the extent of Godard and Gorin's unacknowledged debt to the situationists. The situationist militants, influential beyond their small numbers, appropriated and continued the legacy of Pannekoek and the council communists. Violently opposed to Marcuse's assertion in *One Dimensional Man* that the working class had been "integrated" into the social fabric—irredeemably afflicted with a contingent loss of revolutionary potential—the situationist René Viénet claimed that although "consumer alienation, spectacular passivity, and organized separation have been the major accomplishments of modern affluence," these impediments to change "were challenged by the May uprising . . . the workers entered the struggle spontaneously, armed only with their subjectivity in revolt."[67] *Tout va bien*'s final supermarket spree, in which a tracking shot captures a Communist Party functionary's energetic hawking of his manifesto as well as unaligned workers impulsively looting the well-stocked shelves, concretizes the spirit of "subjectivity in revolt." Of course, it is also clear why more traditional leftists thought that a movement that became infatuated with transient revolutionary eruptions was destined to be short-lived. Viénet's claim that the "occupation movement . . . ended the sleep of the masters of commodities . . . never again shall spectacular society sleep in peace" may now appear overly optimistic, as radicalism *in toto*, both mainstream and "ultra-left,"[68] appears to be in an almost irreversible slump. The penultimate voice-over peroration—"change everything, but where do you start? Everything at once" sums up the ferment of the post-'68 period in France—a desire to turn the world upside down coupled with a realization that this task is far from easy. Invoking Bakhtin's theorization of carnival, some recent commentators have wondered if "May's extraordinary combination of fierce violence with almost complete lack of bloodshed can be understood as a 'fictional intensification of symbolic exchange'—the acting out of the desire for revolution rather than of revolution itself."[69] To a large extent, ruminations of this sort were engendered by the depletion of radical energy in both Europe and the United States from the mid-1970s onward. Nevertheless, *Tout va bien* offers evidence that carnivalesque inversion can also illuminate the impetus for this assault on hierarchy, and need not be viewed as merely an aesthetic phenomenon—a "fictional intensification of symbolic exchange." The striking workers' refusal, for example, to allow their captive boss any more time to relieve his bladder than they are granted themselves is a case in point. Bakhtin maintained that the "lower stratum is mankind's real future,"[70] and the factory occupation that forces the boss to turn his office into an impromptu *pissoir* suggests a possible future where bureaucratic duress is outmoded and unimaginable. Instead of changing "everything at once," the radical left slowly imploded, at least partly as a result of the radical movement splintering into tiny, ineffectual Leninist *groupuscules*.[71] But *Tout va bien* (however frivolous it may now appear to Godard himself) is still noteworthy for its vision of a non-hierarchical society, even though the film's directors were only vaguely aware of its anarchistic implications.

Revolting against Work: Petri's *The Working Class Goes to Heaven*

Despite the fact that occasionally a film, such as *Metello*, charts historical fluctuations in workers' consciousness, the majority of films celebrating antiauthoritarian workers' insurrections do not take strikes, even the anarchosyndicalist "mass strike," as their departure point. For the most part, films by, among others, Petri, Farraldo, and Tanner are more concerned with defying what the anarchist polemicist p.m. terms the "planetary work machine"[72]—the process of industrialization itself—than combating the excesses of specific autocratic bosses. A sophisticated critique of conformist unionism such as Elio Petri's *The Working Class Goes to Heaven* (*La Classe Operaia Va in Paradiso*, 1971) shares Bakunin's desire for the "complete negation of all authority and power" as well as his complementary "negation of the concept of the individual as citizen of the state replaced by the concept of free man [sic]."[73]

Lacking the intricate reflexivity of *Tout va bien*, *The Working Class Goes to Heaven* depicts working-class life in an arguably more nuanced, and unquestionably more disturbing, manner. Studs Terkel concludes that "work is, by its very nature, about violence—to the spirit as well as to the body."[74] Consequently, Petri's portrait of a steelworker, Ludovico Massa (superbly played by Gian Maria Volonté), brutalized by the demands of piecework, is considerably less idealized than the rather bloodless representatives of the proletariat enshrined by Godard and Gorin. Massa cannot fulfill the expectations of either the Communist Party or Maoist students (who would like him to conform to their respective visions of political rectitude) and his frustrations are reflected in his sexism, which is presented as neither exemplary nor particularly shocking, and his willing capitulation to the lure of consumerism. *The Working Class Goes to Heaven* charts Massa's progress from his near-robotic tolerance of his work regime to anguished rebellion; he is neither a revolutionary paragon nor an apolitical boor. The film eschews revolutionary exhortations, and merely suggests how routinized work can cripple both body and mind. Petri's modus operandi privileges showing over telling. He opens the film with a close-up of Massa rising to check the clock, a subsequent shot of the glaring factory lights, and a dramatic pan up Volonté's exhausted face as he complains of a splitting headache.

Instead of instantly becoming a rebel, however, Massa—jocularly christened "Lulu the tool"—initially accepts his fate and becomes, in his own eyes, a rabid "Stakhanovite." This reference to the heroically productive Soviet steelworker from the Donbass region, whose remarkable output was extolled by Stalin during the 1930s, unites supposedly antithetical modes of capitalist and state socialist rationalization. Both systems glorified self-sacrifice, or what Max Weber termed "inner worldly asceticism," an ethic which ostensibly curbed worker dissidence. Yet, as Moshe Lewin points out, Stakhanovism eventually sabotaged efficient production, since "the orientation on supermen had a disorganizing effect, not least of all because of the resentment it produced among workers who were not up to the exploits of the few and begrudged the privileges showered upon the chosen in times of scarcity."[75] Massa is able only tentatively to embody this parody of Herculean productivity because he views himself in thoroughly reified terms—an "individual who is just like a factory, a shit-making factory." He is well aware of the fact that he behaves like a "trained monkey," but prefers brute numbness to the frustration he experiences when anger and sexual desire overwhelm him. An industrial accident provides the catalyst for this tool's massive refusal of the institution of work, and Petri demonstrates to his audience that the regimen of the shop floor is also evident in the alienated sexuality of this worker's relationships with his wife and mistress.

Massa's progression from manic productivity to militant resistance to work brings to mind the Italian left's own traditionally ambivalent view of rationalization, especially as exemplified by the work of Antonio Gramsci. Gramsci has been hailed alternately as a diehard but innovative Leninist and as a man always on the verge of rejecting the Leninist tradition. These antinomies are supremely evident in his 'Americanism and Fordism,' a work that acknowledges that the U.S. version of inner-wordly asceticism "helped to create in the U.S. an historically new type of individual—the 'trained gorilla,'"[76] but, from a somewhat fundamentalist Marxist position, advocates "Fordism as the ultimate stage in the process of progressive attempts by industry to overcome the law of the tendency of the rate of profit to fall."[77] Although *The Working Class Goes to Heaven* was attacked by traditional leftists for its 'confused ideology,'"[78] Petri's coolly undogmatic film unobtrusively explodes the contradictions that Gramsci was unable to successfully resolve in "Americanism and Fordism."

The Working Class Goes to Heaven's none-too-subtle insistence that Lulu's frantic Stakhanovism is a product of his sexual frustration may now seem slightly reductive. It corresponds to a tendency to align radical Freudianism, particularly the work of Wilhelm Reich, with anti-Stalinist radicalism in films such as Marco Bellocchio's *La Cina e Vicina* (*China is Near,* 1967) and Dusan Makavejev's *WR: Mysteries of the Organism* (1971). In any case, the film's equation of mindless work and mechanical sexuality is refreshingly blunt. A close-up of a tool die machine, for example, is followed by a shot of Lulu moaning his desire for a "piece of ass." It also soon becomes apparent that Lulu's one-dimensional view of women as vehicles for his immediate pleasure makes his sex life joyless and perfunctory. The hollowness of Lulu's home life, which he shares with his morose mistress (Mariangela Melato), cannot be regarded as the leisurely antithesis to the grueling assembly line. The constant drone of the television set is apparently the only antidote to an existence that mirrors, rather than relieves, the monotony of factory life. In recent years, Michel Foucault's critique of Reich's isolation of sexual repression as the source of political authoritarianism has deflated the pretensions of those who believed that free-floating libidinal desire held the key to social revolution. Nonetheless, Reich, at least in his early work, did not simplistically believe that "sexual revolution" would irrevocably lead to social and political revolution. Furthermore, left-libertarians such as Maurice Brinton, who paid special attention to Reich's early work, drew links between the anti-

Leninist emphasis on self-activity and the Reichian desire for the eradication of alienated sexuality. This approach argues that workers' "character armor" protects them from suicidal despair, the assumption being that if workers "realized that they were wasting their lives in the service of an absurd system they would either go mad or commit suicide."[79]

Massa's ultimate decision to question an "absurd system" is precipitated by an encounter with a psychiatric bureaucrat who shows a farcical adeptness with the jargon of vulgar Freudianism. According to this shrink's pedantic diagnosis, Lulu's severed finger—the result of a final bout of frenzied industriousness—is emblematic of protracted "castration anxiety." While *The Working Class Goes to Heaven* embodies a post-'68 critique of both the capitalist and socialist variants of the work ethic, it also provides a narrative casing for some of the currents within the "anti-psychiatry" movement that were especially vibrant in France and Italy in the aftermath of the May events. To be sure, earlier in the century a small group of psychoanalysts—Otto Fenichel, Otto Gross, and Wilhelm Reich being perhaps the most prominent "political Freudians"—attempted to unite therapeutic techniques with an empathy for the problems of working class.[80] Yet by the 1960s, conformist psychoanalysis reigned supreme, and Félix Guattari's claim that there is a "profound interaction between individuals and psychopathological problems and the social, political and work context" could seem truly groundbreaking.[81] Of course, the danger of some forms of anti-psychiatry, particularly the brand pioneered by R. D. Laing, resided in a tendency to romanticize the "mad"—the merely neurotic were often dismissed as mundane malcontents—as Byronic "schizos." Petri avoids the pitfalls of this kind of romanticization by consistently bringing our attention to his protagonists' shortcomings. Moreover, Petri's film, being an example of neither inordinate revolutionary optimism nor radical nihilism, does not suggest that either the workers or the mad will necessarily find a niche within an eventual post-communist collectivity.

Lulu's former comrade, Militina, serves as the catalyst who transforms Petri's likable anti-hero into a militant opponent of forced drudgery. Militina ends up languishing in a mental hospital—an antiseptic institution that bears an ironic resemblance to the BAN factory featured in the film. The sequence highlighting Lulu's initial visit to Militina in this peculiarly infernal mental hospital amplifies the film's subtle rhetoric of active negation—the calculated refusal of both the boss's credo and mainstream trade unionism—with particular success. At one point, Militina is proudly informed by Lulu that he has "become a symbol" to the most radical workers. Yet, unsurprisingly, Militina finds it difficult thoroughly to enjoy his newfound iconic status. When asked by his former colleague if at some point he realized that he was

going mad, a close-up of the despondent ex-worker reveals his inner desolation. Militina's combination of anger and passive refusal compels him to
repeat a grim inner scenario of ultimate disillusionment. "Tell me what those
pieces are used for or I'll kill you," thunders Militina at his friend; this howl
of desolation succinctly sums up the nature of alienated labor as elucidated
by disparate commentators, whether the "young Marx" of the *Economic and
Philosophic Manuscripts* or the anarcho-Marxist analysis of Fredy Perlman's
The Reproduction of Daily Life. Militina's resistance to this alienation also
arms him with a salutary cynicism toward the Maoist militants who claim to
be fighting for his and Lulu's liberation. Militina in fact rejects Lulu's gift of
a copy of *Quotations From Mao Tse-Tung*, and his rejection of both capitalist and Leninist platitudes makes him at least an embryonic anarchist. His
desire, however futile, to know the significance of piecework is reminiscent
of the assembly-line alienation meticulously recalled in a memoir by Miklós
Haraszti—a one-time Hungarian dissident who chronicled the factory discipline promoted by a supposedly "liberal" state socialist regime. Haraszti's
lucid memoir *A Worker in a Worker's State* dissolves the dichotomy, always
artificially imposed, between the capitalist West and what was once called
"actually existing socialism":

> Even at work, when I have found the rhythm and become one with the
> machine, thoughts and feelings do not disappear; they change. What dis-
> appears is the direct relationship which unites them with me, the identity
> between me and them. This is very difficult to communicate. The best way
> I can put it is like this: *I* cease to exist. . . . In the end exertion itself ceases
> to exist: there is only a consciousness (or is it a memory) of my exhaus-
> tion. . . . I am the rhythm of the machine, and this perhaps is why, of all
> else from the world outside work, it is sex—of the same inert, impersonal
> character which finds a place in my consciousness. To make love without
> loving: the rhythm drives me on. I *know* what I feel and what I will feel,
> but I do not *feel* it.[82]

While *The Working Class Goes to Heaven* certainly drives home the parallels between alienated labor and alienated sexuality, the film avoids heavy-
handed moralizing by refusing to idealize Lulu. His boorishness toward his
wife and mistress is not whitewashed, but it soon becomes evident that, for
Petri, Lulu's sexism is not merely an individual dilemma. His retrograde attitudes are, above all, a product of a social and cultural nexus. Petri's subtle
indictment of popular culture's complicity with his protagonist's economic
oppression and sexual misery may go against the grain of certain aspects
of postmodern theory. Nevertheless, *The Working Class Goes to Heaven*'s

jaundiced view of television and advertising is not linked to an Olympian contempt for popular culture, although it does not subscribe to the notion that a silver lining, or hidden emancipatory moment, is lurking under the cloudy edges of every mediocre sitcom. Rather than condemning popular culture *tout court*, Petri demonstrates how artifacts representing the most debased forms of mass culture—a beer ad featuring a *Playboy*-style pin-up and an inflatable version of Donald Duck—vapidly reinforce an existence already rendered irrevocably vapid by the routinization of work. It would certainly be reasonable to be alarmed by Andrew Ross's characterization of the Frankfurt School's view of the masses—"a populace of dopes, dupes and robots mechanically delivered into passivity and conformity by the monolithic channels of the mass media and the culture industries"[83]—if it wasn't a misleading caricature of the culture industry thesis. Since many of the northern Italian workers whose experiences are fictionalized in *The Working Class Goes to Heaven* migrated to cities like Turin from a south where folk culture was once particularly fecund, it might be easy to concur with the traditional Frankfurt School analysis that modernity eradicates folk cultures beyond recognition. Nevertheless, the diametrically opposed contention of Néstor García Canclini (writing from a Latin American perspective) that "modern development does not suppress traditional popular cultures"[84] should make us pause before assuming that Lulu's alienation is the product of an irrevocable process of cultural deprivation.

Lulu's eventual disdain for glossy ads and Donald Duck is an earnest, if unfocused, attempt to maintain some measure of personal autonomy (a response, of course, that is only potentially anarchistic) despite unavoidable media onslaught. James Roy MacBean informs us that a San Francisco Festival audience broke into applause after Lulu singlehandedly deflates the Donald Duck toy with his cigarette.[85] This kind of engagement with—and resistance to—popular culture raises certain questions that correspond to later debates concerning the nature of spectatorial resistance: questions are raised that, to a certain extent, coincide with demands for workers' resistance. Can the emancipation of working-class television viewers be achieved by the viewers themselves? Would this resistance constitute a process in which, as Ien Ang proposes, spectators "actively negotiate with textual constructions"?[86] Or is this active "negotiation" an imperceptible micro-resistance that does not combat the "disempowerment . . . which has to be fought by means beyond" the "individual resistance" championed by "active audience methodology"?[87]

Yet if Petri occasionally seems to argue that Lulu's consciousness has been seriously deformed by the detritus of mass culture, he also provides evidence that this fiercely de-romanticized worker has gained insights that enable him to expose the bad faith of both the trade union's pseudo-radicalism and the Maoist left. In many respects, the film's climactic sequences illustrate the vacuum within the post-'68 Italian left—a morass in which the bourgeois left offered only ineffective meliorism and the "ultra-left" promised merely a refurbished version of the Leninist vanguard party. This abyss is concretely driven home after Lulu, fired for his newly politicized rage, is rehired by a factory that fears further direct action by disgruntled workers. A union delegate informs him that "this is the first time a worker fired for politics was hired back . . . we have gained all we set out to achieve . . . especially the control of piece-work." Yet these upbeat sentiments have little resonance for Lulu: after the trade-unionist's peroration, the camera pans left to reveal, from Massa's point of view, an ominous assembly-line panorama. This vision of quotidian doom inspires Lulu's final feverish reverie: he dreams he is dead and prevented from entering the fog-obscured gates of paradise. Despite heaven's seemingly unattainable realm, a vision of Militina spurs Lulu on, urging him to "smash everything and go in." Yet the walls of the workers' paradise remain impenetrable—a once vibrant utopian ideal has petrified into an empty chimera.

From an American perspective, John Zerzan marshals evidence to prove that most of the mainstream U.S. unions did little to oppose Taylorization, and Massa's rejection of both reformist trade unionism and Maoism's supposed alternative is tied to his intuitive belief that even radical organizations harbor a reverence for traditional modes of work.[88] In addition, the fervent resistance to work foregrounded in Petri's film is, in many respects, congruent with the advocacy of acts of insurrectionary defiance, or "zerowork," by the Italian Autonomist movement of the 1970s.[89] During an earlier period, the Turin council communist movement of 1919–1921, for example, sought to move beyond the economic reductionism that still proved a hindrance in the early 1970s. Gramsci, who would later abandon councilism for his own idiosyncratic version of Leninism, claimed that the councils represented a new ideal in which "the form and content of socialist society would be prefigured in the ongoing struggle of workers to transform all aspects of their everyday life."[90] Despite his Marxist veneer, the early Gramsci seems indebted to the uncompromising anarchism of Errico Malatesta, who maintained that we "must distinguish between the revolutionary act which destroys as much as it can of the old regime and puts in its place new institutions, and government, which comes afterwards to halt the revolution and suppress as many of the revolutionary conquests as it can."[91] And anticipating a subsequent phase of Italian history, even as early as 1965 Mario Tronti, from within the Communist Party, anticipates the quasi-anarchistic Autonomist movement by advocating a "strategy of refusal." While refusing to abandon some aspects of orthodox Marxism, Tronti argues that saying no to the work process can constitute a momentary blockage of capitalist value creation; he insisted that "we have worked with a concept that puts capitalist development first and the workers second, and this is a mistake."[92] From Tronti's nuanced recasting of classical productivism, it was just a small step to the strategy of *autoriduzione* (auto-reduction, alternatively referred to as "proletarian expropriations") in which workers continued their factory resistances by selectively refusing to pay exorbitant prices at supermarkets—the inspiration for Dario Fo's *Can't Pay? Won't Pay!*

Ultimately, the polemics surrounding the "revolt against work" debate focused on whether this kind of resistance constituted a truly "new form of struggle" or merely "privatistic discontent."[93] Similar questions could be aimed at *The Working Class Goes to Heaven*. Was Ludovico Massa's disillusion the harbinger of more global tremors within the working class or simply a wail of pain that lacks the potential to transform itself into collective action? Given the fact that working-class quiescence is now widespread in Italy and elsewhere, the seeming pessimism of the film's conclusion might appear bleakly apropos. Yet since talk of "sabotage"[94] and "the abolition of work" is still in the air, it may be too early to throw in the towel and conclude that a strategy of refusal has proved self-defeating.

The Sunday of Life: Seizing "The Right to be Lazy"

> I regard the five day week as an unworthy ideal. . . .
> More work and better work is a more inspiring and
> worthier motto than less work and more pay. . . . It is
> better not to trifle or tamper with God's Laws.
> —John E. Edgerton, President of the National
>   Association of Manufacturers (1926)

During the darkest days of the 1950s, Harvey Swados made an effort to debunk the post–World War II image of workers: complacent individuals who were supposedly "satisfied, doped by TV, essentially middle-class in outlook."[95] Swados maintained that American intellectuals, entranced during the 1930s with fantasies of the heroic worker, were now disillusioned with individuals who they feared had accepted "the same aspirations . . . as middle-class suburbanites." While certain segments of the U.S. New Left continued to believe in the stereotype of the self-satisfied worker, the events of May '68 confirmed the realization that workers were not necessarily the unthinking dupes of their bosses, and undermined the image of the apolitical prole.

If American cinema did not reflect this more nuanced view of the working class, it owed to both Hollywood's and the independent cinema's inability to transcend this sort of stereotype, evident in films such as John Avildsen's *Joe* (1971). It is true that a certain diluted Marcusean tendency claimed that the proletariat had become thoroughly integrated into the mainstream, leaving activist students as the only vanguard. Nonetheless, a lively left-libertarian contingent challenged what Swados termed "the myth of the happy worker."[96]

Paul Schrader's intriguingly muddled *Blue Collar* (1977) was the only Hollywood film of the post-1968 period to suggest that U.S. workers were capable of the same sort of rage against economic and psychic constraints evinced in European films such as *The Working Class Goes to Heaven*. Schrader, a devotee of Bressonian stasis and noir fatalism, would not seem predisposed to making political films. Yet *Blue Collar*'s empathetic portrayal of three (two African Americans and a white Polish American) Detroit automobile workers' only nascently political disgust with bureaucratic unionism—accurately labeled the "politics of resentment"[97] by Schrader—is in many respects a commercial, "psychologized" appropriation of the "ultra-left" skepticism concerning official workers' organizations outlined in Newsreel's tribute to the Detroit-based League of Revolutionary Black Workers, *Finally Got the News* (1969, a collective documentary directed by, among others, Peter Gessner and Stewart Bird).[98] The flawed nature of Schrader's film was evident at the time of its release. The heavy-handed corruption of a fictitious union closely modeled on the "liberal" United Automobile Workers seemed more reminiscent of the thuggish Teamsters, while even Schrader himself admitted that the solidarity between African American and white ethnic auto workers emphasized in *Blue Collar* was more a wish-fulfillment fantasy than a reflection of the de facto segregation that separated black from white in Detroit after the factory gates closed. Schrader, however, indisputably captures the primal rage experienced by workers when a union fails to deliver on its reformist promises. A key sequence features a disgruntled worker, armed with a fork lift and hammer, assaulting a defective beverage-vending machine after the foreman's advice to consult the union representative proves unproductive. The film, moreover, is extremely effective in its efforts to depict the systemic racism that permeated the automobile industry in the post–World War II era, as the burgeoning African American rank and file (estimated to be as much as one-fifth of the industry by the 1960s[99]) found itself frustrated by the power wielded by white bosses and union bureaucrats. It is entirely appropriate that Zeke, *Blue Collar*'s angriest black character (played with manic charm by Richard Pryor), remarks that an automobile "plant" is short for plantation'; it is also duly ironic that his scheme to rip off the union leads to the Pyrrhic victory of being bought off by the same officials who were the targets of his initial subversion.

In the wake of May '68, films such as Faraldo's *Bof* (1971) and Tanner's *Charles—Mort ou vif* (*Charles—Dead or Alive*, 1969) depicted latter-day attempts to seize the "right to be lazy' and celebrate what Hegel called "the Sunday of life." Although Hegel's view of common folk depicted in the Dutch genre paintings he lauds in *The Philosophy of Fine Art* is more than a little patronizing, his claim that "the Ideal itself is not wholly absent from the unperturbed easy way of life"[100] demonstrates at least a salutary distance from what C. Wright Mills once termed the "labor metaphysic."[101] While Hegel thought that an easygoing pastoral life was innocuously charming, the films of Faraldo and Tanner radically revise his qualified endorsement of the "unperturbed easy way of life."

Unlike *Tout va bien* and *The Working Class Goes to Heaven*, *Bof* is a film made by an unashamed anarchist. In fact, Claude Faraldo is a rarity among filmmakers—a disgruntled member of the working class who escaped the daily grind, and eventually expressed his dissatisfaction with the rigors of work by becoming a director. Faraldo's better-known *Themroc* (1973) was widely considered "anarchistic" by critics, but this fable about a worker, played with noteworthy gusto by Michel Piccoli, who lusts after his sister and destroys his fiat in a burst of destructive energy is often distressingly misogynistic. Farraldo's ode to indolence can be seen as an intermittently cathartic, although ultimately slightly puerile, wish-fulfillment fantasy; the film is weighed down by a rather simplistic opposition of stifling gentility and "animalistic rage."

Bof, however, more accurately fictionalized the anti-authoritarian director's own life experience. Faraldo claimed that "up to the age of 23" he was "what could be called average . . . working in a factory and as a delivery man."[102] But when Faraldo was twenty-six, he moved in with a woman who supported him for three years. After experiencing a life of leisure, Faraldo observed that "it doesn't take much to transform a prole into a bourgeois."[103] This general trajectory—from mind-numbing work to semi-Edenic leisure—is discernible in *Bof*. The film's celebration of "dropping out" is characteristic of many countercultural films of the late 1960s and 1970s, but Faraldo's working-class background and sardonic humor make it considerably less sentimental and dated than, say, *Getting Straight* (1970) or *Zabriskie Point* (1970). In fact, Pascal Aubier's more recent short film *Les Trois Coins* (1986), in which a morose worker locks himself in a toilet stall to be lured outside only by a lubricious woman (a wish-fulfillment fantasy that gives audiences the option of taking it literally), evokes much of Faraldo's peculiar synthesis of anti-authoritarianism and slightly smutty—not to mention occasionally sexist—humor.

Bof opens with several sequences elucidating the whole regimen of its protagonist—known simply as the son (Julian Negulesco). In contrast to most films, in which work is merely alluded to or depicted obliquely, if at all, Faraldo features many close-ups of bottles being stacked and lifted. Yet the quasi-documentary quality of these early sequences is soon eclipsed by an almost Renoiresque ambience when *Bof*'s hero quits his job, his father suddenly kills his wife, and this ragtag duo heads to the south of France with wives, girlfriends, and a black street-cleaner in tow. The father's seemingly capricious murder, and the film's casual acceptance of it, typifies Faraldo's often unsavory synthesis of liberatory zeal and cavalier machismo. An aging roué's impromptu reversion to euthanasia—he conveniently claims that his wife was suicidal—allows him to live a life of sexual abandon he could previously only dream about. In any case, Faraldo is obviously interested in provoking audiences with his disrespectful view of traditional familial bliss. At a sequence focusing on a communal dinner, superficially not much different from dinner-table sequences in numerous French films, Faraldo allows the father to vent his pent-up rage against industrial work. "Twenty-five years, minus holidays, tell me how many times I clocked in?" demands this bumbling patriarch in a sequence that precedes his casual murder. From a close-up of his anguished face, Faraldo cuts to a two-shot of the son's wife and the factory boss's daughter illuminated with a perversely red filter. Soon after, father and son are cavorting with these women in bed; immediate gratification and sexual plenitude are apparently fine for working-class men, but the women remain contingencies or conduits for male desires.

The French word "*bof*" has been termed a "verbal shrug" (although it is might be more accurately described as a para-verbal grunt), and this aptly sums up Faraldo's intuitive brand of anarchism. Yet although *Bof* is distinguished by an eagerness to negate the established order, its vision of a possible future—what might be termed the film's capacity for prolepsis—is somewhat adolescent. The father's liberation from years of meaningless work entails an embrace of a regrettably juvenile conception of free love. When the wayward paterfamilias first appears with dinner and the boss's daughter, he exclaims "I bought the croissants, but I stole the broad." It is not so much that Faraldo should be condemned for his insensitivity to women; it is merely that his conception of unfettered sexual pleasure is reminiscent of a tame bachelor party and does not offer a bona fide alternative to repressive family arrangements.

As the film closes, Faraldo frames his narrative with a pastoral long-shot of this newly formed extended family sauntering along a river bank. This sylvan image capitulates many of the contradictions of Faraldo's film—the need for a thoroughgoing social revolution yearned for by workers such as *Bof's* son-and-father duo is all too frequently offset by the stasis that entraps many individuals, despite their radical aspirations.

The critique of industrial servitude highlighted in Alain Tanner's *Charles—Dead or Alive* is grounded in an ironized reflexivity that is quite alien to Faraldo's less-focused assault on bourgeois mores. This tale of an industrialist who abandons his factory to explore countercultural possibilities with some young companions is not completely anomalous—Pasolini's *Teorema* (*Theorem,* 1968), after all, featured a factory owner who suddenly decides to hand over his factory to the workers. Yet unlike films such as *Tout va bien* or *The Working Class Goes to Heaven,* Tanner's film is more contemplative than agitational. Like many of Tanner's films, *Charles—Dead or Alive* is interested in shattering the picture-postcard stereotype of a bucolic Switzerland—the film's cynicism about work also constitutes a critique of Swiss bourgeois complacency.[104] The newfound, guilty radicalism of an affluent Swiss businessman may not seem like a promising departure point for a film; fortunately, François Simon's portrayal of Charles Dé accentuates the character's pensiveness, not his self-pity.

Charles's desire to emulate his young leftist cohorts is rooted in a specific tradition of Swiss radicalism. His guilty conscience is pricked by memories of his grandfather, an anarchist watchmaker from the Jura region who established a Geneva watch factory, which his grandson is now abandoning. The film's measured consideration of the merits of a pre-industrial heritage does not, therefore, emanate from a historical vacuum. The factory was established after the demise of a workers' movement that Bakunin himself once lauded as one of the most promising in Europe. In addition, historian Marianne Enckell notes that the demise of the once vibrant Swiss anarchist movement coincides with a sweeping transition from a society of small craftsmen to mass industrialization.[105] Charles's self-ironic attempt to revive this tradition, moreover, is tempered by the fact that his confession of despair takes place during a television broadcast at the beginning of the film; the protagonist's gentle self-abnegation is inevitably sullied by the mass media's genius for banality and distortion.

Tanner's decision to set his film in the future—the hundredth anniversary of the watch factory that Charles commemorates with a wry melancholy postdates the film's 1969 release by several years—gives the narrative a proleptic dynamism. Of course, the protagonists, being more sullen and low-key than the denizens of *Bof*'s counterculture, are no more paragons of revolutionary ardor than Faraldo's would-be insurrectionists. Charles's friend, Paul, who dutifully recites quotations (meticulously culled from books by Charles's daughter, Marianne) from, among others, Michaux, Benjamin, and Lefebvre, cannot go beyond his cerebral infatuation with rebellion to embrace genuine political commitment. Paul's political and moral hibernation perfectly encapsulates the contemporary Swiss dilemma: Kropotkin's idealized anarchist watchmakers, armed with "sturdy independence, literacy, and devotion,"[106] have been eclipsed by an insular philistinism. Tanner avoids falling prey to a facile opposition between Swiss aridity and countercultural utopian buoyancy; even the radicals cannot escape from Swiss bourgeois homogeneity.

In lieu of a truly democratic, anti-hierarchical movement, Charles and his friends find solace in ritualistic disruptions of the status quo. Perhaps the film's central ritual (in which technology becomes the site of semiotic struggle) is a protracted sequence highlighting Charles's gleeful disposal of his car, a once beloved object that he now considers mere excess baggage. Before pushing his car off a cliff, Charles recites a long text by Henri Lefebvre in which the automobile is condemned as a crucial component of late capitalism's ecological crisis. Lefebvre is well-known for being a mentor to the situationists (although they eventually rejected his mentorship with acerbic scorn), and this giddy recontextualization inevitably reminds us of the heterodox French philosopher's preoccupation with 'the festival.' Jim Leach maintains that Tanner's frequent citation of Lefebvre implies that *Charles* can be 'seen as a contribution to Lefebvre's "revolutionary' plan to . . . resurrect the Festival."[107] Yet Lefebvre's work, while unquestionably provocative, is also inescapably problematic when placed within an anarchist framework. Like Marcuse, Lefebvre reevaluated the "early Marx" and downplayed the economism dear to Leninists. Yet, along with Marcuse, he never thoroughly discarded certain authoritarian shibboleths; his work is peppered with rather vague, but not entirely unflattering, allusions to Lenin.[108] Tanner's last sequence features Charles reciting the last paragraph of Lefebvre's *Everyday Life in the Modern World* as he is speeded to a mental hospital in an ambulance. Given the Swiss need for unimpeded calm, eruptions of "the festive" have apparently been put on indefinite hold. Nevertheless, a blithe dismissal of the Swiss work ethic surfaced again in Tanner's subsequent *La Salamandre* (*The Salamander*, 1971). The film's working-class heroine, Rosemonde, declares that she has "little taste for what is called a trade where one earns an

honest—which means poor—living, where one is at anyone's beck and call
. . . and where freedom means a quick smoke in the shit house."

Slackers and Neo-Nihilists

A more recent film, Richard Linklater's *Slacker* (1991), is not preoccupied
with active resistance to work: the film's world-weary anti-heroes do not
need to be convinced of the work ethic's futility since they take the virtues of
idleness for granted. Linklater describes *Slacker* as "primarily about people
on the fringes of any meaningful participation in society."[109] Yet, unlike Petri
or Faraldo's workers, Linklater's disaffected punks, conspiracy theorists, and
Madonna enthusiasts are, for the most part, downwardly mobile members
of the middle class whose status as "slackers" has not been inspired by the
rigors of the assembly line. Many of the younger "slackers" have a tenuous
relationship to the University of Texas at Austin; dropping out of college is
less strenuous than challenging the factory boss.

A seemingly aimless reworking of *La Ronde,* the film exchanges Schnitz-
ler's bittersweet romantic entanglements for a kind of postmodern flânerie.
The spirit of Linklater's celebration of indolence has certain affinities with
Bob Black's smart-ass neo-anarchism (for example, "Incorrect—Positive
Thinking, Correct—Positive Drinking . . . Incorrect—Dad, Correct—Dada
. . . Incorrect—Atomic Power, Correct—Anomie Power"),[110] since Linklater
rejects "all official systems" and ideologies. Yet Black's "type 3" anarchism—a
synthesis of individualist anarchism and certain strains of post-situationist
thought—is still recognizable as anarchism, even if it delights in its deviation
from the now musty unholy trinity of Proudhon, Bakunin, and Kropotkin.
We can take literally Linklater's detachment from "any kind of ideology(ies)"
and note with amusement his pleasure that *Slacker* has grossed "well over
a million at the box office," not to mention the hundred thousand copies
of *Generation X* sold by his friend Douglas Coupland. Despite its cursory
references to anarchism, the film's protagonists "epitomize the postmodern
sensibility in its purest form, unsullied by divisive memories of the unitary
pre-fragmented society of the past."[111]

Interestingly, the distance traveled from classical radicalism to *Slacker's*
neo-bohemianism is best illustrated by a sequence in which a character,
referred to simply as the "Old Anarchist," pays tribute to Leon Czolgosz,
McKinley's assassin who called himself an anarchist even though other anarchists disavowed him, and offers dubious reminiscences of fighting with
the CNT in Spain. After reasonably venting dissatisfaction with "modern day
Libertarians with all their goddamn selfish individualism," the Old Anarchist

delivers a paean to Austin's most infamous mass murderer, Charles Whitman. Using *Slacker* as his primary text, Patrick Durfee maintains that Linklater's protagonists "interrupt the infiltration of social space by commodity culture," but insists that the Old Anarchist's praise of Whitman "shows how a politics that affirms any and all deformations of administered social space fails to produce a vision that reaches beyond random instances of rebellion."[112] While this old, but not very wise, anarchist's homage to a psychopath is certainly the product of an anti-intellectual politics that celebrates "random instances of rebellion," Durfee fails to distinguish this character's eccentric conception of propaganda by the deed from an anarchist tradition that has little patience for this grotesque parody of direct action. Yet the blurring of distinctions between the Spanish social revolution and apolitical acts of terror is unfortunately not unusual in today's glib postmodernist climate; all too often anarchism is confined to a hip, marginal ghetto where its radicalism is defused by being categorized as merely one more eccentric "alternative" current.

A flâneur at the end of his tether is the protagonist, and undeniable cynosure, of Mike Leigh's *Naked* (1993). Johnny, though working class, is definitely not a proletarian hero. Neither a hero nor a villain, he ends up being both victim and victimizer. There is no "backstory" for Johnny's refusal of work; it is impossible to conceive of this abrasive loner tolerating even a day of the regimen endured by the protagonists of *Tout va bien* or *The Working Class Goes to Heaven*. Although critics unfailingly referred to Johnny as a "drifter" or a "marginal character," unlike most individuals traditionally termed homeless, this Mancunian adrift in London consciously rejects the humdrum annoyances of domestic life. Like Dostoevsky's Underground Man, Johnny celebrates "his own free and unfettered volition . . . inflamed sometimes to the point of madness." While *Naked*'s picaresque, open-ended narrative features many of Johnny's nocturnal strolls around London, this flâneur has none of Walter Benjamin's dispassionate erudition. Instead, his peripatetic jaunts evoke Georg Simmer's more mundane conception of the flâneur: a passive "*spectator* of the never-ending spectacle of crowded urban life."[113]

One of the film's most effective sequences features Johnny's feverish indictment of mindless work. Finding refuge in an antiseptic office building, he alternately befriends—and mercilessly harangues—a gentle nightwatchman named Brian. Brian's stoic acceptance of his dreary job becomes the springboard for Johnny's invective, as well as for his chillingly apocalyptic flights of fancy. "You've succeeded in convincin' me that you do 'ave the most tedious fuckin' job in England," announces Johnny to Brian. Brian's response to his interlocutor's disdain is to reply that at least the job gives him "time and space to contemplate the future" at his leisure. As Leigh highlights a two-shot of his odd duo in eerie, near-noir silhouette, Johnny dismisses Brian's "gleeful preoccupation with the future" and then launches into a ferociously idiosyncratic eschatological tirade, mixing references to Nostradamus and the Book of Revelation with allusions to Chernobyl.

Leigh shares Petri's unwillingness to idealize his working-class protagonist. As the film's voluble catalyst, Johnny spews forth monologues of sometimes breathtaking, if crazed, eloquence, and engages in a series of trysts with troubled women who find themselves initially attracted to his torrent of words but are eventually repelled by his contemptuous abuse. The sex in *Naked* is the complete antithesis of Hollywood's soft-focus coupling—what Nabokov once derided as the "copulation of clichés." In fact, any idea of "sexual union" is alien to *Naked*'s protagonists, since the characters' frantic writhings ultimately accentuate their essential aloneness.

Although Leigh claims that *Naked* "presents a more anarchist view of the world"[114] than his previous *High Hopes* (1988) he also vehemently stresses the point that "he doesn't primarily" regard himself as an anarchist. *Naked*'s despair cannot be reconciled with traditional anarchist concerns. Like *Slacker*, it belongs here almost solely for negative reasons; it is inescapably a film that completely abandons the political debates that preoccupied leftists from the First International and the Paris Commune through World War II. As their careers have progressed, both Leigh, and especially Linklater, became more-mainstream figures whose work could be easily assimilated within the rubrics of "art house" or "indie cinema."

In recent years, enthusiasm for the "refusal" of work has moved beyond the sphere of anarchism to encompass critiques launched by Marxist feminists, "left-accelerationists," and the social democrats ensconced at *Jacobin*. According to Kathi Weeks, who fuses socialist feminism and an anti-work impetus, "work is not only a locus of unfreedom, it is also a site of resistance and contestation."[115] Needless to say, the revulsion toward meaningless work that permeates popular culture is frequently riddled with contradictions and intersperses conservative and anti-authoritarian elements. Mike Judge's *Office Space* (1999), for example, a comedy depicting modern-day serfs at the mercy of the information economy, reflects a deep-seated contempt for tyrannical bosses and bureaucratic inanity. While Judge's film is, as Mark Fisher asserts, cognizant of how corporations "become sclerotized by administrative 'anti-production,'"[116] the director's conservative libertarianism ends up affirming a quiescent status quo. Fisher is on target in identifying the mind-numbing tasks required by the tech company that employs the putative hero Peter (Ron Livingston), as well as the meaningless adornments ("seven pieces of flair") imposed upon his waitress girlfriend, Joanna (Jennifer Aniston) at her restaurant, as part and parcel of a neoliberal preoccupation with bureaucratic regimentation. Yet the cynicism of Judge's right-wing brand of libertarianism comes to the surface at the end as his protagonists' passive-aggressive resistance earns them apolitical, escapist rewards. After the flukish success of an embezzlement scheme that almost goes awry, Peter finds bliss as a construction worker and Milton, the victimized office schlub, retreats to a beach resort.

Both more scabrous and more despairing than *Office Space,* Benoît Delépine and Gustave Kervern's *Louise-Michel* (2008), reinvents anti-authoritarian rage with deadpan gallows humor. The two protagonists' first names invoke the memory of Louise Michel, the anarchist heroine of the Paris Commune of 1871, in ways that will understandably disconcert many earnest anarchists. When the intellectually disabled Louise (Yolande Moreau) discovers that she and her colleagues are suddenly out of work after a duplicitous boss abandons their factory, she urges her comrades to hire a hit man to kill the hated culprit. The contract killer turns out to be Michel (Bouli Lanners), a hopeless bungler who leads Louise on a wacky wild goose chase through France and Belgium until their prey is finally discovered relaxing in Jersey, a notorious tax haven in the Channel Islands.

A film that dispatches clownish and inept anti-heroes to wreak havoc on boorish capitalists involves tricky narrative and political strategies. But as buffoonish as Louise and Michel might be, Delépine and Kervern are undeniably fond of this hapless duo; in an interview, Kervern insists that these marginal characters touch him and his co-director "more than the company bosses and middle-classes, or the literary and artistic circles, who are usually the focus of French films."[117] In addition, as the journalist Fabien Lemercier maintains, Louise and Michel's vertiginous quest is almost impossible to disentangle from the peculiar depersonalization wrought by corporate globalization. While a villainous boss in the nineteenth century would not have strayed from his local estate, contemporary plutocrats, with no visible national allegiances, are free to wander the globe. In the film's most comically transgressive sequence, the ungainly pair simulate the destruction of the World Trade Center with the aid of a scale model, an act that functions as both an absurdist exorcism of this international trauma and a jab at mainstream—and anarchist—respectability.

Jacques Rancière's research on nineteenth-century French workers' movements led him to conclude that "whether in Paris or in Icaria, workers refused to live up to the class mission conferred on them"[118] by intellectuals. Delépine and Kervern's rebels are far from model proletarian insurgents; their antics are not part of a constructive "agenda." Of course, while a strategy of negation might seem appropriate for our current climate of reaction and retrenchment, there are tangible cinematic alternatives to the conservative cynicism of *Office Space* and *Louise-Michel*'s left-leaning nihilism. Naomi Klein and Avi Lewis's *The Take* (2004), a chronicle of the wave of factory occupations that erupted in Argentina in the early 2000s, provides a modicum of hope.

Although Klein and Lewis's earnest account of the twentieth-first century's most vibrant experiment in workers' control does not explicitly reference anarchism, it's an implicit tribute to what has been called "horizontalism," an anti-hierarchal form of self-organization that positioned itself as the antithesis of the top-down mandates of arbiters of austerity such as the International Monetary Fund. *The Take* views the factory occupations that resisted the neoliberal consensus established after President Carlos Menem's economic model proved untenable as both radical and radically pragmatic. The filmmakers celebrate stirring instances of workers' solidarity while also proving that self-managed factories successfully transformed capitalist enterprises in a fashion that eluded bosses in the private sector. What seems clear is that, as Marina Sitrin argues, horizontalism represented not "just a break with parties from formal institutions of power, but also with radical and revolutionary Left parties, from the Peronists to the Trotskyist."[119] Klein's narration also reiterates the taboo-shattering nature of the occupations by emphasizing how they did not resemble the collectivization imposed "from above" in Russia or China but instead exemplified a spontaneous surge to reshape workplaces "from below."

This dynamic is most apparent in the sequences devoted to the takeover of Ceramica Zanón, perhaps the most celebrated factory occupation and the one whose success helps to explicate the larger cultural impact of horizontalism. Sitrin, citing a scene from *The Take* that she believe encapsulates the fervor associated with "recuperating" factories, lauds "a worker practicing with a slingshot, shooting perfectly smooth, round, white balls that are made in the factory."[120] The Zanon workers play David to the Goliath personified by Luis Zanon, the former owner of the factory whose ties to Menem convinces him that he'll be able to regain his expropriated property. The film convincingly argues that Zanon's experiment transcends mere workplace autonomy; the surrounding community is equally energized by the occupation. Self-activity is considered much more vibrant than tepid electoral politics. "Our dreams don't fit on your ballots" is one Zanon worker's rejoinder to the electoral match between the returning candidate and his eventual victorious rival, Néstor Kirchner.

The Take, in a rather traditional vein, occasionally latches on to charismatic interviewees as a device to anchor the struggles it celebrates in lived experience. Freddy Espinosa, a driving force behind implementing "the take" at the Forja San Martin auto parts factory, is the closest the film comes to foregrounding a "protagonist." Klein and Lewis devote a fair amount of screen time to the hardships suffered by Espinosa and his family after Forja San Martin's closing; he can be regarded as an emblem of resilience. Despite employing rather standard journalistic techniques, the film's alternation between the private and public realms is polemically effective. Documenting the hardships endured by Freddy Espinosa and his family rhyme aptly with subsequent sequences recapitulating the eviction of workers from the Brukman suit factory in 2003. The glimpses of muddling through the travails of austerity give way to new chapters of resistance imbued with a sense of optimistic inevitability.

Portuguese director Pedro Pinho's *The Nothing Factory* (2017), a film partially inspired by the militancy of Argentinian workers in the early years of the twenty-first century, features a leftist pundit who proclaims: "if I criticize self-management, it's not because it's too radical, it's because it's not radical enough—it's still a market agent." Pinho's film is a wildly ambitious, somewhat scattershot effort to deal with the legacy of recent European austerity. Like Miguel Gomes's even more far-ranging *Arabian Nights* (2015), *The Nothing Factory* implicitly concedes that a traditional linear narrative is unable to do justice to suffering engendered by the ongoing economic crisis. Only a hybrid form interspersing fictional and nonfictional elements is up to the task. A number of intersecting tributaries flow out of some workers' initial outrage toward an elevator factory's decision to close its gates. Pinho's reflexive structure recalls *Tout va bien*'s playfulness while the earnestness of the protagonists' refusal to succumb to despair is linked to the practical tactics that made possible the self-management schemes of *The Take*.

Taking an actual incident at a Portuguese branch of Otis Elevator as a departure point, Pinho charts the workers' anxieties as machinery removed from the factory appears to presage its closing. This catalyst allows the film to splinter into a number of mini-narratives: the workers' seizure of their own factory is tempered by an account of the impact of this upheaval on a militant named Zé and his wife. Another layer of self-interrogation is unveiled when a filmmaker, Danièle Incalcaterra, arrives on the scene to query activists and attempt to place the ferment within some tangible sociopolitical framework.

The film's tone alternates between pathos and mock-didacticism. In a pivotal scene, Incalcaterra opens his laptop and broadcasts a speech in which a weary commentator concludes that, once the Berlin Wall came down, the welfare state died. This is not a muted defense of outdated state socialism, but an admission that the end of the cold war ushered in a neoliberal regime in which a ragtag group of workers seizing the means of production is less a gesture of revolutionary ardor than one of brute survival. With its nuanced deployment of disparate narrative strategies, *The Nothing Factory* suggests that its heroic Portuguese workers are both emblems of admirable solidarity and blasts from the past inasmuch as the precepts of self-management reflect the limitations of what Weeks labels the "laborist" work ethic.

4. Film and Anarchist Pedagogy

Anarchism in One Classroom:
Educational Reform versus "Deschooling"

> Education is an admirable thing. But it is well to
> remember from time to time that anything worth
> learning cannot be taught.
> —Oscar Wilde, *A Few Maxims for the Instruction
> of the Over-Educated*

Conservatives, liberals, and Marxists have all devoted a considerable amount of energy to evaluating and, in some respects, transforming educational theory and practice. Yet the preoccupation of anarchists with the nuances of pedagogy is unmatched by any other political tendency. It is, of course, difficult to overlook a recent efflorescence of pedagogical theory by non-anarchists, primarily neo-Marxist and post-structuralist writers. The theoretical importance of this work should not be glibly dismissed, but, for better or worse, it is not easy to bridge the gap between postmodern pedagogical theory, primarily the work of academics, and the contributions of anarchist theorists and educators such as Mikhail Bakunin, William Godwin, and Francisco Ferrer. Henry Giroux—to cite the one postmodern figure who has actually displayed familiarity with anti-authoritarian educational traditions—is not entirely wrong to characterize anarchist pedagogues as romantic advocates of "self-fulfillment" who occasionally forget the dynamics of hierarchy and power that anti-authoritarians should be loath to overlook.[1] Nonetheless, despite the fact that traces of anarchist pedagogy linger in the work of the post-modernists, it is surprising that, with rare exceptions, they thoroughly ignore the work of Ferrer, Godwin, and Paul Goodman, as well as the self-emancipatory pedagogy endorsed by anarchist activists such as Emma Goldman and Mikhail Bakunin.

Contemporary anarchist pedagogy began with the work of William Godwin and Max Stirner, and defined itself by a critical engagement with the faux-libertarianism of Jean-Jacques Rousseau's seminal, if contradiction-ridden, educational treatise cum novel *Émile*. "Rousseauistic" has become a synonym for the celebration, or perhaps the fetishization, of a "state of nature." Yet when faced with the demands of civilization, Rousseau proposed an unassailably statist "social contract" that is surprisingly congenial to proponents of autocratic rule—one commentator has even called his political theory, with its rather amorphous notion of the "general will," an example of proto-totalitarianism.[2] Nevertheless, it is undeniable that *Émile*'s pedagogical agenda foreshadows the liberal tradition of Maria Montessori and John Dewey (and, in certain respects, the cognitive psychology of Jean Piaget)—currents with which anarchism has certain affinities, despite its fundamental opposition to these reformers' willingness to accommodate themselves to the established order. Rousseau's view of childhood is both celebratory and paternalistic: *Émile* encourages children to revel in their apparently blissful irrationalism until the onset of puberty. Committed to a truly sentimental education, Rousseau insisted that childhood education should be "purely negative," only concerned with rescuing "the heart from vice and the mind from error."[3]

Although Émile's "negative education" is intended to nurture his eventual self-sufficiency—unburdened with books or moral aphorisms at an early age, he supposedly "gets his lessons from nature and not from men"[4]—his ubiquitous, seemingly benevolent tutor functions as something of a pedagogical puppet master who is always nearby pulling the strings attached to his unwitting pupil. As Jean Starobinski observes, Émile's education may be designed "*for* freedom, but it is certainly not in any authentic sense education by means of freedom."[5] When Émile reaches manhood, his tutor happily plays the role of an offstage Pandarus by arranging his romance and eventual marriage to a woman named Sophie. Even the receptive pupil's "education of the senses" must be masterminded by an enlightened despot.

Michael Smith maintains that Rousseau's fondness for "disguised coercion . . . is a double affront to the child's autonomy" Smith proposes an anarchist critique of Rousseau's elaborate regulation of freedom, suggesting that a more legitimate mode of autonomy can help us distinguish "liberal" or "progressive" teachers from "genuinely libertarian" instructors.[6] William Godwin, for example, sought to reverse the "received modes of education" in which the "master goes first and the pupil follows."[7] Godwin is determined to de-mystify the so-called "helplessness of the child," and, unlike Rousseau, his pedagogy takes pains not to unduly manipulate children's needs and desires. Godwin could be viewed as the first advocate of "free schools" and radical educational reform—an eighteenth-century precursor of radical educators such as Herb Kohl, John Holt, and Jonathan Kozol.

The implications of Young Hegelian Max Stirner's even more radical, al-though less concrete, critique of mainstream pedagogy has still not been completely assimilated by anarchist educators. Stirner's brief treatise *The False Principle of Our Education* bears a striking intellectual resemblance to what eventually became known as radical deschooling. Stirner maintained that "there is everywhere a great abundance of political, social, ecclesiastical, scientific, artistic, moral, and other corpses, and until they are all consumed, the air will not be clean and the breath of living beings will be oppressed."[8] Perhaps because Stirner was a former schoolmaster, he identifies the school with philistinism and draws a distinction between the "educated man" and the truly free individual. Although a myopic reading might merely view Stirner's rage against pedagogy as a symptom of the anti-intellectualism that anarchists are often unjustly (and occasionally justly) accused of, he does not dispute the value of acquiring knowledge, but claims that "through knowledge . . . we become only *internally* free . . . outwardly, with all freedom of conscience and freedom of thought, we can remain slaves and remain in subjection."[9]

While Stirner's polemical fervor corresponded to the early Nietzsche's scorn for the mediocrity of institutional education and remained on a level that was more existential than practical, Bakunin's call for "integral educa-tion"—vocational as well as intellectual training geared to train the "whole man"—focused explicitly on the educational inequities that separated the upper classes from the proletariat. Bakunin's pedagogical agenda entails a slightly coercive form of anti-authoritarianism, preaching that "education must be spread among the masses unsparingly, transforming all the churches, all those temples dedicated to the glory of God and to the slavery of men, into so many schools of human emancipation."[10] With typically brilliant indecisiveness, Bakunin presciently summed up the two major currents within contemporary anarchist pedagogy. At times, he advocated the ideal of universal education, yet, in a distinctly Stirnerian passage, concedes that "up to a certain point man can become his own educator, his own instruc-tor as well as creator."[11] If nineteenth-century and early twentieth-century anarchism exalted the transformative potential of alternative schools, the last thirty years has been marked by a gradual loss of faith in the institu-tional efficacy of all schools, whether mainstream or purportedly "free." In many respects, Ivan Illich's championing of "deschooling" fleshed out the abstractions of *The False Principle of Our Education,* while striving to fulfill its concluding exhortation: "knowledge must die and rise again as *will* and create itself anew each day as a free person."[12]

The utopian socialist Charles Fourier, a figure claimed by both the anarchist and surrealist traditions, formulated an eccentric, if often charming and ingenious, educational practice that was, in many respects, genuinely anti-authoritarian. Truly proto-feminist, he had little use for Rousseau's veneration of the family or Bakunin's occasionally condescending view of women. Consequently, Fourier's seemingly whimsical quest for harmony—"a social order organized so that the gratification of individual desire serves to promote the common good"[13]—spawned an anti-dogmatic pedagogy that assumed children could learn as much from their peers as from their elders.

By 1909 the Spanish government's decision to execute the anarchist educator Francisco Ferrer, founder of the Modern School (subsequently emulated by anarchist pedagogues in western Europe and the United States), proved that even a modest attempt to acquaint students with anti-authoritarian principles could be perceived as a threat by a nervous government. Although the Spanish authorities lamely tried to implicate Ferrer in a plot to assassinate King Alfonso XIII, the regime's unwillingness to yield to international pleas for the educator's release was motivated by their almost primal fear of his advocacy of secular, rationalist education, which, while tame by contemporary standards, alarmed the Catholic educational establishment. The response of Catalonia's anarcho-syndicalist movement to the government and church's intransigence culminated in the "Tragic Week" of 1909—a period encompassing a general strike in Barcelona and the populace's spontaneous violence against the symbols and representatives of Catholicism (according to Joan Connelly Ullman, workers set fire to "forty convents and twelve parochial churches"[14]). Ferrer's martyrdom became emblematic of the central role of alternative pedagogy for committed anarchists.

While later radicals spurned words such as "positivism" and "rationalism" as tokens of conformist ideology, Ferrer's anticlericalism led him to embrace science as the logical antidote to Catholic hegemony. Given the church's hostility to his conception of the classroom as a laboratory for change, it is not surprising that the Spanish authorities greeted with trepidation Ferrer's proclamation that "the child, in order to avoid error," must be taught that it is "essential to admit nothing on faith."[15] For Ferrer, the school could serve as the locus of revolutionary ferment; as Joel Spring observed, he believed that "one could not *wish* a non-authoritarian society into being . . . the Modern School was the beginning of a plan to move in that direction."[16]

This tension between a faith in alternative institutions and a contingent fondness for deinstitutionalization is at the heart of Ivan Illich's polemical strategy. His seminal tract *Deschooling Society* is eminently quotable, and the pungently aphoristic style consciously eviscerates the standard underpinnings of leftist discourse. Although Illich is decidedly a man of the left, and quite sympathetic to the anarchist legacy of, among others, Paul Goodman, he is able to invoke Milton Friedman's call for tuition credits on one page, while on another approving of Fidel Castro's assertion (invoked in 1970) that "by 1980 Cuba will be able to dissolve its university since all of life in Cuba will be an educational experience." True to his calling as an intellectual gadfly, Illich puckishly forages in non-anarchist pastures in order to conclude that "neither learning nor justice is promoted by schooling."[17]

Illich observes that "consumer-pupils are taught to make their desires conform to marketable values."[18] As an antidote to mainstream schooling's hidebound "hidden curriculum," he proposed replacing institutional pedagogy with "learning webs" that would replace compulsory schooling with opportunities for eager students to take advantage of community learning centers and contact peers and "educators at large" who could share skills and specialized knowledge. M. P. Smith is correct to take Illich for task for the legalistic bias of deschooling's penchant for "contractual" learning, its inability to distinguish between the learning needs of children, adolescents, and adults, and a "naivete about power" that "marks him off from the anarchist movement."[19] In addition, there is at times an odd convergence between the interests of presumably anarchistic deschoolers and right-wing homeschoolers, whose anti-statism owes a great debt to the teachings of free-market apostles such as F. A. Hayek. Nevertheless, it is important to note that "by deschooling, Illich does not mean a complete deinstitutionalization as much as a transformation of institutions . . . he refer[s] explicitly to the need for 'new formal educational institutions'"[20]—an aspiration that is perfectly congruent with the aims of anarchist self-activity.

Many anarchists have in fact been resourceful autodidacts, either thoroughly self-educated scholars or nonaligned intellectuals who have surpassed the limitations of their formal education. Proust's conviction that "we do not receive wisdom; we must discover it for ourselves, after a journey through the wilderness that no one else can make for us"[21] is one, rather idealistic, half of anarchist pedagogy's creed. Yet even if the most productive learning is usually self-generated, the ability to cope with or triumph over our inevitably long—occasionally interminable—march through educational institutions has preoccupied many practically minded left-libertarian pedagogues.

Narrative cinema, which has traditionally conceived of the classroom as a cinematic microcosm that can encapsulate the conflicts and contradictions of childhood and adolescence, provides fertile territory for charting the ideological—and often aesthetic—vicissitudes of authoritarian, reformist, and anti-authoritarian education. The ways in which film can both reflect pedagogical currents, and even function as pedagogical practice itself, will occupy us in the next section.

The Classroom Film: Authority, Reform, and Anarchy

Philippe Ariès's thesis that Western culture "invented" the institutions of childhood and adolescence at the end of the Middle Ages has provided a historical departure point for a number of radical pedagogues and theorists. Ariès's claim, disputed by some historians but not definitively disproved, that the concept of childhood innocence itself was a post-Renaissance develop-ment—nurtured by the transition from communal living to what we know now as the nuclear family and the development of an elaborate age-specific etiquette[22]—has been important for an anarchist pedagogy that seeks to challenge the power wielded over children and adolescents. A veneration of so-called childhood innocence proved a double-edged sword; departing "from the doctrine of original sin to the cult of original virtue in the child"[23] was not entirely salutary. The "Romantic child" inspired William Blake's profoundly libertarian work, but it also encouraged a sentimental, regressive acceptance of the inevitability of youthful dependence—and submission. By the nineteenth century, moreover, the treacly clichés of the Romantic child coexisted with a stigmatization of poor and street children as "sav-ages." Hugh Cunningham has demonstrated how the discourse of racism and imperialism in nineteenth-century Britain coincided with attitudes toward impoverished youngsters—children in London's "ragged schools" were termed "as barbarous and brave as North American Indians," while sup-posedly ineducable slum children were described as "street Arabs," "English Kaffirs," and "Hottentots."[24]

Reformist pedagogy tends to disguise its paternalism with more euphemis-tic attitudes and terminology. For Ian Hunter, the "new" liberal pedagogy of the nineteenth century, fashioned by cultural figures such as Matthew Arnold, as well as less-heralded educational bureaucrats like James Kay-Shuttleworth, embraced a form of social control whose influence is still detectable in con-temporary schooling. Arnold, a state school inspector as well as a cultural critic, elucidated reformist pedagogy's contradictory ethos: the moral supervision of children, especially working-class children, who were deemed little better than animals, was tied to "correction through self-expression."[25]

An anarchist critique, therefore, of how "classroom films" represent, and often embody, mainstream pedagogical values must take into consideration the fact that authoritarian education is often accompanied by a concern, however paternalistic, with the inner life and moral development of students. If "making the desire of the pupil rather than the will of the instructor the motive element in learning"[26] is the guiding principle of anarchist education, a survey of classroom films can reveal how representations of faux-libertarianism often alternate with tributes to less-adulterated forms of authoritarian schooling. It may seem presumptuous to consider American pedagogical narratives alongside films from western Europe, since the relatively decentralized American school system contrasts sharply with highly centralized equivalents in countries such as France and Britain. A certain ideological homogeneity permeates schoolroom films: one could, following Bakhtin, speak of a classroom "chronotope," since the schoolroom provides a "transcultural, spatio-temporal matrix"[27] that shapes the genre and its narrative propensities.

Charles Dickens's *Hard Times* is a seminal classroom narrative. The novel could be considered an allegorical response to various pieces of legislation that made schooling increasingly compulsory for working-class children. A decidedly coercive, but supposedly humane and practical, form of education gradually replaced the hardships of child labor. The specter of Mr. Gradgrind, the absurdly utilitarian teacher whom Dickens gleefully caricatures, hovers over many cinematic portrayals of authoritarian teachers. His literal-minded enthusiasm for nothing but the facts can also be discerned in milder depictions of well-intentioned, liberal instructors. *Hard Times* mingles the mundane, empirical realm of Gradgrind's classroom with the more sensual, alluring *demi-monde* of Sleary's circus, its appealing raffishness enhanced by colorful, decidedly non-utilitarian vernacular. The BBC adaptation of *Hard Times* subtly altered the rhythms of Dickens's novel by intercutting the raw vitalism of the circus with the classroom vignettes that open the novel. The integration of Gradgrind's pedantic celebration of facts with the circus and its revivifying vulgarity was so effective that one critic maintained that Dickens had been improved upon.[28] Instead of viewing the classroom and its carnivalesque anodyne as autonomous realms, this adaptation held out the promise that the classroom itself could be carnivalized.

While few of Hollywood's instructors possessed Gradgrind's inadvertent comic brio, many of these films solemnly embraced the educational Messianism that Dickens mocked, and emphasized the schism between classroom sobriety and popular culture with a strident tendentiousness that might have amused him. Richard Brooks's *Blackboard Jungle* (1955) is a paradigmatic example of a film in which a teacher is portrayed as a near-saintly redeemer. In a pseudo-liberal humanist repositioning of the nineteenth-century opposition of crusading pedagogues and "savage" students who need taming, Richard Dadier (Glenn Ford) takes over a turbulent inner-city classroom with the aplomb of a mild-mannered general—a younger, more hirsute version of then–President Eisenhower. Not unmindful of new educational techniques, Dadier one day decides to play some of his cherished Bix Beiderbecke records for his rambunctious class. Yet Dadier's version of hipness is too square for his class of urban pariahs. They prefer rock and roll, and mercilessly smash his vinyl reproductions of white jazz with gleeful abandon. While Dickens satirized Gradgrind's unimaginative pragmatism, Brooks uncritically celebrates Dadier's paternalistic liberalism. By the end of the film, many of the students appear repentant, and are apparently on their way to becoming boringly law-abiding.[29] This rudimentary narrative trajectory—what might be termed a "redemptive model" of pedagogy—is repeated, with occasionally quirky permutations, in scores of films featuring unruly urban students: *To Sir With Love* (1967) (in which Sidney Poitier, cast as a juvenile delinquent in *The Blackboard Jungle*, becomes an African American incarnation of Richard Dadier), Alan Pakula's *Up the Down Staircase* (1967), Lina Wertmuller's *Ciao, Professore!* (1992; a Sicilian version of *The Blackboard Jungle* and equally insufferable), and John N. Smith's *Dangerous Minds* (1995) are among many films that belong to this highly schematic subgenre. *The Blackboard Jungle* and *Dangerous Minds* feature protagonists whose tenure in the military supposedly qualifies them for inner-city teaching duty, but these films' reactionary humanism pales in comparison to John Avildsen's *Lean on Me* (1985), a fictionalized homage to Newark principal Joe Clark, whose idiosyncratic view of school discipline approaches, at least rhetorically, a kind of pedagogical fascism. The ideology of many authoritarian schoolroom films is pithily revealed by the protagonist of Nicholas Ray's *Bigger Than Life* (1956), a deranged schoolteacher who believes that "childhood is a congenital disease and the purpose of education is to cure it."

In the Victorian era, a consensus evolved that the children of the upper classes were also small savages; their educational taming, however, was designed to make them loyal servants of the state and administrators of empire—a process that reached its apogee in the British public school. Robert Stevenson's *Tom Brown's Schooldays* (1940, a reverent adaptation of Thomas Hughes's novel) pays tribute to Rugby headmaster Dr Thomas Ar-

nold (father of Matthew Arnold, and played with stern benevolence by Cedric
Hardwicke), and this example of Hollywood Anglophilia treats Arnold as a
pedagogical deity. Rugby's headmaster was considered a major educational
reformer, since his regime effectively eliminated much of the bullying, haz-
ing, and drunkenness that spurred Arnold on in his crusade to create a
less cut-throat educational environment. Early in the film, he delivers a key
speech in which he pledges that Rugby is "no longer the school of savage
barbarians but of God-fearing young men." Arnold believed that the school
should help to domesticate the fundamentally evil inclinations of young boys;
the institution was not so much a community of scholars as an embryonic
version of the state that the students would eventually rule.

Arnold's moralizing nationalism and fervent championing of the classics
as the core of the public-school curriculum continued well into the twentieth
century. Yet by the time that Mike Figgis remade Terence Rattigan's play
The Browning Version in 1995, Albert Finney's portrayal of the disillusioned
classics master came to seem like a mannered parody of Arnoldian values.
Perhaps the cinematic death knell for the once respected disciplines of Latin
and Greek had been sounded years before by Alf Sjoberg's *Torment* (1944),
in which the Latin master, Caligula, is portrayed as a surrogate Hitler. Years
later, looking back to a period of actual fascism, Fellini's *Amarcord* (1974)
mocked the absurd pretensions of Mussolini's efforts to invoke the grandeur
of ancient Rome in his schools—interrelated sequences feature mischievous
schoolchildren farting and belching their way through a series of fatuous
classes.

The vapid authoritarianism conveyed by the educators featured in Frederick Wiseman's *High School* (1968) is much closer to contemporary trends
in mass education than either the high-flown cadences of Thomas Arnold
or more recent pleas for the redemptive value of self-expression. The film
compresses several months of educational tedium into an ingeniously edited
portrait of an alternately hellish and unintentionally comic typical school day.
Several critics have noted how a shot of a milk truck—emblazoned with the
logo "Penn Made Products"—in the film's opening sequence refers to both
the school's mission to churn out impeccably solid citizens and Wiseman's
sardonic "examination of sexual conditioning and gender definition."[30] Nonetheless, despite some exemplary formal analyses of *High School,* the implications of its sly anti-authoritarian bias have not been sufficiently examined.

According to Edward A. Krug's comprehensive two-volume history of
the American high school, the triumph of what has come to be known as
the "investment theory of education" produced an ideology that exalted
the "need for social control" and promoted "the stern adjustment of the

individual to the group."[31] Yet Krug informs us that this ideology did not become ascendant without a struggle. Through the 1920s, for example, the pedagogic ideals of the Progressive Education Association (an organization that, for the most part, exemplified the reformist agenda of John Dewey) contested, with occasional success, an insidious emphasis on standardization. The proponents of standardization were able to draw ideological sustenance from what Michael Katz labels "the irony of early school reform."[32] Katz chronicles how, in the nineteenth century, the wealthy Massachusetts citizens who promoted compulsory secondary education met resistance from working-class citizens who resented the paternalistic largesse of industrialist magnates. Ultimately, the official ideology triumphed: public schools were proclaimed the embodiment of an egalitarianism ideally designed to level the differences between rich and poor.

High School is anchored in a middle-class milieu where teachers and administrators pride themselves on the excellence of their college preparatory program, but the film's procession of ineffectual teachers and bureaucrats, whether staunchly autocratic or wanly liberal, reflects the routinization of knowledge that can also be found in varying degrees in working-class schools or elite boarding schools. Wiseman repeatedly mingles close-ups of adult instructors with subsequent long-shots and medium close-ups of bored students; a rhythm is established in which the pupils' perhaps unwitting "passive resistance" deflates the pomposities of their instructors. Nevertheless, the film is not preoccupied with ad hominem character sketches—it skewers authoritarian pedagogy with a systematic critique. After all, a protracted sequence in which an English teacher discusses a Simon and Garfunkel song with her unresponsive students—a gauche, if touching, exercise in misguided hipness—is as damning an indictment of the school's hierarchical orientation as the accompanying tirades of a dean of discipline who resembles a particularly ferocious drill instructor. Ultimately, the faculty's good intentions must be dismissed as immaterial, since the oppressiveness of Northeast High School is engendered not merely by flawed individuals. One of *High School*'s most emblematic sequences highlights an exchange between the dean of discipline and a meek student who insists that he should be excused from gym class. The fact that the school must indiscriminately impose a regimen that demands the thoroughgoing submission of body and mind to often irrational edicts brings to mind Foucault's observations in *Discipline and Punish* concerning the "techniques of an observing hierarchy . . . and normalizing judgment"[33]—a standardization that seeped into pedagogy when seventeenth-century schools introduced a battery of regular examinations guaranteeing continuous assessment and surveillance. The attention paid by Wiseman to recalcitrant students who wander the halls without passes records the banalization of the rites of utilitarian humanism. The gap between the high school's liberal idealism and the reality of its schematized boredom is reminiscent of Raymond Williams's summary of *Hard Times*'s anti-utilitarianism: "a reliance on reason, which in the short term was cleansing and liberating, became in a real society an alienation of reason."[34]

The insidiousness of the American variant of "normalizing judgment" might well be Wiseman's theme. At least in a British or European context an acknowledgment of the minutiae of class differentiation leads to an awareness of how education becomes a crucial component of more-generalized social stratification. The distinction made by Basil Bernstein,[35] for example, between the "restricted" linguistic codes shared by working-class students at home and the formalized "elaborated" linguistic code imposed by the school environment (not to mention the inevitable advantages reaped by middle-class students) offers a perspective that is, for the most part, alien to mainstream American sociology. Since the accepted American ideology embraces the leveling of class differences, and an implicit belief in an illusory egalitarianism, the fusion of the aims of the school and the state that *High School* affirms is perhaps more seamless in the United States than elsewhere. When, toward the end of the film, a school official reads a letter from a student eventually killed in Vietnam, which makes tangible connections between the high-school values of citizenship and military self-sacrifice, a perhaps inevitable dilution of John Dewey's pedagogical altruism becomes evident. While even some radicals such as Henry Giroux have promoted a refurbished version of Dewey's model of "citizenship education," the fact that Dewey's most vigorous advocacy of progressive education immediately precedes what might be characterized as a retreat to liberal jingoism—his support of World War I illustrates the fact that liberal educational reform is constantly vulnerable to co-optation.[36] As Stirner proclaimed, education should not promote the production of "useful citizens," but encourage the formation of autonomous individuals who do not, of course, sever themselves from the interests of fellow citizens.

Wiseman's sequel, *High School II* (1994), featured the open classrooms of New York City's Central Park East: the school's concern with "personal relationships between faculty and students"[37] is, at least implicitly, posited as an empathetic alternative to the alienated classroom labor documented in *High School*. Nonetheless, while it is evident that the learning environment is less oppressive at Central Park East than its cinematic precursor, the New York school's pedagogical encounter groups facilitate the production of useful citizens in a kinder, gentler way. Carl Rogers's therapeutic educational model conceived of non-coercive education as a means to self-transformation, not societal change: "when threat to the self is minimized, the individual makes use of opportunities to learn in order to enhance himself."[38] A lengthy faculty meeting, which Wiseman captures in real time, couples a discussion of Advanced Placement scores with faculty repartee imbued with the rhetoric of self-actualization.[39] *High School II* and Central Park East's liberal pedagogy recall Dewey's plea for a "flexible adjustment" of society's institutions[40]—a goal that might result in greater self-esteem but is far indeed from the aspirations of anarchist pedagogy.

If *High School II* makes use of progressive education's platitudes and simultaneously reaffirms the status quo, Jean-Luc Godard's *Le Gai Savoir* (1967) strips Rousseau's *Émile* of its Romantic complacency. As in films such as *La Chinoise* and *Tout va bien,* "Maoist" gauchisme functions as a covert anarchism that the filmmaker steadfastly refuses to acknowledge. A dialogue preoccupied with the aporias of cinematic representation, interspersed with parodically quoted media fragments, *Le Gai Savoir* casts Jean-Pierre Léaud as a protagonist named Émile, who merges new-wave anomie with a naive radicalism, and Juliet Berto as Patricia, a gauchiste who moonlights as a fashion model. Unlike the linear progression of traditional schoolroom films, Godard's film is not an homage to a Messianic pedagogue or an educational technique, but itself functions *as* an exploratory form of pedagogy. Despite an obligatory, quasi-parodic nod to Rousseau, *Le Gai Savoir*'s cinematic pedagogy is actually more reminiscent of Denis Diderot's mordantly comic philosophical dialogues, particularly *Rameau's Nephew* and *D'Alembert's Dream.*

A dialogue such as *Rameau's Nephew,* distinguished by an invigoratingly vertiginous form of argumentation, promotes a salutary philosophical disequilibrium that is far different from Rousseau's schematic liberalism. As Elisabeth de Fontenay remarks, Diderot "undermine[s] the pretensions of the Western male subject to set himself up as the basis of neutral knowledge and sovereign power." Marginal figures such as "the Nun, the blind, Rameau's Nephew . . . destablilize the current order unique in its five manifestations: political, metaphysical, religious, ethical and mathematical."[41] *Le Gai Savoir*'s post-consumerist destabilization of fixed aesthetic categories resembles Diderot's pioneering "open text" much more than the concluding certitudes of *Émile,* a narrative in which the eponymous hero's intellectual journey ends with undialectical domestic solace. Godard's film is closer to the dialectical ironies of Hegel's ironized "unhappy consciousness," a concept profoundly influenced by *Rameau's Nephew.*

Patricia's injunction to "start from zero . . . and see if there are any traces" evokes Diderot's tendency to oscillate between intellectual earnestness and what P. N. Furbank terms "self-subverting" cynicism. The film's playful pseudo-rigor can be taken as a lighthearted indictment of early structuralism's craving for actual rigor. Godard's trademark whispery voice-over, for example, informs us that Émile was shot in the heart during a demonstration, but was saved by a copy of *Cahiers du Cinéma* lodged in his sweater. Godard refuses to choose between cinephilia and a political critique that is more self-lacerating than genuinely didactic.

Émile and Patricia's pedagogical scheme exemplifies this internal tension, since it synthesizes both a poetics and a politics of representation. The first year of their alternative university's curriculum would be devoted to the collection and assessment of sounds and images, the second year would subsequently decompose these sounds and images, while the third would end with a mock-Hegelian synthesis—a creative reconstitution of film and television language. Anarchists can find much to admire in this retooling of *Émile*. Godard's consolidation of Leninism and modernist poetics resembles Julia Kristeva's odd fusion of aesthetic anarchism and dogmatic Maoism.[42] Nonetheless, the film's anti-Stalinism (in an offhand remark, Patricia, a lingerie model, remarks that both the communist *L'Humanité* and the conservative *Le Figaro* publish the same vapid advertisements that pay her rent) and anti-authoritarian homages (Cohn-Bendit's voice is heard on the soundtrack) reveal that Godard did not capitulate to the authoritarian panaceas that full-blown Maoism required.

At times, seemingly anti-authoritarian classroom films conceal a submerged conformist bias. Laurent Cantet's *Entre les murs* (*The Class*, 2008), awarded the Palme d'Or at the Cannes Film Festival by unanimous decision of the jury, and termed a "seamless" movie by president Sean Penn, is a slippery piece of work. It partially reinforces the seemingly benign authoritarianism and facile hero worship inherent in the *Blackboard Jungle* paradigm, while half-heartedly critiquing the teacher hero's charismatic authority. Although *Variety*'s Justin Chang called *Entre les murs* "a welcome corrective" to "Yank" films like the aforementioned *Dangerous Minds*[43] (and the *New York Times*' A. O. Scott likewise bashed the Michelle Pfeiffer potboiler in order to praise the more sophisticated French film), Cantet's film is an admittedly less cheesy, more subtle version of the much-reviled Yank template: in other words, a crowd-pleaser. Certainly not without its charms, Cantet's film is primarily intriguing for the contradictions it embodies, as well as its ambivalent view of the French educational system and the ideological consensus it represents.

Shot in what lazy critics have termed a "documentary style" (but with a glossy, widescreen aesthetic that corresponds to precious few documentaries), Cantet's film makes efforts to maintain an ironic distance from both lived experience and its source material. Perhaps consciously avoiding the embarrassing disparity between documentary idealism and old-fashioned greed that resulted in the gentle rural schoolmaster of Nicolas Philibert's *Être et avoir* (2002) suing for a cut of the film's profits, Cantet's film is securely anchored in the fictional realm. Skillfully dodging James Frey–style fabrications, former junior high-school teacher (and *Cahiers du Cinéma* contributor) François Bégaudeau plays a fictional version of himself based on his autobiographical novel. Self-effacing (in a suspiciously arrogant fashion), Bégaudeau insists in interviews that he is "not a star," merely the "main character" in a supremely democratic film. And in a loose narrative directed by a non-doctrinaire leftist, the emphasis is primarily on the interchanges between the intrepid, but conspicuously flawed instructor and the students, played by appealing non-professionals, in his always lively, multicultural class. The superficial spontaneity of the classroom scenes was the result of meticulous preparation. The cast participated in extended workshops in which—prompted by Bégaudeau's suggestions—extended improvisations formed the basis of the final script.

Many of the predominantly comic interludes in the film's first half do in fact wittily deflect Bégaudeau's hubris—despite the fact that he flaunts this smugness as a strategically ironized badge of honor. As a case in point, a protracted exchange on the affectations of the imperfect subjunctive reiterates how language reflects class stratification in ultra-hierarchical France. The debate on this notoriously thorny slice of French grammar propels the students and their reliably argumentative teacher into a debate in which their arguments, and social roles, almost appear predetermined. The kids, unsurprisingly, complain that "no one speaks like this," while Bégaudeau, perhaps partially with tongue in cheek, vigorously defends the subjunctive as part of the French literary arsenal. In another pivotal scene, Khoumba, an intelligent but consistently irascible student, puts her instructor's patience to the test by refusing to read an excerpt from *The Diary of Anne Frank* aloud in class. Interestingly enough, the debates about *Anne Frank*'s "relevance" to a multiethnic group of students that would probably take place in a North American milieu are sidestepped, and Khoumba's sullenness is viewed as more of a reaction to what she perceives as her instructor's hostility than a tangible critique of French universalism.

While Cantet misses few opportunities to underline his protagonist's flaws, there is ultimately a smugness to *Entre les murs* that allows Bégaudeau to triumph despite the film's ostentatious emphasis on his verbal infelicities and gift for pedagogical self-sabotage. As the movie sputters toward a conclusion that a small group of dissenting critics have rightly categorized as glib, the melodramatic ante is upped, and the good will Cantet has earned by dint of some slight, but charming, vignettes begins to dissipate. A rather trumped-up controversy between the unorthodox teacher, a surly African student named Souleymane, and Esmeralda, a feisty Algerian girl, sucks the life out of what could have been a spirited evisceration of French educational shibboleths.

Esmeralda, somehow the student representative to the school's faculty meeting, becomes enraged that Bégaudeau refers to Souleymane as "limited." Caught off guard, he petulantly dismisses Esmeralda and one of her female pals, as "behaving like skanks." Yet, when the chastened teacher makes his cinematically mandated amends (after initially failing to integrate his gaffe into another grammar lesson), a class discussion summing up the year's achievements features Esmeralda's colloquial tribute to Plato's *Republic*. The clumsiness of this narrative coup de grace is truly startling: slapped on the wrist for political incorrectness, the hapless teacher is re-coronated as an antic philosopher king and avatar of Socratic dialogue.

In the final analysis, the failings of *Entre les murs*—its star's faux humility notwithstanding—can be ascribed to an unwillingness to confront the systemic roots of educational inequality. The charm of Abdel Kechiche's *L'esquive* (2003) resided in the efforts of marginalized kids of North African origin to appropriate classical French literature for their own needs. While their nondescript white teacher stays safely in the background, screen hog Bégaudeau emerges as an insufferable *magister ludi*. The late sociologist Pierre Bourdieu, perhaps the most trenchant critic of French educational privilege, unwittingly located the central quandary of *Entre les murs* in his work on "education and domination" by asserting that the "Jacobin ideology on which the traditional criticism of the teaching system is based, as well as certain traditional criticism of government reform of this system, actually justify the system under the guise of challenging it, as well as justifying the pedagogical conservatism of a number of those who demand these reforms."[44]

Despite indubitably good intentions, Bégaudeau's innovative teaching methods end up "justifying" the structural inequality they seek to circumvent. This sort of indictment would doubtless piss off the self-assured teacher, since he even invokes Bourdieu's terminology in the press book, claiming quite reasonably that "a school . . . is, in the end, discriminatory, unequal, it fabricates reproduction, etc." What Bégaudeau can obviously not admit, however, is that his scenario always puts him center stage as the film's puppet master. As Bourdieu observes, "the school also has a function of mystification

... it persuades those whom it eliminates that their social destiny ... is due to their lack of natural gifts, and in this way contributes to preventing them from discovering that their individual destiny is a particular case of a collective one."[45] Like countless schoolroom movies, *Entre les murs* mystifies the educational process by maintaining that dreary, reactionary classrooms can be transformed by the empathetic, if ultimately condescending, intervention of a heroic teacher. The fact that Cantet is more conscious of these pitfalls than his many Hollywood precursors does not excuse his film's fundamental dishonesty.

Alain Tanner's *Jonas qui aura 25 ans en l'an 2000* (*Jonah Who Will be 25 in the Year 2000*, 1976) is distinguished by a more straightforwardly left-libertarian, if equally reflexive, version of cinematic pedagogy. The film opens with a circular pan of a Geneva statue of Rousseau, accompanied by a solemn voice-over intonation of the philosopher's famous observation—"to be human is to be chained by our institutions." This fragment from *Émile* neglects to inform the audience of the great Romantic's flirtation with authoritarian precepts: his educational theory contains quasi-anarchist components that coexist uneasily with a belief that children need a "national identity" that can instill "patriotic values in its future citizens."[46] Tanner's affectionate and, at times, gently sardonic homage to the post-'68 generation takes the acknowledged father of progressive education at his word, and considers the possibility that individuals are indeed capable of self-liberation. The film revolves around the activities of a commune that must constantly deal with the threat of dissolution, and it is certainly not coincidental that several of the protagonists are educators. For example, the working-class Mathieu's mixture of proletarian militancy and practical agricultural skills imbues him with a status close to Gramsci's yearned for, if rare, "organic intellectual." Of course, the anarchist tradition has often urged the cultivation of both manual and intellectual talents, and Kropotkin's anarcho-communist variant of "integral education" promotes this ideal with noteworthy fervor—"a society where each individual is a producer of both manual and intellectual work; where each able-bodied human being is a worker, and where each worker works both in the field and in the industrial workshop."[47] Significantly, Mathieu organizes and teaches classes in the commune's "free school," and his enthusiasm for teaching the very young can be aligned with Ferrer's belief that radical pedagogy and social transformation are inextricably intertwined.

Despite obvious admiration for Mathieu's educational initiatives, Tanner and screenwriter John Berger decided to devote a considerably larger block of screen time to the high-school classes taught by Marco, Mathieu's more absent-minded fellow Communard. Although *Jonah* hints that Marco embodies an archetypal brand of New Left Marxism, his lecture on the "sausage link" theory of history blends the materialism of a decidedly libertarian Marxism with an anarchistic distrust of progress and alienating work. Marco's lesson, combining playfulness and sobriety, proposes that the "pieces of history" represented by the sausage morsels that he has gleefully cut with a butcher's cleaver can be used to demonstrate the naivete of a belief in uninterrupted progress. Without romanticizing the view of history shared by preindustrial societies, Marco observes that industrial capitalism brought a "new kind of violence," in which the cyclical notion of time shared by agricultural societies was replaced by a hierarchical, standardized notion of time that shaped subjectivity by requiring "clocking in, clocking out."

Marco's discussion of historical discontinuities recalls Fernand Braudel's shift from an emphasis on supposedly "seminal" historical events to a preoccupation with more quotidian patterns of everyday life,[48] and is also reminiscent of the heterodox historiography of Walter Benjamin's Arcades Project. Conversely, the slightly sheepish teacher's pedagogical stance can be aligned with the efforts of Leo Tolstoy—anarchist educator as well as celebrated novelist—to learn from the inquisitive peasant children who attended his short-lived experimental school. One of Tolstoy's most representative educational essays is titled "Should We Teach the Peasant Children to Write, or Should They Teach Us?" This question, seemingly rhetorical but actually heartfelt, sums up some of the contradictions that must be confronted by anti-authoritarian pedagogues such as Marco. Radical educators must resolve the dilemma of refusing to feed students predigested information, while maintaining a committed stance that resists the banalities of tepid pluralism. Like many contemporary proponents of the open classroom, Tolstoy conceived of education as a "conversation . . . an unrehearsed intellectual adventure."[49] Marco's mock-culinary history lessons evokes the holes—the inassimilable fissures—within history; like Benjamin's idiosyncratic materialism, this approach has the potential to foster critical reflection, but is not tainted with autocratic stridency. For Susan Buck-Morss, Benjamin's commitment to a historiography of dialectical images—"a graphic, concrete representation of truth" in which history "cut[s] through without a totalizing frame"—is inspired by his desire to formulate a "philosophy *out* of history" rather than a "philosophy of history."[50] The Benjaminian yearning for a historical method that avoids the teleological certitude of Leopold von Ranke's view of the past—"the strongest narcotic of the nineteenth century"[51]—is not unlike Marco's contention that the identification of history's lacunae—or "holes"—requires a process of patient excavation, since often "no one understood" epochal historical transformations. The resourceful teacher believes that "capitalism is collapsing," but does not partake of the stale temptation to proclaim that revolution is around the corner. In this respect, the tone of Marco's lecture resembles the multilayered ironies that abound in the scripts of Benjamin's radio broadcasts designed for children. Mathieu's disquisition on the "pseudo-oil" crisis offers no panaceas; he even wonders if the students will "still be alive in the year 2000." His wistful resignation resembles Benjamin's materialist chiliasm, his belief that the examination of catastrophe can help us to perceive a "devastating flash or illumination."[52]

While Marco's history lesson and Mathieu's lyrical version of crisis theory both challenge standard liberal and conservative shibboleths, a subsequent sequence featuring Marco's girlfriend, Marie, recasts the suggestive, if epistemologically creaky, model of anarchist education suggested by Tolstoy. Although many of the techniques employed by Tolstoy at his Yasnaya Polyana school have inspired contemporary anarchist educators, his belief that teachers must restore children to a state of harmony that has vanished because of the encroachments of civilization has an idealist resonance that is difficult for many contemporary radical educators to accept wholeheartedly. Marco's efforts to elicit class participation by aligning Marie's personal woes with broader social concerns are congruent with the Tolstoyan assumption that education is essentially conversational, although his spirit of radical doubt bears little resemblance to the quasi-theological ambiance of Yasnaya Polyana. Of course, a teacher's commitment to non-hierarchical education can easily be deflected by students' ennui: Tanner's occasional propensity to pan the faces of Marco's students reveals something less than total mental absorption; during the pivotal history lesson, the camera reveals that some students are genuinely engrossed, while another contingent seems frankly bored. Nonetheless, the plight of Marie, a supermarket cashier in Geneva who invariably violates the law by not crossing the Swiss border to sleep in France after the end of the workday, elicits genuine empathy from Marco's students. Like many radical classrooms, Marco's hovers between emancipatory possibilities and the necessity to deal with more mundane concerns. On the day of Marie's classroom appearance, he announces that, instead of the scheduled examination, the class should "connect" their knowledge of Marie's dilemma with their "own desires." Although this is a slightly strained attempt to establish affinities between the travails of work, the irrationality of legalistic strictures, and the lure of erotic desire, Marco's replacement of pedagogical abstractions with awkward autobiographical ruminations at least partially addresses Roland Barthes's call for a radical pedagogy that combats the "tyranny of imposed meaning."[53]

Marie is eventually fired from her job for providing generous, and un-authorized, "discounts" to the supermarket's elderly and indigent, and the film implicitly endorses her impromptu form of distributive justice. Her magnanimity may seem intuitive, but this spontaneous desire to share the wealth corresponds to a certain minority tendency within nineteenth-century anarchism christened *la reprise individuelle*—individual recovery of products of labor—by Élisée Reclus. According to Reclus's biographer, Marie Fleming, this anarchist theorist and geographer believed that "there was little difference between work within the context of bourgeois society and what the law termed as theft, because both activities resulted in the appropriation of wealth . . . therefore . . . to recover extra-legally the stolen goods was perfectly just."[54] Although some of Reclus's comrades (particularly Peter Kropotkin and Jean Grave) found this an untenable distortion of anarchist tenets, Marie charmingly updates the *reprise individuelle* for a post-'68 era, recalling the situationist Raoul Vaneigem's observation that "pilfering is a normal response to commodity's provocations."[55]

In an analogous spirit, Luc Moullet's brief film *Barres* (1984) explores creative expropriation with comic brio. *Barres,* despite its tongue-in-cheek insouciance, can be considered a pedagogical film, since Moullet painstakingly demonstrates the best way to avoid paying the fare on the Paris metro. The lessons the audience receives in applying chewing gum to turnstiles (a "destabilizer"), dodging transportation authorities, and making fare-dodging a competitive sport are interspersed with facetious titles (outwitting metro surveillance is said to cement "solidarity between classes") and even quotes from Pascal displaced into a truly absurd context. Although *Barres* may seem like an inconsequential jape, the film teaches its audience (a healthy dose of good-natured irony notwithstanding) a useful form of collective resistance.

Jonah's playful refashioning of Brechtian *Lehrstücke* and *Barres*'s reformulation of Proudhon's motto "property is theft" do not merely illustrate modes of pedagogy that could be labeled anarchistic. They also function as pedagogical cinematic exercises that, without excessive heavy-handedness, point the way beyond the entrenched habits endemic to authoritarian forms of schooling. Both films struggled to endorse, and by implication teach, concerted resistance during a period when radical hopes were waning. Jonah, the eponymous child who is the incarnation of Tanner and Berger's utopian hopes, functions as an ambiguous metaphor for the difficulty of adhering to an anti-authoritarian politics and ethics during dark times. While the film rather predictably links Jonah with the soothing sounds of whale music, it resonates also with George Orwell's backhanded tribute to the biblical Jonah's legacy in his essay "Inside the Whale." "Inside the Whale" is a virtuosic feat of devil's advocacy, a perverse celebration of Henry Miller's wholly apolitical sensibility. Yet in a far-fetched rhetorical maneuver, Orwell, perhaps rather condescendingly, termed Miller "a proletarian novelist . . . because his political passivity was close to the actual attitudes of ordinary men."[56] Although Tanner and Berger's sensibility has little in common with Orwell's, *Jonah's* post-'68 radicalism maintains a precarious balance between the anarchist pedagogy of Marco and Mathieu and the New Age proclivities of characters such as Madeleine and Max, whose central preoccupations—innocuous-enough concerns such as astrology and tantric sex—can be traced to these protagonists' disillusionment with political engagement. The film's open-ended pedagogical structure leaves the question of whether Jonah himself will follow in the footsteps of Marco and Mathieu or resist political commitment by remaining inside the whale.

For some viewers, *Jonah's* linkage of pedagogy to a countercultural ethos may seem rooted in a bygone era. Yet, during a period when teachers and students in the United States are fighting an uphill battle to combat the rigid priorities of standardized testing and the "Common Core," a new generation is learning that education is often a form of social control. Like the authoritarian classrooms of *Hard Times*, American public schools in the twenty-first century are focused on teaching only "the facts" and treat students like vessels designed to be filled with information. While this approach may be appropriate for transforming students into passive, obedient citizens, it ignores the importance of play for children and squelches kids' creative potential.

During the 1960s, a vibrant alternative education movement resisted the pieties of authoritarian pedagogy and launched a plea for independent "Free Schools." Much of the ferment in this country was inspired by the 1960 publication of A. S. Neill's *Summerhill: A Radical Approach to Child Rearing,* the manifesto of a Scottish-born schoolmaster whose Summerhill School in the English countryside, although founded in 1921, became synonymous with the burgeoning counterculture's contempt for authoritarian education. In an anthology titled *Summerhill: For and Against* published in 1970, the political demarcations are clearly drawn. The late Max Rafferty, the famously right-wing California state superintendent for public instruction from 1963 to 1971, denounces Summerhill for degrading "true learning to the status of a disorganized orgy." Michael Rossman, on the other hand, a '60s activist known for his participation in Berkeley's Free Speech movement, hails the Summerhill experiment as the harbinger of a "new social order."[57]

Since Neill conceded that Summerhill could not afford to admit poor students, his educational experiment was vulnerable to accusations that it catered exclusively to the wealthy. During the late '60s, Herbert Kohl, whose

36 Children (1967) recounted his experiences while teaching in Harlem, and Jonathan Kozol, the educator who made his name with the memoir *Death at an Early Age: The Destruction of the Hearts and Minds of Negro Children in the Boston Public Schools,* (1967), became advocates for inner city Free Schools, a modification of Neill's pastoral ideal. (Kozol's *Free Schools* [1972] provides tips for educators interested in founding their own alternative schools.)[58] Of course, few of the '60s proponents of Free Schools were familiar with the educational tenets of Francisco Ferrer, even though Ferrer's ideas quickly caught fire in the United States and inspired Modern School offshoots in New York and New Jersey during the early years of the twentieth century. According to Paul Avrich, the author of the definitive history of the American Modern School movement, the graduates of these schools "appear to have carried away a strong cooperative and libertarian ethic, a spirit of mutual aid and individual sovereignty, which has remained with them throughout their adult years, regardless of their politics or occupation."[59]

These historical precedents subtly inform Amanda Rose Wilder's *Approaching the Elephant*, a chronicle of the inaugural year of the Teddy McArdle Free School, a contemporary Free School in Little Falls, New Jersey. Named for the child-seer protagonist of J. D. Salinger's "Teddy," some introductory titles acknowledge the school's debt to Ferrer's anti-authoritarian ideals and reveal that, at the moment of its founding, it was among only a handful of extant Free Schools worldwide since the first appeared on the scene in Barcelona in 1901—the 262nd.[60] It's nevertheless revealing that many film critics, while enthusiastic about Wilder's film, compared the relatively innocuous antics of the kids at Teddy McArdle to the macabre events of *Lord of the Flies* and included ominous references to "chaos in the classroom." As Alexander Khost, the school's director, points out, "since so few people have any sort of knowledge or background in anarchist pedagogy, it's a difficult subject for a documentary as it is a topic so easily taken out of context."[61]

Wrenching the topic out of its context is of course possible because, in the years that have elapsed since the heyday of Free Schools in the '60s and '70s, authoritarian schools have eclipsed alternative schools to become a monolithic norm. Given that both teachers and students find it difficult to escape their authoritarian conditioning, it's not surprising that the classroom ambiance is fraught at Teddy McArdle. Anarchism in one classroom is not an easily attainable goal; utopian experiments have trouble thriving in the midst of dystopian realities. Perhaps the disparity between the idealism of anarchist pedagogy and the gritty, daily struggles of running a school is one reason that critic Matt Zoller Seitz wondered if Free Schools were a "misguided over-correction" to America's "quasi-fascistic school system."[62]

One startling aspect of Wilder's film, which implicitly pays homage to Frederick Wiseman's "reality fictions" and the Direct Cinema of the Maysles brothers and D. A. Pennebaker, is that the evocative black-and-white cinematography and the absence of cell phones, computers, and video games, almost convince us that we're back in the late '60s or early '70s. Direct Cinema's refusal to impose a didactic thrust or guide viewers to a specific conclusion probably explains why the film functions as what Seitz terms a "Rorschach Test." Audience members predisposed to be skeptical of Free Schools will probably have their assumptions confirmed while those sympathetic to anti-authoritarian modes of education will most likely see Teddy McArdle's growing pains as an outgrowth of Neill's belief that "freedom works slowly; it may take several years for a child to learn what it means."[63]

Teddy McArdle's "democratic meetings," which seem patterned on Neill's belief that "the function of Summerhill self-government is not only to make laws but to discuss social features of the community as well," pinpoint the struggles of both the students and faculty to come to terms with what true autonomy means within the framework of an educational community. A spirited little girl named Lucy embodies the contradictions of a student confronted with the challenges faced by the elimination of mandatory classes and the necessity of grappling with the realities of what anarchists term "self-activity" or "self-liberation." At first, Lucy is both cautious and diplomatic. She hesitates to use a saw during woodworking because she fears her mother may not approve and, rather than attack a fellow student's drawing, she merely confesses that it's "not her style." She subsequently comes out of her shell and claims that adults are trying to unilaterally impose their rules on kids. Whether she's right or wrong is immaterial; the minimal "rules" are, after all, meant to ensure everyone's safety. It's nevertheless refreshing that she confirms Neill's assertion that "the . . . General School Meeting is of more value than a week's curriculum of school subjects."[64]

Most reviewers have focused on the film's latter half, which is bound up with the school's decision to expel Jiovanni, a boy who, despite his considerable charm, is deemed a disruptive bully. For some commentators, Teddy McArdle's failure to make Jiovanni a productive member of the community is evidence of its failure. Another, more nuanced way to view the furor over Jiovanni's obstreperous behavior is to understand that Free Schools are always works in progress and that, to invoke a term employed by contemporary anarchists, educational experiments can be viewed as "temporary autonomous zones." Toward the end of the film, Khost admits that, in some respects, Teddy McArdle is "very much" like the school he dreamed of as an unhappy boy in public school and, in some respects "very much unlike" his childhood conception of an antidote to authoritarian schooling. Inasmuch as he succeeded, at least for a brief period, in combating the testing and regimentation that still dominates American schooling, his tenure at the school was much more of a success than a failure.

It perhaps goes without saying that, in recent years, the alternative school paradigm has been co-opted by neoliberal pundits and the religious right. The neoliberal perspective, which often masquerades as enlightened self-interest on behalf of desperate parents, is exemplified by Davis Guggenheim's highly misleading documentary, *Waiting for Superman* (2010). In a fairly covert gambit to discredit public education and promote charter schools, the film celebrates a handful of successful charter initiatives such as Geoffrey Canada's Harlem Children's Zone while numerous charter failures are glossed over. Anarchists, to be sure, have consistently attacked the conformist agenda of American public schools. Nevertheless, many charter schools, often affiliated with corporate chains or religious institutions, are frequently little more than underfunded imitations of their public brethren. In an effort to extricate pedagogy from the false options proffered by this public/private dichotomy, Joseph Todd suggests that anarchist deschooling, or anarchist homeschooling, might be slotted within a category, inspired by the political theorist Nancy Fraser, labeled "educational counter publics." From this vantage point, radical alternatives to mainstream education are extricated from the sterile dichotomies of the private and public realms and emerge as a challenge to both repressive public schools and equally problematic quasi-public charter schools.[65]

Classroom Insurrections and the "Education of the Senses": *Zéro de conduite, L'Atalante,* and *If . . .*

Jean Vigo's *Zéro de conduite* (*Zero for Conduct,* 1933) is one of the few noteworthy films that critics unfailingly consign to the ill-defined category of "anarchist cinema." Vigo's anarchist credentials are often established by allusions to his father's political activities. P. E. Salles Gomes's biography familiarized cinephiles with Eugène Bonaventure de Vigo's (known to his comrades as Miguel Almereyda—a pseudonym meaning "there is shit") adherence to anarcho-syndicalism and pacifism as well as his imprisonment and almost certain murder—the facts of the case are still shrouded in considerable doubt—in 1917. Although Jean Maitron's history of the French anarchist movement dwells briefly on Almereyda's association with anarcho-pacifists such as Domela Nieuwenhuis,[66] Salles Gomes's research revealed the contradictory, and even capricious, nature of his ideological commitments.

Almereyda's political chameleonism is reflected in the shifting positions of *La Guerre Sociale,* the newspaper that he was associated with from 1909 to 1913. Although Almereyda was one of the many anarchists to come to Francisco Ferrer's defense in 1909, his increasingly reformist trajectory took him closer to Jean Jaurès's mainstream socialism, as well as eventual support of World War I—a position admittedly shared by certain "pro-war" anarchists such as Peter Kropotkin and Jean Grave, whose fear of Prussian militarism outweighed their doubts concerning French imperial duplicity.

While Almereyda's militancy, however erratic and inconsistent, influenced his son, it is important to emphasize the truly anarchist components in films such as *Zero for Conduct* and *L'Atalante* (1934) while avoiding mechanical analogies between early twentieth-century French anarchism and Vigo's aesthetic orientation. From an explicitly pedagogical vantage point, *Zero for Conduct* endorses Ferrer's ideal of making education a testing ground for a new social order, even if the film's ludic propensity has little in common with his rationalist educational schemes. In other words, neither Almereyda's early pragmatic, if militant, anarchism nor his later meliorism are tangible presences in *Zero for Conduct,* a film rooted in a utopian conception of childhood that not only looks backward to Fourier, but anticipates the work of radicals such as Paul Goodman, Everett Reimer, and Ivan Illich. Nonetheless, if Vigo shares Reimer and Illich's view that schooling is often no more than incarceration disguised as education, the film's delineation of childhood as an alternative, and perhaps superior, universe of discourse clashes with Reimer's assertion—undoubtedly an embellishment of Ariès's historiography—that "childhood becomes a problem when extended over too many years and too many aspects of life."[67] Paul Goodman's stance, which takes issue with the legalistic arguments of "children's rights" and prefers a promotion of childhood "spontaneity"[68] and creativity, is undoubtedly closer to Vigo's enshrinement of childhood as a lost paradise. As we have seen earlier, a hypostatized image of a romanticized childhood became vulnerable to perils of sentimentality during the Victorian era, and Goodman, among others, is not unaware of this insidious sentimental tradition. *Zero for Conduct,* however, avoids the pitfalls of fetishizing childhood innocence by refusing to present its young protagonists as mere cherubic naifs.

Vigo's distinctive cinematic style helps to reinforce anarchist pedagogy's penchant for fusing an investment in childhood spontaneity with a contingent promotion of social, collective desire. Mainstream cinema's obsession with linear character development is almost wholly discarded in *Zero for Conduct.* Nonetheless, Vigo lovingly details the individual creative desires of a mischievous group of children—pranksters who would be natural candidates for the "little hordes" of Fourier's phalanx. As William G. Simon convincingly demonstrates in his comprehensive textual analysis, the film's paucity of close-ups, Vigo's evident disdain for establishing shots, and his tendency to film much of the action either in long-shot or from peculiarly high or low angles is part of a larger cinematic strategy. Narrative cinema's usual predilection—or at least desire—for near-seamless spatial and temporal coherence is brilliantly undermined.[69]

While Vigo was obviously constricted by a limited budget, the eccentric pacing and editing rhythms that resulted from this imposed restriction produced a film that illustrates, as well as endorses, anarchist pedagogy. The implications, both aesthetic and pedagogical, of this idiosyncratic modus operandi become evident in the film's opening sequence. Both Simon and Salles Gomes emphasize the fact that the film plunges the viewer into the alternative world of childhood: the allowance for a realm of play establishes the possibility of what José Lebrero Stals terms the "utopian toponymy of the childlike . . . a space where impulse is more crucial than intelligibility."[70] The opening sequence of the film, like much that follows, creates an imaginary topos removed from the constraints of adulthood. Eventually, a rather perfunctory sequence highlighting the return of a student named Caussat to the dreaded boarding school is replaced by shots where the dynamism of improvised invention is given full rein, despite the fact that an observant camera remains thoroughly static. When Caussat's traveling companion, Bruel, arrives, a series of magic tricks performed by the newly arrived boy, Caussat's impishly improvisatory performance on a toy trumpet, and some prolonged cigar-smoking that makes a mockery of this adult postprandial ritual initiates the viewer into a realm where the strictures of authority cannot penetrate. Interestingly, one of the boys' teachers, Huguet, is present in the train's compartment, but his contingent relationship to the children is consistently reiterated throughout the film—he essentially functions as a whimsical messenger between the realms of childhood and adulthood. Bruel and Caussat's tricks and pranks—two balloons, for example, that obediently coalesce into female breasts—are the complete antithesis of the utilitarian tasks foisted on pupils in Mr. Gradgrind's classroom. These decidedly non-goal-oriented activities bear a strong resemblance to the practice the situationists labeled *dérive* or drift—"locomotion without a goal . . . in which one or more persons during a certain period drop their usual motives for movement and action, their relations, their work and leisure activities, and let themselves be drawn by the attractions of the terrain and the encounters they find there."[71] Appropriately enough, a commentator in a post-situationist zine explicitly links the *dérive* to childhood, remarking that "the drifter opens the self up to the recesses of intuition, the realm immediately available to the child."[72] In Vigo's film, these "recesses of intuition" are concretely embodied by the smoky train compartment that Caussat, Bruel, and Huguet inhabit.

In contradistinction to this unabashedly liminal space, the depiction of *Zero for Conduct*'s grimly spartan boarding school cements anarchist analogies between school and prison that considerably predate the writings of Illich, Goodman, and Foucault. In the nineteenth century at least, as the biographer of the French anarchist critic Félix Fénéon observes, schools were often built like prisons: "with an inner courtyard, and long straight corridors that a warden at each end could supervise at a glance. . . . In such barracks, built to last, the elite of the nineteenth century learned conformity, order and discipline, so that the best among them could serve a hierarchical, centralized state."[73] Vigo is supremely cognizant of these parallels between schools and prison, and several important sequences featuring nocturnal activities in the school dormitory emphasize the fear and tedium caused by institutional surveillance, as well as the students' efforts to break free from their boorish teachers' control. In *Zero for Conduct*'s initial dormitory sequence, for example, four beds, only three of which are occupied, are seen in long-shot. Before long, Parrain, the creepily silent superintendent, appears and, without saying a word, attempts to foreclose the possibility of schoolboy shenanigans. For the moment, we are merely provided deindividuated portraits of the boys, a decidedly claustrophobic visual style that Vigo employs to express his derisory view of the school's bureaucratic facade. Even when there is a transition to brief snippets of dialogue exchanged between Parrain and his recalcitrant charges, several overhead shots distance the audience from the humorless superintendent's fairly inept exercise of authority.

Vigo's self-consciously Manichean opposition of the repressive school to the liberatory realm outside its perimeter has not gone unnoticed by critics, yet the implications of this dialectic for anarchist pedagogy has not been sufficiently explored. For Allon White, a division between schoolroom and playground reinforces the process of "social reproduction of seriousness," and his Bakhtinian gloss on this phenomenon might almost be seen as an inadvertent analysis of Vigo's contrast between classroom solemnity and playground spontaneity:

> Easy to romanticize (the playground is also the site of bullying and displaced abjection), the playground is nevertheless the site of the "carnivalesque." . . . From the outset, the modern school system is predicated upon the enclosing and exclusion of the carnivalesque from its territory. The serious act of growing up and acquiring knowledge begins by inculcat-

ing the child with a primary law of double exclusion: where knowledge is, play is not; where play is, knowledge is not. . . . The playground/classroom division is a binary opposition which helps to *produce* the Western historical category of intellectual *work*, of serious knowledge.[74]

A sequence from Vigo's original script that was never shot endeavored to illustrate how childhood spontaneity "is constantly being repressed":[75] it would have provided graphic evidence of this socially ingrained "double exclusion." Vigo planned to include an incessant drumroll on the soundtrack, while freezing the frame, as the schoolboys' frolicking reaches its zenith; the kids' natural grace would thereby be arrested and converted into gauche, splenetic movements. Similarly, if we examine sequences that actually exist, the carnivalesque schoolyard is exalted as both a tangible and a quasi-utopian respite from seriousness. Once Vigo moves the camera outside the school's interior, relatively rare close-ups of students—Caussat and Bruel, planning a mini-insurrection—are featured. The boys' animated exchange is followed by a close-up of Tabard, a solitary, near-androgynous boy. Tabard initially seems like a prime candidate for bullying, a victim of what White terms "displaced abjection." Yet at the very point at which Tabard is unfairly suspected of being a "sneak," Huguet appears and assumes the role of both honorary child and antic pied piper. As a tracking movement captures Huguet's exultant impersonation of Chaplin, an already playful conspiratorial ambience is transformed into full-fledged carnivalesque glee. Huguet's mimicry specifically recalls *Easy Street,* a film in which the itinerant tramp is harassed by the police. This allusion is especially apt, since Chaplin is one of the few pop culture icons frequently praised by anarchist critics and educators alike. Some residual elements of this carefree interlude are subsequently integrated into Huguet's own classroom, transgressively violating the seemingly ironclad distinction between classroom and playground. Huguet not only embodies a blithe inversion of Parrain's austere demeanor, but even draws a caricature of the superintendent while walking on his hands. He refuses, moreover, to interfere as his pupils play marbles or cards, or even sleep in class. This may be slightly different from what the anarchist writer and art critic Herbert Read meant by "education through art." But since Read believed that art, as well as aesthetic pedagogy, creatively reconciles "intuition and intellect, imagination and abstraction,"[76] we might well view Huguet's unorthodox classroom tactics as an unwitting tribute to Read's twentieth-century appropriation of Schiller's "play instinct." Simon notes that Vigo's use of an extended panning shot in this sequence "has the effect of accepting the havoc . . . showing it as something natural."[77] The insurrectionary nonchalance of this classroom's meticulously orchestrated chaos is in fact reinforced by the lack of quick cutting and reaction shots, and fosters, in an admittedly hyperbolic fashion, what Read considers the first aim of aesthetic education—the preservation of "the natural intensity of all modes of perception and sensation."[78] Yet Vigo's film is remarkable for conveying a less-compromised version of this "natural intensity" than Read himself, an essayist whose allegiance to the more rarefied currents within modernism (particularly noticeable in a tense but enduring relationship with T. S. Eliot) tended slightly to compromise his anarchism.

As a film that might be considered an example as well as an illustration of anarchist pedagogy, *Zero for Conduct* is, unsurprisingly, not kind to individuals who attempt to stifle spontaneity. The film's unswerving anti-authoritarianism is most tellingly conveyed in a brief sequence in which the diminutive headmaster chastises Tabard. A sudden tilt of the camera transforms his rambling paternalistic lecture into an incoherent rant; a seemingly benign patriarch starts raving like a lunatic, ironically invoking the specter of "neurotics and psychopaths." The insane headmaster's concern for the mental health of the baffled student is not only a spectacular example of projection, but is also akin to what Nietzsche termed ressentiment, since the headmaster not only seems to envy the children's spontaneity, but also appears to consider "uniformity a virtue"[79]—he would undoubtedly like to impose the "morality of the herd" on the captive student body. The children's subsequent pillow fight, captured in oneiric slow-motion, is Vigo's aesthetic response—and liberators' antidote—to classroom anomie.

Although a Nietzschean "transvaluation" of herd morality often has conservative rather than radical implications (despite the fact that many anarchists were devout admirers of his work, particularly Emma Goldman), *Zero for Conduct* begins with mere disdain for the bogus virtues of uniformity, but reaches its climax with a radical, if prototypically childlike, rebellion against the established order. The schoolboy's final gesture of revolutionary defiance transforms what some might have viewed as a random series of vignettes into a specifically anarchist critique. At a staid Alumni Day celebration, with representatives of the church and state (a bishop and governor) in attendance, recalcitrant students interrupt the proceedings with catcalls, hurl shoes and homemade weapons at the guests of honor, and make their escape to freedom through the school's roof. Clearly, this joyous rebellion is not merely a negation of one school's dismal regimen, but an attack on authoritarian pedagogy that fuses anti-clerical and anti-statist motifs. Yet despite the fact that the film's ending implicitly conceives of something like an educational variant of Bakunin's autonomous commune as the antidote to repressive schooling, it is not surprising that the open-ended conclu-sion leaves unanswered the question of whether an alternative educational structure or comprehensive "deschooling" offers the most anarchistic solu-tion. Alan Lovell seems to understate the radical implications of *Zero for Conduct*'s ending when he claims that the "status quo has been disturbed but not overthrown."[80] It is true that child-centered pedagogical coups, like the adult political equivalents, might only replace one corrupt, entrenched hierarchy with another. Yet Vigo's film punctures the ideological presupposi-tions of mainstream pedagogy with more success than many sober tracts.

Vigo's final film, *L'Atalante* (1934), can be considered a companion piece to *Zero for Conduct,* since the former film's promotion of the "education of the senses" enhances the latter film's antinomian form of radical pedagogy. The plot is deceptively simple. Jean (Jean Dasté) and Juliette (Dita Parlo), a newlywed couple, take an excursion down the Seine on a dilapidated barge. When Jean, the barge's lackadaisical skipper, is separated from the sprightly Juliette in Paris, the couple are reunited through the intervention of Jean's curmudgeonly colleague, Père Jules (Michel Simon). Despite the film's osten-sible preoccupation with personal fulfillment rather than social transforma-tion, Jean and Juliette's amorous progress is actually inextricable from the particularities of the social fabric. When Juliette becomes separated from her husband, Vigo's camera pans to the unemployed workers who were certainly an unavoidable presence in Depression-era Paris. Vigo's anti-authoritarian political stance is illustrated in a sequence that highlights a thief's attempt to steal Juliette's purse as she buys a railway ticket. For a short time, Vigo's focus is diverted from his protagonist to events more conventional directors would consider peripheral. The middle-class crowd swoops down upon the thief as if they mean to lynch him, the well-fed take their revenge upon a scruffy renegade. Vigo's empathy seems to be split between the downcast Juliette and her pathetic assailant; his ability to extend his compassion beyond a narrow universe of discourse makes his film complex as well as radical.

If the frequently fractious lovers provide *L'Atalante* with its amatory center, Père Jules, played by the extravagantly eccentric Michel Simon, appears to serve as Vigo's benignly grotesque alter ego. Père Jules speaks nostalgically of his days in Caracas "during the revolution," and a tattooed nude on his body contains initials for the slogan "Mort aux vaches" (literally, "Death to cows"—French slang for denouncing the police, "cows" being roughly equivalent to the American epithet "pigs"), which was a motto long cherished by the French poor, and, as Salles Gomes reminds us, adopted by "anarchists in the 1890s."[81] Simon's garbled diction seems only to enhance the character's childlike exuberance: Jules's characteristically anarchist gusto has a kinship with the transgressive revelry of *Zero for Conduct*. Whether Jules is modeling an apron for Juliette or balancing a cigarette in his navel, he exemplifies a life force that corresponds with Vigo's penchant to thumb his nose at all things respectable. Père Jules's magnificently cluttered cabin, with its dusty gramophone and unclassifiable bric-a-brac, serves as a metaphor for a film that is defiantly unclassical and proudly disorganized, or at least not subservient to conventional cinematic teleology. Although his role in reuniting the lovers eventual proves pivotal to the film's highly unschematic structure, the screen time devoted to the frequently half-intoxicated Père Jules's antics does not advance the plot.[82] Marina Warner reduces Jules's role to that of an archetypal "magical helper,"[83] yet his fusion of hedonism and undogmatic radicalism might well be considered exemplary, and could also be hailed for its heterodox pedagogical merit. Diderot, for example, in *Jacques the Fatalist,* praises the "true oracles of Babcic, or the gourd," who can "only be understood through the neck of a bottle."[84] The notion that sagacity can coexist with drunkenness goes against the grain of the puritanical discourse of mainstream pedagogy, but a heretical Western tradition that includes avatars of Babcic, such as Diogenes, Rabelais, and Diderot, tolerates, and even sanctions, a more corporeal mode of learning that might well include the amiably gruff, and astutely tipsy, Père Jules.

True to his anarchist origins, Vigo presents an ambiguous portrait of urban life. A certain anarchist tradition spurns the metropolis as an embryonic "necropolis." Another important current that extends from the Paris Communards of 1871 to contemporary Lower East Side squatters maintains that urban milieus can be reclaimed and revitalized through concerted direct action. Despite the economic ravages that Vigo refers to in *L'Atalante,* the film is something of an urban pastoral. Père Jules expresses a certain ambivalence toward cities when he moans that "the less time we spend in town the better." Yet even he sings the praises of "Paris, city of sin and delight." Jean and Juliette, moreover, are completely captivated by Paris. A peddler flirting with Juliette, the glittering store windows that beckon her, and the cabarets, street urchins, and fortune-tellers that the director lovingly depicts are all emblems of a utopian affirmation that coexists with the poverty and sordidness that are never repressed.

Zero for Conduct and *L'Atalante* belong to an important strain of undogmatic, radical pedagogy. Nevertheless, many critics and filmmakers have found it difficult to resist the temptation to praise Vigo's films as examples of supposedly transhistorical lyricism. Julien Temple's *Vigo—Passion for Life* (1998) is a particularly egregious example. Temple's film largely depoliticizes Vigo and depicts him as a combination of Rimbaudian Romantic and proto-punk rocker. Superficially faithful to the facts recounted in Salles Gomes's biography, Vigo's anarchist lineage is primarily invoked in order to explain the budding filmmaker's oedipal anxiety concerning the murky details of his father's death and anguish engendered by a distant mother. A fleeting glimpse of an issue of *La Guerre Sociale* notwithstanding, the focus is on the intense love affair between Vigo (played unconvincingly by British actor James Frain) and his wife Elisabeth Lozinska (a.k.a. Lydou; impersonated by the French actress Romane Bohringer), a Polish woman the filmmaker met while being treated for tuberculosis at a sanatorium in 1926. The film's hodgepodge of clashing accents and misbegotten madcap episodes appear designed to depict the zaniness of anarchist bohemians; the burdens of political commitment are summed up when Lydu's mother comments on her daughter's turbulent marriage: "That's what you get for marrying an anarchist." Forced merriment notwithstanding, the film is not antic enough to ignore Vigo's indebtedness to anarchist pedagogical traditions. When an anarchist comrade of Vigo's, whose elaborate tattoos bring to mind Père Jules' in *L'Atalante,* encounters a child, he reflects that anarchists envision a world where "teachers will learn from children . . . and parents will not tell children what to do."

Lindsay Anderson's *If . . .* (1968), on the other hand, often hailed as a British reinterpretation of *Zero for Conduct,* suggests something of a critical conundrum since it's neither an example of radical art per se nor a movie that can be dismissed as unabashed commercialism. Curiously enough, while the rhetoric of Anderson's film is at times more strident than Vigo's, *If . . .* is a film in which ostensibly militant sentiments are ultimately defused by essentially conservative trepidations. Anderson frequently called himself an anarchist, but the vagueness of his "anarchy," set alongside the apolitical longing for community exemplified by his study of John Ford, makes it clear that the anti-authoritarianism of *If . . .* is largely the result of a pessimistic disdain for modernity that is not accompanied by a vision of a future. Of course, the imagination of a more genuinely anarchistic director such as Buñuel is also lured by negation and a disgust with the less savory aspects of modern life; but films such as *L'Âge d'or* and *Viridiana* fuse the urge to negate accepted mores with an affirmative transvaluation of established values. *If . . .,* despite a sporadically effective satirical acerbity, opposes malevolent authority figures with cynical rebels who largely mirror, despite wide-eyed rhetoric, the venality of their supposed foes.

Vigo's educational critique is largely successful because of its brilliant marriage of radical style and content. Conversely, *If . . .*—a film in which the archaic, upper-class conventions of the British public school provide allegorical fodder for an indictment of contemporary Britain—suffers from lack of focus because of its reliance upon a nihilistic anti-hero, Mick Travis (played with impish aplomb by Malcolm McDowell), who is an exemplar more of disengagement than of any actual anarchist current.[85] After declaiming that "the world will end very soon" with "black bodies turning into ash," Mick concludes that "violence and revolution are the only pure acts." Lounging around in his room, festooned with nude pin-ups and posters of Mao, Mick's apocalyptic ruminations sum up the film's hedge-betting; apparently, we are meant to acknowledge the perverse allure of these sentiments while simultaneously muttering our disapproval. While Anderson realizes that "people persistently misunderstood the term anarchistic," and "think it just means wildly chucking bombs about,"[86] Mick's pseudo-radicalism appears inspired by a mere inversion of his school's reverence for God and country.

The "anarchism" of *If . . .* may be ill-defined, but Anderson's rather impersonal direction of David Sherwin's script often functions like a coy subversion of Matthew Arnold's famous antitheses—culture and anarchy. As Gerald Graff observes, the twentieth century has inherited the pedagogical, and cultural, quagmire that Arnold analyzes: "a loss of common understandings that had been taken for granted by a social elite."[87] The categories of culture and anarchy are so nebulous that they are nearly self-deconstructive, but Arnold's use of the word "anarchy," with its vague disdain for Jacobinism apparently alludes to the growing ire of the working class, while "culture" is conceived of as a modern integration of ancient erudition with a modern, statist pragmatism capable of defusing radical passions. To a large extent, this agenda is similar to the ideology of the nineteenth- and twentieth-century British public school that is the object of satire in *If . . .*; Anderson's implicitly anti-Arnoldian barbs are among the film's strongest moments. The housemaster's injunction, "work, play, but don't mix the two," mimics Arnold's contention that the antinomies he names "Hebraism" and "Hellenism"—terms wrenched from their historical contexts that vaguely refer to the domains of morality and art—must remain in equilibrium, but should never precipitously converge. Yet both Arnold's Victorian ardor, as well as the public-school ideology partly influenced by its prescriptions, visibly implode as this nightmare version of *Tom Brown's Schooldays* progresses. If Arnold viewed education as an important bulwark against "philistinism"— admittedly another term he fails to define with much precision—the liberal elitism of *If . . .*'s headmaster seems to combine the smugness of *Culture and Anarchy*'s disdain for the rabble (called the "populace" by Arnold) with a pronounced philistine disregard for traditional pedagogical pursuits. As a long-shot captures the energetic young headmaster sauntering down the campus walk, he muses that "education in Britain" resembles a "chic Cinder-

ella . . . scantily clad and interfered with." Mingling sexist jibes with mixed
metaphors, he urges that the school's stringent standards keep pace with the
world of television, mini-skirts, and "the huge sacrifice" of Britain's wars.
Arnold's high-minded desire for a common culture may have been given a
left-wing spin by the critiques of Richard Hoggart and Raymond Williams,
but it has become more common for *Culture and Anarchy*'s modernizing,
and essentially conservative, impulses to congeal into the technocratic gusto
personified by Anderson's headmaster. After the slightly crazed educator's
peroration, in which he proclaims the school an "exciting place," a cut to a
stained-glass window featuring a Tudor patriarch's stern visage illustrates,
in cinematic shorthand, the transition from hierarchical values to a more
fluid hybrid culture. Inevitably, Arnold's vision of canonical wisdom has
been superseded by a popular culture that is alternately, and sometimes
simultaneously, democratizing and reifying.

In what is perhaps the crowning inanity of *Culture and Anarchy*'s opaque
rhetoric, Arnold contends that the English "reliance on muscular Christianity, . . . on coal, on wealth," is "wholesomely counteracted by culture . . .
drawing the human race closer to perfection."[88] In flights of self-consuming
verbiage, Arnold both distances himself from bourgeois values and elevates
the disinterestedness that bourgeois culture both pays tribute to and ultimately inhibits. These schizoid cultural imperatives, important components
of the English public school's ideological coloration, permeate many of *If . . .*'s
vignettes. Despite the supposedly exalted intellectual standards of Anderson's
archetypal public school, anti-intellectualism is the norm, and sports possess
a near-sacramental value. The classroom sequences, instead of showcasing
what Arnold termed "the best that is known and thought in the world," regale
us with semi-absurdist pedagogical non sequiturs: a history master bases
his entire lesson around one of J. H. Plumb's more gnomic utterances, while
a cleric's mathematics lesson is taken up more with furtive fondling of his
pupils than with trigonometry. Although the teachers are merely sad and
ineffectual, the student prefects or school "whips" are sadistically jingoistic.
At one point, Denson, a whip whose sneering hauteur proves repellent to
Mick, defends his dictatorial regime by proclaiming that he "serves the nation." The whips' propensity to coat their yearnings for schoolboy power with
altruistic maxims recalls the imperialist idealism of Rudyard Kipling's poem
"If"; Kipling's exhortation prodding Britain to accept its imperial destiny
reaches its crescendo in the poem's penultimate line, "Yours is the Earth
and everything that's in it." As a recent study by Robert J. C. Young makes
clear, Arnold's conception of culture cannot be divorced from imperialism's
racialist preoccupations; Young stresses the affinities between the scientific

"harmonizing power" that Arnold "ascribes to culture itself" in *Culture and Anarchy* and the racialist philology that serves as ideological ballast in his lesser-known work on Celtic literature.[89]

A few of Anderson's cinematic embellishments subtly undermine the imperial longing for racial homogeneity. As Mick's rebelliousness intensifies, the recurrent strains of an African mass, *Missa Luba,* on the film's soundtrack link the hero's potentially radical mischievousness with a desire to escape the constricting accoutrements of the British "culture" extolled by *Culture and Anarchy.* Yet *If . . .*'s rather unwieldy pastiche of Brecht[90] and Buñuel often seems to borrow heavily from more mild, traditional attacks on public schools, particularly novels such as Alec Waugh's *The Loom of Youth.* Mick's anti-authoritarianism, as well as the film's concluding *putsch,* is in many respects more an aesthetic than a political phenomenon; *If . . .,* despite its radical patina, shares an affinity with Waugh's extremely demure critique of public schools, an apolitical indictment of schoolboy athleticism and a chaste celebration of repressed adolescent homosexuality. Elizabeth Sussex notes that Anderson harbored a great deal of affection for the school—Cheltenham College[91]—that inspired his film, and a sequence in which the near-fascistic whip Rowntree gazes at a young boy, Bobby Phillips, oddly resembles Waugh's gentle churlishness, a reminder of the difficulty of "break[ing] loose from the humbug embrace of the Victorian/Edwardian age."[92] Even Summerhill largely derived its appeal from inverting the conventions of the public school, the nominal bad object of progressive education's discourse. Neill, although well-versed in the work of Wilhelm Reich, was also familiar with socialist and anarchist traditions,[93] a fact that differentiated his pedagogical rebellion from the primarily libidinal revolution implemented by Mick at the end of *If . . .* Unlike *Zero for Conduct* or *L'Atalante, If . . .* provides a schematic portrait of largely pre-political anarchist impulses, but its half-hearted riposte to the status quo and restrained, derivative style prevent the film from being a bona fide example of cinematic anarchist pedagogy.

Homo Academicus and the Dilemma of the Anarchist Intellectual

Without accusing himself of outright hypocrisy, the anarchist academic Kingsley Widmer once remarked that American universities "are hardly appropriate places for anarchists . . . for among the obvious criteria for libertarians of almost every shade would be opposition to hierarchy, to large bureaucratic control, to direct service of the state, to exploitative corporate subservience."[94] This implicit autocritique is shared by many anarchist and Marxist intellectuals who flourish or languish in academia. Yet from a pedagogical vantage point, the specific quandary of the anarchist intellectual involves inevitable dual loyalties: to the radical kernel within actually existing universities on the one hand, and the related impulse to apply the arguments of militant deschooling to the university's bureaucratic apparatus on the other. In fact, both serious and popular studies devoted to the contemporary plight of intellectuals are usually distinguished by attempts to divide, with varying degrees of accuracy and cogency, the intelligentsia into opposing camps with divergent interests and ideologies. Consequently, for Zygmunt Bauman, intellectuals can be divided into "legislators" and "interpreters," while Antonio Gramsci differentiates between "traditional" and "organic" intellectuals; Russell Jacoby perceives a widening chasm between "academic" and "public" intellectuals, while Bruce Robbins—implicitly taking issue with J. P. Nettl's claim that "any meaningful concept of intellectual must . . . be free of all forms of institutional attachment"—opposes an ideal of a supposedly "cosmopolitan," but nonetheless radically engaged, academic intellectual to what he considers the chimerical celebration of free-floating, unattached intellectuals. At times, these competing categorizations and demarcations—all formulated by commentators who are themselves academics—appear to partake of varying degrees of self-justification and self-flagellation. Yet a writer like Jacoby believes that academics' self-legitimation reeks of bad faith, while Robbins maintains that the very effort of academics to critique the professionalization of intellectuals is itself an example of misguided self-deception.[95] Conversely, Widmer, the anarchist academic torn by ambivalence, unsurprisingly blames what he perceives as an ongoing academic malaise on the division of labor produced by increasing professionalization and specialization.

Whatever the strengths and weaknesses of these disparate positions, it is indisputable that they are fundamentally continuations of the late-nineteenth-century debates between Marx and Bakunin. Bakunin's musings on the role of intellectuals can often be obliquely discerned in contemporary efforts to disentangle the pedagogical value of committed intellectual discourse from the impediments of bureaucratic inertia. Some of the contradictions of recent debates, moreover, can be traced to analogous contradictions within Bakunin's own work; Paul Avrich's study of Russian anarchists, for example, stresses the fact that, unlike Marx, Bakunin "assigned a major role to . . . disaffected students and intellectuals, alienated from the existing social order and from the uneducated masses as well."[96] Nonetheless, he mistrusted positivists such as Comte, as well as Marxists, labeling them "priests of science" who represented a "privileged church of the mind and superior education."[97]

Although Bakunin's mistrust of scientific hegemony can be discerned in the musings of contemporary radical ecologists and libertarian socialists, H. G. Wells's belief that "technicians, scientific workers, medical men . . . aviators, and operating engineers" represented "the best material for constructive revolution in the West"[98] was, for many years, the dominant current in mainstream left discourse. One version of Wells's technological utopia, albeit a cartoonish, hyperbolic variant, can be disinterred from William Cameron Menzies's film *Things to Come* (1936). Although Wells thought that all of his reservations concerning supposedly benign technocratic dictatorships were excised from the script by Menzies, this fanciful version of scientism run amok is undoubtedly the pop culture version of the positivist priesthood postulated by thinkers like Comte. Of course, a less-reverential view of the cult of science can be found in the Marx Brothers' *Horse Feathers* (dir. Norman Z. McLeod, 1933), in which colleges that care for little else but winning football games bear the names of two of the most revered nineteenth-century scientists—Huxley and Darwin. The idea that intellectuals represent a new priestly class—the subject of extensive theoretical elaboration by Pierre Bourdieu, nominally a Marxist—has its roots in Bakunin's railings against savants. In a similar vein, Alvin Gouldner observes "how the Frankfurt School converges . . . with Bakunin . . . Jürgen Habermas's quest for the 'ideal speech situation' . . . is a literal descendant less of Marx than of Bakunin's struggle against the New Class's educational privileges."[99]

Although Habermas's domination-free "ideal speech situation" has often been castigated as an ersatz utopian ideal—a souped-up version of an academic seminar—several films chronicling the evolution of the student movement and the New Left provide concrete evidence of tangible aspirations toward a "speech situation" that would at least be somewhat more ideal than the illiberal "liberalism" that provoked the ire of 1960s radicals. Mark Kitchell's *Berkeley in the Sixties* (1991) featured moving footage of Mario Savio, the Berkeley Free Speech movement's most influential "leader" (although Savio himself spurned such appellations), urging his comrades to "put [their] bodies on the levers" of the bureaucratic machine that was engendering unprecedented alienation among affluent members of the younger generation: the group groomed to be the future power elite. The Newsreel Collective's *Columbia Revolt* (1968), a film in which the personal testimonies of students involved in mass occupations take on the character of mini-epiphanies, gave voice to members of the embryonic "knowledge class" questioning the premises of the multiversities that embraced them as future leaders. The resistance of Berkeley students to University of California president Clark Kerr's view of his institution as a "knowledge factory" inspired Carl Davidson to promote "student syndicalism." Just as "the syndicalist unions worked for industrial democracy and workers' control," Davidson urged that students agitate for "student control," not a tepid "liberalization" that reflected mere paternalistic concern.[100]

If it seems that Davidson's merging of the tradition of working-class syndicalism with the concerns of students at an elite university was audacious (and oxymoronic only if one thinks that there is something irrational about the supposed beneficiaries of corporate capitalism taking up the cudgel of institutional resistance), even more difficult conundrums confront celebrated intellectuals and academics who constructively bite the institutional hand that feeds them. The career of Noam Chomsky, probably the best-known American intellectual and academic with anarchist sympathies, exemplifies the spirit of what could be labeled faculty syndicalism, since, as a pathbreaking social scientist, he has made a serious effort to undermine the ideology shared by our contemporary "priests of science." Chomsky's explicitly Bakuninist refusal to fulfill his expected function as a "savant" has even been termed "anti-intellectual." Nevertheless, Chomsky has proudly embraced anarchism's propensity to deny any "position of power or privilege to the intelligentsia," since, if anarchism were realized, "people whose major professional concern is knowledge and the application of knowledge would have no special opportunity to manage the society."[101]

Given Chomsky's reluctance to don the vestments of the intellectual secular priesthood, his near-canonization in Mark Achbar and Peter Wintonick's documentary *Manufacturing Consent: Noam Chomsky and the Media* is—despite the filmmakers' unassailably good intentions—slightly odd. The film's opening image—a Canadian shopping mall's huge bank of television monitors broadcasting interviews with Chomsky as pedestrians saunter by—ably sums up *Manufacturing Consent*'s own stylistic and political limitations. Throughout the film, the filmmakers make an admirable case that intellectual discourse need not be rarefied and inaccessible. Apparently, the multiscreen display of the calm, lucid intellectual's image aims to confound our preconceptions, radicalizing a medium that is most often used for commercial purposes. But as the film progresses, it becomes increasingly difficult—despite the filmmakers' stated desire to turn conformist postmodernist irony into a form of populist critique—to view this kind of gimmickry as a form of de-reification. Chomsky, despite his earnest desire to reject the power traditionally offered to celebrated intellectuals, is constructed as a star. This odd transmutation of the media critic into documentary star became the focus of a skeptical review of the film by Paul Mattick Jr,[102] a piece that provoked an unusually intense riposte from Achbar and Wintonick, no doubt because they were particularly queasy that a leftist and fellow Chomsky admirer felt scant admiration for their film's aesthetic strategies. In fact, *Manufacturing Consent's* crowd-pleasing approach is not alone as a valiant if not entirely successful attempt to render intellectual discourse in populist terms. In certain respects, the film unwittingly recapitulates many of the paradoxes of intellectual life, and it is not difficult to link the film's aesthetic to certain ongoing pedagogical quandaries. A radical—particularly an anarchist—intellectual, such as Chomsky, must straddle the extremes of Max Weber's chimerical ideal of a university that maintains circumscribed, value-free disciplines and Bourdieu's claim that post-'68 academics who, *pace* Weber, decided to embrace an *engagé* classroom stance could not escape the professional demands of their "*habitus*—a series of shared social dispositions and cognitive structures."[103] The journey from Weber's view of academia to Bourdieu's traverses the distance from modern optimism to a skeptical reductionism that is indebted to both neo-Marxism and a certain strain of postmodern thought. Weber thought that the "dissemination of value-judgments" encouraged "the continuing power of conservative circles over university education."[104] But in an era when university life foregrounds an ongoing battle between defenders of conservative tradition and the representatives of the postmodern left, Bourdieu's *homo academicus* finds himself mired in a university bureaucracy that preoccupies itself with "cultural production . . . whose oldest paradigm is obviously the church."[105]

Being neither a conservative intellectual nor an exponent of neo-Marxism or postmodernism, Chomsky finds himself in a somewhat anomalous position. He obviously cannot posit an absolute continuity between his scientific work and his politics, since such naive intellectual conflations have led to the horrors of Lysenko's "socialist biology" and Stalin's Soviet linguistics. Yet, as a disciple of Bakunin, Chomsky can obviously not assume that scientific inquiry can possibly remain "value-free." C. P. Otero remarks that Chomsky's "cartesian linguistics," "if developed into a science, might give definitive justification for the sort of society Bakunin had in mind."[106] Whether intentionally or not, Achbar and Wintonick undermine this effort by their prominent inclusion of a clip in which the dean of studies of Malaspina College in British Columbia unironically invokes the *New York Times Book Review's* characterization of Chomsky as "arguably the most important intellectual alive today" when introducing him to a student audience. Although, after striding to the lectern, Chomsky himself deflates the pomposity of this description by pointing out that the *Times* commentator also derided his "terrible" views on foreign policy, the film's celebratory view of this activist intellectual is not far from the hyperbolic prose of journalistic encomiums.

In a mood of slight self-aggrandizement, Bourdieu alludes to Marx's obser-vation that "some individuals managed to liberate themselves so completely from the positions assigned to them in a social space that they could compre-hend that space as a whole, and transmit their vision to those who were still prisoners of that structure." He drily suggests that "the sociologist" can obtain a greater sense of the totality "without thereby laying claim to such absolute vision."[107] Although Chomsky himself is much too modest to assume that he inhabits an empyrean vantage point outside the nexus of domination, many of the filmmakers' attempts to fuse MTV-like glibness with documentary probity seem to enshrine Chomsky as an intellectual sovereign who has in fact extricated himself from the "apparatus of domination" through a sheer act of will; one man's individual heroism, not a systemic dilemma, becomes the primary focus. On a superficial, mildly amusing level, this surfaces in a sequence in which footage of Chomsky out-debating the Dutch minister of defense is intercut with a clip of a boxer knocking out his opponent.

The film's incorporation of snippets from Chomsky's televised debate (ac-tually a polite exchange on Dutch television) with Michel Foucault, however, misses an opportunity to assess the respective contributions of these thinkers without being blinded by starry-eyed hype. Oddly, in a film that portrays Chomsky in near-hagiographic terms, a brief section that features a clip from the debate on Dutch television fails to convey the fatuousness of many of Foucault's political pronouncements. To be sure, Chomsky's faith in the boundless potential of enlightened—and Enlightenment-style—rationalism might well be questioned, even if he makes an extremely cogent case for this tradition's essentially radical impetus. Legitimate doubts concerning the viability of Cartesian rationalism notwithstanding, viewers of *Manufactur-ing Consent* have no idea of the odd amalgamation of Nietzsche and Mao subscribed to by Foucault in this debate, a much cruder political critique than the more nuanced analysis presented in books such as *Madness and Civilization* and *Discipline and Punish*. In portions of the exchange not in-cluded in this film, Foucault responds to Chomsky's reiteration of classical anarcho-syndicalist precepts and his belief that "a fundamental element of human nature is the need for creative work" by uncritically invoking Mao Tse-tung's distinction between "bourgeois human nature" and "proletarian nature." He argues, in an ultra-Leninist fashion, that the proletariat's need to command power is more important than the possibility that a just society might emerge from that seizure of power.[108] Foucault reveals a surprising blind spot in failing to acknowledge his paradoxical juxtaposition of radical philosophical skepticism with Leninist (if his deference to Mao is not a mere rhetorical gesture) authoritarian certitude.[109] In all fairness, at a later date, when Maoism was no longer in vogue, Foucault's longing for "the intellectual who will destroy whatever is obvious and universal and who will seek out and reveal the weak spots, the openings, the lines of force . . . to be found amidst the constraints of the present day" seems implicitly anarchistic, even if these sentiments are far removed from Chomsky's brand of radicalism.[110]

Foucault believed that it was salutary that "intellectuals have given up trying to be prophets," and, despite a divergent philosophical position, Chomsky's Bakuninist strain imbues him with a skeptical view of members of the "knowledge class." While it is possible to isolate his linguistic theory as unquestionably groundbreaking, he would be the first to acknowledge that his anarcho-syndicalist views are not original, but part of a vital, still-evolving tradition. *Manufacturing Consent,* however, tends to downplay Chomsky's participation in a community of scholars by including interview footage that emphasizes his prodigious intellect, not his affinities with other intellectuals. This tendency is especially blatant in a brief audio clip from a BBC interview with Chomsky conducted by Jonathan Steinberg, in which the linguist–activist replies that he did most of the essential research for his important demolition of the standard view of the Spanish Civil War, "Objectivity and Liberal Scholarship," when he was twelve years old. For the most part, it is quite possible for viewers to have the mistaken impression that Chomsky's libertarian socialism is sui generis, when in fact he has often stressed his indebtedness to the tradition of Bakunin, Goldman, and Rudolf Rocker.

As Mattick points out, the film's most valuable sequences detail the media's shameful neglect of U.S. complicity with human rights violations in East Timor. These sequences focus less on Chomsky's individual genius than does the bulk of the film; a sober investigative drive that resembles the energetic muckraking of now-defunct publications such as *Covert Action Quarterly* and the *Lies of Our Times* briefly supplants the obsession with one man's, unquestionably admirable, career. Unlike much of *Manufacturing Consent,* the goal of the East Timor sequence is closely aligned to the work of media analysts such as Herbert Schiller and Chomsky himself, as well as scrappy media collectives such as Paper Tiger Television.[111] Perhaps not coincidentally, Paper Tiger has often produced tapes featuring frequently scathing critiques of institutions and media organs by anarchists such as Murray Bookchin and Tuli Kupferberg, who share much of Chomsky's demystifying verve.

Some years ago, Alvin Gouldner delineated the paradox of the modern university's function as "the single institution from which most . . . ideologues derive their livings," while also being "the largest single site for the production and storage of *anti*-establishment ideologists . . . of *both* science and ideology"[112] "Anti-establishment ideologists" like Chomsky must now navigate between the university, at once extremely insular and intimately tied to the state, and a public sphere in which the traditional ideal of community is eroding. To alleviate this communal erosion, Gouldner, influenced by the Frankfurt School, advocated a "media critical politics," while in the 1990s Mark Dery proposed "culture jamming"—direct action against "an ever more intrusive technoculture whose operant mode is the manufacture of consent through the manipulation of symbols."[113] While the film entitled *Manufacturing Consent* can be viewed as partly a portrait of an intellectual who self-consciously attempts to deploy (to use Bourdieu's terminology) his "cultural power" to deflate the pretensions of the state's own more formidable power, it fails to examine reflexively its infatuation with the aura of celebrity that surrounds even so-called "oppositional" thinkers. It may not be advisable to put our faith wholly in the pronouncements of intellectuals, since in the post-1968 period we have witnessed the tragicomic trajectory of, among others, André Glucksmann and Bernard-Henri Lévy—chroniclers of the zeitgeist who went from uncritical cheerleading for Althusserian Maoism to equally unnuanced trumpeting of the gospel according to Solzhenitsyn. Neither what Karl Mannheim termed an "unattached" intellectual nor a professional cog in the wheel of a vanguardist "interpretive community," Chomsky has skillfully avoided being seduced by either right-wing or left-wing authoritarianism.

In the post-Occupy era, anarchist academics such as the anthropologist David Graeber, among others, have also succeeded in bypassing the pitfalls of being mired in the role of "Homo Academicus." After being denied tenure at Yale for reasons that were unassailably political, Graeber has skillfully navigated between academia and activism (for example, support of the Rojava Revolution as well as well as Occupy.) The example of Graeber, as well as the careers of a host of lesser-known anarchist academics, proves that the Chomsky enshrined in *Manufacturing Consent* is not an anomalous lone wolf.

Pedagogy beyond the Classroom: Dutch Squatting and the Battle of Tompkins Square Park

Anarchists have often fused pedagogical aspirations with larger economic and social goals. For this reason, anarchist pedagogy extends far beyond the confines of the classroom or academic conference. Paulo Freire's concept of *conscientização* ("the awakening of critical consciousness"[114]) is supremely applicable to the educational pursuits of anarchists. Freire's interest in teaching literacy skills to the Brazilian poor is inseparable from a belief that learners should "make history," while continuing to be transformed by the world they inhabit.

A similar effort to fuse anti-authoritarian pedagogy with activist concerns can be observed in some of the videotapes chronicling the Dutch squatters' movement directed by Hanneke Willemse and Jan Groen, members of the Kontrast collective. Produced in the early 1980s, these ad hoc documentaries—with names that are defiant, such as *Two Years of Resistance,* or mournful, such as *You Can't Live in a Tank*—possess an intentionally provisional quality; often shown to small squatters' affinity groups planning a strategy for the future, they were not designed to have enduring aesthetic importance but were intended for short-term pedagogical purposes. *Two Years of Resistance,* for example, was made during a period of two years, and the filmmakers occasionally changed their focus in response to feedback they received from screening the work in progress at cafés and meeting halls. It could be termed an instructional tape, since it provides practical advice on how to occupy a house, unite members of a squat, and resist police intervention. This tape is significant for documenting a transitional period within the ranks of the Dutch squatters, a period when morale was low since police informers had infiltrated many of the squats. The movement appears to have had isolated moments of triumph, as well as considerable periods of internecine conflict and dissent. Since the movement was at a low ebb, a particularly despondent squatter comments that, despite democratic aspirations, one can find oneself acquiring certain assumptions but eventually "overthrowing" them owing to an increasing feeling of "senselessness." Quite reasonably, he observes that the "senseless repression of the squatters" movements became an excuse for a general repression of social movements.

Een vondelbrug te ver (*A Vondelbridge Too Far*), on the other hand, a film chronicling the police evacuation of squatters from Amsterdam's Vondelstraat in 1980, is considerably more upbeat, despite the fact that it conveys the anguish of an equally demoralizing period of resistance. A more affirmative tone is struck because of the unusual amount of cooperation between videographers and subjects; there is no pretense of false objectivity. One young man comments that the "squatters want to control their own images . . . creating a 'symmetry' between activism and 'the filmmaking process.'"Although the tape documents the government's almost completely successful evacuation of the Vondelstraat squats, the fact that many of the participants remain determined to seize buildings in other neighborhoods and make concrete links between their plight and "the conditions of immigrants and workers" amplifies this temporary setback for colleagues and potential recruits, and proves that even a seemingly crushing defeat can retain at least a pedagogical importance—debate is encouraged within a community that actively influences the content of these documentaries.

Although Clayton Patterson, the videographer whose tape *Tompkins Square Park Police Riot* (1988) contained incontrovertible evidence that an August 1988 mêlée at one of New York's countercultural landmarks was instigated by the police, had a considerably different relationship to his subjects than the Dutch collective (like the better-known Rodney King tape, this documentary was not part of a programmatic movement or affinity group, but was shot fortuitously), his work could also be considered an example of anarchistic community pedagogy. One of our wittiest journalists once observed that "these days, all art aspires to the condition of real estate."[115] Writing about the art scene in the 1990s, I observed that, although it's not difficult to concede that Steven Spielberg's films have become the cinematic equivalents of Trump Tower, the same sort of aesthetic gentrification is apparent in the tendency of even the supposedly "oppositional" realm of the avant-garde to be sucked into the high-priced real estate of swanky gallery "spaces." In the twenty-first century, much of this pseudo-oppositional energy has been diverted into faux-utopian schemes that conceived of the internet as a virtual film where artistic creativity can flourish. Nevertheless, as Astra Taylor points out, the yen to have a constantly accessible flow of free online "content" is tied more to right-wing libertarianism than it is to anything resembling a new definition of the "commons."[116]

Patterson's work, however, despite being shot on a format considered clunky in the digital era, can be cited as an intriguing counterexample. His nearly four-hour video chronicle of what might be considered an embryonic "urban revolution" cannot be facilely assigned to any one of the now moldy subdivisions of political documentary. Patterson's tape, however unwittingly, explodes Louis Marcorelles's distinction between American direct cinema's rather naive appeal to authenticity and the quasi-Brechtian strategies of directors such as Jean Rouch.[117] The tape shares direct cinema's concern with immediacy and the contours of the "life-world," but Patterson's low-key, but still apparent, participation in the spirit of communal solidarity as a member of the Lower East Side community is very different from the anthropological detachment of filmmakers such as Pennebaker and Leacock. Patterson is neither a leader nor a bystander but part of the struggle, and his unwillingness to hide behind a veil of passionless objectivity gives his tape, despite its transparent artlessness, a kinship with the Rouch–Godard tradition of committed reflexivity. Nineteenth-century writers and commentators such as Henry Mayhew, and recent documentarians such as Frederick Wiseman, have attempted to explicate urban strife from the clinical perspective of the outsider.[118] Patterson's tape is distinctive in that it is the work of a community activist who, in a casually pedagogical spirit, informs the community of the results of homelessness and corporate greed (the most recent fruits of what has been called "the recapitalization of the city") without the condescension of the traditional participant-observer. Patterson's compulsion to expose himself to the consequences of the riot makes him vulnerable to the police aggression he is chronicling, and a police assault on fellow video artist Paul Garrin[119] is in fact a prominent sequence in Patterson's tape.

Despite the fact that many Lower East Side activists might be labeled "lifestyle"[120] rather than working-class anarchists, there is little doubt that 1988's summer of discontent represented an attempt, however inchoate and untheorized, to puncture the logic of capital. Undoubtedly, as Colin Ward is at pains to point out, squatters' movements, particularly in Europe, have "taken a variety of forms . . . in Turin . . . a bitterly fought working-class struggle . . . in Berlin, a battle against redevelopment for the well-off . . . in Amsterdam a manifestation of the counterculture."[121] The New York squatters' denunciation of gentrification shares much with the anarcho-punk alliance of West Germany's Autonomen movement and the last gasp of the 1960s alternative culture in Amsterdam. In certain respects, this type of anarchist self-activity is reminiscent of the desire to reappropriate social space that inspired both the French Revolution and the Paris Commune of 1871. The Commune, for example, urged the "permanent intervention of citizens in communal affairs, by the free expression of their ideas and the free defense of their interests." Manuel Castells's[122] contention that the Commune was a movement not of the industrial proletariat but of an eclectic agglutination of social groups that directed their rage against the gendarme and landlord rather than the corporate boss has echoes in the quintessentially urban tenor of the Tompkins Square Park events. Anarchist internationalism prompted a dissident group in Poland to express solidarity with the Lower East Side's "alternative culture people,"[123] proving that what Edward Soja labels the "politics of spatiality"[124] unites East and West.

Many of these currents, particularly the radical urbanism of squatting and the anarcho-punk alliance, coalesce in *Tompkins Square Park Police Riot*. In many respects, Patterson's realization of the democratic possibilities of video technology satisfies Douglas Kellner's criterion for the development of a pedagogy to develop "critical media literacy"—the nurturing of "oppositional subcultures and alternatives to media culture."[125] True to an oppositional conception of media pedagogy, the tape provides a remarkably accurate portrait of the ebb and flow of state violence. Sporadic, seemingly spontaneous outbursts are evident, as well as eerily quiet lulls. Patterson's lightweight camera is in almost constant motion, and at times we are presented with a frenetic blur of pavement, blue uniforms, horses, and blood. As the tape progresses, several basic patterns of visual choreography emerge. The camera zooms in to capture the impact of police attacks, remains in close-up for the testimony of witnesses, and pans from stone-faced police on horseback to animated demonstrators to illustrate the chasm between an indigenous population and what amounts to an occupying army. The occasional low-angle shots—and the perpetual drone of an overhead helicopter—remind the spectator of the programmatic nature of the violence, engendered more by meticulously planned surveillance than by the impetuous errors of judgment invoked by Mayor Koch and Police Commissioner Ward. The numerous shots of police vans interspersed throughout Patterson's tape are not gratuitous. *The Shadow*, a Lower East Side anarchist newspaper, reported evidence of police "trouble"[126] several days before the police riot, revealing that violence "from the bottom up" is often spontaneous; violence ordained from above is rarely the result of mere brute instinct. The tape's soundtrack records many of these contrasting motifs. Slogans such as "Hell no, we won't go" (the antiwar chant displaced into another context) and "Horse shit out of the park" have a near-incantatory quality, while the police retorts of "Clear the street" and "Do you think this is some fucking game?" seem both half-hearted and impersonal.

In many respects, recent video guerrillas such as Clayton Patterson have partially fulfilled Hans Magnus Enzensberger's prognostication that the "new media" have the potential to be deployed as a "means of production," not merely "means of consumption." Enzensberger felt that this transition from passive consumption to an active process in which citizens could become "agents of history" was contingent upon a socialist transformation.[127] In the midst of an analysis of the strengths and weaknesses of the Dutch squatters' movement, Stephen Englander comes to the conclusion that "debilitating re-cuperation was . . . facilitated by naive, uncritical, and sacrificial engagement with the media." If *Tompkins Square Park Police Riot* can be regarded as an example of media pedagogy that transcends the boundaries of the classroom, it is because this tape remained on the periphery of the mainstream media, refusing to contribute to its capacity for endless recuperation.[128] Like many examples of community video, Patterson's work should inspire restrained optimism; his successful experiment in guerrilla video confirms the veracity of Élisée Reclus's view that "Geography is not an immutable thing. It is made, it is remade every day; at each instant, it is modified by men's actions."[129]

An Avant-Garde Pedagogy?

The rupture between reformist pedagogy and the anarchist alternative can be illustrated with the assistance of two prototypical cinematic examples:

François Truffaut's *L'Enfant sauvage* (*The Wild Child,* 1969) and Luis Buñuel's *Las Hurdes* (*Land Without Bread,* 1932). Truffaut's fictionalized re-creation of the "wild boy of Aveyron's saga" is an archetypal narrative of Enlightenment meliorism. Early in Truffaut's film, the transition from untamed, arboreal landscape, an early home for "wild child" Victor, to Dr. Jean Itard's study, well stocked with diagrams of the human brain and other documents of the empirical sciences, foregrounds the unquestioned authority of the humane, redemptive teacher. Armed with the discoveries of Locke and Condillac, the indisputably well-intentioned Itard has little doubt that his teaching will tame his student's "savagery." Itard regards himself as the pedagogical conduit who will allow his charge to acquire language and become a mature, responsible member of society. *Land Without Bread,* on the other hand, reveals the exploitative rationale that often lies behind the facade of reformist education. Buñuel's documentary exposé of the conditions suffered by the inhabitants of one of Spain's poorest, most isolated regions mocks the pretensions of a curriculum, approved by the "liberal" Republic of the early 1930s, in which children are encouraged to forget their hunger pangs and remember that they "should respect their neighbor's property" and concentrate on the fact that "the sum of the angles of a triangle is equal to two right angles." As Freddy Buache suggests,[130] this parody of documentary propriety can be viewed as an allegorical response to the Republic's betrayal of its supposedly humane mission—a betrayal that entailed unyielding hostility to the CNT and the aspirations of anarcho-syndicalists. An article in the anarchist journal *Libertarian Education* observed that "liberal education results in the tacit acceptance and defense of established values . . . and sees the need to be civilized as the broad-based need to become more middle-class," while anarchist education "sees the freedom to be human as necessarily lying with the liberation of society from class."[131] *The Wild Child* is essentially a Rousseauistic fable—"the reflective master takes it upon himself to facilitate the unreflective life of the child, until such time as the pupil is ready for initiation in the art of reflection."[132] Moving beyond liberal humanism, *Land Without Bread* assails the process of "cultural reproduction" triggered by a distorted, if nonetheless recognizable, version of the Enlightenment legacy.

Recent exemplars of postmodern theory generally espouse a more cautious pedagogical credo.[133] Whatever the limitations or vagaries of "applied grammatology," this educational approach was implicitly forecast by avant-garde filmmakers. The Lettrist director Isidore Isou's *Traité de bave et d'éternité* (*Venom and Eternity,* 1951)[134] is an example of applied grammatology *avant la lettre.* Isou's film is a mock-bildungsroman in which the young protagonist deserts the classroom for the refuge of the cinema. Despite the fact that the hero clings to a rather conventional aestheticism, his expulsion from the Communist Party is one of the film's pivotal events: a crisis of conscience (the character refers to his "lost salvation" in voice-over) that looks forward to the next generation's disillusionment with the conservative strictures of the PCF. The young cinephile loathes both Hollywood and Soviet cinema, and his unquestionably pedagogical suggestion of a cinematic "anti-grammar" has obvious parallels with the attempts to reformulate cinematic language in the wake of the eruption of 1968, *Venom and Eternity* spends considerably more time smashing venerable avant-garde idols like Breton and Cocteau than searching for concrete political alternatives to Stalinism. Its "anti-grammar," like Ulmer's, is radical on the level of the signifier, but remains essentially a flamboyant performance.

Instead of being dazzled by academic thespians, it is likely that children, adolescents, and university students will continue to bypass traditional hierarchical education, as well as its supposedly radical avant-gardist variant, by making their own films and videos. Tuli Kupferberg and Sylvia Topp's collections of children's writings were a literary forerunner of this now embryonic tendency, even if Kupferberg admitted that the selections were often made to please adult tastes.[135] In the 1990s, as video technology became more widely disseminated, a film such as Ilan Ziv and Peter Kinoy's *Teen Dreams* (1994) illustrated the inevitable gulf between adult sensibilities and the young video documentarists, laudably given the opportunity to transcribe their own dreams and anxieties. Ziv and Kinoy encouraged the young "video storytellers"—a homeless young woman, a young man from Philadelphia who survived life in a gang, and an East Harlem teenager who plans a reconciliation with his father—to recount their experiences with unsparing honesty. Even if the teenagers' contributions remain, compared to commercial productions, unpolished and noteworthy for their raw immediacy, there is still the fact that professional, if not particularly slick, editing alters the result. Without denying the producers' good intentions, it is also true that Kinoy and Ziv are credited as the nominal *auteurs,* despite the fact that they continually deferred attention to their young protégés.

The subsequent ascendancy of social media in the 2000s at least allowed young people some nominal opportunities to circumvent established channels—without even the assistance of well-meaning adults. For example, Vine, a now-defunct mobile app enabled teenagers to craft frequently amusing six-second videos and, according to one commentator, "served as a much-needed way for communities of color to mock and respond to stereotypes about themselves, while safely expressing anxiety about police violence, racism, and other threats to black lives."[136] While a fair amount of Vine's content was frivolous or apolitical, it did offer an enclave for African American young people to respond to police violence and was, in its own humble fashion, a junior adjunct of Black Lives Matter.

Even if documentaries like *Teen Dreams* and *Harlem Diary* (1995) were compromised forms of cinematic self-activity and Vine was a short-lived phenomenon, the precedent of pre-cinematic forms of pedagogical resistance might pave the way for a new subgenre in which young people will chronicle their own lives without the mediation of well-meaning outsiders. Stephen Humphries's *Hooligans or Rebels?*, an oral history of British working-class children's resistance to educational norms in the late nineteenth and early twentieth centuries,[137] reveals a previously little-known legacy of school strikes, rebellious truancy, and "subversion of the syllabus" that offers a pedagogical equivalent to the post-syndicalist resistance to work, especially since Humphries draws overt analogies between worker absenteeism and the students' desire to "lark about." A radicalizing spirit is located in activities condemned by middle-class educators, social workers, and educators as irresponsible hooliganism. Today, resistance to bureaucratic modes of schooling have become increasingly necessary, as the growth of standardized testing and charter schools has to a degree fulfilled Gilles Deleuze's observation that the old centralized educational model would eventually be replaced by "frightful continual training . . . continual monitoring of worker-schoolkids or bureaucrat-students."[138]

Concrete Utopia, the Emancipated Spectator, and *La Commune*

Released on the cusp of the twenty-first century, Peter Watkins's *La Commune (Paris, 1871)* (2000) is an exemplary case study in how radical cinema can coincide with anarchist pedagogy and an ethics and aesthetics of self-emancipation. If, as certain critics assert, *La Commune* refashions motifs derived from Brecht, Godard, and the situationists,[139] the film also presents a revivified model of radical spectatorship that is arguably closely aligned to the paradigm Jacques Rancière labels "the emancipated spectator." In Rancière's formulation, a conception of a truly emancipated spectator does not assume, à la Brecht or Guy Debord, that spectators are innately passive and need to be goaded to shed the veil of ideological mystification. Emancipation is defined as the "blurring of the boundary between those who act and those who look; between individuals and members of a collective body."[140]

To a certain extent, Rancière's conception of the emancipated spectator is a postmodern retooling of aspects of liberatory pedagogy that span from

Francisco Ferrer to Paulo Freire. And a cinematic corollary of Rancière's anti-hierarchical inversion of the roles of schoolmaster and student is at the heart of Watkins's project.

Although the Paris Commune is sometimes written off as a catastrophic defeat, it endures as an emancipatory moment that remains pertinent for the anti-authoritarian left. The fascination of *La Commune* resides in Watkins's effort to merge an aesthetics of self-emancipation with the historical memory of the Commune, a seventy-two-day historical interlude that illustrated the importance of revolutionary self-organization in the history of workers' movements. Both elegiac and prescient, the film's pedagogical strategy is not mired in revolutionary nostalgia but seeks, in the spirit of Ernst Bloch's "concrete utopia," to "negate the present and anticipate the possible future."[141] Watkins's method of historical reportage, a modus operandi in which actors coordinated the writing of the script and were in ongoing dialogue with their colleagues concerning the film's polemical thrust, ruptured, as Antoine de Baecque observes, the "traditional relationship between 'filmer' and 'filmed' and redefined 'performance' as a form of political and active participation in the film, which in turn explicitly incorporated the personal experience of every member of the cast."[142] Consequently, there's a convergence between Watkins's egalitarian production process and a Communard's affirmation, when interviewed by the slyly anachronistic "Commune TV," (the conservative government position is represented by "Versailles TV") that "proletarians will finally claim their rights and the fruits of their labor" and "the workers will be bosses." The insurrectionary ambience possesses certain affinities with what Max Blechman labels "revolutionary romanticism"—an emphasis on the liberatory dimension of aesthetics that can be traced from Schlegel and Novalis through Guy Debord.[143]

Anarchism is, in many respects, the absent presence in *La Commune*. The historian David Armitage labels Watkins's epic "an anarchist masterpiece."[144] But Watkins never explicitly references anarchism in his voluminous annotations on the film that can be consulted on his website. Of course, it's ironic that the Trotskyist critic David Walsh's largely dismissive review of the film reiterates Watkins's anarchist credibility more convincingly than Armitage's encomium. Walsh's Leninist perspective leads him to sneer at both the film's spontaneist bias and, in a display of ideological hauteur, Watkins's refusal to endorse the concept of a vanguard party that could have—supposedly—safeguarded the Commune's gains. Walsh is disconcerted by the film's supposed anarchist impetus, generated by celebrating the Commune's "spontaneity, lack of centralization, political amorphousness so . . . we infer that the Parisian workers government is being raised, falsely, as an alternative to the Soviet state established in Russia in 1917."[145] Rather perversely, Walsh's attack functions as a validation of Watkins's agenda.

Even a perfunctory look at the complex historical record confirms the Commune's ideological multifariousness; the participants included Jacobins, Proudhonists, Blanquists, and moderate Republicans. Yet, during the aftermath of the Commune, both Bakunin and Kropotkin assessed its achievements from a respectful distance. Even Marx, in *The Civil War in France,* hailed the Commune's assault on the "centralized" French state. Bakunin declared himself a "supporter of the Paris Commune above all because it involved a courageous and whole-hearted rejection of the State. He mused that "its subsequent suppression . . . ha[s] lent it an even more momentous effect on the imagination and in the heart of the proletariat of Europe."[146] Kropotkin, whose anarcho-communist ideals resonated with some of the more radical Communards, was more cautious in labeling the insurrection "a first attempt" that did not break with "the tradition of the State" and, because it was crushed by Adolphe Thiers' reactionary Versailles government, inevitably failed to "proclaim the independence and free federation of Communes."[147] It's telling that Louise Michel, the symbol of female militancy during the Commune, only formally became an anarchist after she was subsequently exiled to New Caledonia. During the Commune's ferment, her position was close to the Blanquists, whose socialism was both voluntarist and invested in the capacity of a revolutionary elite to promote revolutionary change.

As a cinematic hybrid that fuses documentary and fictional techniques, *La Commune* is noteworthy for avoiding the textbook clichés that usually litter standard historical accounts of the Paris Commune. The anarchist director Armand Guerra's early stab at a cinematic tribute to the events of 1871 (*La Commune,* 1914) is, by comparison, a rather staid historical pageant. Guerra's stiffly choreographed tableaux vivants chronicle the key chapters in the Commune's rise and fall, particularly the opportunity for a revolutionary socialist government introduced by the vacuum offered by France's disastrous war with Prussia, the radicalized National Guard's defense of the cannons left by the Prussians during the siege of Paris—weapons that Thiers's Versailles government wanted to seize—and the declaration of the Commune on March 18. Paradoxically enough, the true anti-authoritarian tenor of the Commune only surfaces in Guerra's epilogue commemorating a 1911 gathering of former Communards that includes the vibrant presence of the anarchist Nathalie Lemel.

Watkins's *La Commune,* without explicitly labeling itself anarchist, is less preoccupied with the "great men"—or even the "great women"—of the Commune and more concerned with reconstructing radical history from the

"bottom up." Luminaries such as Jules Vallès and Louise Michel are only mentioned in passing. Resisting sensationalism, *La Commune* does not tackle the
largely discredited claim that a significant number of militant women were
branded as *pétroleuses,* "incendiaries" who gleefully set fire to the Tuileries
and other monuments.[148] Watkins even avoids depicting the Communards'
destruction of the Vendôme Column, a hated symbol of Napoleonic militarism—an event that almost seems tailor-made for a historical film.

While the conspicuous role of women as Commune supporters is highlighted, the emphasis is less on heroic leaders like Michel or Elisabeth Dmi-
trieff than on the yearnings of ordinary working-class women caught up in
the revolutionary maelstrom. Appropriately enough, the female denizens of
the eleventh arrondissement interviewed by Commune TV emphasize the
potential of pedagogy to instill revolutionary values. One woman extols the
"hunger for knowledge" and insists that "everyone has a right to an education"; another proclaims that "we want schools for girls to read." The ruse
of on-the-street, nineteenth-century televised interviews allows Watkins to
avoid protracted didactic sequences outlining the historic role of women in
the Commune. Women workers not only demanded equal pay and education for girls—they were also committed activists and participated in the
battle to secure the cannons on March 18 from the troops dispatched from
Versailles.[149] As Kristin Ross underlines, the *Women's Union for the Defense
of Paris and Aid to the Wounded* "became the Commune's largest and most
effective organization."[150] At an early juncture in the film, Watkins also hails
the transition from the suffocating Catholic classrooms of Napoleon III's
regime to a secular educational model. A young woman exults in the demise
of religious schooling she heartily "loathes . . . that only teaches obedience
to authority." A teacher, Mary-Louise Beauger, who resigned her post in a
Catholic institution, recounts how her refusal to hew to Catholic dogma,
which required her to inform girls they must be resigned to working as
"seamstresses and nothing more," radicalized her. These sentiments reflect
an implicitly anarchist sensibility inasmuch as they fuse anti-clericalism
with pleas for "integral education" that Ross traces to Fourierist, as well as
Bakuninist, influences. Following Rancière, Ross concludes that, unlike the
pedagogical meliorism that pervades the mainstream French Republican
tradition, radical pedagogy during the Commune endeavored to "separate
the logic of the emancipation from the logic of the institution."[151]

La Commune's eagerness to provide viewers with multiple explanations of
historical events also belies a pedagogical imperative. For the partisans of the
status quo at Versailles TV, the Commune's murder of two generals and emissaries of Thiers—Claude Lecomte and Jacques Leon-Clément Thomas—ex-

emplifies the savagery of the mob while, alternately, the radicalized members of the National Guard believe that this sort of direct action is an essential part of a popular insurgency. Watkins's strategy has nothing to do with liberal pluralism or the desire to inform viewers of "both sides." The tension between the establishment Versailles TV, which is almost a proto-Fox News outlet, and the Communards often involves sequences featuring workers and militants that actively negate the premises of the Versailles talking heads. A case in point is the film's treatment of the co-operatives established in April 1871. "F. Foucart," a right-wing commentator on Versailles TV (played by a Royalist historian), condemns the economic organization of the Commune (particularly the establishment of cooperatives) as impractical and steeped in demagogy. The sequences that follow invert Foucart's calumnies by illuminating the scope of the Communards' economic self-activity. Machinists exult that they're "now the bosses" and discuss establishing a collective and reopening the foundry. Explanatory titles remind the audience of the efforts of Augustin Avrial and Leo Frankel to launch the cooperatives. In a more conventional historical chronicle, leaders such as Avrial and Frankel would be foregrounded. For Watkins, they're almost footnotes, and the workers' process of coming to terms with their newfound autonomy takes precedence. In pedagogical terms, this phenomenon is akin to what Freire labeled the "actualization of potential."

As Hamish Ford maintains, Watkins is less interested in demonizing Versailles TV and enshrining Commune TV than he is in conveying the limitations of what he calls the "Monoform"—the one-way communication that excludes the audience and is tacitly accepted as an endemic component of the modern media landscape.[152] A fairly glaring example of sanitizing the news occurs when some of the Communards advocate the formation of a "Committee of Public Safety," an entity whose name echoed the despotic centralism of Robespierre and the Jacobins of 1789. Gérard, the Commune TV broadcaster played by Watkins's son, wants to broach the details of internal debates within the Communes surrounding this reversion to an authoritarian tradition. But Aurélie, his colleague, prefers to suppress this controversy and nervously yells, "Cut!"

The device of interweaving the glib showmanship of television news with the Commune's growing pains take on a new earnestness as Watkins's self-reflexive approach acknowledges his own disdain for the modern equivalents of Versailles TV—and, in some respects, the flawed "alternative" of Commune TV. Slightly more than midway through the film, titles announce that the film's participatory ethos is anathema to the "global media." Escaping this stranglehold of the "Monoform" resulted in actors becoming researchers and commentators onscreen, a process that enabled them to construct cogent links between their characters' plights and their own lives. One actress, for example, is furious about the failure of French schools to teach history in a manner that enables children to connect the past to current quandaries. Disparate personae—actor, researcher, spectator, historian—are fused. Of course, even the most mainstream historians invoke the shibboleth of the "usable past." But Watkins radicalizes the cliché of the usable past by blurring boundaries in a salutary fashion; as in the contours of Rancière's emancipated spectator, "what is involved is linking what one knows with what one does not know; being at once a performer deploying her skills and a spectator observing what these skills might produce in a new context among other spectators."[153]

Watkins's respect for his actors' political consciousness is not unlike the Commune's own passion for grassroots debate; the ongoing polemics were part of an ambiance that resulted, in Stuart Edwards's formulation, "the whole city becom[ing] a public forum for political discussion and action . . . the clubs claimed to express . . . popular sovereignty and to act as centers of political intelligence and education."[154] Some of the intellectual excitement savored by the members of these clubs is revealed in an actor's reflection that what "impressed" him about the Commune, despite its ostensible failure, was the avenues of inquiry opened up by this one catalytic historic event. For the actors, the Commune's inveterate ability to provoke intellectual controversy outweighs the occasionally petty criticisms launched at the ad hoc government's military strategy and political tactics by Lenin and his cohorts during the political ferment of the subsequent century.

The frequent self-referential musings of *La Commune*'s protagonists on the film's production process take several forms. At times, actors resist conflating their own perspectives with those embraced by their characters. Toward the end of the film, an actress playing Marguerite Lachaise pauses to consider the ethical import of her character's actions. Lachaise, a member of the International, encouraged her neighbors to recommend the execution of Charles de Beaufort, a National Guard member suspected of collaborating with Versailles. The actress ponders the moral dilemma posed by Lachaise's intervention and interrogates her firebrand character's endorsement of summary execution. She finds her nineteenth-century alter ego's impulses understandable—if not thoroughly defensible. Other meditations on the propensity of the present to echo the past are less character-driven and more of a gloss on the film's pertinence to inequities spawned by the age of corporate globalization. Actors and explanatory titles drive home the parallels between the Commune's agenda and a workers' uprising in Algeria in 1871, as well as the

March 1996 occupation of Saint-Ambroise Church by 324 undocumented African workers ("*sans papiers,*") who demanded asylum in France. (During the Commune, Saint-Ambroise housed the "Club des Prolétaires," a group frequently at odds with the less radical edicts of elected officials.)

Since the Commune ended with summary executions, massive deportations, and estimates of twenty to thirty thousand participants murdered, how can hope be extracted from an insurrectionary interlude that, by all appearances, failed and triggered unprecedented bloodshed from the Versailles authorities? (The historian John Merriman asserts that the massacre of Communards anticipates the mass "state repression" of the twentieth century.[155]) Watkins's implicit response to radical pessimism is to provide us access to the testimony of a Parisian worker who, in the throes of mayhem, proclaims that the Commune made the world aware of a certain ideal of freedom. From this vantage point, the failure of this great experiment also possesses pedagogical import as an event that encapsulates "prefigurative" politics— a historical example that can be newly reappropriated and reinvented in a multitude of contexts.

In the final analysis, *La Commune* is as much about usurping aesthetic norms as it is about defying political taboos. For Watkins, the dreaded "Monoform" embodies all of the limitations of Hollywood cinema—"the densely packed and rapidly edited barrage of images and sounds, the "seamless" yet fragmented modular structure which we know so well."[156] His antidote to this bland template—a leisurely film with ten minute sequence shots and occasional pauses when the screen goes dark—combines the aesthetic rigor of European art cinema with an older tradition of agitprop. "Passivity" is perhaps the dirtiest word in Watkins's lexicon, and his rhetoric aimed at combatting the narcotizing effects of the media recalls Benjamin's desire for authors to become producers and Enzensberger's hope that consumers will become producers. Exasperated by the public's limited access to *La Commune,* Watkins established a group called Rebond pour la Commune designed to distribute the film to alternative venues and make it available on video. This sort of outreach, although in some respects a product of Watkins's dismay that the French network ARTE only broadcast the film once at a very late hour, also produced a kind of anarchist feedback loop wherein other artists have been inspired by *La* Commune's own example to initiate their own projects. For example, Philip Rizk, an American filmmaker based in Cairo, admits that *La Commune* was "the greatest influence on *Out on the Street,*" the film he co-directed with Jasmina Metwaly.[157] A 2013 project initiated by the architect and writer Léopold Lambert posits an alternate reality in a New York where the citizens have embraced a modern-day equivalent of the Paris

Commune—a schema with a family resemblance to *La Commune*'s synthesis of research, art, and activism.[158]

It's important to realize that *La Commune* is not a radical landmark that emerged *ex nihilo*. Various theatrical and cinematic ventures can be considered precursors of *La Commune*'s participatory ethos. Watkins's affinities with anarchism are concretized in his relationship with Armand Gatti, an avowed anarchist theater and film director whose working method no doubt influenced *La Commune*'s concerted blurring of the boundaries between life and art. *La Commune* was shot on the site of Gatti's former workshop, a site that once housed the studios of film pioneer Georges Méliès. More importantly, Gatti's working methods anticipate Watkins's; one example is a 1972 production of *La Colonne Durruti* at the Catholic University of Louvain, an exercise in "collective theatre" that encouraged students to conduct independent research on the anarchist militia leader and generated a text that, according to Gatti's biographer, delineated "seven different images" of this iconic figure.[159] *La Commune*'s efforts to dissolve the boundary between the director, traditionally stereotyped as an autocratic figure, and his cast also recalls the egalitarian aspirations of Chris Marker's *A bientôt j'espère* (1968), a documentary on a strike in a French textile factory that inspired Marker to provide workers with cameras to chronicle their own experiences.

The pedagogical thrust of Gatti, Marker, and Watkins could be termed offshoots of what Chiara Bottici labels "imaginal politics."[160] Bottici's term endeavors to transform the concept of imagination from mere passive aesthetic contemplation into a variant of praxis that can undermine the status quo. While no one work of art can perform this task single-handedly, *La Commune* is one of the most provocative examples of anti-authoritarian pedagogy as art to date.[161]

5. The Elusive Anarchist Aesthetic

Art is the last refuge of scoundrels.
—Tuli Kupferberg

ALL OF THE LEADING anarchist figures—Proudhon, Bakunin, Kropotkin, and Goldman—joined forces with influential figures from the arts. And members of the nineteenth and twentieth centuries' aesthetic avant-gardes often aligned themselves with anarchists. For Donald Drew Egbert, this alliance can be attributed to "the highly individualistic, anti-official, and artistically revolutionary nature of so much avant-garde art since the late eighteenth century."[1] Yet although there have often been ties between aesthetic radicals and the libertarian left, it is not likely that necessary and sufficient conditions for the production of "anarchist art" will ever be formulated. A monolithic anarchist aesthetic must be dismissed as elusive and dubiously essentialist: unlike the Marxist aesthetic, the anarchist conception of art is not "normative," but "is presented in the form of a *project* which leaves the door wide open to the future."[2]

Peter Bürger's contention that the "avant-garde" traditionally seeks to break down the boundaries separating art and life, while challenging the autonomous status of the "institution of art" traditionally embraced by modernists (cherished by, among others, Theodor Adorno[3]), is eminently applicable to nearly all confluences of art and anarchism.

There is, however, more than a superficial similarity between the notion of a political "vanguard" party and the concept of an aesthetic avant-garde. Perhaps naively, Adorno assumed that a strict separation of art and life could prevent an authoritarian coalescence of art and politics. He believed that "art without autonomy would lose its negative, critical force and become a mere instrument for either political activism or affirmative decoration of the status quo."[4] Yet Adorno's conception of a disinterested critical art is less typically anarchist than Percy Bysshe Shelley's eloquent defense of an anarchist imagination, a radical transmutation of the redemptive view of art endorsed by the Romantic movement. *A Defence of Poetry,* which M. H. Abrams labels "our greatest general statement about the indispensable role of art and of imagination in achieving the highest values in life, civilization, and the modern and political and economic state,"[5] is certainly not in tune with the more modest goals of contemporary aesthetic radicalism. And even a commentator with a profound sympathy for Shelley's Romantic anarchism concedes that he was essentially an aristocratic radical with an imperfect understanding of the poor, oppressed individuals to whom he pays tribute in his work.[6] Shelley's idealist aesthetic, fueled by a concern to "champion the resources of creative immanence"[7] (most famously encapsulated in his assertion that "poets are the unacknowledged legislators of the world"), may seem light years away from some contemporary anarchists' denunciation of art as "an enemy of the people."[8] But the Romantic exaltation of the poet is merely the idealistic precursor of the recent avant-garde's disillusioned contempt for the institution of art—antithetical versions of the desire to negate "the means—ends rationality of the bourgeois everyday."[9]

By the 1980s, the "neoists," whose post-situationist avant-gardism displays utter contempt for the creativity prized by the Romantics, severed their ties to Shelleyan idealism: their panegyrics to plagiarism assault a "culture that finds its ideological justification in the 'unique.'"[10] This tiny avant-garde group's anti-art activities (which recall a tongue-in-cheek retread of the work of Dadaist Hugo Ball) might be viewed as an eccentric response to Raymond Williams's critique of Shelley's need to isolate art as a "superior reality."[11] Yet even the neoist attempt to deliver a definitive death knell to "autonomous art," with its assumption that artist-activists will take responsibility for the delegitimation of art and facilitate a convergence of art and life, is at best a simple inversion of the "Romantic ideology." The odd phenomenon of artists willing their own obsolescence is clearly not a universal tendency within the avant-garde. The older Shelleyan paradigm has often reasserted itself in contemporary avant-garde practice; among other examples one can cite the references to "Prometheus Unbound" in Jonas Mekas's *Guns of the Trees* (1961)[12] and the place of pride given to Shelley as one of Julian Beck's precursors in Sheldon Rochlin's *Signal Through the Flames: The Story of the Living Theater* (1983).

Early attempts to formulate an anarchist artistic praxis were far removed from the antics of dadaists and neoists. Proudhon's anarchist aesthetic ideology is a case in point: his anti-authoritarianism did not impede his formulation of a rigidly prescriptive aesthetic. His *Du Principe de l'art et de sa destination sociale* (1865) argues that a realist aesthetic represents the zenith of artistic achievement: in other words, "the artistic faculty perceives pre-existing beauty, rather than creates it."[13] Proudhon thought that Courbet's work was an exemplary union of the artistic faculty with radical political aspirations. Courbet himself welcomed this judgment: Meyer Schapiro concludes that "Courbet's feeling of superiority as an artist was justified for him by his indigenous relation to the masses."[14] Realism is notoriously difficult to define, but for Courbet it entailed a near-positivist disdain for previous classical and Romantic artistic models (which supposedly hindered a faithful reproduction of the nuances of nature) and a faithfulness to peasant, artisanal traditions—an aesthetic agenda that corresponds to the political goals of Proudhonian anarchism. As James Henry Rubin emphasizes, Proudhon's enthusiasm for Courbet's realism was intimately tied to a belief in historical progress. The rejection of aesthetic artifice was fused with radical art's "concomitant role in the inevitable flow of social development."[15] Proudhon viewed "art . . . the search for the beautiful and the perfecting of truth" as essential to the "final evolution of the worker, the phase which is destined to bring the Circle of Nature to a glorious close."[16] Unlike Kant, he did not prize art for its "purposeful purposelessness": form was always subservient to the "question of content."[17]

Nothing could be further from the Proudhon/Courbet exaltation of realism than the symbolist aesthetic's obliviousness to "the real." Yet, by the end of the nineteenth century, many symbolists, whose hermetic fondness for the doctrine of *l'art pour l'art* was diametrically opposed to the Courbet/Proudhon marriage of realism and radicalism, "were sympathetic to, or actually involved in, the growth of anarchism."[18] The symbolist poet Pierre Quillard, for example, bridged private reverie and radical social change by insisting that "whoever communicates to their brothers in suffering the secret splendor of his dreams acts upon the surrounding society in the manner of a solvent, and makes all of those who understand him, often without their realization, outlaws and rebels."[19]

Abstract debates concerning Romanticism, realism, symbolism, and surrealism are not obvious topics for discussion in the cinema. But at least superficial hints of this desire to merge aesthetic provocation with political rebellion, which extends from Rimbaud's participation in the Paris Commune to the alliance of the surrealists with the anarchists of *Le Libertaire* in the 1950s, are evident in films that deal with the antics of so-called "bohemians." The term "bohemian" has become a rancid cliché, beloved by hack writers who yearn for a quick way to pigeonhole anything considered arty and slightly marginal. Nevertheless, bohemianism—"a country without boundaries"[20]—has often been associated with anarchism. In 1895, for example, Hugh Strutfield raged at "decadent literature" as "cultural anarchism": he concluded that "the unbridled licentiousness of your literary decadent has its counterpart in the violence of the political anarchist . . . the one works with the quill, the other with the bomb, and the quill is the more dangerous weapon of the two."[21] Admittedly minor films such as Aki Kaurismaki's *La Vie de Bohème* (1993) and Agnieszka Holland's *Total Eclipse* (1995) recycle popular stereotypes of both the eccentric artist and the deranged anarchist.

Kaurismaki's film never mentions anarchism, but his affectionate parody of the bohemian milieu can help us to understand conflicts within anarchism between aesthetic radicals and working-class anarcho-syndicalists such as Sam Dolgoff, who pilloried "half-assed artists and poets who object to organization and want only to play with their belly buttons."[22] This adaptation of Henri Murger's 1851 novel *Scenes from Bohemian Life,* with its wily caricatures of talentless if nonetheless endearing poets and artists, is a farcical riff on anti-work themes: instead of celebrating the revolt of disgruntled industrial workers, Kaurismaki mocks the self-imposed indolence of individuals whom Dolgoff and his comrades derided as "parlor anarchists."

Kaurismaki's surprisingly faithful adaptation of the Murger novel appears designed to encourage protracted audience head-scratching. Is the film a tribute to bohemian resourcefulness or a sly critique of a motley assortment of bullshit artists? The film's compromised synthesis of deadpan facetiousness and apparently earnest sentiment convinces us that Kaurismaki's ironic sensibility is often at war with a weakness for the same lachrymose sentimentalization of poverty that permeates *La Bohème,* Puccini's opera based loosely on Murger.

La Vie de Bohème, despite some fairly perfunctory efforts to update Murger, is essentially a series of comic vignettes inspired by the now rather musty avant-gardist aspiration to fuse art and life. Murger's dramatis personae are only slightly transmogrified. The Albanian painter Rodolfo (a departure from the indelibly French poet, Rodolphe, of the novel, who resembles a particularly melancholy basset hound as played by the Finnish actor Matti Pellonpaa), the irascible poet Marcel (Andre Wilms), and the John Cage–like composer Schaunard prove quite artful in their attempts to cadge meals and evade the landlord's wrath. They prove woefully inadequate, however, when confronted with blank canvases, writing tablets, and composition paper. Kaurismaki freely borrows the idiosyncrasies that Murger bequeathed to his characters, but ups the comic ante by transforming the nineteenth-century author's gentle indictments of artistic pretension into full-blown absurdist set pieces. A turgid-sounding five-act play entitled *The Avenger* in Murger becomes Marcel's twenty-one-act mega-masterpiece in the film. Murger alludes to some vaguely preposterous paintings. Kaurismaki, conversely, relishes the opportunity to display Rodolfo's amusingly hideous neo-expressionist monstrosities. Kaurismaki's apolitical sensibility prevents him from drawing analogies between his protagonists' foibles and the current nostalgia for—and commodification of—bohemia.

What, then, is the pertinence of Kaurismaki's gentle jab at the foibles of latter-day bohemians to the aesthetic aspirations of anarchists? A rationale for including *La Vie de Bohème* in this context becomes clear if we examine the debates concerning the socioeconomic significance of bohemia that have preoccupied scholars in recent decades. The Marxist art critic T. J. Clark made a controversial distinction between radical and conformist factions within bohemia: the subculture detailed in Murger's novel was dismissed as a degraded, privatized form of bohemianism, while the radical artists and poets who aligned themselves with the revolution of 1848 were termed genuine bohemians.[23] For Jerrold Seigel, these categories were overly glib: his influential book on bohemianism characterizes Murger's vision of bohemia as a "representation of both a passageway into bourgeois society and a permanent form of separation from it." From our perspective, however, it would do little good to commit ourselves fully to one of these polemics. The many anarchists who evinced a faith in both radical art and politics could be seen as inheritors of the mantle of "true" bohemianism prized by Clark, but it is equally difficult to deny that all forms of bohemianism have become, as Seigel maintains, "part of the history of a developing bourgeois consciousness and experience."[24] In any case, there has often been an intimate relationship between the frequently hermetic activities of bohemia—the "sobriquet for those artists, poets, and libertines living on the fringes of the newly industrialized society"[25]—and anarchism's communal ethos.

Unfortunately, *Total Eclipse,* Holland's shallow fictionalization of Arthur Rimbaud and Paul Verlaine's poetic exploits and doomed romance, does little to illuminate the political ramifications of poetic revolt. Christopher Hampton's arch script makes several fleeting references to Rimbaud's support of the Paris Commune, but the film is primarily determined to portray the bickering poets as the nineteenth-century equivalents of rock stars. Holland and Hampton's narcissistic focus is perhaps best summed up by a speech by Verlaine in which he berates Rimbaud for following him to London. Rimbaud's decision to tag along with his older mentor is termed another stage in a "private odyssey" that will allow the young poet to "graze on the upper slopes of Parnassus." However, biographical evidence reveals that Rimbaud's poetic activities were never purely the product of private reveries. It is true, as

Wallace Fowlie notes, that Rimbaud did not want to *be* a worker: he merely wanted to help the "workers who were dying in the battle of Paris."[26] But the spirit of his poems inspired by the days of the commune (particularly *Les Mains de Jeanne-Marie,* which pays tribute to the working-class women who took part in the Commune's street battles) is far indeed from *Total Eclipse*'s schlocky depictions of poetic navel-gazing. The separation of radical bohemians from the class whose interests they purport to serve continues to plague avant-garde art. One particularly egregious example is the work of Nick Zedd—a self-proclaimed outlaw filmmaker whose hip nihilism tended to taint his endorsement of anti-authoritarian goals in films such as *Police State* (1987).

Bakunin, the prototypical man of action, had little time for Rimbaudian inwardness and aesthetic formulations; he was not at all enamored of his friend Wagner's *Kunstreligion.* Nonetheless, his materialist *cri de coeur* in *God and the State*—"the idea of God . . . is the most decisive negation of human liberty, and necessarily ends in the enslavement of mankind, both in theory and in practice"[27]—might well have served as Luis Buñuel's aesthetic credo. Although an entire study could be devoted to anti-authoritarian motifs in Buñuel's work, some brief remarks can illustrate how two of his films—*L'Âge d'or* and *Viridiana* (1961)—reveal a creative distillation of traditional anarchist preoccupations, such as anti-clericalism and anti-statism.[28]

Buñuel's relationship to actually existing anarchism was certainly ambiguous. While he was friendly with many Spanish anarchist literary figures (*Las Hurdes* was financed by one of his anarchist acquaintances, Ramón Acín[29]), he felt he was "not good enough"[30] to be an anarchist. He always identified himself as a surrealist, and was closer to the communists than the CNT during the Spanish Civil War. There is little doubt, though, that he would have appreciated Bakunin's reverence for Satan as "the eternal *reunité,* the first free-thinker and the liberator of the world."[31] A capacity for revolt is in fact the catalyst for all varieties of anarchism, and Stirnerian and Kropotkinite, as well as Bakuninist, themes are conspicuous in *L'Âge d'or* (1930), his second—and final—collaboration with Salvador Dalí (who subsequently voiced his disapproval of the film's anti-clerical bias).

The early sequences of this "unique exaltation of total love"[32] parody the founding of imperial Rome. A Stirnerian veneration for "self-ownership" coexists with the animosity toward both clerical and governmental authority that suffuses both Stirner's and Bakunin's work.[33] More specifically, a sequence detailing the disruption of the regime's ceremonial founding by a completely self-absorbed, lustful couple ably demonstrates how Stirner's supposedly asocial anarchist individualism logically dovetails with Bakunin's social, collectivist anarchism. The assembled dignitaries—"soldiers, priests, monks, nuns, policemen and silkhatted civilians"—are startled to find their proceedings interrupted by "a man and woman rolling in the mud, in lascivious embrace."[34] This collision of the forces of order and unstoppable passion is, for all intents and purposes, a surrealist transmutation of Stirner's diatribe against Christianity. *The Ego and Its Own* excoriates a Christianity

> aimed to deliver us from a life determined by nature, from the appetites as actuating us . . . and so has meant that man should not let himself be determined by his appetites. . . . The Christian does not hear the agony of his enthralled nature, but lives in "humility." . . . But, if the flesh once takes the floor, and its tone is "passionate," indecorous; not "well-disposed," "spiteful" (as it can not be otherwise) then he thinks he hears voices against the devil . . . and is justly zealous against them.[35]

Since the couple in *L'Âge d'or* does not suppress their appetites and are blatantly "indecorous," the crowd feels compelled to quell their passion by separating them and dragging the woman away. Soon after, the film's equation of state power with offal is made graphic with a punning use of sound and image the sound of a flushing toilet and a shot of "lava" which most audiences perceive as excrement. If Stirner is convinced that the theocratic intolerance of erotic love lampooned in *L'Âge d'or* robs us of our autonomy, Bakunin believes that the collusion of church and state evident in this sequence perpetuates "the enslavement of humanity"[36] and forestalls social revolution.

Buñuel felt that *Viridiana* and *L'Âge d'or* were the films he "directed with the greatest feeling of freedom." *Viridiana*, however, converts *L'Âge d'or*'s avant-gardist, excremental vision into a more concrete indictment of the moral stasis endured by Spaniards under Franco. In addition, the film intersperses surrealist motifs with themes borrowed from the tradition of seventeenth-century Spanish baroque literature. José Antonio Maravall's masterly survey of the Spanish baroque establishes the fact that this epoch's cultural life was dominated by two overarching, interrelated topoi: "the madness of the world" and "the world turned upside down." Maravall, however, is adamant in claiming that this aesthetic pandemonium was merely a safety valve that ultimately reinforced the power of the state.[37] *Viridiana* is distinguished by its appropriation of familiar baroque concerns for insurrectionary purposes; unlike the work of the seventeenth-century writers discussed by Maravall, Buñuel's film seeks to negate, not affirm, the dominant order.

Like Buñuel's earlier critique of Christian piety, *Nazarin* (1958), *Viridiana* features a sympathetic portrait of a protagonist whose enthusiasm for an egalitarian form of Christianity proves hubristic. The title character delays her vows in order to visit her lecherous uncle, Don Jaime. The first part of the film is one of Buñuel's most extended exercises in blasphemy: Viridiana's saintly masochism (her luggage includes a wooden cross, nails, and a crown of thorns) is undermined by Don Jaime, who rapes his niece while she sleeps. Her brutal introduction to the ways of the world gives way to comic altruism as she organizes the local beggars into a commune based on Christian principles. The predictably disastrous results underscore the differences between Viridiana's patronizing charity and the self-liberation that Kropotkin believed would be the result of anarchist communism. Kropotkin maintained that "when working men are liberated from wage slavery . . . there is no doubt . . . that the needs of all will be fulfilled."[38] But Viridiana's coercive communalism is merely a product of her spiritualized narcissism. The "comic but clumsy . . . cross-cutting" between "images of manual work" and the "effete hypocrisy of Viridiana's beggars at their *angelus*"[39] reiterates Buñuel's view that religious devotion is incompatible with genuine self-liberation.

The famous beggars' banquet toward the end of the film could be construed as a Rabelaisian version of Kropotkin's suggestions for mass peasant expropriation of food, land, and dwellings in *The Conquest of Bread*. This sequence, which culminates in one of Buñuel's most famous images—a scatological parody of da Vinci's *Last Supper*—celebrates the beggars' final adieu to their ascetic regime. Buñuel's debt to the medieval fascination with "the grotesque" is merged with a surrealist belief in the inextricability of aesthetic frisson and social revolution. Benjamin observed that surrealism reintroduced Europe to "a radical concept of freedom that had remained dormant since Bakunin's influence waned: a liquidation, moreover, of a sclerotic-liberal-moral-humanistic ideal of freedom."[40] The sequence's most memorable shot—a beggar woman taking a group "snapshot" by lifting her skirt—crystallizes Buñuel's assault on moralistic ideals of freedom. This "utterly obscene gesture"[41] blasphemes against both Christianity's chaste reverence for "divine sight" and the liberal rationalist view that reform can be implemented through enlightened, hierarchical social policy. Both Christians and the secular conservative and liberal elite fear lumpen rebelliousness, and this shot literalizes—and celebrates—this threat with erotic finesse. Buñuel has had his imitators, but many subsequent filmmakers' so-called "transgressiveness" is little more than hollow self-aggrandizement.

Profoundly indebted to anarchism, libertarian Marxism, as well as surrealism,[42] the Situationist International (despite a fury toward the surrealists that can only be termed Oedipal) helped to revive the "radical concept of freedom" pioneered by Breton and Bakunin. The situationists were plagued by an ambivalent attitude toward the aesthetic avant-garde. The Situationist International attacked previous avant-garde movements "for a failure to carry through a critique of religion to which the "left" (avant-garde art and thought) . . . was heir."[43] When, in 1962, Guy Debord decided to dissociate himself (and the French situationists) from his German and Scandinavian comrades,[44] the rationale for the split was based on a newfound militancy (influenced by anarchist and council communist tenets) that questioned any attempts to confine art to an autonomous sphere.[45] Yet as Simon Ford points out, Debord and René Viénet's continued commitment to film makes it clear that "the Debordist 'SI' never really excluded the possibility of producing cultural artifacts."[46]

Although the situationists had only contempt for what they considered the ossified politics of the French Anarchist Federation, they often made positive references to Bakunin and the CNT–FAI. Yet Debord's most famous film, *La Société du spectacle* (*Society of the Spectacle*, 1973, a cinematic adaptation of his manifesto of the same name), reveals how his anti-authoritarianism manifested itself in oracular pronouncements that gave this potted version of his treatise a quasi-authoritarian tenor. To a certain extent, the film's potpourri of found footage and hectoring voice-over can be ascribed to Debord's queasiness with film itself. Since the spectacle is described as the "concrete inversion of life"—the false consciousness that results when the commodity "completes its colonization of social life"[47]—cinema cannot be exempted from the critique of the spectacular economy. Yet Thomas Levin cautions that "a facile collapsing of cinema and the spectacle" prevents us from considering "the possibility of an alternative sort of cinematic activity incompatible with the economy of spectacle, a nonspectacular, anti-spectacular . . . cinema."[48] In *Society of the Spectacle*'s most effective sequences, Debord's aesthetic intransigence coincides with his political militancy; a case in point is the film's most explicit homage to anarchism—the collision of footage from Eisenstein's avant-garde Bolshevik epic *Battleship Potemkin* (1925) with a lengthy quotation from Durruti, the left-libertarian foe of Bolshevism.

Debord and his colleagues were intent on "creating situations" capable of disrupting the "false totality" of the spectacle. Unfortunately, the didactic drone of his narration in *Society of the Spectacle* tends to give the film the feel of a classroom lecture.[49] While Debord's best-known film often resembles traditional self-absorbed avant-gardism more than a utopic, "antispectacular" alternative, his cinematic *détournement* ("the reuse of pre-existing artistic elements in a new ensemble for parodic or critical purposes"[50]) is most intriguing when the appropriation of pop culture artifacts inadvertently subverts its supposed argument. A clip from Nicholas Ray's *Johnny Guitar,* which features an exchange of quips between Joan Crawford and Sterling

Hayden, wittily undermines Debord's assertion that "when art becomes independent, represents its world with dazzling colors, a moment of life has
grown old and it cannot be rejuvenated with dazzling colors."[51] Nevertheless,
the interweaving of footage chronicling seminal moments of unadulterated
spectacle—the Beatles greeting their fans, stills from Marilyn Monroe's last
unfinished film—with Debord's analysis that celebrities constitute "a spectacular representation of a human being" is strikingly similar to aspects of
Richard Dyer's analysis of the allure of stardom. But Dyer's elucidation of
the star-making apparatus—a construct generated by "promotion publicity,
films, and commentary/criticism"[52]—acknowledges the transient pleasures,
as well as the reified displeasure, that can be derived from passive star-gazing.
Although not much more than an in-joke, René Viénet and Gerard Cohen's *La Dialectique peut-elle casser des briques?* (*Do Dialectics Break Bricks?*,
1973)—a *détourned* martial arts film that gutted the original soundtrack
and replaced its grunts and idiotic dialogue with paeans to council communism—was a less dour example of situationist cinema.

Despite Debord's jaundiced view of popular culture, the music industry
took pleasure in cannibalizing many of his ideas. Most famously, Malcolm
McLaren's synthesis of entrepreneurial savvy and ill-digested chunks of situationist theory had an indelible impact on the Sex Pistols' brand of punk rock.
The paradox of an attempt to critique the spectacle with a baldly "spectacular" apparatus is almost boringly obvious, but several commentators, most
notably Greil Marcus, Neil Nehring, and Jon Savage, are unusually kind to
McLaren.[53] Nehring's study is especially attuned to the relationship of punk
to classical anarchism (many of whose representatives are endlessly irritated
by such comparisons): he is convinced that McLaren and the Sex Pistols
"managed the transformation of the negative and profane into a positive,
genuinely disruptive force." Nehring is eloquent in his claims that the Sex
Pistols created a "working-class Bohemia," but his refusal to consider how this
refurbished bohemianism has been recuperated by members of the media
who have never read a word of Debord is disconcerting.

The Sex Pistols themselves seemed infinitely more aware of the cynicism
that coexisted with, and could not be separated from, the more subversive
aspects of their subcultural project. This awareness is obvious in the opening
sequence of Julien Temple's *The Great Rock 'n' Roll Swindle* (1979).[54] A lesson
in "how to manufacture your own group" is interrupted by a re-creation of the
Gordon Riots of 1780, billed as the eighteenth-century version of "Anarchy
in the UK." E. P. Thompson characterized the Gordon Riots, an outpouring
of radical Protestant fury against wealthy Catholics, as an event that must
be deemed a "mixture of manipulated mob and revolutionary crowd"—at-

tacks on banks were accompanied by "indiscriminate orgies of drunkenness, arson, and pickpocketing."[55] A parallel tension between radical potential and crass manipulation is also evident in the Sex Pistols' own aesthetic praxis. They remain remarkable, however, for their ability consciously to appraise the conformist implications of their own work.

Vastly less solemn than Debord's films, Craig Baldwin's *Sonic Outlaws* (1995) documents whimsical varieties of American *détournement*. The pranksters profiled in Baldwin's documentary unite an improvisatory blend of Yippie-style anarchism with a post-situationist conviction that "creative jests . . . evoke a liberation of experiences . . . and challenge the authority of appearances."[56]

The antics of Negativland, an experimental rock group who found themselves in a legal quagmire when one of their acoustic collages aroused the ire of the recording industry, provide the initial focus of *Sonic Outlaws'* examination of DIY "creative jests." The offending record, "U2/Negativland," featured an impish sound mix—outtakes of the seemingly genial disk jockey Casey Kasem cursing the Irish rock group U2, overlaid with computer-generated strains of the band's hit single "I Still Haven't Found What I'm Looking For." This home-grown version of situationist *détournement* was not appreciated by Island Records, U2's label. Condemning the single as an example of "deceptive packaging and copyright infringement," a federal judge "issued a temporary restraining order . . . demanding that the band and its label [SST Records] turn over to the plaintiffs [Island Records and Warner/Chappell] all 6,000 copies of the single."[57]

Negativland's Mark Hosler terms his group's work an "outgrowth of growing up in a media-saturated world," and their critique of the music industry's corporate cynicism certainly meshes with the anarchist avant-garde's belief that "plagiarism" can be deployed to "enrich human language" and promote "collective . . . progressive social transformation."[58] Hosler's enthusiasm for what fellow aural prankster John Oswald calls "plunderphonics" also leads him to a pragmatic endorsement of a liberal interpretation of the "fair use" doctrine, which usually only sanctions "free appropriation in certain cases of parody or commentary."[59] Negativland's guerrilla aesthetics may seem to have little in common with the concerns of classical anarchism, but their modest challenges to corporate power are certainly examples of concerted direct action.

Baldwin's homage to connoisseurs of collage is itself a documentary collage. Negativland's battle with U2 is only one link in *Sonic Outlaws'* associative chain, and the frantic editing allows for skillful transitions to the analogous activities of the Billboard Liberation Front[60] (artists who specialize in *détourned* versions of billboard advertising), the Barbie Liberation Organization (feminists who delight in sabotaging the "gendered" ideology of children's toys by switching the taped messages of Barbie and GI Joe dolls), and the Tape Beatles' satirically garbled versions of television programming. Despite these groups' indebtedness to a post-situationist mindset, they could also be evaluated as eccentric exemplars of anarchist pedagogy. Groups like Negativland may not have succeeded in thoroughly collapsing art into life, but their critiques of the spectacle at least partially eradicate the difference between aesthetic play and non-hierarchical education and self-education. The participatory aesthetic of the Billboard Liberation Front and the Barbie Liberation Organization suggests the possibility of combining creative activism with the dissemination of alternative information. The film, however, does not confront a central contradiction: it appears to endorse some of its participants' desire to assume composite identities (for example, some post-neoists decided to all call themselves either "Monty Cantsin" or "Karen Eliot") even as they are implicitly hailed as cultural heroes. Heroic individualism is often smuggled into antithetical discourses through the back door.

Although Baldwin's "sonic outlaws" were pre-internet phenomena, they look forward to the many varieties of "culture jamming" that emerged in the digital era. Many radical pranks that went viral, while not necessarily explicitly anarchist in nature, reveal an anti-authoritarian orientation endemic to the variety of culture jamming known as "media jujitsu": "asymmetrical semiotic warfare, whereby media-makers draw from the arsenal of domination in order to turn the power of the dominant media against domination itself."[61] This kind of puckish subversion is on display in counterhegemonic media interventions such as Yes Men member Andy Bichlbaum's impersonation of a Union Carbide spokesperson on a BBC broadcast, during which he announced that Dow Chemical, Union Carbide's parent company, planned to liquidate the corporation and use the profits to fund research and turn over $12 billion in profits to the victims of the 1984 Bhopal disaster. Given both entities' continual refusal to accept full responsibility for a "tragedy" (a word that transforms a man-made catastrophe into a metaphysical event; in the wake of the disaster, Union Carbide settled a lawsuit for a paltry 470 million dollars) caused by mismanagement at a Union Carbide factory, the Yes Men's indictment of corporate malfeasance could be characterized as needed virtual remediation, not a mere satirical prank.

Other types of media jujitsu entail creative disruptions of the spectacular milieu of mass entertainment. When, after the dissolution of Occupy Wall Street, the movement's former headquarters at Zuccotti Park were repurposed for an episode of *Law and Order: SVU,* Occupy members staged an action they labeled "Mockupy." Objecting to being reified as fodder for vicarious amusement, the Occupiers chanted "We are a movement, not a TV plot."

The legacy of Occupy is treated more obliquely in several of the footage tours de force crafted by the anonymous collective that calls itself the Anti-Banality Union. During an era where the "remix," the "mashup" and the "supercut" have become internet staples, it's understandable these latter-day descendants of *détournement* have been greeted with skepticism by recent commentators. McKenzie Wark, for example, remarks that "[W]here remix bows down before the mower of recuperated desire and merely makes a fetish of it, *détournement* has no such reverence."[62]

Whether the Anti-Banality Union deploys the "spectacle against itself" in the service of "autonomous desire" is debatable; their projects are more straightforwardly agitational (if not precisely agitprop) than the *détourned* films of Rene Viénet esteemed by Wark. What is clear, however, is that the Anti-Banality films, or what the mainstream media invariably refer to as their "supercuts," confront the post-Occupy political malaise with energetic archival scavenging that reveals political "wish fulfillment" fantasies embedded in ostensibly escapist Hollywood entertainment.

Police Mortality (2013), one of Anti-Banality's most celebrated works, presents compelling evidence that a number of police epics, when judiciously recycled, endorse the dissolution or self-destruction of so-called "law enforcement." The collective argues "that there's a kernel of liberation in all of these Hollywood narratives, and the destruction of New York, and the police destroying themselves from within, are both maybe sublimated forms of revolution, or maybe ideas of revolution that insinuate themselves into Hollywood in these masked forms."[63] This dexterous recontextualization of cop sagas foregrounds both the vigilantism and repression endemic to self-styled arbiters of justice, as well as the loathing of the police force that is easily identified as a barely submerged strain within popular culture. Within this schema, the "People's Revolutionary Strike Force" that menaces "Dirty Harry" Callahan in *The Enforcer* and are branded as mere psychopaths, emerge as an emblem of resistance. On the other hand, a sci-fi satire such as Paul Verhoeven's *RoboCop* (1987) requires little ideological massaging. Verhoeven's speculative fiction proved eerily prophetic inasmuch as it predicts the hyper-militarization of the police and its collusion with the corporate sector. In a paradoxical narrative coup de grace, the efforts to make old-guard cops redundant results in a mass strike by the men in blue. The more muddled ideological landscape of *The Dark Knight Rises* nevertheless depicts a NYPD at war with itself. With a facetious sleight of hand, *Police Mortality* transforms dystopia into utopia and constructs a prefigurative vision by envisioning the destruction and/or self-eradication of the police.

By locating emancipatory elements in even the most reified Hollywood detritus, the Anti-Banality Union identifies the seeds of resistance within popular culture.

The decentralized aesthetic initiatives of the groups immersed in media jujitsu is typical of the almost total rejection by anarchists of the Wagnerian model of the *Gesamtkunstwerk*: most examples of contemporary cinema abjure the synaesthetic ideal of aesthetic totality. Of course, in some respects an earlier generation of anarchists' anti-statism was permeated by a desire to create what Josef Chytry termed an aesthetic state—"a social and political community that accords primacy, although not exclusiveness, to the aesthetic dimension in human consciousness and activity."[64] An anarchist incarnation of this ideal reached brief fruition in the Bavarian Republic of 1918–1919 when literary figures like Ernst Toller joined forces with activists such as Gustav Landauer.[65] Yet in an era when the seizure of power by anarchists has not seemed a tangible possibility, to say the least, filmmakers and video artists have been largely concerned with concrete local or topical issues that lack—or consciously ignore—the Romantic pretensions of an earlier generation of anarchists, who viewed art as transcendent and redemptive.

Nick Macdonald's *The Liberal War* (1972), a critique of the ideological underpinnings of the Vietnam War that is as much autobiographical reflection as documentary, is a paradigmatic example of the post-Romantic anarchist impulse. Made by a committed anarchist in his own apartment, the film is exemplary for its modesty. This stripped-down combination of documentary and autobiographical reflection adheres to the goals of anarchist pedagogy with a bare-bones aesthetic, which avoids the heavy-handed editing and sentimental rhetoric that Macdonald abhorred in "liberal" documentaries such as Peter Davis's *Hearts and Minds*.[66]

The Liberal War indicts the liberal statist ideology that provided the ideological sustenance for the Vietnam conflict. Avoiding conventional documentary rhetoric, the film defamiliarizes the Kennedy–Johnson bad-faith appeals to democracy with narration written from the vantage point of an anarcho-communist narrator who resides in a post-revolutionary society. He must explain the imperialist war of the 1960s to his disbelieving comrades. Vietnam becomes an eerie abomination, part of a past "long before the humanist spirit of anarchism engulfed the world and gave power over the self to every child, woman, and man." The "liberal war" thus emerges as the negation of the projected anarchist communist future.

Macdonald's avowedly "poor" cinema contrasts its own pedagogical thrust with the official culture of Harvard University, which produced "most of the architects of the war," among them men such as Robert McNamara and McGeorge Bundy. Macdonald's anti-Harvard interlude is followed by a shot in which he tears up his own Harvard diploma, thereby acknowledging his own familiarity with the ideology of liberalism.

If it is possible to chart the anarchist aesthetic's trajectory from the belief in poet-seers (which is still apparent in some commercial and art films) to less narcissistic critiques of the media, can we locate analogous phases within the history of anarchist film criticism? Although anarchist film criticism is even more difficult to classify than anarchist-inspired cinema, it is possible to draw a rough sketch (if not a precise "periodization") of anti-authoritarian critical tendencies. If we start with the post–World War II period (there is very little substantial anarchist commentary on film before that era), three distinct approaches can be outlined: a critical orientation, strongly reminiscent of—if not usually consciously aligned with—the Frankfurt School's mass culture thesis, which dismisses most Hollywood films as irredeemable sludge; a more concrete "Enzensbergerian" orientation, which actually predates the publication of Enzensberger's essays; and articles and books that reflect the influence of post-structuralist thought and postmodern genre theory.

Emma Goldman is reported to have attacked movies as "the opium of the masses,"[67] and her contempt for the cinema reflects her distinctive oscillation between a Nietzschean, quasi-elitist individualism and a more traditionally anarchist advocacy of radical democracy. A similar unease with popular culture (without the attendant Nietzschean baggage) is evident in many of the articles devoted to movies in small American anarchist journals such as *Why?, Resistance,* and *Retort* during the 1940s.

"A Night at the Movies," for example (published by *Resistance* in 1949 and apparently written by the antiwar activist Daniel De Wees),[68] lamented the fact that a trip to the local cinema during the late 1940s could never consist of simple escapist entertainment—even a simple outing to see a comedy culminated in a barrage of cold war paranoia:

> You go to the movies on that night. Nothing much to do, and a movie is as good a place as any to kill a couple of hours. . . .
>
> News of the World. . . . And you are only minding your business and here to see a comedy, but here are planes, speeches, rockets, and bombs. . . . Your memory goes back to other movies on other nights when burning Japanese soldiers were flung on the screen and they clapped . . . a military parade, soldiers, sailors, WACS and Waves, guns, planes and tanks. . . .

> Surely nobody believes this crap any more—but the cold dead faces around
> you believe. They believe.

While De Wees's article simply regrets the fact that popular entertainment
cannot escape being contaminated by political reaction, another *Resistance*
contributor, Jackson Mac Low, strikes a recognizably Adornian chord in
his essay "The Human Condition: Hunger-Art and the Hungry Artists."[69]
The article starts out with a well-deserved swipe at T. S. Eliot (resplendent
on 'the cover of *Time* . . . carrying his face in an incredibly vulgar, pink and
gold 'symbolic' landscape"), but its subsequent complaint that most Hollywood films "remain on a level of trashiness seldom approached by even
the Roman circuses" recalls Patrick Brantlinger's conviction that "from the
left, "bread and circuses" has proved a useful phrase for helping to explain
and condemn the processes by which capitalism has managed to deflect "the
proletariat" from its goal."[70]

Dwight Macdonald, whose intellectual journey took him from youthful
communism to middle-aged Trotskyism and finally to his own idiosyncratic
form of anarchism, also agreed that the bulk of Hollywood films should be
banished to the trash pile. Nevertheless, since Macdonald has been caricatured as a pessimistic snob, it is important briefly to examine his broader
cultural assumptions before focusing on his film criticism.[71]

Macdonald's postmodern critics seem to forget that his superficially "mandarin" stance was, at least initially, a reaction to the arid doctrines of "socialist realism" and "proletarian fiction" promoted by the Communist Party's
cultural commissars. Socialist realism presented itself as populist, but there
is little doubt that the work of now (deservedly) forgotten novelists such as
Clara Weatherwax had no more appeal for most members of the working
class than the novels of Proust and Kafka, championed by Macdonald and
his colleagues at the *Partisan Review*. It is unfortunate, however, that Macdonald's justified disdain for bureaucratic control of the arts blinded him
to the fact that not all film and literature tied to the Popular Front (if not
the Party itself) could be dismissed as mediocre: as several scholars point
out, *Citizen Kane* was as much a product of this broad-based left–liberal
alliance as turgid proletarian novels.[72] Harvey Teres makes the case that the
Partisan Review's disenchantment with the Communist Party was as much
a product of dismay over the Stalinist betrayal of the Spanish Revolution as
"disagreements over . . . cultural matters."[73]

Yet to conclude that Macdonald's hostility to Stalinism is no better than
"Cold War anti-Communism"[74] ignores his consistently anarchist perspective. It is true that, during the 1950s, Macdonald lent his support to the Con-

gress for Cultural Freedom and, even more embarrassingly, "chose the West" in a debate with Norman Mailer.[75] But by 1960, Macdonald was lecturing on anarchism to the early chapters of SDS and was subsequently conspicuous in his support for the Columbia radicals during the 1968 strike.[76]

It does remain slightly perplexing that Macdonald made no attempt to align his anarchism with his film criticism—an attempt that was made, however unsuccessfully, by the writers at *Resistance* and *Why?* This may have been merely the result of the journalistic milieu that produced the bulk of his film reviews, or it could perhaps be judged the most regrettable result of his fondness for the undialectical rubrics of high and low culture. Macdonald's invective is not confined to domestic examples of supposed masscult and midcult: he also lambasts films by Visconti and Fellini that he regards as bloated white elephants. To his credit, he generously supported independent features such as Robert Frank's *Pull My Daisy* (1959) and John Cassavetes's *Shadows* (1961).[77] For the most part, however, Macdonald saves his enthusiasm for modernist works by Antonioni and Resnais, which are the cinematic equivalents of the writers most prized by his colleagues at *Partisan Review; Hiroshima Mon Amour* (1959) is considered sophisticated enough to be compared "with Joyce, with Picasso, with Berg and Bartok and Stravinsky."[78] Resnais's artistry is rarefied enough to win Macdonald's praise, while Otto Preminger's *The Cardinal* is exiled to the same aesthetic Siberia as the collected works of Pearl Buck and the monthly selections of the Book-of-the-Month Club. As Umberto Eco remarks, "for MacDonald 'avant-garde' is synonymous with 'high' art, the only domain of value; any attempt to mediate its results must be bad, for the very simple reason that the average man, the citizen of modern industrial civilization who requires such mediation, is beyond help."[79] But one (admittedly extreme) contemporary riposte to Macdonald's view of mass culture is John Fiske's tome, which obsequiously thanks the "producers and distributors"[80] of commercial television—seems to invert, rather than remedy, the terms of the ongoing debate surrounding popular culture's viability.

The film reviews published in the French Anarchist Federation's journal, *Le Libertaire*, constitute an eccentric exception to these critical strands. For example, in 1950, Georges Goldfayn attacked the French distributors of Buñuel's *Los Olvidados* (1950) for retitling the film *Pitié pour eux:* "It is not pity but revolution that the forgotten ones have need of," complains Goldfayn. Louis Bedouin chastised Charlie Chaplin for accepting an award from the Parisian police; the comedian whose anti-authoritarianism was marked by a derisive view of the police in early films such as *Easy Street* is taken to task for his surprising about-face. True to its anti-clerical roots, *Le Libertaire* also savaged Bresson's *Diary of a Country Priest* (1951) in a review by Ado Kyrou entitled "The Cinema Has No Need of God."[81]

Several of the articles published in the British anarcho-pacifist newspaper *Peace News* during the early 1960s mark a transitional phase within anarchist film criticism: the reviews and articles written by Alan Lovell still cling to some of the same cultural preferences that permeate Macdonald's work, even though they cannot help but reflect the growing influence of the *politique des auteurs*.

Alan Lovell's 1962 musings on "the importance of criticism" are imbued with a Kropotkin-like social concern (although Lovell's primary concern is threat of nuclear war, not capitalist exploitation) and an aversion to Hollywood—"the world . . . populated exclusively by beautiful men and women, living in luxurious surroundings."[82] Most of the article is devoted to a pained consideration of the flawed realism[83] of John Schlesinger's *A Kind of Loving*. The "exhibitionism" of the *mise-en-scène*, the editing's "showy restlessness," and current "sociological clichés" are said to derive from the same "drabness and defeat" that paralyzed Britain during the "struggle against the bomb." The earnest moral urgency is miles away from Macdonald's breezy tone, but Lovell's objections to Schlesinger's middlebrow realism are close in spirit to Macdonald's rage against "midcult."[84] On the other hand, an article written only months later finds Lovell coming to terms with "the great power of the American cinema . . . the area of myth."[85] Even though Lovell ultimately concludes that Hitchcock and John Ford are inferior to Renoir and Ozu, allowance is made for the possibility of a critical practice capable of analyzing the Hollywood cinema without condescension.

Some of Paul Goodman's essays on film could be categorized as less-elegant renderings of the same anti-mass-culture arguments that were Macdonald's stock in trade. In fact, Goodman moves beyond glib pronouncements on the moribund state of the cinema and looks forward to the media criticism of Chomsky, as well as scores of lesser-known anarchist scribes. A 1963 article, "Is Little TV Possible?"[86] ponders the vast expense of even "educational television" (as it was then known). A subsequent article calls for the creation of "decentralized" media outlets. Goodman's "proposal to countervail brainwashing"[87] has never been enacted, but numerous scrappy guerrilla video organizations keep alive his hopes that "little media" can contribute to a genuine "schola videotica."

Some years ago, a manifesto on "anarchist art" proclaimed that "if a work of art is to be truly anarchist, its means corresponding to its ends, it must be anarchist in its plot, anarchist in its images, or anarchist in its form."[88] It is exceedingly difficult to say authoritatively what anarchist plots, images, and forms are or should be: they are constantly in flux and subject to revision. Still, as this discussion has confirmed, there are certain motifs and tropes that recur within an ever-evolving anarchist aesthetic. Anarchist cinema often zeroes in on salutary moments of negation—not unlike the moment when the protagonist of John Carpenter's *They Live* (1988) dons a pair of shades and immediately perceives the reified nature of late capitalist society when confronted with billboards revealing hidden messages such as "obey and consume." In addition, the beggars' banquet scene in *Viridiana* and the scatological montage sequences in *WR* crystallize a tradition that Robert Stam celebrates as the "transmogrification of the negative"—an irreverent strain that pays homage to writers such as Rabelais and filmmakers like Buñuel and Makavejev who "valorized the grotesque body and the lower social and bodily stratum."[89] As we face an uncertain future, the aesthetic uplift offered by the power of negative thinking is strangely inspirational.

Afterword

WHEN I WAS RESEARCHING *Film and the Anarchist Imagination* in the 1980s and 1990s, left intellectuals and academics dismissed anarchism as either passé or quaint. The words "anarchism" and "anarchist," particularly when paired with cinema, generated quizzical stares and unabashed head scratching. During a visit to the International Institute of Social History in 1987, I told a fellow researcher (a specialist in the no-doubt-fascinating history of Dutch social democracy) that I was focusing on film and anarchism. Without warning, he started to laugh uncontrollably; no explanation was provided.

The first edition of this book was published in 1999, several months before the Seattle demonstrations protesting the World Trade Organization's Ministerial Conference. Although similar protests had already taken place in European cities such as Cologne and London, the so-called "Battle in Seattle" marked the resurgence of an anarchist presence in American mainstream discourse. Not since the "Red Scare" of the early twentieth century had anarchists been more visible—or more vilified—in the mass media. In the years that followed, there was an efflorescence of scholarly publications on anarchist theory and history. Academics reassessed the classical anarchist tradition, often from a post-structuralist perspective; disparate versions of "post-anarchism" were thrashed out in anthologies,[1] as well as in the pages of *Anarchist Studies,* an academic journal founded in 1993 that became increasingly more prominent—while remaining a whipping boy occasionally vulnerable to attack by anarchists who find academia inherently suspect. Rare anarchist films, once only available to researchers able to travel thousands of miles to archives, became downloadable through Stuart Christie's Anarchist Film Channel.

Unicorn Riot, an online source of radical news, does not label itself as specifically anarchist on its website. Still, their self-identification as a "decentralized media collective" that sustains itself without corporate support more or less redefines the ideals of an ongoing anarchist media tradition. Livestreaming events such as the anti-capitalist demonstrations at the G20 summit imbue coverage of activist hot spots with a "you are there" immediacy. Young people who would have once discovered anarchism by perusing the standard surveys by George Woodcock or Daniel Guérin were instead introduced to anarchist thought and practice by outlets such as Indymedia or Crimethinc. They might also consult the "A is for Anarchy" videos disseminated by submedia.tv, which present short, accessible guides to basic concepts such as "direct action" and "mutual aid." For example, "Heatscore" of submedia emphasizes the "easily digestible"[2] quality of his site's Crimethinc-inspired films; whether the films are commendable for their lack of jargon and accessibility—or questionable because of what certain commentators have termed their residual anarcho-individualism and indebtedness to middle-class rebelliousness—is a quandary that critics must confront.

Anti-authoritarian artists, who usually reject Leninist injunctions to rally around a vanguard party, have often found themselves in sympathy with aesthetic avant-gardes. David Graeber's "The Twilight of Vanguardism" maps the peculiar history of a much-maligned keyword by demonstrating how avant-garde movements, particularly the furiously schismatic surrealists and situationists, frequently parodied political vanguardists by expelling members for real or imagined aesthetic heresies, a mock-Stalinist mindset engendered by "insane sectarianism." For Graeber, a radical anthropologist, the saving grace of these farcical exercises in authoritarianism coordinated by so-called anti-authoritarians resides in the hope that radical artists, armed with a fervent belief in the need for "non-alienated production," will humble themselves sufficiently to both critique their own hubris and learn from the "most oppressed" (and frequently most anti-hierarchical) people on earth—that is, the indigenous.[3]

Navigating the occasional conflict between anarchism's appeal for avant-gardists with its concomitant need to appeal to what Kropotkin termed the "constructive activity of the masses"[4] is one of the central paradoxes that confront any critic determined to take on debates between inveterate modernists and diehard populists. One of the most surprising critiques of *Film and the Anarchist Imagination* involved one reviewer's claim that I was oblivious, or even hostile, to popular cinema or what academics occasionally term, with wide-eyed veneration, "the popular"—despite my blatant contention that the anarchist aesthetic was irrefutably "elusive" and not monolithic. This critique partially stems from my acknowledgment of an entity identifiable as the culture industry, despite the intrinsic amorphousness of the term and the admittedly unhelpful refusal of Theodor Adorno and Max Horkheimer to dissect specific examples of popular culture, and my qualified appreciation of some aspects of Dwight Macdonald's aesthetic stance. Yet my defense of Macdonald's anti-Stalinist acerbity toward Popular Front sentimentality was tempered by a disappointment that he failed to align his film criticism with his anarchist sensibility. These caveats were conveniently ignored in a blanket dismissal of Macdonald's complex and contradictory corpus that sought to equate my own perspective with the author of *Against the American Grain*'s denunciation of "masscult" and undiluted enthusiasm for high art. From this vantage point, I'm accused of opposing "popular film for mass consumption" and privileging "what one could call 'art films' (low-budget features with relatively limited distribution)" and documentaries, thereby formulating an implicit link between the anarchist aesthetic and an avant-garde aesthetic.[5]

The paradoxical nature of these assumptions becomes clear when perusing Isabelle Marinone's introduction to *Cinémas libertaires, au service des forces de transgression et de révolte*,[6] an anthology that, unlike *Film and the Anarchist Imagination*, does unequivocally argue that anarchist cinema is synonymous with the avant-garde and pigeonholes my study as little more than a tribute to anarchist "heroes and martyrs." Perhaps the confusion lies in a certain category mistake: one critic maintains that my implicit disdain for popular cinema leads me to ignore the charms of popular melodrama, while another rather patronizingly implies that an interest in historical representation and standard genres such as the biopic makes me immune to the allure of the genuine strains of "transgression and revolt." The truth is that I have a great respect, and fondness, for Hollywood popular cinema. As Gilberto Perez makes clear, Hollywood was producing decidedly non-kitschy films such as *Young Mr. Lincoln* (1939), and *Mr. Smith Goes to Washington* (1939) at the same time that mandarin leftists such as Clement Greenberg were dismissing American commercial cinema tout court.[7] The anarchist critic's quandary of course involves balancing their affection for classic Hollywood cinema with the realization that this tradition is, for the most part, unalterably opposed to anti-authoritarian precepts. In fact, as early as 1934, the noted anarcho-syndicalist José Peirats's manifesto, *Para una nueva concepcion del arte: Lo que podria ser un cinema social*, paid tribute to the technical and aesthetic achievements of key Soviet and American directors while retaining hopes for a "social cinema" that, as his biographer Chris Ealham points out, could provide a "counterpoint to the 'moral code' of Hollywood and the 'belligerent tendencies' of cinema under the Nazis."[8]

Setting aside Hollywood's fairly routine hostility to anti-authoritarian politics, it's obvious that fissures within its ideological edifice surface occasionally. John Farrow's *Five Came Back* (1939), to choose one example, is a taut B movie that, like many films written by screenwriters destined to be blacklisted (in this case, Dalton Trumbo), smuggles subversive themes into a superficially formulaic genre film. Farrow and Trumbo have great fun with a fairly routine tale of a group of airline passengers en route to Panama who became stranded in the jungle after a crash. The film's portrayal of an altruistic anarchist was, for its time, almost unprecedented.

In any case, if enshrining the avant-garde as inherently anarchist was one of my priorities, I would certainly have devoted some space to Man Ray's films—even though, Man Ray's sympathy with anarchism notwithstanding, I would have found it difficult to find a plausible link between his Dadaist forays and anarchist principles.

Of course, Jesse Cohn's suggestion that scholars tackle the history of anarchist "resistance culture,"[9] particularly popular culture fashioned within the anarchist community itself, delineates provocative terrain that, at least on paper, avoids the sterile antinomies of fetishizing the popular on the one hand and giving uncritical obeisance to hermetic avant-gardism on the other. In a provocative essay devoted to the realm of "anarchist cultural studies," Cohn exhorts his readers to explore "precisely what made anarchism" the object of "mass appeal (and for whom); of what the limits of anarchist possibility really were, and why, of the possibilities manifested by earlier experiments in the construction of an anarchist popular culture from the parodic songs of Joe Hill to Armand Guerra's short-lived "Cinéma du Peuple film cooperative."[10] This is a laudable goal, but, as with some of the CNT films such as *Aurora de Esperanza* that Cohn lavishes with qualified praise elsewhere, the aspirations of Guerra's collective were often more noteworthy than its achievements. I'd be the first admit that the imperatives of film criticism often undermine other considerations in *Film and the Anarchist Imagination*. The book's central conundrum—or if you like, aporia—resides in the fact that it is essentially a work of film criticism that also aligns its agenda with anti-authoritarian political sentiments. Call it perversely anti-intentionalist, but for better or worse, films made by non-anarchists such as Petri and Buñuel are often more convincingly anarchist in spirit and execution than films made by well-intentioned anarchists.

Despite the fondness of many anarchist academics for popular culture, the most salient examples of twenty-first-century anarchist cinema and media have not originated from Hollywood or even from the increasingly conformist realm of so-called independent cinema. Although it's best to avoid facile dichotomies, there's clearly a widening gap within anarchist-inspired visual culture between what, in reference to Clayton Patterson's *Tompkins Square Park Police Riot,* I term "provisional" activist media and the avant-gardist tendency that still covertly believes in art as redemptive, even as it outwardly endorses an "anti-art" agenda.

In *Anarchy and Culture: The Aesthetic Politics of Modernism,* David Weir argues that "the infusion of anarchistic principles into artistic practice—particularly individualist anarchism" led to a profound impact on nineteenth- and twentieth-century modernist and avant-garde culture.[11] Perhaps because Weir's book was published in 1997 before the resurgence of anarchist activism, he insists on a strict demarcation between the "cultural success" of anarchism and its "political decline." This distressingly Manichean account was, several years later, challenged by Allan Antliff's account of early twentieth-century American avant-garde painters in *Anarchist Modernism* that assumes more of a symbiosis between artistic creation and political activism.[12] Nathan Jun, who takes a stab at formulating a specifically anarchist film theory, contends that anarchists should champion a "cinema of liberation" that rejects both hermetic avant-gardism and commercial endeavors to "appropriate" mainstream cinema for radical purposes. Jun wants to avoid relegating anarchist cinema to either "the commodity form . . . or a mere vehicle for propaganda."[13]

Huw Wahl's *To Hell With Culture: A Film About Herbert Read* (2014) reminds us of a brief era when anarchism did in fact become closely associated with the avant-garde. The film argues, quite convincingly, that Read, the mandarin advocate of what might reasonably termed a modernist "vanguard" and one of the co-founders of London's Institute of Contemporary Art, infused his aesthetic credo with an anarchist impetus at a time when anarchism was profoundly unfashionable in Britain. Interweaving archival footage of a television interview with Read conducted by George Woodcock with various testimonies from art historians, a portrait of a fascinatingly contradictory figure emerges. Despite Read's paradoxical status as a putative country squire who accepted a knighthood, Jerry Zaslove hails him as a thinker who was forgotten as Marxism became ascendant—and whose broadsides against mass culture share affinities with the non-dogmatic Marxism of the Frankfurt School.

For the majority of the interviewees, *To Hell With Culture,* the manifesto that gives the film its name, is a central text in fusing anti-authoritarian Marxism with an anarchist ethos that personifies what Michael Löwy terms "romantic anti-capitalism,"[14] a current that extends from William Blake to the surrealists and situationists. For the majority of the interviewees in *To Hell*

With Culture, Read's work functions as an antidote to the "commodification of culture"; in a special issue of *Anarchist Studies* that embellishes the film's arguments, Matthew S. Adams strikes a Kropotkin-like note by maintaining that, "As Read rebuilt Britain in his imagination, he saw a country beginning a long experiment with mutual aid and participatory democracy, and perceived the shoots of a new culture slowly germinating in its fields, factories, and workshops."[15] A fragment of Read's lecture on the "surrealist object" also reiterates his romantic antinomianism—a belief that "the imagination," implicitly an anarchist imagination, can transform banal emblems of everyday life into aesthetic artifacts, Towards the end of the film, a section outlining the precepts of Read's manifesto, *Education Through Art,* drives home the point that championing aesthetic "self-creation" among the young negates an inert conception of culture that restricts art to the realm of hidebound institutions such as museums and the egotism of professional artists.

It might not be too hyperbolic to claim that post-1999 anarchist film culture is less preoccupied with the schism between high and low culture than with dividing lines between collective, frequently anonymous, unsigned work and traditional auteur-driven cinema. To be sure, contradictions abound even in the most anti-authoritarian corners of the internet where sites often feature both anonymous works that inspire activists, as well as films, both short and feature length, that are signed and reflect a specific directorial sensibility. What unites most of these films, though, is their widespread availability online. In this respect, the video work of online anarchist collectives belong to what Robert Stam labels the "vast planetary archive of ideas and strategies" that form the "aesthetic commons."[16] In addition, the accessibility of a "planetary archive" democratizes, even if it doesn't efface, the disparity between high modernist works imbued with a Marcusean "negativity" and activist work designed with more pragmatic goals in mind.

Perhaps the most celebrated unsigned anarchist video artifact of the new century is *The Potentiality of Storming Heaven,* a twenty-eight-minute account (disseminated online by submedia) of a 2008 uprising in Athens (some anarchists, as well as vehement anti-anarchists, call it, with varying amounts of disdain, irony, and affection, "riot porn") that followed the police murder of a young man named Alexis Grigoropoulos in the city's Exarcheia district. Images of confrontations between protestors and cops, fires being set, and rocks being thrown are accompanied by pithy slogans and testimonies from young participants in the action. One slogan that sounds more like an invocation is repeated twice—"the ghost of freedom always comes with the knife between its teeth." A young militant asks rhetorically—"Why do we burn?" He answers plaintively: "because we're commodities." Intertitles instruct viewers to resist the society of the spectacle.

Potentiality's sentiments echo the rhetorical tenor of the Situationist International's "The Decline and Fall of the Spectacle-Commodity Economy." For the SI, the Watts riots, denounced by respectable commentators on the right and left as irresponsible (a typical newspaper headline contains the admonishment: "protest devolved into rioting") were bound up with a rebellion against the commodity, a cri-de-coeur attributable to the despair of "worker-consumers." More recently, Joshua Clover's *Riot. Strike. Riot: The New Era of Uprisings*[17] attempts to undermine the predictable indictment of rioting as nihilistic and antithetical to constructive activism. Aiming for a materialist analysis, Clover notes that, once the riots that preceded what E. P. Thompson termed the "making of the English working class" in the seventeenth and eighteenth centuries subsided, spontaneous insurrections were replaced by mass strikes as an industrial economy took hold in the nineteenth century. During an era when "creating value beyond the point of production" has become a priority—that is, the "financialization" of capitalism—the riot has again become the central mode of social protest.

While *The Potentiality of Storming Heaven* is intriguing as an online found object documenting a political riot, *Breaking the Spell* (1999), whose authorship is often assigned to a trio of directors, represents a more conventional template for agitprop video. The quandary of evaluating what the mainstream press considers violence—that is, property destruction—looms large in this "on the ground" chronicle of the WTO events and their impact upon both the anarchist community and skeptics in the mainstream press. Compared to *Potentiality*, *Breaking*'s structure is closer to a traditional documentary inasmuch as there's a clear juxtaposition between two universes of discourse. Much of the film harnesses footage of the WTO demonstrations in Seattle and interviews with participants in order to implode the mainstream media's tendency to equate property destruction with "violence." These more or less straightforwardly polemical sequences stand in contrast to a more self-reflexive component of the film in which anarchists based in Eugene, Oregon ponder the significance of the WTO events and are interviewed by a *60 Minutes* correspondent about the controversies surrounding the Black Bloc's activities. The fact that Christopher Robé named his study of anarchist video activism *Breaking the Spell* indicates how pivotal the WTO ferment was to both DIY videography and the contemporary anarchist movement.[18] In the *60 Minutes* episode, an activist named Shelley observes that watching television and being exposed to corporate logos can put "you in a daze . . . when that's shattered, it breaks a spell." Breaking the spell becomes synonymous with crossing a line and embracing what might be deemed a twenty-first-century equivalent of propaganda by the deed. Quite predictably, assaults on property condemned by liberals such as Medea Benjamin in 1999 look forward to Chris Hedges's similar rant at the time of Occupy Wall Street in 2011.

A certain amount of confusion concerning the precise authorship of *Breaking the Spell* reflects its status as a film wedged between the complete anonymity of online "riot porn" and a full-fledged documentary effort. The credits attribute the direction to Tim Lewis, Robé highlights the role of Tim Bream, while some online credits foreground a collaboration between Lewis, Bream, and a rather mysterious figure named "Sir Chuck A. Rock." When I queried Robé about these disparities, he replied: "there is always a tension in many of these anarchist communities (as well as Left communities as a whole) between collective effort and individual recognition, utopian aspiration and pragmatic concerns. Media-making is seen as a means for a greater good and also as a badge of recognition and perhaps professional advancement." Not surprisingly, the contradictions of our culture can be found lodged within these ambiguities."[19] Given that very few critics or academics are willing to forfeit "individual recognition," it's also very difficult to be sanctimonious about these ambiguities.

Stuart Townsend's conspicuously earnest *Battle in Seattle* (2007) attempted to explain the intricacies of anti-corporate protest to a wider audience. Unfortunately, although Townsend cites *The Battle of Algiers* (1966) and *Medium Cool* (1969) as influences, his film, as critics pointed out, frequently resembles a slightly more enlightened version of Paul Haggis's *Crash* (2004).

As in *Crash,* a grab bag of strangers collide, and they endure privation while learning predigested life lessons. Although the travails of a harried liberal mayor (based loosely on former Seattle mayor Paul Schell), a world-weary NGO representative, and a cop who regrets pummeling a protestor need not concern us, the depiction of the activists, particularly an impassioned anarchist named Lou (played with requisite amounts of anger and spunk by Michelle Rodriguez), provides ample evidence of the paradoxes that emerge when anti-authoritarian politics becomes fodder for mainstream entertainment. Despite being a passionate advocate of direct action, Lou—perhaps in the spirit of spurious "balance"—is preoccupied with condemning the supposedly violent tendencies of her fellow anarchists. Lou clearly references the activities of the Black Bloc and apparently believes that this group's most famous "transgression"—the smashing of Starbucks windows—renders it hopelessly violent and outside the pale. But, as David Graeber observes, "Journalists have a fairly idiosyncratic definition of 'violence' . . . so even if one protestor damages a Starbucks window, one can speak of violent protests, but if police then proceed to attack everyone present with tasers, sticks, and plastic bullets, this cannot be described as violent."[20] And as a group of anarchists wrote in an anonymous broadside against Townsend's film, an entire swath of anti-hierarchical protest, which includes grassroots groups like "Food Not Bombs," is overlooked in *Battle in Seattle*. Townsend is, alas, more interested in gooey humanist uplift than the nuts and bolts of direct action.

Maple Razsa and Pacho Velez's *Bastards of Utopia* (2010), in which the filmmakers doubled as participant observers (Razsa is a Harvard-trained anthropologist) immersed in the life of a small group of Zagreb-based anarchists during the early years of the twenty-first century, adds a more ruminative tinge to the resurgent anarchism explored in *Breaking the Spell*. Sharing the experience of Croatian activists during alternating exhilarating and disillusioning interludes results in a nuanced portrait of a community occasionally at odds with itself as internecine quarrels surface. As Razsa observes,

> the longitudinal nature of the project, as well as the enormous resources of time we were able to put into the film with academic support, working our way carefully through 200 hours of footage mark clear differences in the conditions of production we enjoyed in contrast to many more quick and dirty activist productions that respond to the urgent questions of the day, rather than the larger arc of movements ups and downs. But I think in some way we also were reacting against the "riot porn" focus only on radical acts of militant defiance by nameless and masked anarchists and toward understanding confrontational protest as one important moment in a much more varied life of political commitment that also includes many less dramatic and more quotidian forms of politics.[21]

Weaned on punk rock and the anti-corporate globalization movement, *Bastards'* young communards have rediscovered a left-libertarian tradition that remained submerged during the state socialist era. Repulsed by the excesses of consumer capitalism, the young militants must also come to terms with both the unfortunate legacy of Tito's authoritarian regime and the ravages of neoliberalism. Their solution is to strive for implementing utopian goals in the here and now instead of waiting for some radiant anarcho-communist future—an approach that recalls, however unwittingly, Colin Ward's practical interpretation of Kropotkin's notion of mutual aid in *Anarchy in Action*. This strategy involves such traditional anarchist alternatives as communal living, seizing abandoned property for squatting, and operating a free store to feed and clothe the less privileged members of the community.

One of the virtues of the "longitudinal" nature of Razsa and Velez's project is that it allows them to explore some of the subtle tensions within the anti-authoritarian movement. Fistra and Dado, young men who favor militant direct action, are somewhat put off by their female comrade Jelena's willingness to collaborate with more moderate NGOs such as the World Social Forum. Razsa's *Bastards of Utopia: Living Radical Politics After Socialism*, a book-length ethnographic study that is, in many respects, a companion volume to the film, fleshes out some of these contretemps. Although Jelena is initially willing to join forces with "moderate" antiwar NGOs at the time of the Iraq War (and endures the wrath of her colleagues), Razsa's book recounts how a mistrust of these organizations surged by the time his three protagonists travel to Thessaloniki to protest the EU summit in 2003. Within the film, Jelena critiques Fistra's machismo, which apparently makes him doubt that she'll be effective during street actions. His jibes are ultimately eclipsed, rather paradoxically, by Jelena's reassessment of confrontational tactics after her experience with her affinity group in Thessaloniki. Razsa's summing up of these events, in a chapter entitled "Feeling the State on Your Own Skin," allows for a more comprehensive analysis of internal debates—especially Jelena's "anarcha-feminist" skepticism toward what is termed "performative violence" within their affinity group.

Razsa's book, a bravura example of thick description, complements his and Velez's film by providing an analytical gloss on transient moments that illuminate the participants' fears, as well as their regrets. For example, only several brief sequences in the film document the formation, and eventual demise, of the activists' "Free Store" in Zagreb. A pragmatic exercise in prefigurative politics—and a Croatian oasis within consumer capitalism that is made possible by a squat in a building owned by a supermarket chain—falls victim to heavy-handed police tactics. This disillusioning incident, as well as a retrospective interview with Jelena in London, illuminates the consequences of burnout in the anarchist community. Razsa's chapter on the dissolution of the Free Store does not, however, depict anarchists wallowing in despondency. On the contrary, Fistra (referred to as Rimi in the book, which somewhat takes on the tenor of anthropological metafiction) maintains that the failed venture taught him to understand the preparation for "struggling for what is not yet," an "important experience" for the collective.

Labeled a "live participatory film" by its directors, Razsa and Milton Guillen's *The Maribor Uprisings*, (2017) also explores the consequences of direct action in post-Communist eastern Europe. Razsa and Guillen convey the ferment of the third Maribor uprising of December 2012. Maribor, Slovenia's second-largest city, was a bustling industrial center during the heyday of the former Yugoslavia. In 1988, as a foretaste of the years of austerity to come, the city was plagued by an economic crisis and workers fought back by organizing a general strike. According to Gal Kirn, this led to one of the few genuine Yugoslavian experiments in self-management that "was organized from below and had relatively lasting effects." By 2012 Maribor was plagued by unemployment and the local population became fed up with the city government's pervasive corruption. This disgust reached its apogee when Mayor Franc Kangler established radar traps that ensnared twenty thousand people in a city comprising one hundred thousand inhabitants. When it was confirmed that Kangler was receiving kickbacks from the private contractor responsible for the radar traps, the once quiescent residents of Maribor began to emulate other, more ballyhooed struggles. In truth, the speed trap imbroglio was merely the catalyst for a more diffuse series of rebellions against austerity and the post-socialist neoliberal regime.

Unlike *Bastards of Utopia, The Maribor Uprisings* is less concerned with seasoned activists, or even avowed anarchists, than the struggles of ordinary citizens, many newly energized and unfamiliar with radical politics. The film's conceptual ruse embeds two videographers, one female and one male, in the most hectic moments of the third uprising. They essentially function as participant observers and narrate the events to the audience as they sift through their own reminiscences of experiencing the impact of state repression on Maribor residents, who, "once viewed the police as their allies and protectors."

The participatory component of *The Maribor Uprisings,* in which the audience must choose between two options that often entail either plunging into confrontations with police or retreating from the action, might seem superficially gimmicky. After all, in video games or rather tame narrative experiments, this sort of "participation" is often merely an excuse for facile manipulation or a symptom of anemic storytelling. For Razsa and Guillen, the choices we're invited to make are less about the narrative pleasures to be derived from nonfiction than an effort to familiarize spectators with the "sensorial" or visceral immediacy of direct action. At an early juncture in the film, spectators are asked if they want to "follow the hay" (an unflattering reference to Mayor Kangler's hard-to-believe claim that more than one hundred thousand Euros thought to be ill-gotten gains were actually accrued from the sale of hay on this farm) with protestors gathered at the city's Liberty Square to a more militant demonstration at the Municipal Building or refrain from direct action. The audience I saw the film with voted for following the hay, an unsurprising decision in light of the inevitable inclination of both film audiences and crowds to gravitate toward excitement, or the inclination of activists to challenge authority on a visceral level. In the book version of *Bastards,* Razsa employs Jane Gaines's concept of "political mimesis" as a conduit to examine the strengths, and contingent limitations, of "riot porn." According to Gaines's perspective, viewers sympathetic to specific political viewpoints can be mobilized in solidarity with social movements by films that titillate as much as they instruct.[22] While Razsa rightly concludes that the implications of "political mimesis" need to be fleshed out with a deeper understanding of historical contexts, the audience's yen for immediate confrontation confirms that immersion in street action can be either a prelude, or an accompaniment, to either more nuanced political consciousness or an understanding of historical precedents. *The Maribor Uprisings* offers testimony outlining popular discontent; a young man named Aleš describes how he and his friends endure constant police harassment. One of the film's narrators describes how the uprisings functioned as an antidote to the despondency recounted by alienated young people and workers, a release of tension on a mass scale: "We were overwhelmed by feelings of solidarity; it was love at the barricades."

This ecstatic afterglow is challenged in some of the reflective concluding sequences that consider the aftermath of the uprisings and the political upheaval that followed. Participants in the uprisings and sympathizers attest to the fact that, although Kangler and the prime minister were removed from office, no significant structural reforms were enacted and the ravages of austerity were not eradicated.

Another documentary subgenre—the essay film—is supremely congruent with the anarchist project since, according to Adorno, the essay form subverts "totalities of truth" and promotes productively heretical musings.[23] One of the salient characteristics of the classical essay from Montaigne to Adorno encompasses a freedom of invention that allows for indulgence in a digressive aesthetic.

A purposeful digressiveness is one of the delights of Adam Kossoff's *The Anarchist Rabbi* (2014), an essay film that uses the London years of the German-born anarcho-syndicalist Rudolf Rocker to shed light on a little-known era of British anarchism in the late nineteenth and early twentieth century. The title of Kossoff's elegiac documentary is a bit of a tease for viewers unfamiliar with Rocker's career. An activist in London for a good chunk of the late nineteenth and early twentieth centuries, Rocker's alliance with the city's East End Jewish radicals (the non-Jewish Rocker even learned Yiddish in order to edit several Yiddish-language newspapers) led to him becoming known as a secular "rabbi." Narrated by the actor Steven Berkoff, Kossoff's film employs voice-over that resuscitates Rocker's ghost and allows him to point out the key locales, as they appear today, crucial to the London anarchist milieu (with brief forays to Liverpool and Brighton) of more than a hundred years ago. Channeling the voice of Rocker for a new generation, Kossoff's main target is historical amnesia. Mourning the fact that urban renewal and gentrification obliterate the traces of a radical legacy, the film is a powerful meditation on the potency of a subversive "hidden history." To cite but one of many examples, Louise Michel, renowned for her participation in the Paris Commune, once lived on a street in the now-fashionable Fitzrovia neighborhood; shoppers in contemporary London are doubtless oblivious to the fact that bombs, which were planted by a police spy in the basement of her house, resulted in the arrest of several anarchists denounced as foreign agitators. Kossoff does not, however, fret over an irretrievable past—he reiterates Rocker's essentially optimistic conviction that "I am an anarchist not because I believe that anarchism is the final goal, but because there is no such thing as a final goal."

Kossoff's cine-essay starts out with a quote from Jacques Derrida, which surmises that future historians will rely on "specters" for illuminating the past; an approach that is certainly part of *The Anarchist Rabbi*'s agenda. Radical flânerie is foregrounded as a number of anarchist landmarks, mostly in the East End of London, are traversed in the spirit of conscientious psychogeography. Some of the anarchists invoked by Kossoff are even less part of the radical historical consciousness than Rocker, who is at least known to activists and historians. For example, Benjamin Feigenbaum,[24] who William Fishman termed a "master of anti-religious satire,"[25] is cited as the film invokes the Jewish anarchist propensity to brandish ham sandwiches in front of synagogues on Yom Kippur, the *ne plus ultra* of a certain brand of anticlericalism. Moving on from rhetorical gestures to the rhetoric of violence, the Greenwich Observatory, near the site of where, in 1894, a French anarchist blew himself up while apparently attempting to plant a bomb, becomes the cynosure that underlines how fear of propaganda by the deed helped to fuel anarchist caricatures during a period where foreigners and anarchists were both deemed enemies of the state.

An experimental "biodoc"—Abigail Child's *Acts and Intermissions* (2017) on Emma Goldman—shares many of the concerns of the essay film and the hybrid documentary. Known for her avant-garde films, Child began her career in documentary. *Acts and Intermissions* bridges the gap between hardcore avant-gardism and agitprop while abjuring biographical clichés. Interspersing archival footage, contemporary cell-phone footage, and staged reenactments, the film charts the pertinence of Goldman's legacy to contemporary neoliberal America by avoiding a traditional hagiographic approach (as can be observed in Mel Bucklin's PBS documentary, *Emma Goldman: An Extraordinarily Dangerous Woman, 2004*) Despite incorporating large chunks of Goldman's *Living My Life* into the film via captions and voice-over, her radicalism becomes a vehicle for forging links between the inequities of the past and the equally dispiriting inequities of the twenty-first century.

Child's use of what is sometimes called "macro montage," an approach also favored by feminist filmmakers such as Sara Gomez and Su Friedrich, enables her to create a visual ripple effect in which the militancy of the past segues effortlessly into contemporary struggles. Goldman's account of the 1912 Lawrence, Massachusetts textile strike is juxtaposed with shots of a twenty-first-century sweat shop. Goldman's preoccupation with police infiltration of the anarchist movement aptly rhymes with shots of a computer surveillance unit that evokes the condemnation of government snooping in Laura Poitras's *Citizenfour* (2014). Realizing that a comprehensive biographical portrait of Goldman is both unachievable and undesirable, the film sifts through highlights of Goldman's life without any pretense to comprehensiveness. The attempt on Henry Clay Frick's life by her lover, Alexander Berkman, is given precedence over Goldman's controversial empathy (although not support) for Leon Czolgosz, President McKinley's assassin. Debates that raged within the anarchist community concerning Goldman's romance with Ben Reitman, the so-called "king of the hobos," are elided. A shot of Reitman (played on screen by the filmmaker Bradley Eros) hints that he is a charming rogue. Goldman's anarchist colleagues, however, condemned him as an "opportunist," a scoundrel and, according to certain accounts, a possible police informer.[26] Yet because there's an incommensurability between straightforward biography and *Acts and Intermissions'* playful reinterpretation of Goldman's legacy, these elisions are integral to this bio-doc's aesthetic. Child adopts a modified version of the editing style employed in her less blatantly polemical avant-garde work to create a documentary emphasizing a radical continuity between past and present. There is not only a through line between, say, Berkman and Goldman's rage toward Henry Clay Frick and the demonstrations against Walmart, the personification of punitive labor practices in twentieth-first-century America, that are captured in cell phone video footage. The two eras are implicitly inextricable and fused.

Child's film, like similarly experimental efforts by Kelly Gallagher and Leslie Thornton, address, whether directly or obliquely, debates concerning the viability of what might be termed "intersectional anarchism." Mimicking more-traditional leftists, some anarchist commentators argue that intersectionality is a "liberal" appeal to identity politics that ignores the dynamics of class struggle. Another polemical strain insists that the feminist and anti-racist concerns of intersectionality are easily applicable to anarchism and can help to combat macho "manarchist" and insular, white middle-class tendencies within the anti-authoritarian movement.

Bereft of special pleading, Gallagher's short animated film, *More Dangerous Than a Thousand Rioters* (2016), is a heartfelt attempt to rehabilitate the reputation of Lucy Parsons, a woman of color whose legacy has been appropriated by syndicalists, anarchists, and Communists. Perhaps because Parsons often remained in the shadow of her husband Albert Parsons, one of the Haymarket martyrs executed in 1887—as well as because she collaborated with the Communist Party during the last decades of her life (whether she became a member of the party is a matter of historical dispute)—she is a somewhat underappreciated figure within anarchist circles.

Gallagher sidesteps these ideological entanglements by suggesting that Parsons's life can serve as an inspiration to beleaguered organizers in the age of Trump. An admirer of the gritty visual style of Lizzie Borden's *Born in Flames,* she employs an artisanal approach to animation that spurns CGI and favors the "homemade" artistry of collage and stop motion. Interspersing photographs and graphics with abstract pattern, the visual track is unostentatious enough to focus attention on the narration—a pithy, six-minute chronicle of Parsons's trajectory from birth on a Texas plantation to her passionate support for the "Great Railway Strike of 1877," as well as her neglected status as one of the founding members of the IWW. Parsons's shifting political affiliations make it impossible to anoint her an "anarchist" heroine. But Gallagher's film wisely refuses to take sides in hair-splitting debates between anarchists and communists. Even though Emma Goldman branded Parsons an "opportunist" for her willingness to work with communists, her 1884 manifesto, "To Tramps," a broadside that urges the "the unemployed, the disinherited, and the miserable" to dismantle the "industrial system," is probably more indicative of her true sensibility than certain compromises made subsequently at a time when anarchism was considered defunct.[27]

The vicissitudes of gender fluidity, class, and intellectual radicalism are confronted in an admittedly less-direct fashion in Leslie Thornton's two films on Isabelle Eberhardt, *There Was an Unseen Cloud Moving* and *The Great Invisible.* The films, hybrids that synthesize faux documentary elements and stylized dramatic reenactments, recount Eberhardt's still-controversial life in an elliptical, nonlinear fashion. Eberhardt, a Swiss woman known as the "cross-dressing heiress," converted to Islam and lived as a man in North Africa in the late nineteenth century. Touted as a daring adventurer and transgressive feminist and damned as an Orientalist whose interest in Islam smacks of misguided romanticism, Eberhardt is a classic shapeshifter. Thornton's films share family resemblances with other anarchist "bio-docs" since Eberhardt's worldview was greatly influenced by her equally eccentric father, and tutor, an anarchist named Alexandre Trophimowsky. As chameleon-like as his daughter, Trophimowsky, a former Russian Orthodox priest, is referred to as "tyrannical" in *The Great Invisible,* even though he is also celebrated as a benign patriarch whose rigorous home schooling ensures Isabelle's erudition and no doubt triggered her rebelliousness. One biographer calls him a Tolstoyan pacifist anarchist, while another categorizes him as a "Bakuninist." Superficially a peripheral figure, Trophimowsky is crucial to unraveling Eberhardt's career (he taught her Arabic and nurtured her interest in Islam) since, like her, he both defied Western Victorian norms and betrayed a soft spot for the "exotic" vision of Islam popularized by Pierre Loti's novels. A rather incongruous scene in *The Great Invisible* depicts him denouncing café bombings, the variant of propaganda by the deed endorsed by renegade anarchists like Émile Henry and Ravachol. The relationship of this debate to his daughter's exploits is rather tenuous, but, if nothing more, his political radicalism can be viewed as the progenitor of her sexual radicalism.

Blurring fiction and documentary should not be viewed as a trendy postmodern response to hidebound cinéma verité clichés. Želimir Žilnik, one of the leading filmmakers of the Yugoslavian Black Wave, was already interspersing fictional and nonfictional elements as early as the 1960s. Žilnik's first feature, *Early Works* (1969), which earned him early acclaim when it won the Golden Bear at the Berlin Film Festival, focused on a group of young people determined to revive the emancipatory spirit of the "early Marx" (hence the reference to "early works"—that is, the *Economic and Philosophic Manuscripts of 1844*) despite the bureaucratic morass of Tito's Yugoslavia. Inasmuch as the young protagonists embrace sexual abandon as much as anti-authoritarian socialism, *Early Works* shares some family resemblances with Makavejev's less-despondent meld of anti-Stalinism and psychosexual critique (Žilnik was Makavejev's assistant on *Love Affair of a Switchboard Operator*). Seemingly challenging ideological complacency with their revolutionary fervor, the small cell self-destructs—the brutal attempted rape and attempted murder of a young female revolutionary tellingly named "Jugoslava," imposes a pessimistic gloss on the film's initially hopeful challenge to Titoism from the left. The protagonists are caught in an ideological stranglehold; anti-authoritarian radicalism, clearly inspired by the Belgrade student uprising of 1968, becomes a form of self-immolation.

For many on the anti-Stalinist left, the promise, and ultimate failure, of Yugoslavian Communism resided in the unfulfilled promise of its vaunted experiment in workers' self-management. Anarchist commentators were often cognizant of the contradictory nature of "self-management" in the former Yugoslavia—the yawning chasm between the promise of the concept of a participatory workers' democracy and its actual role as a cog in the machinery of state socialism. Fredy Perlman, writing in the same year that *Early Works* was released, railed against the "ideology of self-management," which "continues to serve as a mask for a commercial-technocratic bureaucracy which has successfully concentrated the wealth and power created by the Yugoslavian working population."[28]

These contradictions are rejiggered and recontextualized in Žilnik's *The Old School of Capitalism* (2009), a doc-fiction fusion that ponders the peculiar legacy of post-Communism in a Serbia still smarting from the scars of Slobodan Milošević's authoritarianism and the foibles of privatization. It's telling that the chorus of "The International" is heard on the soundtrack of both the opening and closing sequence of *Old School*; the realignment of left-wing priorities in a country coping with the ravages of neoliberalism is a key element of Žilnik's alternately impassioned and playful film. According to Branka Ćućrić, the tainted heritage of the "pseudo-participation" of workers' self-management, a strategy that became part and parcel of a "post-Fordist" economy, suffuses both *Old School* and many of other Žilnik's films that depict the hardships of marginalized groups from the former Yugoslavia.[29] In an interview addressing *The Old School of Capitalism*'s ideological tapestry, Žilnik observes that a new formation of young anarcho-syndicalists recognizes that the ideals of Yugoslavian self-management, however compromised, "silently embraced anarchism . . . the idea that the state will wither away and expire and be replaced by workers' associations."

Old School's dramatic catalyst involves the rage of workers, embittered about the privatization of factories under Milošević and their subsequent abandonment by negligent owners who declare bankruptcy and leave their former employees in the lurch. In a scenario inspired by protests in the Serbian city of Zrenjanin, the workers' anger is soon enough channeled into efforts to ambush the boss and his wife in their home—and eventually to kidnap the head of the factory and his associates. The disgruntled workers' initial confrontations possess a distinctively comic flavor. Furious men donning American football helmets and shoulder pads convey a zany pandemonium bordering on slapstick.

Not until an articulate anarchist organizer suggests a more concerted form of direct action does the plan to ambush the factory boss and his

cronies gather steam. Žilnik's predilection for casting nonprofessional actors whose political views correspond to the positions advocated by their
characters is reflected in the choice of Ratibor Trivunac to play an anarchist
who decries both the capitalist status quo and reformism, as well as the
casting of Branimir Stojanovic, a Lacanian psychoanalyst and "Communist
without a party" as Tivunac's antagonist. Many of the debates in the film
center around the advisability and plausibility of direct action, as well as
the ability of intellectuals and activists to transform the consciousness of
workers, whose discontents coexist with lingering resentments engendered
by the scars of ethno-nationalism. Trivunac remains thoroughly optimistic, however, throughout these interchanges and maintains his conviction
that the workers can challenge the ideological stranglehold impeding their
revolutionary impulses.

The clashes between Stojanovic and Trivunac not only involve disagreements concerning the nature of workers' agency and consciousness—they
also stem from almost intractable tactical differences. Stojanovic is wary
of Trivunac's scheme to kidnap the boss and his associates since he doesn't
believe that kidnapping is a political act.[30] More importantly, since he maintains the workers "sided with those who humiliated them for twenty years,"
he is skeptical about prospects to transform their consciousness in one fell
swoop, Trivunac, on the other hand, remains convinced that agitation can
inspire the workers to adapt a "revolutionary practice." In some respects, this
contretemps recapitulates many debates between Leninist critics of "spontaneism" and anarchists such as Errico Malatesta, who believed that "partial
uprisings, local revolts, and propaganda by the deed were useful in forming
a revolutionary consciousness."[31]

Žilnik delights in interweaving actual incidents with fictionalized interludes. Vice President Joe Biden's state visit to Belgrade in May 2009 spurs
Trivunac on to burn an American flag in front of the visiting dignitary's
motorcade. What at first appears to be a mere jape becomes a catalytic event.
Trivunac's audacity galvanizes many of the skeptical workers and convinces
them that his radicalism amounts to more than idle rhetoric.

The upshot is that Trivunac inadvertently becomes a martyr, something
on the order of Rachel Corrie, during an attempt to encourage workers on
a privatized farm to resist. Killed by a plow on the orders of the boss, it is
tempting to conclude that this downbeat ending resembles *Early Works'*
cataclysmic final scenes. But Žilnik's specific brand of hybridism, a synthesis
of documentary-style reportage and mock-documentary polemicizing, is
intrinsically open-ended. Žilnik began his film by shooting demonstrations
in Belgrade spearheaded by the Independent Workers Union of Serbia, He

eventually scrapped part of his scenario and some of the film's footage after deciding to incorporate confrontations between Truvanic and Stojanovic into the film. (Lazar Stojanovic, no relation to Branimir, impersonates the latter's father and represents the a liberal, anticommunist stance.)[32] Instead of short-circuiting optimism, *Old School Capitalism* instead depicts the end of one chapter in an ongoing, still-evolving struggle.

Most of the high-profile documentary efforts to chronicle the Occupy movement—the American protest movement designed to combat structural inequality and the excesses of finance capital—proved less innovative and trenchant than Žilnik's ingenious meld of fiction and documentary. *99%: The Occupy Wall Street Collaborative Film* (2013), a film credited to nine directors, fails because its good intentions iron out most of the internal tensions that made Occupy Wall Street, as well as its offshoots in other U.S. cities and abroad, a fascinatingly contentious aggregation of voices. Despite thinking of itself as radical, *99%*'s politics are resolutely liberal and reformist. Of course, the muddled nature of this documentary overview is fairly unsurprising. In *Translating Anarchy: The Anarchism of Occupy Wall Street,* Mark Bray ponders the incongruity of Al Gore and Nancy Pelosi endorsing the goals of Occupy despite the fact that at least a third of the participants identified themselves as anarchist. Although David Graeber is often cited as a major influence on the Occupy movement, and Graeber is credited with first suggesting that Occupy appropriate the travails of the 99% as a catchphrase, Bray observes that the slogan "was so successful because it reclaimed a sense of class conflict under a political guise . . . the notion of the 99% was exceptionally inclusive and thereby allowed middle-class and (even some upper class) people to feel like they were just as much 'The People' as anyone else."[33]

The vacuity of misapplying the 99% rubric is obvious in the film of the same name. The anarchist impetus behind Occupy is ignored and an interview with Micah White attempts to convince viewers that what Ramon Glazov of *Jacobin* terms the "bizarre ideology"[34] of *Adbusters* was the moving force behind Occupy. Naomi Wolf trashes the modus operandi of the General Assembly and strivings toward achieving consensus—a methodology she claims has never worked. The journalist Matt Taibbi and the "social epidemiologist" Richard Wilkinson discuss the nuances of income inequality with sound bite–worthy nimbleness, even though no aspect of the pundits' analyses goes beyond social democratic bromides. Vague references to a "decentralized" model of democracy are bandied about and fleeting references to anarchist participation in Occupy Oakland are thrown out in a somewhat gratuitous manner that doesn't negate the film's more or less liberal-reformist orientation.

Experimental filmmakers with no obligation to spoon-feed the public fared better in documenting Occupy in a more-meditative and less-reductive manner. Jason Livingston's short film *#Rushes* provides an alternative to what the filmmaker himself labels "populist agitprop." The two versions of the film deploy contrasting reflexive strategies designed to challenge standard representations of dissent and on-the-spot reportage of street activism. Offering a glimpse of a festive protest cum celebration commemorating the first anniversary of Occupy Wall Street in 2012, Livingston juxtaposes the culture-jamming antics of the Jellyfish Brigade with familiar scenes of police intimidation and use of force. Demonstrators dressed in whimsical costumes holding signs such as "No Fossil Fuels . . . Frack Wall Street, Not Water" highlight the march's blend of earnestness and carnivalesque glee; the differences in tone are reinforced by, on the one hand, the satirist Reverend Billy's comic spiel and, on the other, the unironic politicking of perennial presidential candidate Jill Stein and Cheri Honkala, her 2012 vice presidential candidate.

Forsaking digital for 16mm with in-camera edits, the initial version of *#Rushes* was projected silently to live audiences. Refusing to bombard the audience with riot porn clichés, talking heads, voice-over—or even the ambient sounds of a demonstration—Livingston instead solicited a running commentary from the audience at various screenings and encouraged a participatory ethic and aesthetic. His decision to shoot in 16mm and move away from the more au courant DSLR aesthetic evolved from his antipathy toward consumerist pressure to abandon "technologies deemed obsolescent."

Although Livingston's regarded his stripped-down aesthetic—and his promotion of audience participation—as "Occupy poetics," a screening at UnionDocs in Brooklyn convinced him to launch an extended autocritique of his own neo-Brechtian assumptions concerning "active spectatorship." Despite the fact that *#Rushes* inspired some animated responses from audiences (particularly a frenetic screening at Squeaky Wheel in Buffalo that Livingston loved because it engendered a "lot of talking" over the silent images), he feared "that by encouraging 'participation' (i.e. talking) without sufficient direction on my part, I was inadvertently disavowing my role as the maker (not that it's much power in the end . . .), and actually promoting a very, very vague participatory democracy that felt all too much like upper management's penchant for Doodle polls, or asking workers for 'input.'"[35]

Livingston's ambivalence toward his own attempt to emulate Occupy-style egalitarianism one microcinema at a time convinced him to accompany the film with narration, later transformed into a series of memes embedded in a second version of the film, that undercuts the celebration of a participatory ethos with what he terms a "warm antagonism." Warm antagonism might be defined as playful self-laceration, almost a parody of the type of self-criticism that was once de rigueur among authoritarian leftists. In the self-*détourned* version of *#Rushes,* Livingston proclaims: "Against participation, not because participation denies the primary role of the artist in any give work and thus projects an anti-hierarchical fantasy . . . but because participation itself is a bureaucratic imagination." While there's a tongue-in-cheek aspect to Livingston's self-indictment, the cadences of his manifesto also undermine the pieties of "active spectatorship" and the hallowed entity known as the "emancipated spectator." In certain respects, the alternative film world's penchant for participatory events might constitute a farcical equivalent of the pseudo-participation that anarchists mock when confronted with liberal or bureaucratic-socialist experiments in self-management. From another perspective, the film's dialogue with its audience, and with itself, is close to the kind of "auto-ethnography" that David Graeber proposes as a riposte to the vanguardist sensibility.

The irreverent cultural scavenging of the Anti-Banality Union, discussed in chapter 5, is far different from the more earnest work of anarchist-inflected filmmakers such as Žilnik, Kossoff, and Razsa. But all of these filmmakers, united by a commitment to anti-hierarchical values, engage in salutary self-scrutiny. For filmmakers who value autonomy, horizontality, and self-management, an ethical film practice becomes inseparable from their aesthetic goals. In the early seventies, during the height of Italian autonomism, the filmmaker Alberto Grifi movingly confessed in a prologue to his influential documentary, *Anna* (1975) that he and his co-director Massimo Sarchielli failed to align their belief in self-management and autonomy to their ethically slippery depiction of a pregnant, drug-addicted teenager. "Massimo maintains that we exposed the decay of institutional systems, but ultimately we should have done something more. While living with Anna, we should have criticized ourselves as an institution, we should have self-managed and tried to find alternative solutions, or to create within and among us, relations that were radically different."[36] Grifi's admission of failure is also an important critical intervention that reminds us that a cinema based on anti-authoritarian principles is obliged to constantly interrogate both its aesthetic and ethical underpinnings.

Self-scrutiny and introspection are perhaps inevitable during an era of political retrenchment when right-wing populism is in the ascendancy and the precepts of radical democracy are under assault. Without even mentioning the word anarchism, Astra Taylor's *What Is Democracy?* (2018) raises the question of whether radical democracy can have a resurgence at a time when democratic hopes are being squelched across the globe. Taylor implicitly poses the question: can the ideal of radical participatory democracy—that originated in the ancient Athenian polis[37]—be revived at a historical juncture where neo-populism has accelerated regressive trends to resuscitate authoritarian cults of personality? Taylor's contemporary Greek interlocutors enshrine the democratic possibilities of the Greek *agora* while Cornel West reminds us that the dystopian challenges of Plato and Dostoyevsky, who explain the seemingly irrational desire of citizens to, in Erich Fromm's phrase, "escape from freedom," remain pertinent.

Taylor acknowledges that anarchism is a vital "absent presence" in *What is Democracy?* "Among other things the film grew out of my experience with Occupy, which was an anarchist formation. And it had to be—at that point in time (and in the '90s) anarchists were the only people on the left who ever did anything. Occupy was an attempt to model democracy directly, and the movement refused to make demands of the state. I'm generally pretty skeptical of the idea of direct democracy defined as consensus decision making. And while I'm attracted to this idea of prefigurative politics, I also think we need to put pressure on the state—we can't only operate outside (because under capitalism, there is no outside). So those were some of the things on my mind as I began thinking about the film and democracy as a guiding theme. But as the movie ultimately shows, the Occupy movement in Greece did just that. They occupied, rioted, built a party, and not only made demands of the state but took state power—and look where that got them. The Greek anarchists I know were hardly surprised by Syriza's failure."[38]

The Greek austerity crisis functions as a litmus test for the limitations of mere electoral democracy in Taylor's film. Despite the Greek electorate's desire to refuse compliance with Angela Merkel and the IMF's demands for austerity, the prime minister, Alexis Tsipras, and Syriza capitulate to their demands. This incident becomes an object lesson in the seemingly immovable resistance to democratic demands evinced by a neoliberal establishment.

What is Democracy?'s most impressive set piece is devoted to dissecting a fourteenth-century fresco housed in Siena's Palazzo Pubblico, *The Allegory of Good and Bad Government*. With the aid of the autonomist Marxist Silvia Federici, the fresco's high-minded aspirations are unmasked as a covert defense of income inequality. The upright burghers in the "good government" panel could well be construed as unethical plutocrats while the miscreants representing "bad government" are potential revolutionaries. In addition, Federici makes clear that the fresco excludes the sphere of "reproduction," the so-called domestic realm that governs sexuality and work performed by women.

If radical democracy failed in contemporary Greece, the concept still has resonance in the modern revamping of the civil rights movement and popular mobilizations against police violence. The convergence between African American activism and the anarchist ethos represents a little-known attempt to mediate between two seemingly contradictory traditions. For example, the former Black Panther Ashanti Alston, weaned on the black nationalism of the sixties, ardently believes that nationalism and anti-statism can coexist productively.[39] (Like a number of thinkers, he also perceives affinities between traditional African communalism and anarchism.) In addition, a decentralized movement such as Black Lives Matter, without explicitly referencing anarchism, is fueled by a passion for direct action and skepticism toward electoral politics. In any case, the agenda of BLM—concern over the excesses of the carceral state and racist police violence—is certainly congruent with anti-authoritarian impulses. Kropotkin addressed the question of whether prisons are necessary in the last chapter of *In Russian and French Prisons* and concluded:

> Unhappily, hitherto our penal institutions have been nothing but a compromise between the old ideas of revenge, of punishment of the "bad will" and "sin," and the modern ideas of "deterring from crime," both softened to a very slight extent by some notions of philanthropy. But the time, we hope, is not far distant when the noble ideas which have inspired Griesinger, Krafft-Ebing, Despine, and some of the modern Italian criminalists, like Colajanni and Ferri, will become the property of the general public, and make us ashamed of having continued so long to hand over those whom we call criminals to hangmen and jailers.[40]

Far from taking up Kropotkin's challenge to abolish prisons, the United States has increasingly become a carceral state. Michelle Alexander's *The New Jim Crow*, which inspired Ava DuVernay's *13th* (2016), documents how the "war on drugs" under a series of U.S. presidents helped to replicate the morass of racism and impoverishment that followed Reconstruction during the Jim Crow era. According to Elizabeth Hinton, the American carceral state is bipartisan and all-encompassing; she reminds us that the "United States is the largest incarcerator in the world. We are 5 percent of the world's population, but we hold 25 percent of the world's prisoners, and the incarceration rate for black males is higher than that of Russia. It's out of control."[41]

As Brett Story's elegantly conceived, occasionally elliptical *The Prison in Twelve Landscapes* (2016) demonstrates, the contours of imprisonment in the United States are no longer limited to brick and mortar edifices. Rather than confining her investigation of mass incarceration to lambasting prison

conditions, Story's documentary, which is often more meditative than re-
ductively journalistic, illustrates Hinton's assertion that the American prison
industrial complex has promoted the "criminalization of urban space." With a
certain amount of restrained mordant wit, the vignettes generated by Story's
mosaic-like structure provide evidence that the landscapes of prisons have
invaded the everyday lives of Americans with far-reaching economic, political, and social consequences.

Instead of advocating piecemeal prison reform, *Twelve Landscapes* limns
the contours of a carceral society that, in step with the dystopian scenario of
Foucault's *Discipline and Punish,* enshrines social control and surveillance.
For example, the film ponders the plight of Charisse Davidson, a Missouri
woman who languishes in jail for three days after failing to affix her garbage
lid properly. Keeping the populace in line is often more important than fighting crime. Another quasi-surreal sequence captures the perspective of a Cali-
fornian female inmate recruited to combat forest fires. While firefighting is an
onerous task, it's also evident that it's frequently easier for prisoners to obtain
employment under duress than it is for civilian job hunters to land compa-
rable jobs. Story, moreover, focuses on the way in which a carceral ethos is
intimately linked to the structure of the American economy. An interview
with a Bronx entrepreneur, who owns a small business devoted exclusively to
making household products to the specifications of the prison bureaucracy,
confirms the porous boundaries between the market and the cost-benefit
analyses endemic to prison culture. A sequence shot at the sprawling Quicken
Loans campus in Detroit is slightly more cryptic. A friendly employee offers
Story a breathless tour of the premises, but despite his cheerful demeanor,
he represents a corporation that benefits the rapacious schemes of Quicken's
founder, Dan Gilbert, and accelerates the impoverishment of Detroit's public
sector. According to a blistering article in *Jacobin*,[42] downtown Detroit is
saturated with surveillance cameras provided by Gilbert; public space has
become irredeemably carceral.

Another subtle jab at the tendency of disciplinary regimes to insinuate
themselves into the public realm occurs in a sequence devoted to sex offenders confined to a pocket park in Los Angeles. Story argues that this effort to
separate urban denizens from a category of offenders considered the lowest
of the low reinforces how "moral panics" manifest themselves within the
flux of urban life.[43]

The transmutation of rage concerning mass incarceration and police violence into direct action can be discerned in a number of films that merge
investigative journalism with accounts of the evolution of Black Lives Matter's
strain of direct action. Craig Atkinson's *Do Not Resist* (2016), like many films

belonging to this subgenre, opens in Ferguson, Missouri after the community uproar generated by the police killing of Michael Brown. But Atkinson's film takes the Ferguson events as a departure point to examine the increasing militarization of the police in the United States—a concrete elaboration of Story's argument that it's increasingly difficult to distinguish American civil society from the terrain of a prison.

In many respects, *Do Not Resist* lays out the ideological impediments that an anti-authoritarian resistance to prisons and police violence must confront. Exhibit A is Dave Grossman, one of the leading American police trainers, who, in an unwitting inversion of anti-police rhetoric, claims that the police themselves must "fight violence with superior violence—righteous violence." As evidence of how persuasive Grossman's argument is to frightened communities, Atkinson includes footage of a Concord, New Hampshire city council meeting in which a few brave representatives oppose the supposed benefits of the government's 1033 program that transfers military equipment to local police departments. Their fellow counselors, who view armored vehicles as a boon to law enforcement, outvote them handily. Even more chillingly, the criminologist Richard Berk endorses preventive measures eerily close to the dystopian notion of "pre-crime" elaborated by Philip K. Dick in "The Minority Report." Claiming scientific objectivity, nothing—race, class, purported antisocial tendencies—proves off-limits in Berk's efforts to use newfangled demographics as tools of surveillance and social control.

Sabaah Folayan and Damon Davis's *Whose Streets?* (2017), which recounts the birth of Black Lives Matter during the protests against Michael Brown's killing in Ferguson, Missouri, is devoted largely to the consequences of the militarization of the police. While not specifically anarchist, BLM borrows from a tradition of direct action that fueled the civil rights movement, as well as the anti-nuclear protests of the '70s and '80s and Occupy Wall Street. The film's pivotal pronouncement is rapper Tef Poe's assertion that "this ain't yo momma's civil rights movement." Poe's retort to the injunctions of "leadership" is a broadside fired squarely at the old civil rights bureaucracy exemplified by the NAACP and putative leaders such as Al Sharpton. In many respects, the old guard civil rights leaders' refusal to engage in direct action is what led many to conclude that an organization like Black Lives Matter was necessary. It's also true that movements devoted to prisoner resistance have long been allied with anarchism, and activists from the ranks of insurrectionary prisoners see natural affinities between their work and the Black Lives Matter agenda.[44]

Attempts to criminalize dissent are highlighted in the film's treatment of one of BLM's founders, Brittany Ferrell, who spent months trying to clear herself of accusations of property damage caused to a SUV during a demonstration in Ferguson. Ferrell's agonizing legal wrangles are complemented by the saga of "Copwatch" videographer David Whitt, who is subject to persistent police harassment and intimidation.

Although Keeanga-Yamahtta Taylor's *From #BlackLivesMatter to Black Liberation* relies on Marxism, not anarchism, for its analytical framework, her antipathy to simplistic reformist solutions to police violence is not unlike the positions advocated by anarchists, who reject liberal gradualism. Taylor's desire to "transform this country in such a way that the police are no longer needed to respond to the consequences"[45] of inequality resonates with the analysis of anarchist proponents of "Copwatch" such as Richard Modiano, who maintained some years ago that this resurgent watchdog organization "aspires to create revolutionary alternatives to policing, prisons, and systems of domination, exploitation, and oppression."

The upshot is that several documentaries that tackle the specter of police terror conclude, either implicitly or explicitly, that the abolition of the police should be the most important item on the radical agenda. Peter Nicks's *The Force* (2017), for example, a vérité account of efforts to reform the Oakland, California police, ultimately implies that the rot in Oakland is systemic, and good-faith promises to clean up the department and quell police violence and incompetence are more or less futile. In 2014 Sean Whent is installed as the chief of police and, for a short time, is hailed as a golden boy. But, by 2016, he is ousted by Mayor Libby Schaaf after a sexual abuse scandal. Even though Nicks's observational approach fails to provide much context for the morass Oakland finds itself in, it's clear from the film that activists were never convinced that Whent's superficially liberal zeal could have much of an impact on gratuitous assaults against members of the black community. Police violence continued apace during his tenure and, as one commentator observed, the officers' acceptance of sexual favors from an underage sex worker reinforced the continuing stigma wrought by criminalizing prostitution.[46]

If abolishing the police is not explicitly endorsed in *The Force,* which straddles liberalism and an embryonic critique of it, Julie Perini, Jodi Darby, and Erin Yanke's *Arresting Power: Resisting Police Violence in Portland, Oregon* (2015) presents a blueprint for combating the crimes of those charged with enforcing the law and openly advocates the abolition of police. Walidah Imarisha, a longtime Portland activist, in fact sets a utopian tone early in the film by asking: "What would a world look like without police?"

While *The Force* is bereft of context, *Arresting Power* suffuses its painful chronicle of police homicides in Portland with a host of interviews with historians and activists, as well as first-hand testimonies by victims. Wrongly pegged as an unproblematically "liberal" city by those unfamiliar with its history, Portland retains the scars of being in a state created as a refuge for white people. As Kristian Williams, the author of *Our Enemies in Blue*, emphasizes, formal police forces in the Northwest, as well as the South, are the descendants of slave patrols designed to quell slave rebellions.[47]

This grim historical background augments the film's painstaking documentation of a plethora of police killings, mostly of unarmed African Americans, from the late twentieth century to the early decades of the present century. Perini, Darby, and Yanke's decision to intermittently scratch 16mm film stock is intended as an illustration of the collective trauma engendered by each killing. As each name of a victim appears on the screen, the audience is confronted with the residue of these accumulated traumas. A handful of cases are meticulously detailed: for example, the fate of Aaron Campbell, a mentally ill man shot on the same day of his brother's death, is narrated with the use of archival police radio tapes; Kendra James, shot to death after the car she was riding in was stopped; Tony Stevenson, a former Marine felled by police after he intervened to stop a robbery and was mistaken for a criminal himself.

The film, however, is ultimately more preoccupied with resistance than victimhood, and *Arresting Power*'s interviewees pay tribute to a host of organizations that fought back over the years—the Portland Black Berets, Black Justice Committee, the Portland Community Liberation Front, and Portland Cop Watch. The collective rage that animates these groups is succinctly expressed by Patrisse Khan-Cullors in her memoir: "when cops kill, there is the presumption that the killer is in the right, that his or her decision was reasoned and necessary and done in the name of public good and safety . . . despite the fact that cops were created in this nation specifically *and solely* to hunt Black people seeking freedom."[48]

By contrast, migrants from various parts of the world—often condescendingly lumped into a rubric personified by the phrase "the defining human rights issue of our time"—are rarely granted even a modicum of agency in the various films, usually documentaries, consumed with their plight. Most of the well-intentioned liberal-humanist films devoted to the international migrant crisis usually depict the dispossessed as passive victims or objects of pity. In *Sea Sorrow* (2017), the ostensibly radical Vanessa Redgrave relies primarily on the testimonies of politicians, writers, and NGO representatives, not migrants themselves, to craft a shallow film on the refugee crisis. The perspective of the undeniably empathetic Ai Weiwei is tangible in the title of his film on the migrant crisis—*Human Flow* (2017). Ruminations on "human flow" tend to flatten out specificities and isolate a generalized malaise that loses sight of political malfeasance. Despite genuflecting to the power of "resistance," Ai's insistence that "human movement will neither stop nor fully disappear because it is tied to human nature" is, to say the least, problematic. "As long as humans exist," he muses, "there will be a human flow because we are animals with free will." Such bromides tend to consecrate an ineradicable "human condition."

Sylvain George's *May They Rest in Revolt* (*Figures of War*) (2010) jettisons the platitudes of liberal condescension by employing an idiosyncratic admixture of essayistic strategies, stylized vérité naturalism, and lyrical interludes to highlight the rebellious spirit of migrants in Calais, France's notorious "jungle" encampment. George, who has a background as a social worker and views conflicts between refugees and an insensitive bureaucratic state through the lens of Giorgio Agamben's concept of "bare life," aspires toward a revivified "humanism" that allows room for lived experience and genuine opposition to racism to thrive. Jay Kuehner terms this a humanism "in which a person's potential is held and recognized."[49]

Paradoxically enough, the entry point into George's hymn to resistance is an allusion to the mythic power of Exodus leavened with Walter Benjamin's revolutionary fervor. Fleeting glimpses of Mt. Sinai are juxtaposed with a telling fragment of Benjamin's "Critique of Violence" that hails the merits of "divine violence." As Howard Eiland and Michael Jennings observe, Benjamin's reflections were the "product of more general research into anarchism"; for Eiland and Jennings, the essay "apostrophizes the erasure of all current forms of state power."[50]

Benjamin's famously difficult meditation on violence, which belongs to an early phase of his work in which his radicalism draws from Marxist, anarchist, and "messianic" sources, implicitly indicts the violence of legality and endorses a sharp rupture from "administrative violence" while allowing the possibility of "sovereign violence." Within this framework, the migrants from the Middle East and Africa featured in *May They Rest in Revolt* actively contest the subordinate status they must endure in Europe and assert their sovereignty with small, but potent, acts of rebellion. Although Kuehner admits that the verité components of George's film are unavoidably "voyeuristic," the migrants' visceral anger, captured by a roving hand-held camera, differentiates this film from more complacent projects. A pivotal scene highlights a man attempting to scrape fingerprints off his hand with a razor, a gesture of defiance towards a regime of digital surveillance that threatens displaced populations.

The film culminates in a confrontation between police and inhabitants of the makeshift "jungle." This is not merely a pitched battle between defenseless victims and representatives of the state. The attack on refugees reflects the ideological stance of Éric Besson, the government minister responsible for immigration under President Nicolas Sarkozy. Despite Besson's hatred for immigrants and the demolition of the encampment and the dispersal of the undocumented, the "jungle" rose again several years later and was then demolished again in 2016. State power cannot obliterate the rage of these migrants, who denounce their status as "slaves." The assault on migrants continues under Emmanuel Macron, whose immigration bill of 2018 was designed to limit applications for asylum and allows for provisions to hold children in detention.

The *Nakba* ("catastrophe"), during which seven hundred thousand Palestinians were forced to emigrate in 1948 after the establishment of the state of Israel, still constitutes one of the most profound migrant crises of the last hundred years. The Palestinian struggle is often part of the contemporary anarchist agenda, even though a group such as Anarchists Against the Wall,[51] which participated most notably in actions against the Lebanon incursion in 2006 and the war on Gaza in 2008, includes both anarchists and non-anarchists. As early as 1971, the anarchist filmmaker Nick Macdonald's *Palestine* zeroed in on the settler colonialist nature of the Israeli state. In an essay film that simulates a dinner-table conversation on the inequities of Zionism, Macdonald intercuts images of the My Lai massacre in Vietnam with a discussion of the massacres of Palestinians in Deir Yassin and Kafr Qasim during the '40s and '50s.

Of all the films dealing with the Nakba and related topics, Eyal Sivan and Michel Khleifi's *Route 181: Fragments of a Journey in Palestine-Israel* (2004) is by far the most courageous and aesthetically satisfying. A film with almost no chance of being commercially distributed in North America, *Route 181* has had a troubled history. In what a press release calls an "unprecedented move," a screening scheduled for March 2004 at Le Festival du Cinéma du Réel was abruptly cancelled. The festival's co-sponsors disseminated a statement defending their action by asserting that the film posed "a risk to public order" and arguing that, despite being the product of a collaboration between an Israeli filmmaker and his Palestinian cohort, it might even encourage "anti-Semitic and anti-Jewish statements and acts in France."

Just as Anarchists Against the Wall unites dissident Israelis and Palestinians, *Route 181,* a collaboration between an Israeli and a Palestinian filmmaker, attempts to dissolve nationalist clichés by unearthing a submerged history. For both Israelis and Palestinians who believe that certain suppressed elements of Zionist history should be brought to light, this epic documentary represents a triumph of conscience over expediency and is about as far from an incitement to anti-Semitism as one could imagine. As leisurely—and as subtle—a polemic as Robert Kramer's similarly episodic *Route One/USA* (1989), Sivan and Khleifi's documentary is actually a carefully structured road movie that, during a four-and-a-half-hour running time, retains a kernel of utopian optimism despite the pessimism evinced by many of the interviewees.

The filmmakers' decision to retrace the route of the 1947 UN Partition plan, quickly abandoned after the 1948 war, captures the grim origins of the ongoing crisis with mordant irony. This trek—from the south of Israel near Gaza to the north near the Lebanese border—evokes an ambiguous historical past. On the one hand, the Partition might be rightly pilloried as an attempt on the part of the imperial powers to carve up Palestine and shortchange the indigenous population; on the other, the thoroughgoing abandonment of the dream of a binational state that was once embraced by secular Jews such as Hannah Arendt, Noam Chomsky, and I. F. Stone represents a lost opportunity for peaceful co-existence. Alternately, but even more importantly, the emphasis on post-1948 travails highlights the chasm between Israel's enshrinement of a "war of independence" and liberation and the Palestinian elegy for the Nakba, a period of dispossession and devastation. In some respects, *Route 181*'s unabashed focus on a host of former Arab villages now transformed into Israeli communities is enough to arouse the ire of diehard Zionists. But a reiteration of historical data that has even been acknowledged by Benny Morris, a staunchly Zionist historian often mislabeled a "post-Zionist," would not be enough to make this film's stance distinctive. Sivan and Khleifi explore how many Israelis appear to both affirm and disavow this legacy of dispossession, and the relationship of this apparent political schizophrenia to the ongoing historical impasse within Israel/Palestine.

In fact, one of the film's most revelatory sequences pithily interweaves past historical woes and the contemporary snare of self-inflicted historical amnesia. At the museum of Kibbutz Yad Mordechai, an elderly, Polish-born Israeli tour guide (and former "pioneer") maintains that, unlike recent Jewish settlers, "we didn't colonize." There is, however, an odd slippage between his assertion that Arabs merely "fled" to Gaza during 1948 and his de facto admission that Arabs were expelled. He goes on, moreover, to bemoan the increasing birth rate of the Arab population and expresses his fear that Israel's Jewish character might eventually be endangered. These calumnies are followed by a shot of a statue that greets visitors at another kibbutz, which the filmmakers describe on their website as a "Stalinist-looking monument"—a reminder that the ideology of the earliest Zionist settlers encompassed both an Old Left emphasis on class consciousness and a racist view of their Arab neighbors that differed little from the views of right-wingers such as Ariel Sharon.

Most of the Sephardim—Jews from Arab countries—who emigrated, or were forcibly repatriated, to Israel after 1948 were less than entranced by the discourse of Labour Zionism elucidated by the Polish tour guide. Unlike much of the historical literature and the majority of documentary films that address the Israeli-Palestinian crisis, *Route 181* offers a nuanced view of the Sephardic community. As Ella Shohat argues in *Sephardim in Israel: Zionism from the Standpoint of its Jewish Victims*, "Although Zionism claims to provide a homeland for all Jews, that homeland was not offered to all with the same largess. Sephardi Jews were first brought to Israel for specific European-Zionist reasons, and once there they were systematically discriminated against by a Zionism that deployed its energies and material resources differentially, to the consistent advantage of European Jews and to the consistent detriment of Oriental Jews." While even Peace Now, a group often assumed to be at the forefront of Israeli liberalism, has often stigmatized Sephardi Jews as reactionary and inflexibly anti-Arab, Sivan and Khleifi recognize that Arab Jews in Israel actually represent an important link to the historical past and a bridge to reconciliation between Israelis and Palestinians. For example, early in the film, a weary Palestinian man recalls that "Jews lived among Arabs in Arab countries for many years. . . . [The] problem isn't between Jews and Arabs, but between occupiers and occupied." This lament is soon followed by an interview with an Iraqi Jewish grocer, whose positive memories of his childhood in Iraq and fondness for Arabic is accompanied by a pronounced cynicism toward his government. Near the end of Sivan and Khleifi's pilgrimage, a Moroccan woman recounts her youthful recruitment in the late '50s as a "broom" by the Israeli government—an agent instructed to lure fellow Jews to Israel. She concludes that she was "hoodwinked" by the Israelis; as Shohat explains, "From the early days of Zionism, Sephardim were perceived as a source of cheap labor that had to be maneuvered into immigrating to Palestine." Finally, in a blunt coda, a Tunisian Jewish woman, still distraught over the death of her son in Lebanon, blurts out that "Sharon and Arafat should be shot with their mothers"—a sentiment that might be shared by both Jews and Palestinians who only feel disgust for the bureaucratic machinations of so-called "leaders."

North American indigenous filmmakers are as likely as Palestinian directors to condemn their own fraught relationship with settler colonialism. For Zach and Adam Khalil, ethnographic filmmaking itself reflects a colonialist mindset, and their hybrid documentary, *Inaate/Se [It shines a certain way.*

to a certain place/it flies./falls] (2016), lodges a multifaceted critique of how the Ojibway tribe's history has been hijacked by patronizing ideological assumptions, as well as distorted by films that view indigenous history as either folkloric ephemera or alien terrain that require "decoding." Adam Khalil explicitly allies himself with th.e "politics of refusal" outlined in Audra Simpson's *Mohawk Interruptus*.[52] Although the category of "refusal" summons up the legacy of the Frankfurt School, particularly Marcuse's injunction to negate a one-dimensional society, Simpson is more focused on a more specific type of disdain for ideological homogeneity. Her primary case study is the Kahnawà:ke Mohawk's adherence to the laws of the Iroquois Confederacy and refusal to grant sovereignty to the United States or Canada. This refusal to acknowledge Canadian or American sovereignty is tantamount to negating the power and allure of the state.

The Khalils' strategy of refusal also leads them to carnivalize documentary conventions by embracing a collage-like style that, in a ludically Brechtian fashion, separates the elements of traditional linear documentary into constituent parts and allows them to collide with each other. Their riposte to ethnographic platitudes in *Inaate/Se* involves intermixing archival documentary footage, interviews, animation, and parodic interludes. The birch bark scrolls of the Anishinaabe Seven Fires Prophecy emerges as a bulwark against colonialist subjugation. The Seven Fires Prophecy also decries environmental devastation, and this eco-radicalism is at the heart of much indigenous radicalism, whether in Canadian protests against tar sands pipelines or American resistance at Standing Rock. The Seven Fires Prophecy never, however, becomes fetishized as a mythical, or for that matter, mystical remnant of a heroic past. The Khalils eschew this sort of monologism by placing explications of the prophecies in dialogue with sequences demystifying the Jesuit version of indigenous history encased in Sault Saint Marie's "Tower of History" and a zany indictment of Jesuitical pieties that features a priest donning a death mask. Another crucial strand foregrounds an encounter with "Wild Bill," an alcoholic indigenous man who lives a solitary life on an island, embodying a stoic autonomy that rejects the respectability that society usually demands of so-called "role models."

Of course, it's important to avoid a facile false equivalence between anarchists and indigenous activists. On the surface, both camps would seem to share a radical refusal to capitulate to the demands of the state, as well as a preoccupation with decentralized self-organization. Nevertheless, as one commentator observes, many indigenous activists are wary of anarchism's Eurocentric perspective and anarchists' occasional attempts to impose their own circumscribed view of democratic procedure on struggles within another context.[53] When even anarchism can come under suspicion of impersonating a hegemonic ideology, it appears self-evident that there are many paths to dismantling hierarchical societies.

Nevertheless, despite the pervasive skepticism of the parliamentary left, the yearning for radical democracy remains resilient. As James Miller observes, "the Arab Spring's desire for the power of organizing without organization" was "an anarchist's dream come true."[54] The distance, however, between the Arab Spring's altruism and its brutal aftermath is undeniable. Nate Levey, Luhana Carvalho, and Matt Peterson's *Scenes From a Revolt Sustained* (2015) exalts the Tunisian Revolution as a "new form of communication," a rupture with previous revolts that merely sought to replace one dictatorial regime with another. Opening with a Straubian traveling shot traversing an urban landscape, the voice-over insists that the "social war" in Tunisia was wholly "driven by its people," not its elites. Overturning the regime of President Zine El Abidine Ben Ali, who had himself come to power after he supplanted Habib Bourguiba in a bloodless coup, ultimately led, despite the contributions of the anarchist-tinged Disobdience, to the rise to power of Ennahda, the Tunisian equivalent of the Muslim Brotherhood. *Scenes'* postmortem dispassionately observes that the revolution was more akin to an insurrection, or "revolt," that failed to achieve its anti-authoritarian goals. A visit to Thala, a small town where activists occupied the local police station in 2011 and instituted self-government,[55] is a reminder of submerged revolutionary aspirations that might resurface at any opportune moment.

Notes

Introduction

1. See, for example, John McGowan, *Postmodernism and its Critics* (Ithaca, N.Y. and London: Cornell University Press, 1991). Referring primarily to post-structuralist thinkers, McGowan identifies anarchism exclusively with "negative liberty."

2. See Pietro Ferrua, *Anarchists in Films* (Portland, Ore.: First International Symposium on Anarchism, February 17–24, 1980). See also the collectively edited brochure *Cinéma et anarchie,* which contains brief entries on many films from the silent period to the recent past that feature anarchist protagonists (Geneva: Centre International de Recherches sur l'Anarchisme [CIRA] 1984). I should note that these pamphlets contain source material of great value to scholars; I benefited from them enormously. For a study of *"anarchist cinema"* (although the term is never precisely defined) that focuses on the films of Buñuel, Vigo, and Franju, see Alan Lovell, *Anarchist Cinema* (London: Peace News, 1962).

3. This observation is from the introduction to David Goodway, ed., *For Anarchism: History, Theory and Practice* (London and New York: Routledge, 1989), p. 1. Similarly, David Miller, a social-democratic advocate of market socialism who is unsympathetic to most anarchist aims, confesses that "of all the major ideologies confronting the student of politics, anarchism must be one of the hardest to pin down." See his *Anarchism* (London: J.M. Dent, 1984), p. 1.

4. For a definition of "negative liberty," see Isaiah Berlin, *Four Essays on Liberty* (Oxford, U.K. and New York: Oxford University Press, 1969), pp. 122–31.

5. See, for example, Peter Skalnik, ed., *Outwitting the State* (vol. 7 of the Political Anthropology Series, New Brunswick, N.J.: Transaction Publishers, Rutgers University, 1989). In a review of this book, Neal Keating sums up one contemporary anarchist perspective by asserting that "the State is historically less the inevitable cumulation of some kind of quasi-mystical process of evolution, and much more the occasional aberration intruding upon thousands of years of otherwise non-alienated

human interactions." See Keating's "Outwitting the State Takes a Different Kind of Power," in *Anarchy: A Journal of Desire Armed* 33 (Summer 1992): 15.

6. John Henry Mackay, *The Anarchists: A Picture of Civilization at the End of the Nineteenth Century*, trans. George Schumm (Boston: Benjamin R. Tucker, 1891), p. 131.

7. Alan Ritter, *Anarchism: A Theoretical Analysis* (Cambridge, U.K.: Cambridge University Press, 1980), p. 28.

8. William Godwin, *Enquiry Concerning Political Justice and its Influence on Modern Morals and Happiness* (Harmondsworth, U.K. and New York: Penguin, 1976), p. 758.

9. David McClellan postulates that "Stirner took Hegel's views as his basis and then worked out his own philosophy by criticizing everything that was positive in Hegel's critics, Bauer, Feuerbach, and Marx—whose criticisms, according to Stirner, were never pushed far enough. Hegelianism was thus at an end: Stirner only used the form not the content of the Hegelian system and, like all the Young Hegelians, was most fascinated by the dialectic." See McClellan's *The Young Hegelians and Karl Marx* (Aldershot, U.K.: Gregg Revivals, 1969), p. 119.

10. George Woodcock, *Anarchism: A History of Libertarian Ideas and Movements* (Cleveland and New York: World Publishing, 1962), p. 105.

11. Daniel Guérin, *Anarchism*, trans. Mary Klopper (New York and London: Monthly Review Press, 1970), pp. 27–33.

12. Goldman is quoted in Bonnie Haaland, *Emma Goldman: Sexuality and the Impurity of the State* (Montreal and New York: Black Rose Books, 1993), 83. See also Goldman's essay "The Individual, Society, and the State," in Alix Kates Shulman, ed., *Red Emma Speaks: An Emma Goldman Reader* (New York: Schocken Books, 1982), pp. 109–23.

13. Gilles Deleuze hails Stirner for penetrating "to the truth of the dialectic in the very title of his great book: *The Ego and Its Own.*" See Deleuze's *Nietzsche and Philosophy*, trans. Hugh Tomlinson (New York: Columbia University Press, 1983), 160. See also Jacques Derrida's respectful treatment of Stirner in *Specters of Marx: The State of Debt, the Work of Mourning, and the New International*, trans. Peggy Kamuf (New York and London: Routledge, 1994).

14. Max Stirner, *The Ego and Its Own*, edited by David Leopold (Cambridge, U.K. and New York: Cambridge University Press, 1995), p. 281.

15. John Clark, *The Anarchist Moment: Reflections on Culture, Nature, and Power* (Montreal: Black Rose Books, 1984), p. 127.

16. E. H. Carr, *Michael Bakunin* (London: Macmillan, 1937), p. 131.

17. Franco Venturi, *Roots of Revolution*, trans. Francis Haskell (New York: Grosset & Dunlop, 1966), p. 4.

18. Sam Dolgoff, ed., *Bakunin on Anarchism* (Montreal: Black Rose Books, 1980), p. 349.

19. Bakunin is quoted in Julius Braunthal, *History of the International 1864–1914*, trans. Henry Collins and Kenneth Mitchell (London: Thomas Nelson, 1966), 139. See also George Lichtheim's analysis of the First International's internal debates in

Marxism: An Historical and Critical Study (New York: Columbia University Press, 1964), pp. 100—111.

20. J. Frank Harrison, *The Modern State: An Anarchist Analysis* (Montreal: Black Rose Books, 1983), p. 77. Harrison believes that these "two trends in the TWA" have "been simplistically" characterized "as a conflict between Bakunin and Marx." He argues that their "general goals were the same: the destruction of property, exploitation, and the State . . . their differences lay in the question of tactics." See also Brian Morris, *Bakunin: The Philosophy of Freedom* (Montreal: Black Rose Books, 1993).

21. Paul Thomas, *Karl Marx and the Anarchists* (London and Boston: Routledge & Kegan Paul, 1980), p. 341. Thomas consistently takes Marx's side against a variety of anarchist critics.

22. Paul Avrich, for example, argues that Fanon's *The Wretched of the Earth,* "with its Manichean vision of the despised and rejected rising from the depths to exterminate their colonial oppressors, reads as though lifted out of Bakunin's works." See Avrich's *Anarchist Portraits* (Princeton, N.J.: Princeton University Press, 1988), p. 7. Arif Dirlik recounts how early twentieth-century Chinese radicalism was influenced by anarchism. "Marxism, with its preoccupation with the proletariat, had a blind spot toward the peasantry and ignored 80 percent of the world's population." See Dirlik's *Anarchism in the Chinese Revolution* (Berkeley and Los Angeles: University of California Press, 1991), p. 238.

23. Kropotkin is quoted in Martin A. Miller's introduction to P. A. Kropotkin, *Selected Writings on Anarchism and Revolution* (Cambridge, Mass.: MIT Press, 1970), p. 24. Recent critical and biographical studies of Kropotkin have enriched our knowledge of his immersion in the same Narodnik currents that animated Bakunin's early development. See Martin A. Miller, *Kropotkin* (Chicago and London: University of Chicago Press, 1976); and Caroline Cahm, *Peter Kropotkin and the Rise of Revolutionary Anarchism: 1875–1886* (Cambridge, U.K. and New York, Cambridge University Press, 1989).

24. Cahm, *Peter Kropotkin,* p. 61.

25. For a consideration of the role of human nature in classical anarchist theory, see Peter Marshall, "Human Nature and Anarchism," in Goodway, ed., *For Anarchism,* pp. 128–49.

26. After Kropotkin's death, Errico Malatesta faulted his former mentor for his "rigorously mechanistic" scientific materialism. See "Peter Kropotkin—Recollections and Criticisms of an Old Friend," anthologized in Vernon Richards, ed., *Malatesta: Life and Ideas* (London: Freedom Press, 1977), p. 264.

27. This is from Anthony Kenny's discussion of language games in *Wittgenstein* (Cambridge, Mass.: Harvard University Press, 1973), p. 163.

28. David Weir has maintained that modernism represents the aesthetic fulfillment of the anarchist political agenda. See Weir's *Anarchy and Culture: The Aesthetic Politics of Modernism* (Amherst: University of Massachusetts Press, 1997).

29. See Todd May, "Is Post-Structuralist Theory Anarchist," in Danielle Rouselle and Süreyyya Evren, *Post Anarchism: A Reader* (London and New York: Pluto Press, 2011), p. 44.

30. Saul Newman, "Post-Anarchism and Radical Politics Today," in Rouselle and Evren, *Post Anarchism*, p. 63.

31. See Tadzio Mueller, "Empowering Anarchy: Power, Hegemony and Anarchist Strategy," in Rouselle and Evren, *Post Anarchism*, pp. 75–94.

32. Allan Antliff, "Anarchy, Power, and Post-Structuralism," in Rouselle and Evren, *Post Anarchism*, p. 160.

33. Ruth Kinna, "Field of Vision: Kropotkin and Revolutionary Change," in *Substance* 36, no. 2 (2007): 113.

Chapter 1. Anarchism and Cinema: Representation and Self-Representation

1. See, for example, Hobsbawm's disparaging comments on anarchism in "Reflections on Anarchism," in *Revolutionaries: Contemporary Essays* (New York: Pantheon Books, 1973), 72–91.

2. Robert A. Rosenstone, *Visions of the Past: The Challenge of Film to Our Idea of History* (Cambridge, Mass. and London: Harvard University Press, 1995), p. 238.

3. For a discussion of stereotypes that goes beyond simple binarisms, see Ella Shohat and Robert Stam, *Unthinking Eurocentrism: Multiculturalism and the Media* (London and New York: Routledge, 1994), pp. 178–219.

4. Bryan Cheyette, *Constructions of "the Jew" in English Literature and Society: Racial Representations, 1875–1941* (Cambridge, U.K. and New York: Cambridge University Press, 1993), p. 268.

5. For an attempt to contextualize patterns of African American representation and self-representation within the framework of little-known racist statements made by, among others, Hegel and Kant, see Henry Louis Gates Jr., *Figures in Black: Words, Signs, and the Racial Self* (Oxford, U.K. and New York: Oxford University Press, 1987).

6. Anne McClintock, *Imperial Leather: Race, Gender, and Sexuality in the Colonial Context* (London and New York: Routledge, 1995), p. 50. McClintock's discussion of nineteenth-century pseudo-science is largely derived from Stephen Jay Gould's *The Mismeasure of Man* (London and New York: W.W. Norton, 1981).

7. Marcus Graham, "Anarchism, Capitalism, and Marxism," *Resistance*, August–September, 1949, 3.

8. Marion Meade insists that Keaton disliked Chaplin's socially conscious comedy, and is confident that Buster was unremittingly hostile to anarchism. Nonetheless, she rather cryptically observes that contemporary audiences were probably uncomfortable with the comic violence in *Cops*, since they presumably thought it in bad taste. See Marion Meade, *Buster Keaton: Cut to the Chase* (New York: HarperCollins, 1995). From a completely different perspective, Franklin Rosemont ignores the film's stereotypical anarchist and proclaims *Cops* a "wildly anti-cop film," citing Buster's split-second decision to hurl the bomb toward the crowd of police and politicians. See Rosemont's article "A Bomb-Toting, Long-Haired, Wild-Eyed Fiend: The Image of the Anarchist in Popular Culture," in Dave Roediger and Franklin Rosemont, eds., *Haymarket Scrapbook* (Chicago: Charles H. Kerr, 1986), p. 209.

9. For a detailed account of the anarchist sources for *The Iceman Cometh,* see Virginia Floyd, ed., *Eugene O'Neill at Work: Newly Released Ideas for Plays* (New York: Frederick Ungar Publishing, 1981), pp. 299–300.

10. One great historical irony is the fact that Paul Brousse, an influential formulator of the doctrine of propaganda by the deed, went on to be an earnest reformist within the French Socialist Party. For an account of Brousse's career, with special attention given to the status of propaganda by the deed within the First International, see David Stafford, *From Anarchism to Reformism: A Study of the Political Activities of Paul Brousse within the First International and the French Socialist Movement 1870–90* (Toronto: University of Toronto Press, 1971).

11. See, for example, Isaiah Berlin, *Russian Thinkers* (London and New York: Penguin Books, 1977), pp. 214–16; Paul Avrich, *The Russian Anarchists* (Princeton, N.J.: Princeton University Press, 1967), pp. 37–38; E. H. Carr, *The Romantic Exiles: A Nineteenth-Century Portrait Gallery* (Boston: Beacon Press, 1961), pp. 290–310.

12. For an anarchist condemnation of "bourgeois Nechayevism," see Sam Dolgoff, "The Relevance of Anarchism to Modern Society," anthologized in Terry M. Perlin, ed., *Contemporary Anarchism* (New Brunswick, N.J.: Transaction Books, 1979), p. 38. For the quintessential conservative account of "anarchist" terrorism, see Walter Laqueur, *The Age of Terrorism* (Boston and Toronto: Little, Brown, 1987).

13. Pomper writes that "textual analysis suggests that Bakunin was responsible for the style and some of the substance of the first seven paragraphs, but Nechaev injected into them his extreme asceticism and fascination of martyrdom. The second section, comprised of four paragraphs contains some Bakuninist phraseology but is substantively mainly Nechaev's work. The third and lengthiest section is almost certainly Nechaev's, both stylistically and substantively, whereas the last section appears to be wholly Bakunin's." See Philip Pomper, *Sergei Nechaev* (New Brunswick, N.J.: Rutgers University Press, 1979), p. 90. Michael Confino presents the most convincing case that Bakunin had little or nothing to do with the final draft of the *Catechism.* See his introduction to Michael Confino, ed., *Daughter of a Revolutionary: Natalie Herzen and the Bakunin–Nechayev Circle,* trans. Hilary Sternberg and Lydia Bott (Lasalle, Ill.: Library Press, 1973), pp. 9–42.

14. Malatesta is quoted in Nunzio Pernicone, *Italian Anarchism: 1864–1892* (Princeton, N.J.: Princeton University Press, 1993), p. 84.

15. The 1877 insurrection followed on the heels of the previous failed insurrection of 1874 in Bologna. Pietro Cesare Ceccarelli, an ally of Cafiero and Malatesta, admitted that his comrades "could not hope to win . . . we wanted to commit an act of propaganda." Ceccarelli is quoted in Richard Hostetter's account of this episode in *The Italian Socialist Movement I. Origins (1860–1882)* (Princeton, N.J. and Toronto: D. Van Nostrand, 1958), p. 377.

16. This is from Malatesta's essay "Anarchism and Violence," anthologized in Errico Malatesta, *The Anarchist Revolution: Polemical Articles 1924–1931,* edited by Vernon Richards (London: Freedom Press, 1995), p. 61.

17. He writes that "the defection of the mass of the working class had been one of the reasons for the recourse to terrorism." See Guérin, *Anarchy,* p. 75. Ulrich Linse

concludes that "the violent repression of Bakuninist insurrections in the 1870s by
State authorities had resulted in the wave of assassinations thereafter. He views the
yen for propaganda by the deed as an intermediary phase within the history of anarchism, wedged between the eclipse of old-style Proudhonism and Bakunism and
the advent of libertarian syndicalism." See Linse's articles "Propaganda by Deed" and
"Direct Action," anthologized in Wolfgang J. Mommsen and Gerhard Hirschfeld,
eds, *Social Protest, Violence and Terror in Nineteenth- and Twentieth-Century Europe*
(New York: St Martin's Press), pp. 201–29.

18. Mirbeau is quoted in Peter Marshall, *Demanding the Impossible: A History of
Anarchism* (London: HarperCollins, 1992), p. 438. For more on Mirbeau's relation-
ship to French anarchism, see Reg Carr, *Anarchism in France: The Case of Octave
Mirbeau* (Manchester: Manchester University Press, 1977).

19. Mark Polizzoti, Breton's biographer, writes that in 1913, Breton was "unfamiliar
with the theoretical texts of anarchism and Socialism." Breton's praise of Henry is
also quoted by Polizzoti; see his *Revolution of the Mind: The Life of Andre Breton*
(New York: Farrar, Straus & Giroux, 1995), pp. 15–17.

20. Paul Avrich, *The Haymarket Tragedy* (Princeton, N.J.: Princeton University
Press, 1984), p. 61.

21. Richard Drinnon, *Rebel in Paradise: A Biography of Emma Goldman* (Chicago
and London: University of Chicago Press, 1961), p. 81.

22. Félix Dubois, *The Anarchist Peril* (London: T. Fisher Unwin, 1894), p. 213.

23. Charles Musser, *Before the Nickelodeon: Edwin S. Porter and the Edison Manufacturing Company* (Berkeley and Los Angeles: University of California Press, 1991).

24. Bryon R. Bryant, "When Czolgosz Shot McKinley—A Study in Anti-Anarchist
Hysteria," *Resistance* 8, no. 3 (December 1949): 5.

25. Many of these lost films are either mentioned or briefly discussed in Pietro
Ferrua, *Anarchists in Films* (Portland, Ore.: First International Symposium on Anarchism, February 17–24, 1980), or *Cinema et anarchic* (Geneva: CIRA, 1984).

26. Robert J. Goldstein's research revealed that this American "anarchist scare"
was precipitated by several specific "outrages." These included the murder of a priest,
Father Leo Heinrichs, in Denver by an Italian immigrant named Giuseppe Aliaa,
who claimed to have been influenced by anarchist anti-clericalism, and the attempted
murder of a police chief in Chicago by a Russian Jew who the police maintained had
ties to anarchist circles. See Goldstein's article "The Anarchist Scare of 1908: A Sign
of Tensions in the Progressive Era," *American Studies* 15, no. 2 (April 1974): 55–87.

27. Richard Schickel, *D. W. Griffith: An American Life* (New York: Simon & Schuster, 1984), p. 136. For a more historically acute analysis of *The Voice of the Violin*,
see Scott Simmon, *The Films of D. W. Griffith* (New York and Cambridge, U.K.:
Cambridge University Press, 1993), pp. 49–51.

28. Lombroso's views on anarchists are summarized in Gina Lombroso-Ferrero,
Criminal Man: According to the Classification of Cesare Lombroso (Montclair, N.J.:
Paterson Smith, 1972), p. 305. In a parallel vein, a 1908 American newspaper fumed
that anarchists were as "worthless as rats and far more dangerous"—their "damnable
doctrine . . . conclusive proof of insanity." For a reference to this editorial from the

San Francisco Chronicle, February 27, 1908, and Goldstein, "The Anarchist Scene of 1908," p. 61.

29. Kevin Brownlow, *Behind the Mask of Innocence* (Berkeley and Los Angeles: University of California Press, 1990), p. 432.

30. *Moving Picture World,* March 13, 1909, p. 310.

31. André Salmon, *Le Terreur noire: Chronique du mouvement libertaire* (Paris: Jean-Jacques Pauvert, 1959).

32. I have not been able to screen Philippe Fourastie's *Les Anarchistes ou la bande à Bonnot* (France–Italy 1968), a fictionalization of the notorious gang's adventures. A brief description can be found in Ferrua, *Anarchists in Films,* p. 11. Some documentary footage of the Bonnot Gang was included by Nicole Védrès in her documentary, *Paris 1900* (1947).

33. Richard Parry, *The Bonnot Gang: The Story of the French Illegalists* (London: Rebel Press, 1987), p. 25.

34. The allure of Fantômas is made explicit in a passage in which a young man named Charles Rambert is depicted as awestruck as he contemplates the fact that "one man can commit so many crimes, and that any one man . . . can foil the cleverest devices of the police." A shocked magistrate replies to this tribute by admonishing the boy as "mad . . . absolutely mad. . . . You would not hesitate to put the heroes of crime and the heroes of law and order on one and the same pedestal." See Marcel Allain and Pierre Souvestre, *Fantômas* (New York: Ballantine Books, 1986), pp. 18–19.

35. For a meticulous account of the actual historical incidents and personages that inspired Conrad's novel, see Norman Sherry's *Conrad's Western World* (Cambridge, U.K.: Cambridge University Press, 1971), pp. 228–334. See also Paul Avrich's "Conrad's Anarchist Professor: An Undiscovered Source," *Drunken Boat* 2 (Winter–Spring 2001): 227–32.

36. Paula Marantz Cohen, *Alfred Hitchcock: The Legacy of Victorianism* (Lexington: University Press of Kentucky, 1995), p. 31. In a parallel vein, Balzac modeled the character of Vaturin on the real-life François-Eugène Vidocq, "the ex-convict who became the founder of the French Sûrete." See Rayner Heppenstall's introduction to Honoré de Balzac, *A Harlot High and Low* (London and New York: Penguin Books, 1970), p. viii.

37. Irving Howe, *Politics and the Novel* (Greenwich, Conn.: Fawcett Publications, 1967), p. 85. Howe also believes that Conrad's disdain for anarchism was at least partly the result of a compulsion to negate memories of his father's zealous Polish nationalism—a creed that was as devoted as anarchism to its own version of direct action—and assume the demeanor of a proper Englishman.

38. Jason E. Smith, "Portugal and the Future," *Stan Douglas, The Secret Agent* (Brussels: Ludion, 2015), pp. 147–57.

39. In summarizing Hitchcock's work on the final sequence of the original *The Man Who Knew Too Much,* biographer John Russell Taylor, like many commentators, assumed that the Sidney Street gang were actually anarchists. See Taylor's *Hitch* (London: Faber & Faber, 1978), p. 126.

40. John Quail, *The Slow Burning Fuse: The Lost History of the British Anarchists*

(St Albans, U.K. and London: Paladin Books, 1978), p. 267. The British anarchist Nellie Dick confirms Quail's view that the Sidney Street affair was a non-anarchist shoot-out. See John Pether, "A Conversation with Nellie Dick," *Raven* 2, no. 2 (October 1988): 163–64.

41. Richard Watts Jr., review of *Soak the Rich, New York Herald Tribune*, February 5, 1936.

42. For a sympathetic account of Sabate's activities, see Antonio Tellez, *Satiate: Guerrilla Extraordinary,* trans. Stuart Christie (London: Elephant Editions, 1974).

43. Charles Bernheimer, *Figures of Ill Repute: Representing Prostitution in Nineteenth-Century France* (London and Cambridge, Mass.: Harvard University Press, 1989), p. 208.

44. Goldman writes that only "a complete transvaluation of all accepted values ... coupled with the abolition of industrial slavery" will lead to the eradication of prostitution. See Goldman's essay "The Traffic in Women," anthologized in *Anarchism and Other Essays* (New York: Dover Publications, 1969), p. 194. Interestingly enough, conservative historians of ideas—like the filmmakers who link brothels and anarchists—often perceive continuities between radicalism and illicit sexual pursuits such as prostitution and pornography. The notoriously dyspeptic Paul Johnson, for example, claims that nineteenth-century radical publishers inveterately became pornographers when their politics became bankrupt. See the fulminations of Johnson's massive opus *The Birth of the Modern 1815–1830* (New York: Harper Perennial, 1970), p. 872.

45. See Giuseppe Fiori, *L'Anarchico Schirru condannato a morte per l'intenzione di uccidere Mussolini* (Milan: Mondadori, 1983).

46. See Simon's comments in his introduction to Lina Wertmüller, *The Screenplays of Lina Wertmüller,* trans. Steven Wagner (New York: Quadrangle/New York Times Book, 1977), pp. xvi–xvii.

47. Millicent Marcus, *Italian Film in the Light of Neorealism* (Princeton, N.J.: Princeton University Press, 1986), p. 327.

48. Kingsley Widmer, "Notes on some Recent Anarchisms," *Social Anarchism* 21 (1995–1996): 23.

49. Gina Blumenfeld and Paul McIsaac, "Lina Wertmüller: You Cannot Make the Revolution on Film," anthologized in Dan Georgakas and Lenny Rubenstein, eds, *The Cineaste Interviews: On the Art and Politics of the Cinema* (Chicago: Lakeview Press, 1983), p. 133.

50. This phrase is culled from William Van Wert's critique of *Love and Anarchy.* Van Wert assails Wertmüller for portraying Tunin as a "psychic anarchist." See his article "Love, Anarchy and the Whole Damn Thing," *Jump Cut,* May–June 1974, 8–9.

51. Irving Louis Horowitz, *Radicalism and the Revolt Against Reason: The Social Theories of Georges Sorel* (Carbondale and Edwardsville: Southern Illinois University Press, 1961), p. 169.

52. This remark is included in the unsigned leaflet "Fear and Powerlessness," unpaginated. An excerpt from this handout is included in Howard J. Ehrlich, Carol E. Ehrlich, David De Leon, and Glenda Morris, eds, *Reinventing Anarchy: What Are*

Anarchists Thinking These Days? (London and Boston: Routledge & Kegan Paul, 1979).

53. Nora Sayre, review of *Nada Gang* (American release tide), *New York Times,* November 3, 1974.

54. The Red Brigades were, of course, far from being anarchists of any sort. For an analysis of their political perspective, see Spartacus, "The Red Brigades: Between Stalinism and Leftism," *Root and Branch* 9 (1979): 41–50. A recent documentary by Marco Bellocchio, *Broken Dreams—Reason and Delirium* (1995), features some fascinating newsreel footage of this era, as well as interviews with veterans of the Red Brigades.

55. Gianfranco Sanguinetti, *On Terrorism and the State: The Theory and Practice of Terrorism Divulged for the First Time,* trans. Lucy Forsyth and Michael Prigent (London: Aldgate Press, 1982), p. 56.

56. Jill Forbes, *The Cinema in France: After the New Wave* (Bloomington and Indianapolis: Indiana University Press, 1992), p. 161. For another favorable view of *The Judge and the Assassin,* see Daniele Bion, *Bertrand Tavernier: Cinéaste de l'émotion* (Milan: 5 Continents, 1984), pp. 60–71.

57. Ward then goes on to contrast "old man McCabe's" anarchism with Paul Goodman's conception of "autonomy" See Colin Ward, "Anarchist Notebook: Simple Men and Complex Realities," *Freedom,* January 28, 1995, p. 5.

58. Malatesta urges "the free participation of all, by means of the spontaneous grouping of men according to their requirements and their sympathies, from the bottom to the top, from the simple to the complex . . . a social organization would emerge the function of which would be the greatest well-being and the greatest freedom for everybody. This ideal bears no resemblance to the world view of the isolated terrorist that Hartley apparently considers an archetypal anarchist. See *Malatesta's Anarchy,* trans. Vernon Richards (London: Freedom Press, 1974), p. 31.

59. For an account of Segui's activities, see Murray Bookchin, *The Spanish Anarchists: The Heroic Years 1868–1936* (Chico, Calif. and Edinburgh: AK Press, 1988).

60. Andrej Grubacic and David Graeber, *Anarchism, Or The Revolutionary Movement Of The Twenty-first Century* (2004). Online at https://theanarchistlibrary.org/library/andrej-grubacic-david-graeber-anarchism-or-the-revolutionary-movement-of-the-twenty-first-centu.

61. Stephanie Zacharek, "V for Vendetta," Salon.com, March 17, 2006. https://www.salon.com/2006/03/17/vendetta/.

62. Peter Bradshaw, "V for Vendetta," *Guardian,* March 16, 2006.

63. Gabriella Coleman, *Hacker, Hoaxer, Whistleblower, Spy: The Many Faces of Anonymous* (London and New York: Verso Books, 2014), p. 271. The Guy Fawkes mask, moreover, became an emblem of international dissidence that surfaced in Occupy Wall Street, the Arab Spring, and anti-government protests in Thailand. See Monica Nickelsburg, "A brief history of the Guy Fawkes mask," *The Week,* July 3, 2013. http://theweek.com/articles/463151/brief-history-guy-fawkes-mask.

64. Parry, *Bonnot Gang,* p.11.

65. Ross Douthat, "The Politics of the Dark Knight Rises," *New York Times,* July

23, 2012, https://douthat.blogs.nytimes.com/2012/07/23/the-politics-of-the-dark
-knight-rises/; Slavoj Zizek, "The Politics of Batman, *New Statesman,* July 23, 2012,
https://www.newstatesman.com/culture/culture/2012/08/slavoj-žižek-politics
-batman.

66. Saul Newman, "Voluntary Servitude Reconsidered: Radical Politics and the
Problem of Self-Domination," *Anarchist Developments in Cultural Studies* 1 (2010):
32.

67. Colin Campbell, *The Romantic Ethic and the Spirit of Modern Consumerism:
New Extended Edition* (Basingstoke, U.K.: Palgrave Macmillan, 2018), p. 306.

68. From the press notes for *Ceux qui font les revolutions á moitié non't fait que
se creuser un tombeau,* cited in Richard Porton, "The Toronto International Film
Festival," Cineaste.com, Winter 2016, https://www.cineaste.com/winter2016/toronto
-international-film-festival-2016/.

69. See "Translating Anarchy": An Interview With Mark Bray, http://occupywallst
.org/article/translating-anarchy-occupy-wall-street/.

70. Michael J. Schaack, *Anarchy and Anarchists: A History of the Red Terror and
the Social Revolution in America and Europe* (Chicago: F.J. Schulte, 1889), p. 387.
Schaack is referring to the Haymarket defendants.

71. Bob Black, for example, reminds us that the individualist "Tucker defended
the Haymarket anarchists when the collectivist Most repudiated them, receiving
for his gutlessness a horse-whipping from Emma Goldman." He also points out
that the "'individualist" Joe Labadie was a union activist and that the "19th century
'individualists' like Tucker referred to themselves as socialists and interacted intellectually and practically with Fourierists, feminists, atheists, Marxists and all kinds of
radicals." See Black's essay "The Call of the Wild(e)," in *Friendly Fire* (Brooklyn, N.Y.:
Autonomedia, 1992), pp. 183–84. A study of American anarchism by the German
writer Ulrike Heider delineates "an Anarcho-Capitalist family tree" beginning with
Max Stirner and including John Henry Mackay, Benjamin Tucker, Josiah Warren,
and Lysander Spooner. Heider's distortions parallel the misconceptions dissected
by Black in his essays. See Ulrike Heider, *Anarchism: Left, Right, and Green* (San
Francisco: City Lights, 1994), esp. pp. 95–99. For a review critical of Heider, see Allan
Antliff, "Varieties of Anarchism?" *Alternative Press Review* 2, no. 3 (Winter 1996):
73–74. For a work of political philosophy that melds individualism with anarcho-
communism, see L. Susan Brown, *The Politics of Individualism: Liberalism, Liberal
Feminism and Anarchism* (Montreal and New York: Black Rose Books, 1993). For
a critique of Brown, see Murray Bookchin, "The Democratic Dimension of Anarchism," *Democracy and Nature: The International Journal of Politics and Ecology* 3,
no. 2 (1996): 2–3.

72. Martin Henry Blatt, *Free Love and Anarchism: The Biography of Ezra Heywood*
(Urbana and Chicago: University of Illinois Press, 1989), p. 55.

73. See, for example, the introduction to Frank H. Brooks, ed., *The Individualist
Anarchists: An Anthology of Liberty (1881–1908)* (New Brunswick, N.J. and London:
Transaction Publishers, 1994), p. 9.

74. For a comprehensive account of the Chicago anarchists and their trial, see

Paul Ayrich, *The Haymarket Tragedy* (Princeton, N.J.: Princeton University Press, 1984). See also Philip S. Foner, ed., *The Autobiographies of the Haymarket Martyrs* (New York and London: Pathfinder, 1976). Daniel Guerin admires the fact that the "Chicago Martyrs called themselves 'politically anarchists, and economically communists or socialist.'" He regards this as "surely their originality and one of their merits." See his essay "Marxism and Anarchism," anthologized in David Goodway, ed., *For Anarchism: History, Theory; and Practice* (New York and London: Routledge, 1989), p. 121. See also Bruce Nelson, *Beyond the Martyrs: A Social History of Chicago's Anarchists 1870–1900* (New Brunswick, N.J. and London: Rutgers University Press, 1988). For a screed against the Haymarket defendants first published in 1890, see George N. McLean, *The Rise and Fall of Anarchy in America* (New York: Haskell House Publishers, 1972).

75. See David Wieck, "Strange Anarchy," *Social Anarchism* 3, no. 2 (1983): 16–20. Lenny Rubenstein also remarked that the film's denial "of the violent side of anarchism . . . blandly smacks of a desire to make a film acceptable for PBS." See his review in *Cineaste* 13, no. 1 (1983): 26.

76. Sacvan Bercovitch, *The Rites of Assent: Transformations in the Symbolic Construction of America* (New York and London: Routledge, 1993), p. 19.

77. David De Leon, *The American as Anarchist: Reflections on Indigenous Radicalism* (Baltimore: Johns Hopkins University Press, 1978), p. 131.

78. David Wieck, "Strange Anarchy," p. 17.

79. David S. Reynolds, *Walt Whitman's America: A Cultural Biography* (New York: Alfred A. Knopf, 1995), p. 144. As an example of Whitman's baffling combination of radical individualism and obeisance to American tradition, Reynolds cites Whitman's "excoriation" of the Fugitive Slave Law and his concomitant belief that "fugitive slaves must be returned to their owners because the Constitution demanded it."

80. Karl Hess, "Rights and Reality," *Our Generation* 20, no. 1 (Fall 1988): 71–77.

81. Reichert maintains that "anarchists of a later era who attacked Tucker for his alleged indifference to the plight of the working classes missed the point that his passive resistance was as much based upon distrust of organized government as was that of the bomb throwers." See William O. Reichert, *Partisans of Freedom: A Study in American Anarchism* (Bowling Green, Ohio: Bowling Green University Popular Press, 1976), p. 163.

82. This omission is also mentioned in Leslie Fishbein's insightful critique of the film. See her article "Anarchism as Ideology and Impulse: *Anarchism in America* (1981)," *Film and History* 13, no. 1 (February 1983): 17–22.

83. This is George Woodcock's observation in "The Anarchist as Conservative," anthologized in Peter Parisi, ed., *Artist of the Actual: Essays on Paul Goodman* (Metuchen, N.J. and London: The Scarecrow Press, 1986), p. 32.

84. Marshall, *Demanding the Impossible,* p. 641.

85. Steimer, an uncompromisingly radical Russian émigré, was arrested (together with four compatriots) in 1918 for distributing leaflets protesting American intervention in the Russian Revolution. She and her fellow defendants were convicted under the Sedition Act of 1918, and their conviction was upheld in a famous Supreme Court

case that inspired Justice Oliver Wendell Holmes to write one of his most noteworthy dissents. Steimer and the others were deported, at their own expense, to Russia in 1921. For an account of the case that examines its place in American legal history, as well as providing an excellent historical overview of immigrant anarchism, see Richard Polenberg, *Fighting Faiths: The Abrams Case, the Supreme Court, and Free Speech* (New York: Viking, 1987). A transcript of *Anarchism in America*'s interview with Steimer is reprinted in Mollie Steimer and Senya Fleshin, *Fighters for Anarchism: A Memorial Volume,* assembled and edited by Abe Bluestein (Minneapolis: Libertarian Publications Group, 1983).

86. For Dolgoff's view of *Freie Arbeiter Stimme*'s form of trade unionism, see Sam Dolgoff, *Fragments: A Memoir* (Cambridge, U.K.: Refract Publications, 1986), pp. 24–28.

87. For a translation of this open letter by Nathan Chofshi, see "State versus Commune in Israel," *Resistance* 9, no. 3 (April 1951): 12–13.

88. Curiously enough, Eleanor Antin's postmodern shtetl film *The Man Without a World* (a deliberately anachronistic Yiddish silent film made in 1992 to resemble the efforts of cineastes such as Joseph Green) features a debate between Jewish anarchists and Zionists in turn-of-the-century Russia.

89. Michael Renov, "Toward a Poetics of Documentary," in Michael Renov, ed., *Theorizing Documentary* (New York and London: Routledge, 1993), p. 31. According to Renov's poetics, *Anarchism in America* "persuades and promotes," but fails to "analyze and interrogate."

90. Richard J. F. Day, *Gramsci is Dead: Anarchist Currents in the Newest Social Movements* (London and Ann Arbor, Mich.: Pluto Press, 2005), p. 69.

91. Bruce Robbins, "The Young Karl Marx," *Politics/Letters* (March 19, 2018), http://politicsslashletters.live/reviews/young-karl-marx/.

92. Hal D. Sears, *The Sex Radicals: Free Love in High Victorian America* (Lawrence: Regents Press of Kansas), p. 272.

93. Raymond Durgnat, *WR—Mysteries of the Organism* (London: British Film Institute, 1999).

94. See For Ourselves, *The Right to be Greedy: Theses on the Practical Necessity of Demanding Everything,* at http://libcom.org/library/right-be-greedy-theses-practical -necessity-demanding-everything (theses 6 and 8).

95. Peter Marin, "The New Narcissism," anthologized in *Freedom and Its Discontents: Reflections on Four Decades of American Moral Experience* (South Royalton, Vt.: Steerforth Press, 1995), p. 45.

96. Durgnat, *WR,* p. 23.

97. Ibid., p.33.

98. See Thomas A. Stanley, *Osugi Sakae: Anarchist in Taisho Japan* (Cambridge, Mass. and London: Council on East Asian Studies, Harvard University, 1982).

99. David Desser, *Eros Plus Massacre: An Introduction to the Japanese New Wave Cinema* (Bloomington and Indianapolis: Indiana University Press, 1988), p. 212.

100. See Terence Kissack, *Free Comrades; Anarchism and Homosexuality in the United States, 1895–1917* (Oakland, Calif.: AK Press, 2008), p. 4. Contemporary

anarchist equivalents of these pioneering figures have superimposed the tenets of academic queer theory upon the sex radicals' original assault on sexual repression and puritanism. The anthology *Queering Anarchism* (Oakland, Calif.: AK Press, 2012), for example, endorses a political perspective that "refuses to acquiesce to the mainstream codification of LGBT identity."

101. Inkoo Kang, "'The Misandrists' Film Review: Bruce LaBruce Sends Up Feminist Ideology in Dated Satire," *The Wrap*, May 23, 2018, https://www.thewrap.com/the-misandrists-film-review-bruce-labruce/).

102. All quotes from LaBruce are from Richard Porton, "Wake Up and Smell the Estrogen: An Interview with Bruce LaBruce," Cineaste.com (Fall 2018). https://www.cineaste.com/fall2018/wake-up-and-smell-the-estrogen-bruce-labruce.

103. For example, Michael Schaack, a police captain who helped to investigate the Haymarket bombings, described a gathering of women anarchists in the 1880s in the following way: "In many of the smaller meetings held on Milwaukee Avenue . . . a lot of crazy women were usually present, and whenever a proposition arose to kill someone or blow up the city with dynamite, these "squaws" proved the most bloodthirsty." See Schaack, *Anarchy and Anarchists,* p. 207.

104. This is Andreas Huyssen's phrase. In a critique of post-structuralism, he wonders whether its aversion to "the subject" jettison[s] the chance of challenging the *ideology of the subject* (as male, white, and middle-class) by developing alternative and different notions of subjectivity." See Huyssen's "Mapping the Postmodern," in Linda J. Nicholson, ed., *Feminism/Postmodernism* (New York and London: Routledge, 1990), p. 264.

105. Siren, "Who We Are: An Anarcho-Feminist Manifesto," in *Quiet Rumours: An Anarcha-Feminist Anthology* (London: Aldgate Press, 1982). This is an anthology with essays by, among others, Peggy Kornegger and Marian Leighton that does not list a specific editor. "Anarcha-feminism" is a variant of "anarcho-feminism" that was occasionally employed.

106. See Margaret S. Marsh, *Anarchist Women: 1870–1920* (Philadelphia: Temple University Press, 1981), pp. 65–99. Marsh surveys well-known figures such as Voltairine de Cleyre and Emma Goldman, as well as more obscure women anarchists like Helena Born and Lois Waisbrooker. As early as 1903, de Cleyre raged at "the subordinate cramped circle, prescribed for women in daily life, whether in the field of material production, or in domestic arrangement, or in educational work." See Paul Avrich, *An American Anarchist: The Life of Voltairine de Cleyre* (Princeton, N.J.: Princeton University Press, 1978), p. 159.

107. D'Héricourt is quoted in Edith Thomas, *The Women Incendiaries,* trans. James and Starr Atkinson (New York: George Braziller, 1966), p. 25.

108. Ibid., p. 147.

109. Richard Stites, *The Women's Liberation Movement in Russia: Feminism, Nihilism, and Bolshevism: 1860–1930* (Princeton, N.J.: Princeton University Press, 1978), p. 132.

110. See Kropotkin's article, "An Appeal to Artists," in Émile Capouya and Keitha Tompkins, eds, *The Essential Kropotkin* (New York: Liveright, 1975), p. 23.

111. For an analysis of Tkachev's far-ranging influence on Russian radical traditions, see Deborah Hardy, *Petr Tkachev: The Critic as Jacobin* (Seattle and London: University of Washington Press, 1977).

112. Stites, *Women's Liberation Movement in Russia,* p. 9. For Zasulich's impact on Emma Goldman, see Goldman's *Living My Life: An Autobiography* (Salt Lake City: Peregrine Smith, 1982), p. 28.

113. Zasulich is quoted in Jay Bergman, *Vera Zasulich: A Biography* (Stanford, Calif.: Stanford University Press, 1983), p. 170.

114. Figner quoted in Margaret Maxwell, *Narodniki Women* (New York and London: Pergamon Press, 1990), p. 110.

115. Ethel Mannin, *Women and the Revolution* (New York: E.P. Dutton, 1939), p. 31.

116. The most informative history of the Red Army Faction is Stefan Aust, *The Baader–Meinhof Group: The Inside Story of a Phenomenon,* trans. Anthea Bell (London: Bodley Head, 1985). Baader–Meinhof member Bommi Baumann recounts how he read the anarchist classics as well as Marx and Lenin during his tenure with the organization. See Baumann's *How It All Began/Terror or Love* (London: Pulp Press, John Calder, 1977).

117. This is Rainer's description of her aesthetic program, quoted by B. Ruby Rich in "Yvonne Rainer: An Introduction," anthologized in Yvonne Rainer, *The Films of Yvonne Rainer* (Indiana and Bloomington: Indiana University Press, 1989), p. 23.

118. Robert Stam, *Subversive Pleasures: Bakhtin, Cultural Criticism, and Film* (Baltimore and London: Johns Hopkins University Press, 1989), p. 5. Stam is actually discussing Rainer's *The Man Who Envied Women* (1985) in this passage.

119. David Wieck, *The Negativity of Anarchism* (Paris: Interrogations, n.d.), p. 52.

120. Zasulich, for example, eventually denounced Leninism after the October Revolution. See also the chapter on Zasulich in Maxwell, *Narodniki Women,* pp. 3–49.

121. For an analysis of Lacanian theory's "terroristic effects," see Peter Starr, *Logics of Failed Revolt: French Theory after May '68* (Stanford, Calif.: Stanford University Press, 1993), esp. pp. 196–202.

122. Berkman is quoted in Candace Falk, *Love, Anarchy, and Emma Goldman* (New York: Holt Reinhart & Winston), p. 181.

123. Ibid.

124. For a discussion of "free indirect subjectivity," see Naomi Greene, *Pier Paolo Pasolini: Cinema as Heresy* (Princeton, N.J.: Princeton University Press, 1990), pp. 123–25.

125. "Free indirect discourse" was especially prized by Pasolini, although Gilles Deleuze suggests that he borrowed this form of aesthetic heterogeneity from Bakhtin. See Gilles Deleuze, *Cinema I: The Movement-Image,* trans. Hugh Tomlinson and Barbara Habberjam (Minneapolis: University of Minnesota Press, 1986), p. 73.

126. Nollau is quoted in David Kramer, "Ulrike Meinhof: An Emancipated Terrorist?" anthologized in Jane Slaughter and Robert Kern, eds, *European Women on*

the Left: Socialism, Feminism, and the Problems Faced by Political Women, 1880 to the Present (Westport, Conn.: Greenwood Press, 1981), p. 213.

127. Rainer made this admission during a telephone interview with the author (May 1996).

128. Amy Taubin, "Review of *Born in Flames*," *Village Voice*, November 15, 1983, p. 61.

129. See George Bernard Shaw, "Neither Communist Nor Individualist Anarchism," anthologized in Leonard I. Krimmerman and Lewis Perry, eds, *Patterns of Anarchy: A Collection of Writings on the Anarchist Tradition* (Garden City, N.Y.: Doubleday, 1966), pp. 500–514.

130. Zeke Teflon's *The Complete Manual of Pirate Radio* (Tucson, Ariz.: See Sharp Press, 1993) is a widely distributed manual that contains useful practical advice for creating "an alternative to corporate-controlled newspapers and magazines, the insane howling on religious radio and TV stations, the reactionary pap on commercial stations and the innocuous animals—and British accents—on "public" (government-owned) stations." For aesthetic approaches to guerrilla radio, see the essays in Neil Strauss, ed., *Radiotext(e) (Semiotext(e)* 16, no. 6 (1993). For a journalistic glimpse at a New York pirate radio station, see Peter Spagnuolo, "Steal this Radio," *Shadow* 38, May–June 1996, p. 4.

131. Mark Poster, *The Second Media Age* (Cambridge, U.K.: Polity Press, 1995), p. 57.

132. For a brief history of the Provo movement, see Rudolf de Jong, "Provos and Kabouters," anthologized in David E. Apter and James Joll, eds., *Anarchism Today* (London: Macmillan, 1971), pp. 164–80.

133. The quotations are from the author's unpublished telephone interview with Lizzie Borden (May 17, 1996). Borden also discussed the film's anarchist elements in an interview conducted by Alexandra Devon for the anarcho-feminist publication *Kick It Over* 18 (Spring 1987): 1–3. An excerpt from this interview was also published in *Anarchy: A Journal of Desire Armed* 16 (Summer 1988): 9.

134. Teresa de Lauretis, *Technologies of Gender: Essays on Theory, Film, and Fiction* (Bloomington and Indianapolis: Indiana University Press, 1987), p. 139. Bakhtin's discussion of the novel's ability to refract authorial intention is pertinent in this context. See M. M. Bakhtin, *The Dialogic Imagination: Four Essays,* trans. Caryl Emerson and Michael Holquist (Austin and London: University of Texas Press, 1981), p. 315.

135. For an account of "the subject in process" that is also critical of post-structuralist shibboleths, see Paul Smith, *Discerning the Subject* (Minneapolis: University of Minnesota Press, 1988).

136. Bookchin is quoted in Marshall, *Demanding the Impossible,* p. 617.

137. Ibid.

138. See Colin Ward, *Anarchy in Action* (New York and Evanston, Ill.: Harper & Row, 1974), p. 28.

139. Peggy Kornegger, "Anarchism: The Feminist Connection," anthologized in

Howard J. Ehrlich, ed., *Reinventing Anarchy, Again* (San Francisco and Edinburgh: AK Press, 1996), p. 161.

140. Freeman's article, "The Tyranny of Structurelessness," is anthologized in Jo Freeman and Cathy Levine, eds, *Untying the Knot: Feminism, Anarchism, and Organization* (London: Dark Star and Rebel Press, 1984).

141. A remark by Borden in the author's unpublished telephone interview.

142. These sentiments are found in a letter from Goldman to Berkman, dated November 23, 1928, contained in Richard and Anna Maria Drinnon, ed., *Nowhere at Home: Letters from Exile of Emma Goldman and Alexander Berkman* (New York: Schocken, 1975), pp. 95–96.

143. For one women's jaundiced account of the *Class War* militants as radicals living in "a "Boy's Own Paper" fantasy world," see Claudia (C. S. Walton), *The Rebel's New Clothes* (London: CW Publications, 1992), p. 18.

144. This strain of left-libertarian thought is best exemplified by the work of Silvia Federici and more recently, Melissa Gira Grant. See, for example, Morgane Merteuil, "Sex Work Against Work," *Viewpoint Magazine*, October 31, 2015. https://www.viewpointmag.com/2015/10/31/sex-work-against-work/; and Melissa Gira Grant, *Playing the Whore: The Work of Sex Work* (London and New York: Verso, 2014).

Chapter 2. Cinema, Anarchism, and Revolution: Heroes, Martyrs, and Utopian Moments

1. This is from Nomad's essay on Malatesta in *Rebels and Renegades* (New York: Macmillan, 1932), p. 1.

2. For an analysis of *A Fistful of Dynamite*, see Christopher Frayling, *Spaghetti Westerns: Cowboys and Europeans, From Karl May to Sergio Leone* (London: Routledge & Kegan Paul, 1981), pp. 183–86.

3. Hobsbawm observes that "social banditry has an affinity for revolution, being a phenomenon of social protest, if not a precursor or potential incubator of revolt. In this it differs sharply from the ordinary underworld of crime." See Eric Hobsbawm, *Bandits* (Harmondsworth and New York: Penguin Books, 1965), p. 98.

4. Blackburn is quoted in Thom Anderson, "Red Hollywood," in Suzanne Ferguson and Barbara Groseclose, eds, *Literature and the Visual Arts in Contemporary Society* (Columbus: Ohio State University Press, 1985), p. 154.

5. Russell and Dell are quoted in Theodore Draper, *The Roots of American Communism* (Chicago: Ivan R. Dee, 1989), p. 128.

6. Peter Marshall, "Human Nature and Anarchism," in David Goodway, ed., *For Anarchism: History, Theory, Practice* (New York and London: Routledge, 1989), p. 147.

7. For the most comprehensive biography of Hill, which nonetheless raises more questions than it answers, see Gibbs M. Smith, *Labor Martyr: Joe Hill* (New York: Grosset & Dunlap, 1969).

8. Salvatore Salerno makes a convincing case that many IWW members were well aware of European syndicalist traditions. See Salerno's *Red November/Black*

November: Culture and Community in the Industrial Workers of the World (Albany: State University of New York Press, 1989).

9. See, for example, Richard Schickel, "A Pair of Mangled Legends," *Life*, November 26, 1971, p. 8; and Vincent Canby, "Joe Hill," *New York Times*, October 25, 1971. See also Francis Shor, "Biographical Moments in the Written and Cinematic Text: Reconstructing the Legends of Joe Hill and Buffalo Bill," *Film and History* 14, no. 3 (1984): 61–68.

10. Scorsese's film is a rather fanciful version of *Boxcar Bertha: An Autobiography*, as told to Dr. Ben L. Reitman (New York: Amok Press, 1988). Reitman, known as a "Hobo King," was linked to the anarchist movement through a protracted affair with Emma Goldman. This relationship earned Reitman—and, to a certain extent, Goldman—the enmity of many anarchists: Reitman was often dismissed as a parasite and insufficiently political. For an account of Goldman's romance with Reitman, as well as passages from their love letters that were not discovered until the 1980s, see Candace Falk, *Love, Anarchy, and Emma Goldman* (New York: Basic Books, 1980), pp. 333–400.

11. Gibbs Smith found evidence that "Hill was reportedly in charge of enlisting IWW members from Los Angeles" for the Magónists' rebel army. See Smith, *Labor Martyr*, p. 53.

12. James D. Cockcroft, *Intellectual Precursors of the Mexican Revolution 1900–1913* (Austin and London: University of Texas Press, 1968), p. 186. See also John M. Hart, *Anarchism and the Mexican Working Class, 1860–1931* (Austin and London: University of Texas Press, 1978).

13. Wayne Hampton regards Hill and several more contemporary folksingers as a "guerrilla minstrel" who "promotes the cause of the working class." See Wayne Hampton, *Guerrilla Minstrels: John Lennon, Joe Hill, Woody Guthrie, Bob Dylan* (Knoxville: University of Tennessee Press, 1986).

14. Robert Cantwell, *When We Were Good: The Folk Revival* (Cambridge, Mass. and London: Harvard University Press, 1996), p. 91.

15. In response to a query asking if Wilkerson was familiar with films like *The Wobblies* and *Joe Hill*, he responded, "My interest came pretty strictly from growing up in Butte, hearing all the stories and rumors. I saw those films (well before I made mine, not as research) but I found them rather self-defeating, failing to match radical content and form in any meaningful way and obstructing their effect in the process. I was much more inspired by [Sanitago] Alvarez and Third Cinema and struggling to enact those kinds of practices in the context of my home landscapes and political concerns. Of course, I have somewhat different ideas now, but that was a long time ago." email from Wilkerson to author, December 30, 2015.

16. Neil Young uses the phrase "one-man-band" in a *Sight & Sound* piece on Wilkerson. See Neil Young, "Left to His Own Devices," *Sight & Sound*, December 2015.

17. See Arnold Stead, *Always on Strike: Frank Little and the Western Wobblies* (Chicago: Haymarket Books, 2014), pp. 121–25.

18. Peter Rachleff, "An Injury to One: A Film by Travis Wilkerson," *Monthly Review*

Online, August 1, 2005, https://mronline.org/2005/08/01/an-injury-to-one-a-film-by -travis-wilkerson/.

19. Naomi Klein, *This Changes Everything: Capitalism vs. The Climate* (New York: Simon & Schuster, 2014), p. 295.

20. Stewart Bird, Dan Georgakas, and Deborah Shaffer, *Solidarity Forever: An Oral History of the IWW* (Chicago: Lake View Press, 1985), p. 23

21. See Herbert B. Ehrmann, *The Case That Will Not Die: Commonwealth vs. Sacco and Vanzetti* (Boston: Little, Brown, 1969).

22. Paul Avrich, *Sacco and Vanzetti: The Anarchist Background* (Princeton, N.J.: Princeton University Press, 1991), p. 243. Nunzio Pernicone wrote that "you must bear in mind that Montaldo's film is probably more interested in saying something about the Pinelli case than in providing an accurate account of Sacco and Vanzetti" (letter from Pernicone to author, June 29, 1986). Perhaps Peter Bondanella had the Pinelli case in mind when he wrote that "disturbing parallels between the situation during the Red scare of the 1920s in America and contemporary Italy may not be noticed by the non-Italian viewer of the film, but Montaldo employs them skillfully in a discourse about the corrupt nature of political power that recognizes no national frontiers." See Peter Bondanella, *Italian Cinema: From Neorealism to the Present* (New York: Continuum, 1988), pp. 333–34. For more on the relationship of the Pinelli case to *Accidental Death of an Anarchist,* see David Hirst, *Dario Fo and Franca Rame* (New York: St Martin's Press, 1989), pp. 42–43.

23. See Avrich, *Sacco and Vanzetti,* pp. 50–51, 134–36.

24. Vanzetti's 1924 letter to Evans is anthologized in Marion Denman Frankfurter and Gardner Jackson, eds, *The Letters of Sacco and Vanzetti* (Secaucus, N.J.: Citadel Press, 1956), p. 109.

25. See Francis Russell, *Sacco and Vanzetti: The Case Resolved* (New York: Harper & Row, 1986), esp. pp. 64–86.

26. See Luigi Galleani, *The End of Anarchism?,* trans. Max Martin and Robert D'Attilio (Orkney, U.K.: Cienfuegos Press, 1982), p. 64.

27. See Emma Goldman, *My Disillusionment in Russia* (Gloucester, Mass.: Peter Smith, 1983); Alexander Berkman, *The Bolshevik Myth* (London and Winchester, Mass.: Pluto Press, 1989).

28. Christopher Lasch, *American Liberals and the Russian Revolution* (New York and St. Louis: McGraw Hill, 1962), pp. 129–30.

29. Otto Rühle, *The Struggle against Fascism Begins with the Struggle against Bolshevism* (London: Bratach Dubh Editions, 1981), p. 20.

30. See Victor Serge, *Year One of the Russian Revolution,* trans. and ed., Peter Sedgwick (London: Pluto Press, 1992).

31. Boris Pasternak, *Doctor Zhivago,* trans. Max Hayward and Manya Harari (New York: Pantheon Books, 1958), p. 220. For an analysis of Pasternak's "quarrel with Marxism," see Sidney Monas, "Russian Literature and Individual Autonomy," in Donald W. Treadgold, ed., *Soviet and Chinese Communism: Similarities and Differences* (Seattle and London: University of Washington Press, 1967), pp. 255–87.

32. Eastman is also quoted as patronizingly describing anarchism as "a natural

philosophy for artists. . . . It is literary not scientific-an emotional evangel, not a practical movement of men." He complained that anarchists "have no appreciation of the terrific problem of organization involved in revolutionizing the entire world." See William L. O'Neill, *The Last Romantic: A Life of Max Eastman* (New York and London: Oxford University Press, 1978), pp. 93–94.

33. Letter from Emma Goldman to Bayard Boyesen, February 24, 1923, Emma Goldman Papers, University of California at Berkeley.

34. Kropotkin is quoted and the distinction between state communism and anarchist communism is discussed in Joan Burbank, *Intelligentsia and Revolution: Russian Views of Bolshevism 1917–1922* (New York and Oxford, U.K.: Oxford University Press), pp. 99–105. Burbank writes that, despite his harsh criticisms of Lenin, he "never renounced" a "belief in the progressive nature of the Russian revolution; to do so would have called into question the entire positivist foundation of his philosophical system." An account of Kropotkin's meeting with Lenin in 1919 is anthologized in P. A. Kropotkin, *Selected Writings on Anarchism and Revolution,* ed. Martin A. Miller (Cambridge, Mass.: MIT Press, 1970), pp. 325–32.

35. Andrew Sarris, "A Man, a Woman, and, Oh Yes, a Revolution," *Village Voice,* December 2, 1981, p. 64. Historians continue to debate whether Reed was "disillusioned" with Bolshevism before his untimely death. Robert Rosenstone argues that since he "was driven to Bolshevism by world events and his own needs and goals, Reed had embraced it as a philosophy that allowed him to make sense of his own experience, and he would not have abandoned it easily." See Robert A. Rosenstone, *Romantic Revolutionary* (Cambridge, Mass. and London: Harvard University Press, 1990), p. 379.

36. For an insightful critique of *Reds,* see Robert Rosenstone's "*Reds* as History," in Rosenstone, *Romantic Revolutionary,* pp. 83–108.

37. Goldman, *Living My Life,* p. 740. The second volume of Alice Wexler's biography of Goldman upset many anarchists with her assertion that "in the end, the anarchists, and Goldman herself, suffered most from their obsessive anti-Communism and anti-Marxism." Her claim that Trotsky (known to anarchists as the "butcher of Kronstadt") "offered [a] more far-reaching critique of Stalinism" proved particularly distressing. Her defense of the Soviet New Economic Policy (NEP) seemed especially peculiar, since even most Leninists admit that the NEP represented a partial retreat from the goals of the revolution. In the anarchist newspaper *Fifth Estate,* Goldman scholar David Porter attacked Wexler's "apologia for Leninism." See Alice Wexler, *Emma Goldman in Exile: From the Russian Revolution to the Spanish Civil War* (Boston: Beacon Press, 1989), pp. 234–45; David Porter, "Emma Goldman in Exile: New Book Distorts History and a Life," *Fifth Estate* 24, no. 3 (Winter 1990)): 24–25. Wexler defended her views in a letter and Porter replied in "An Exchange—Emma Goldman and the Russian Revolution, *Fifth Estate* 25, no. 1 (Summer 1990): 26–27.

38. Maurice Brinton, *The Bolsheviks and Workers' Control-1917 to 1921, the State and Counter-revolution* (Detroit: Black and Red, 1975), p. 41.

39. Leonard Schapiro, *The Origin of the Communist Autocracy* (Cambridge, Mass.: Harvard University Press, 1977), p. 187.

40. See, for example, Ida Mett, *The Kronstadt Comwmu* (London: Solidarity Press, 1967); Paul Avrich, *Kronstadt 1921* (New York and London: W.W. Norton, 1974); Israel Getzler, *Kronstadt 1917–1921: The Fate of a Soviet Democracy* (London and Cambridge, U.K.: Cambridge University Press, 1983).

41. See P. Arshinov, *History of the Makhnovist Movement 1918–1921,* trans. Lorraine and Fredy Perlman (London: Freedom Press, 1987); Voline, *The Unknown Revolution (Kronstadt 1921, Ukraine 1918–1921),* trans. Holley Cantine (New York: Libertarian Book Club, 1955).

42. Alexandre Skirda's biographical study of Makhno is entitled *Nestor Makhno: Le Cosaque de l'anarchie* (Paris, 1982).

43. Paul Avrich, *Anarchist Portraits* (Princeton, N.J.: Princeton University Press, 1988), p. 118.

44. Stites also mentions that "the satanization of Makhno [was] employed . . . in circus spectacle, operetta, and the marvelous film comedy *Wedding at Malinovka* (1967). See Richard Stites, *Russian Popular Culture: Entertainment and Society since 1900* (Cambridge, U.K. and New York: Cambridge University Press, 1992), pp. 57–58. For more information on *Little Red Imps,* see Jay Leyda, *Kino: A History of the Russian and Soviet Film* (New York: Collier Books, 1960), pp. 248–49. Isaac Babel's diaries include a brief reference to Makhno: see Babel's *1920 Diary,* edited with an introduction and notes by Carol J. Avins (New Haven, Conn. and London: Yale University Press, 1995), p. 37.

45. With the help of Stephen Cole of the Emma Goldman Papers at the University of California, Berkeley, I have ascertained that the scenario was probably written by Berkman while living in Berlin in 1924 during the early phase of his exile. Berkman often met with Makhno during this period, and a letter from Berkman to Pauline Turkel (September 24, 1924, collection of the Tamiment Library, New York University) makes reference to several drafts of a scenario we both assume is *Batko Voilno.*

46. For biographical details on this phase of Makhno's life, see Voline, *The Unknown Revolution,* p. 86.

47. See, for example, the letter from Goldman to Berkman, August 20, 1924, as well as a letter from Goldman to Stella Ballantine, also August 20, 1924, in which a manuscript that seems to be *Batko Voilno* is referred to in passing. Both letters are from the Emma Goldman archive of the International Institute of Social History (Amsterdam). Thanks to Stephen Cole of the Emma Goldman Papers (University of California at Berkeley) for making me aware of these letters.

48. Meltzer's observations appear in his introduction to Ricardo Flores Magón, *Land and Liberty: Anarchist Influences in the Mexican Revolution,* edited by David Poole (Orkney, U.K.: Cienfuegos Press, 1977), p. 2.

49. John A. Britton, *Revolution and Ideology: Images of the Mexican Revolution in the United States* (Lexington: University Press of Kentucky, 1995), pp. 210–11.

50. Dan Georgakas, "Still Good After All These Years," *Cineaste* 7, no. 2 (1967): 15–16. Georgakas considers the film admirably anti-authoritarian, despite its well-known inaccuracies—e.g., Zapata's horse was a sorrel, not a white horse. In the same

issue, Peter Biskind condemns the film as anti-communist propaganda. See Biskind, "Ripping Off Zapata Revolution Hollywood Style," pp. 11–12.

51. Edward W. Said, *Culture and Imperialism* (New York: Alfred A. Knopf, 1993), pp. 66–67.

52. See Ulli Diemer, "Anarchism vs. Marxism: A Few Notes on an Old Theme," in *Anarchism vs. Marxism* (Somerville, Mass.: Root and Branch Mini-Pamphlet), pp. 1–11.

53. See Weil's "Reflections Concerning the Causes of Liberty and Social Oppression," in *Oppression and Liberty* (Amherst: University of Massachusetts Press, 1973), pp. 43–46. For an intriguing amalgamation of anarchist and Marxist motifs, see Jacques Camatte, *This World We Must Leave,* edited by Alex Trotter (Brooklyn, N.Y.: Autonomedia, 1995).

54. See, for example, Gerald Brenan, *The Spanish Labyrinth: An Account of the Social and Political Background of the Spanish Civil War* (Cambridge, U.K.: Cambridge University Press, 1960). For an account of medieval Spanish communalism that predates the anarchist communism of the 1930s by several centuries, see Stephen Haliczer, *The Comuneros of Castile: The Forging of a Revolution, 1475–1521* (Madison: University of Wisconsin Press, 1981).

55. Murray Bookchin, *To Remember Spain: The Anarchist and Syndicalist Revolution of 1936* (Edinburgh and San Francisco: AK Press, 1994), p. 42.

56. See Pierre Broué and Émile Témime, *The Revolution and the Civil War in Spain,* trans. Tony White (Cambridge, Mass.: MIT Press, 1970); Burnett Bolloten, *The Spanish Revolution: The Left and the Struggle for Power during the Civil War* (Chapel Hill: University of North Carolina Press, 1979).

57. Noam Chomsky, "Objectivity and Liberal Scholarship," in *American Power and the New Mandarins* (New York: Pantheon Books, 1969), p. 73.

58. Although this unflattering view of anarchism is voiced by a character in Hemingway's anti-fascist play *The Fifth Column,* it apparently corresponded to his own viewpoint. Stephen Cooper reveals how Hemingway supported the "suppression of subversive or unreliable elements in the Republican camp." The passage from *The Fifth Column* is quoted in "Anarchists in Fiction," unsigned article, *Anarchist Review* 1, no. 5 (1980): 47. Cooper's remark appears in Stephen Cooper, *The Politics of Ernest Hemingway* (Ann Arbor: University of Michigan Press, 1987), p. 93.

59. David Mitchell, *The Spanish Civil War* (New York: Franklin Watts, 1983), p. 133.

60. CNT leaflet, *Sobre la collectivización públicos en nuestro ciudad,* December 24, 1936 (collection of the International Institute of Social History, Amsterdam).

61. Julio Pérez Perucha et al., *El Cine de las Organizaciones Populares Republicanas entre 1936 y 1939* (22 Cetermaen Internacional de Cine de las Organizaciones Populares Republicanas entre 1936 y 1939, December 1980).

62. See Román Gubern, *1936–1939: La Guerra de España en la pantalla* (Madrid: Filmoteca Española, 1986), p. 17. See also José Maria Caparrós Lera, "The Cinema in the Spanish Civil War, 1936–1939," *Film and History* 16, no. 2 (May 1986): 35–46.

63. After the defeat of Republican Spain, *Aurora de Esperanza and Nosostros soms*

asi were banned by Franco's regime. See Peter Besas, *Behind the Spanish Lens: Spanish Cinema Under Fascism and Democracy* (Denver: Arden Press, 1985), p. 19.

64. Abel Paz, *Durruti: The People Armed,* trans. Nancy Macdonald (Montreal: Black Rose Books, 1976), p. 74.

65. See Annette Michelson, "The Kinetic Icon in the Work of Mourning: Prolegomena to the Analysis of a Textual System," *October* 52 (Spring 1990): 17–38.

66. Vernon Richards, *Lessons of the Spanish Revolution* (London: Freedom Press, 1983), p. 182.

67. These remarks were made in a conversation between Durruti and the German anarcho-syndicalist Rudolph Rocker. See Paz, *Durruti,* p. 110.

68. See Ronald Fraser, *Blood of Spain: An Oral History of the Spanish Civil War* (New York: Pantheon Books, 1979), p. 72. Amazingly enough, after the CNT signed a pact with the UGT (the socialist trade union who were under the aegis of the Communist Party in Catalonia) in late 1936, the "Russian consul in Barcelona . . . expressed 'the greatest admiration for the Catalan workers, especially the anarcho-syndicalists." After Durruti's death, "Jose Diaz, on behalf of the Communist Party, sent a telegram of condolence." See David T. Cattell, *Communism and the Spanish Civil War* (Berkeley and Los Angeles: University of California Press, 1956), pp. 126–27. As Fernando Claudin documents, the Spanish Revolution took the Soviet Union by surprise, and the unpredictable fluctuations of official Soviet policy reflect Stalin's initial bewilderment. Inevitably, Claudin concludes that "Stalin's Spanish policy . . . provides the most obvious example of the sacrifice of a revolution to the interests of Soviet *raison d'état.*" See Claudin's *The Communist Movement: From Comintern to Cominform-Part One, The Crisis of the Communist International,* trans. Brian Pearce (New York and London: Monthly Review Press, 1975), p. 242. See also Hans Magnus Enzensberger, *Anarchy's Brief Summer: The Life and Death of Buenaventura Durruti,* translated by Mike Mitchell (New York, London, and Calcutta: Seagull Books, 2018.)

69. In a December 1936 letter, Goldman wrote to her niece Stella Ballantine that "you will hear my voice in the Durruti film" (Emma Goldman collection, New York Public Library).

70. Marcel Oms, *La Guerre d'espangne au cinéma* (Paris: Les Éditions du Cerf, 1986), p. 69.

71. Leval claimed that war "represented destruction and extermination," while anarchism entailed "creation and harmony" See Bolloten, *The Spanish Revolution,* pp. 252–53. As an example of Durruti's military style, Bolloten quotes an anecdote from an anarcho-syndicalist refugee periodical in which the militia leader, instead of shooting two deserters who flee the front in panic, assures them that "here no one is under compulsion." As a result, they supposedly "asked to return to the front and fought with unexampled heroism."

72. In a letter of March 2, 1937 to Stella Ballantine, Goldman discusses her frustration at not being able to obtain prints of Frank's *Fury over Spain* to show for propaganda purposes in London, although she had been promised copies by the German anarchist Augustin Souchy. On August 1, 1937, Goldman wrote to Ethel

Mannin that "Frank left me his picture (*Fury over Spain*)." She found it "powerful" and observed that it conveyed the CNT-FAI's spirit as she "could never hope to do by word of mouth or even pen." She reports arranging a "free showing" in London, but complains of the film's "flammable" condition and exhibition and projection costs. Both letters are in the Emma Goldman collection of the New York Public Library. For more on Goldman's activities in Spain, see the letters anthologized in David Porter, ed., *Vision of Fire: Emma Goldman on the Spanish Revolution* (New Paltz, N.Y.: Commonground Press, 1983).

73. See Howard Rushmore, "'Will of a People': Film of Spain's *No Pasaran*," *Daily Worker*, February 11, 1939, p. 18; James Dugan, "Film on Spain," *New Masses*, February 21, 1939, pp. 29–30.

74. Hugh Thomas, *The Spanish Civil War* (New York: Simon & Schuster, 1961). Thomas responded to his anarchist critics by adding twenty pages on the revolutionary experience and agrarian collectivization in the 1977 edition. Yet even these amendments damn the anarchists with faint praise. For a thorough critique of the 1977 edition, see Richards, *Lessons of the Spanish Revolution*, pp. 242–50.

75. See Franz Borkenau, *The Spanish Cockpit: An Eye-witness Account of the Political and Social Conflicts of the Spanish Civil War* (Ann Arbor: University of Michigan Press, 1971).

76. See Trilling's introduction to George Orwell, *Homage to Catalonia* (Boston: Beacon Press, 1952), p. 3. Two authors, International Brigade veteran Bill Alexander and historian Robert Stradling, maintain that Orwell suffered from myopic political judgments and question *Homage to Catalonia*'s historical accuracy. Both authors evince a palpable distaste for the anti-Stalinist left. See Bill Alexander, "George Orwell and Spain," and Robert Stradling, "Orwell and the Spanish Civil War: A Historical Critique," in Christopher Norris, ed., *Inside the Myth. Orwell: Views from the Left* (London: Lawrence & Wishart, 1986), pp. 85–125. For a response to Stradling and Alexander, see Peter Monteath, Problematizing History: Orwell's Spanish Experience," *Melbourne Historical Journal* 20 (1990): 112–15. Raymond Williams's famously astringent book on Orwell nonetheless terms *Homage to Catalonia* "an unforgettably vivid personal account of a revolution and civil war." See Williams's *George Orwell* (New York: Columbia University Press, 1971), p. 59. The attacks on Orwell anthologized in the Norris book are also refuted in Victor Alba and Stephen Schwartz, *Spanish Communism versus Soviet Communism* (New Brunswick, N.J. and Oxford, U.K.: Transaction Books, 1988), pp. 280–99.

77. Bolloten, *Spanish Revolution*, p. 251.

78. For an account of this event, see E. H. Carr, *The Comintern and the Spanish Civil War*, edited by Tamara Deutscher (New York: Pantheon Books, 1984), p. 36.

79. Nin is quoted in Broué and Témime, *The Revolution and the Civil War*, p. 170. For more on agrarian collectivization from an anarchist perspective, see Sam Dolgoff, ed., *The Anarchist Collectives: Workers' Self-Management in the Spanish Revolution, 1936–1939* (New York: Free Life Editions, 1977); and Gaston Leval, *Collectives in the Spanish Revolution*, trans. Vernon Richards (London: Freedom Press, 1975). See also Graham Kelsey's *Anarchosyndicalism, Libertarian Communism and the State: The*

CNT in Zaragoza and Aragon, 1930–1937 (Dordrecht, Boston, and London: Kluwer Academic Publishers, 1991), p. 161.

80. Letter from Lisa Berger to the author, November 1995.

81. For a summary of Carrillo's position, as well as Josep Maria Solé i Sabaté's view (a historian associated with an institute backed by the Parti Socialist Unificat de Catalunya, PSUC) that the film "does not stand up historically," see Andy Dugan, "The Hidden Story of the Revolution," *New Politics* 6, no. 1 (Summer 1966): 74.

82. Abe Smorodin, "*Land and Freedom*: A VALB View"; Martha Gellhorn, "This is Not the Spain I Knew," *The Volunteer,* Spring 1996, pp. 14, 22. Smorodin and some other Lincoln Brigade veterans regretfully believe that the film "represents the triumph of George Orwell's view of the war." See Lewis Beale, "'Taking a Shot at 'Land and Freedom': N.Y. Vets Attack a New Film that Puts Down their Anti-Franco Fight in 1936," *Daily News,* March 14, 1996, p. 52.

83. Rocabert is quoted in Jonathan Steele, "The War that Spain Tried to Forget," *Guardian Weekly,* October 15, 1995, p. 35.

84. Richard Porton, "The Revolution Betrayed: An Interview with Ken Loach," *Cineaste* 22, no. 1 (1995): 31. See also Jean-Loup Bourget, Lorenzo Codelli, and Hubert Niogret, "'Milicien plutôt que soldat': entretien avec Ken Loach," *Positif* 416 (October 1995): 73–79.

85. Gerard Noiriel, "For a Subjectivist Approach to the Social," in Jacques Revel and Lynn Hunt, eds, *Histories: French Constructions of the Past,* trans. Arthur Goldhammer et al. (New York: New Press, 1995), p. 584.

86. For a brief assessment of Montseny's contributions to the Spanish Revolution from a feminist perspective, see Shirley Mangini, *Memories of Resistance: Women's Voices from the Spanish Civil War* (New Haven, Conn. and London: Yale University Press, 1995), pp. 46–49, 172–74. Helen Graham claims that radical women like Montseny challenged the Republic's "patriarchal order." See Graham's "Women and Social Change," in Helen Graham and Jo Labanyi, eds, *Spanish Cultural Studies: An Introduction* (Oxford and New York: Oxford University Press), pp. 99–116.

87. Robert W. Kern, *Red Years/Black Years: A Political History of Spanish Anarchism, 1911–1937* (Philadelphia: Institute for the Study of Human Issues, 1978), p. 217.

88. Román Gubern, "The Civil War: Inquest or Exorcism?" *Quarterly Review of Film and Video* 13, no. 4 (1991): 112.

89. See José Peirats, *Anarchists in the Spanish Revolution* (Detroit: Black and Red, 1974), pp. 292–301. Camillo Berneri, reportedly murdered by emissaries of the Communist Party during the May Days, challenged Montseny in 1937 by asking if "the anarchists are in the Government for the purpose of being the vestals of a fire about to be extinguished, or whether they are there henceforth to serve as a Phrygian Cap for some of the politicians who are flirting with the enemy or with the forces anxious to restore 'The Republic of the Classes.'" See Berneri's "Open Letter to Federica Montseny," in Vernon Richards, ed., *Spain and the World* (London: Freedom Press, 1990), p. 118.

90. Faure is quoted in Juan Gómez Casas, *Anarchist Organization: A History of*

the FA.I., trans. Abe Bluestein (Montreal and Buffalo: Black Rose Books, 1986), p. 204.

91. David Mitchell, *The Spanish Civil War* (New York: Franklin Watts, 1983), p. 46.

92. George Esenwein and Adrian Shubert, *Spain at War: The Spanish Civil War in Context, 1931–1939* (London and New York: Longman, 1995), p. 132.

93. Martha A. Ackelsberg, *Free Women of Spain: Anarchism and the Struggle for the Emancipation of Women* (Bloomington and Indianapolis: Indiana University Press, 1991), p. 148.

94. Ibid., p. 118.

95. Instead of engaging in melodramatic raids on brothels, the Mujeres Libres set up *liberatorios de prostitución* in order to facilitate the "social readaptation" of prostitutes. See Mary Nash, *Defying Male Civilization: Women in the Spanish Civil War* (Denver: Arden Press, 1995), pp. 163–65.

96. Albert Meltzer, *I Couldn't Paint Golden Angels: Sixty Years of Commonplace Life and Anarchist Agitation* (Edinburg, San Francisco, and London: AK Press, 1996), p. 275.

97. Jonathan Rosenbaum, Review of *El Sopar, Chicago Reader:* https://www.chicago reader.com/chicago/el-sopar/Film?oid=1057598.

98. Antony Beevor, *The Battle Over Spain: The Spanish Civil War, 1936–1939* (New York and London: Penguin, 2005.)

99. Email from Christie to author, March 26, 2017.

100. Michael Knapp, Anja Flach, and Ercan Ayboga, eds., *Revolution in Rojava: Democratic Autonomy and Women's Liberation in Syrian Kurdistan* (London: Pluto Press, 2016).

101. See Gilles Dauvé and T.L., "Rojava: Reality and Rhetoric," *Libcom,* May 17, 2016. https://libcom.org/library/rojava-reality-rhetoric-gilles-dauvé-tl.

102. Email to author, November 23, 2018; See also Önder Çakar, Rojava Film Commune, and Hito Steyerl, "I don't have time!," *e-flux journal* 86 (November 2017). https://www.e-flux.com/journal/86/162859/i-don-t-have-time/.

103. See Gwilym Mumford, "Jake Gyllenhaal to play anarchist joining the fight against Isis," *Guardian,* March 24, 2017, https://www.theguardian.com/film/2017/mar/24/jake-gyllenhaal-daniel-espinosa-isis-syria-film-drama.

104. Hito Steyerl, "The Articulation of Protest," trans. Aileen Derieg, *Transversal,* September 2002, http://eipcp.net/transversal/0303/steyerl/en.

105. Benjamin, quoted in Susan Buck-Morss, *The Dialectics of Seeing: Walter Benjamin and the Arcades Project* (Cambridge, Mass. and London: MIT Press, 1989), p. 186.

106. Mikhail Bakunin, "Preface to Second Instalment of *L'Empire Knouto-Germanique* (June–July 1871)," in Eugene Schulkind, ed., *The Paris Commune of 1871: The View from the Left* (New York: Grove Press, 1974), p. 221.

107. Anthony Masters, *Bakunin: The Father of Anarchism* (London: Sidgwick & Jackson, 1974), p. 260.

108. Gianni Statera, quoted in Robert V. Daniels, *The Year of the Heroic Guerilla* (New York: Basic Books, 1989), p. 165.

109. John McCole, *Walter Benjamin and the Antinomies of Tradition* (Ithaca, N.Y. and London: Cornell University Press, 1993), p. 142.

110. Benjamin is quoted in O. K. Werckmeister, "Walter Benjamin's Angel of History, or the Transfiguration of the Revolutionary into the Historian," *Critical Inquiry* 22, no. 2 (Winter 1996): 258.

111. David Gross, *The Past in Ruins: Tradition and the Critique of Modernity* (Amherst: University of Massachusetts Press, 1992), pp. 7, 61.

112. Richard Philpott, "Brownlow's Gance," *Framework: A Film Journal* 20 (1983): 13. Referring to historians like Christopher Hill and E. P. Thompson, Iain Chambers struck a somewhat similar note when he critiqued the rediscovery of seventeenth-century radical traditions for hewing to a peculiarly British "intellectual refusal of industry, urbanization, and modernity." Chambers complained that these historians concluded that "there was little to be said for the present, except its rejection." Of course, the danger remains that Chambers's postmodernism will reject the past *tout court*. See Jain Chambers, *Border Dialogues: Journeys in Postmodernism* (London and New York: Routledge, 1990), pp. 39–40.

113. Jonathan Rosenbaum, "Journal," *Film Comment,* January–February 1976, p. 2.

114. C. B. Macpherson, *The Political Theory of Possessive Individualism: Hobbes to Locke* (Oxford, U.K. and New York: Oxford University Press, 1962), p. 264.

115. Kenneth Rexroth, *Communalism: From Its Origins to the Twentieth Century* (New York: Seabury Press, 1974), p. 146.

116. Verina Glaessner, "Winstanley: An Interview with Kevin Brownlow," *Film Quarterly* 20, no. 2 (Winter 1976–1977): 22.

117. See Christopher Hill, *The World Turned Upside Down: Radical Ideas During the English Revolution* (London and New York: Penguin Books, 1972), pp. 128–36.

118. For parallels between Winstanley's seventeenth-century Protestant millenarianism and twentieth-century Catholic liberation theology, see Christopher Hill, *The English Bible and the Seventeenth Century Revolution* (London and New York: Penguin Books, 1993), pp. 447–51.

119. R. H. Tawney, *Religion and the Rise of Capitalism* (London: John Murray, 1926), p. 256.

120. For more on the Ranters, see A. L. Morton, *The World of the Ranters* (London: Lawrence and Wishart, 1970). This character is played by Sid Rawle, who, according to Brownlow, founded a commune in Kerry inspired by the Ranters' example. See *Winstanley* press book (1975, n.p.). From George M. Schulman's somewhat anachronistic vantage point, Winstanley "tries to instruct [the Ranters] about sublimation, but they unnervingly attest to the sanctity of what is being sublimated, about which he is ashamed or ambivalent." See Schulman's *Radicalism and Reverence: The Political Thought of Gerrard Winstanley* (Berkeley and Los Angeles: University of California Press, 1989), p. 206. For Winstanley's view of the Ranters, see Jerome Friedman, *Blasphemy, Immorality and Anarchy: The Ranters and the English Revolution* (Athens, Ohio and London: Ohio University Press, 1987), pp. 277–78.

121. Hill, *World Turned Upside Down*, p. 319.

122. David W. Petegorsky, *Left-Wing Democracy in the English Civil War: A Study of the Social Philosophy of Gerrard Winstanley* (New York: Haskell House Publishers, 1972), p. 67.

123. See Peter Marshall, *Demanding the Impossible: A History of Anarchism* (London: Harper Collins, 1992), pp. 96–107. Marshall give us a quintessentially anarchist view of Winstanley. Hill, for example, treats *The Law of Freedom* with considerably more respect.

124. Hill, *World Turned Upside Down*, p. 134.

125. Michael Walzer, *The Revolution of the Saints: A Study in the Origins of Radical Politics* (Cambridge, Mass.: Harvard University Press, 1965), p. 315.

126. Robert Stam and Ismail Xavier, "Transformations of National Allegory: Brazilian Cinema from Dictatorship to Redemocratization," in Robert Sklar and Charles Musser, eds, *Resisting Images: Essays on Cinema and History* (Philadelphia: Temple University Press, 1990), p. 280.

127. Ernst Bloch, *Heritage of Our Times,* trans. Neville and Stephen Plaice (Berkeley and Los Angeles: University of California Press, 1991), p. 97.

128. Simone Pétrement, *Simone Weil: A Life,* trans. Raymond Rosenthal (New York: Pantheon Books, 1976), p. 361.

129. Franco Moretti, *Modern Epic: The World System from Goethe to Garcia Márquez* (London and New York: Verso, 1996), pp. 56–57.

130. Dan Georgakas remarks that "the major persona is not the Macedonian who conquered the known world of his time but a figure from Greek folklore. The legend of this Alexander originated in the 1400s during the struggles with the Turks. Kept alive in oral tradition, the Alexander legend centers on the national yearning for a liberator." See Georgakas' "*O Megalexandros,*" in Frank Magill, ed., *Magill's Cinema Annual, Foreign Series,* Vol. IV (Englewood Cliffs, N.J.: Salem Press, 1985), p. 1997.

131. Dominique Eudes, *The Kapetanios: Partisans and Civil War in Greece, 1943–1949,* trans. John Howe (New York and London: Monthly Review Press, 1972), jacket flap copy.

132. Ibid., p. 9.

133. In reviewing *Modern Epic,* Terry Eagleton paraphrases Moretti's view of the modern epic: "very long, very boring, virtually unread, and doesn't really work." Despite its considerable virtues, *O Megalexandros* could well be characterized as a film that is very long, occasionally boring, and virtually unseen (outside of Greece, where it was actually quite successful at the box office). See Terry Eagleton, "Mixed Baggy Monsters," *Times Literary Supplement,* June 21, 1996, p. 26.

134. Tony Mitchell, "Angelopoulos' Alexander," *Sight and Sound* 49, no. 2 (Spring 1980): 85. See also Tony Mitchell, "Animating Dead Space and Dead Time" (article on film and interview with Angelopoulos), *Sight and Sound* 50, no. 1 (Winter 1980–1981): 29–33.

135. This piece was published as an editorial in *Cahiers du Cinema* 216, October 1969. An English translation is included in Nick Browne, ed., *Cahiers du Cinema:*

1969–1972—The Politics of Representation (Cambridge, Mass.: Harvard University Press, 1990).

136. For a discussion of expressive totality in the work of Althusser and Étienne Balibar, see Martin Jay, *Marxism and Totality: The Adventures of a Concept from Lukács to Habermas* (Berkeley and Los Angeles: University of California Press, 1984), esp. pp. 161–63.

137. See Noël Carroll, "Filming History," *Soho Weekly News*, October 12, 1978, p. 64.

138. See, for example, Serge Toubiana, "Les Arpenteurs," and Serge Daney, "Chantez le Code," in *Cahiers du Cinema* (May–June 1976). See also Alan Sutherland, "Anarchism in Practice: An Interview With Jean-Louis Comolli," *Peace News*, March 25, 1977, pp. 15–16. Another useful piece with certain affinities to my analysis is Reynold Humphries and Geneviève Suzzoni, "Anarchism vs. Reality," *Jump Cut* 12–13 (December 1975): 30–32.

139. For a thorough critique of Comolli's brand of Althusserianism during his *Cahiers* period, see D. N. Rodowick, *The Crisis of Political Modernism: Criticism and Ideology in Contemporary Film Theory* (Berkeley and Los Angeles: University of California Press, 1994), pp. 74–85.

140. For more information on this book, see Jean-Louis Comolli, *Une Commune anarchiste au Brésil en 1890: Dossier d'un film* (Paris: Daniel et Cie, 1976).

141. This passage from *Statism and Anarchy* can be found in Sam Dolgoff, ed., *Bakunin on Anarchism* (Montreal: Black Rose Books, 1980), pp. 326–27.

142. Jacqueline Rose's remarks on the film appear in "The Cinematic Apparatus: Problems in Current Theory," an article anthologized in Teresa de Lauretis and Steven Heath, eds, *The Cinematic Apparatus* (New York: St Martin's Press, 1980), p. 178.

143. Michel de Certeau reflects on both *La Cecilia*'s utopian hopes and its ultimate failure by considering the role of songs in the film. He notes: "in J. L. Comolli's film *La Cecilia*, the anarchist songs form the counterpoint to the events that gradually destroy, as it develops, the socialist commune founded in Brazil by Tito [*sic*] Rossi: the songs remain intact and, in the end, from the very ruins of a history restored to order, these songs rise again, escaping from the battlefield of defeat, lifting up a voice that will bring to life, elsewhere other movements." See de Certeau's *The Practice of Everyday Life*, trans. Stephen Rendall (Berkeley and Los Angeles: University of California Press, 1984), p. 17.

144. Chryssoula Kambas, "Benjamin's Concept of History and the French Popular Front," *New German Critique* 39 (Fall 1986): 89. Kambas's quotations from "Theses on the Philosophy of History" can be found in Walter Benjamin, *Illuminations*, edited with an introduction by Hannah Arendt, trans. Harry Zohn (London: Collins/Fontana Books, 1973), p. 261.

145. Benjamin, *Illuminations*, p. 263.

Chapter 3. Anarcho-Syndicalism versus the "Revolt against Work"

1. Paul Avrich, *Anarchist Voices: An Oral History of Anarchism in America* (Princeton, N.J.: Princeton University Press, 1995), p. 4.

2. See, for example, Joyce L. Kornbluh, ed., *Rebel Voices: An I.W.W. Anthology* (Chicago: Charles Kerr, 1988). The most comprehensive history of the IWW, especially concerning the pre-1917 period, is Melvyn Dubofsky, *We Shall Be All: A History of the Industrial Workers of the World* (Chicago: Quadrangle Books, 1969). For some observations on sabotage tactics and neo-Luddism, see Kirkpatrick Sale, *Rebels against the Future* (Reading, Mass.: Addison-Wesley, 1995).

3. See E. J. Hobsbawm, *Primitive Rebels: Studies in Archaic Forms of Social Movements in the 19th and 20th Centuries* (New York: W.W. Norton, 1965).

4. See Temma Kaplan, *Anarchists of Andalusia, 1868–1903* (Princeton, N.J.: Princeton University Press, 1977). Jerome Mintz's meticulously researched account of the Casas Viejas uprising, one of the pivotal events preceding the outbreak of the Spanish Civil War, also refutes Hobsbawm's "millenarian" view of peasant anarchism. See his *The Anarchists of Casas Viejas* (Chicago and London: University of Chicago Press, 1982).

5. Michael Seidman, *Workers Against Work. Labor in Paris and Barcelona during the Popular Fronts* (Berkeley and Los Angeles: University of California Press, 1991), pp. 45–46. It is interesting to contrast this renewed glorification of work with the New Deal's neglect of workers' demands for shorter hours in favor of increased productivity. For an account of this strategy within Roosevelt's labor policy, see Benjamin Kline Hunnicutt, *Work Without End: Abandoning Shorter Hours for the Right to Work* (Philadelphia: Temple University Press, 1988).

6. Herbert Marcuse, "Socialism in the Developed Countries," *International Socialist Journal* 2, no. 8 (April 1965): 150.

7. Daniel Bell, *The Coming of Post-Industrial Society* (New York: Basic Books, 1973), p. 163. For an early work that is distinguished by considerable empathy for the plight of the assembly-line worker, see Bell's *Work and Its Discontents* (Boston: Beacon Press, 1956).

8. See Dolgoff, "The Relevance of Anarchism in Modern Society," in Terry Perlin, ed., *Contemporary Anarchism* (New Brunswick, N.J.: Transaction Books, 1979), p. 41. For a critique of Bell's "technocratic social theory," see Trent Schroyer's review of *The Coming of Post-Industrial Society* in *Telos* 19 (Spring 1974): 162–76. See also Michael Rogin, "Pa Bell," *Salmagundi* 57 (Summer 1982).

9. Herbert Marcuse, *One Dimensional Man* (Boston: Beacon Press, 1964), p. xiii.

10. Paul Mattick, "The Limits of Integration," in Kurt H. Wolff and Barrington Moore Jr, eds., *The Critical Spirit: Essays in Honor of Herbert Marcuse* (Boston: Beacon Press, 1967).

11. Harry Braverman, *Labor and Monopoly Capital* (New York and London: Monthly Review Press, 1974).

12. Ibid., pp. 359–74.

13. Craig R. Littler, *The Development of the Labour Process in Capitalist Societies* (London: Heinemann Educational Books, 1982), p. 26. Of course, Marx did observe that "in all countries of Europe it has now become a truth . . . that no improvement of machinery, no appliance of science to production . . . will do away with the miseries of the industrial masses." Marx is quoted in Roman Rosdolsky, *The Making of* Marx's Capital, trans. Pete Burgess (London: Pluto Press, 1980), p. 304.

14. See, for example, "Industrialization and Capitalism in Max Weber," in Herbert Marcuse, *Negations: Essays in Critical Theory* (Boston: Beacon Press, 1968), p. 223.

15. William Leiss, *Under Technology's Thumb* (Montreal and Kingston, Ont.: Mc-Gill-Queen's University Press, 1990), p. 46.

16. Lewis Mumford, *The Myth of the Machine: The Pentagon of Power* (New York: Harcourt Brace Jovanovich, 1970), p. 165. It is possible to argue that Mumford's humanism suggests a false dichotomy between nature and culture. This may be at the root of philosopher Todd May's complaint that anarchism is "a humanist naturalism . . . which posits a human essence." Nonetheless, as was argued in chapter 1, not all anarchists are convinced that there is something approximating "human essence." See May's *The Political Philosophy of Poststructuralist Anarchism* (University Park: Pennsylvania State University Press, 1994), p. 63.

17. Two of the most influential texts have been Clastres's *Society Against the State* and Diamond's *In Search of the Primitive*. See Clastres and Diamond, *In Search of the Primitive* (New Brunswick, N.J. and London: Transaction Books, 1987). Marshall Sahlins's research convinced him that hunter-gatherers (he used the Arnhem Land hunters as his primary example), contrary to popular assumptions, enjoyed an extraordinary amount of leisure and had little reverence for work. See Marshall Sahlins, *Stone Age Economics* (New York: Aldine, 1972), pp. 18–21.

18. See John Zerzan, *Future Primitive and Other Essays* (Brooklyn, N.Y. and Columbia, Mo.: Autonomedia, and *Anarchy: A Journal of Desire Armed*, 1994).

19. See Dennis West, review of *Rebellion in Patagonia*, *Cineaste* 10, no. 1 (Winter 1979–1980): 50–52.

20. Osvaldo Bayer, *Anarchism and Violence: Severino Di Giovanni in Argentina—1923-1931* (London: Elephant Editions, 1987).

21. See Rudolf, Rocker, *Anarchism and Anarcho-Syndicalism* (London: Freedom Press, 1988). Ed Andrew reminds us that Malatesta "considered 'anarcho-syndicalism' a bastard term: 'either it is the same as anarchy, and is therefore a term which only serves to confuse matters, or it is different from anarchy and cannot therefore be accepted by anarchists.'" Andrew concludes that "anarcho-syndicalism then results from a dialectical unity, not a simple identity of anarchism and syndicalism." See Ed Andrew, *Closing the Iron Cage: The Scientific Management of Work and Leisure* (Montreal: Black Rose Books, 1981), pp. 154–55.

22. Rocker, *Anarchism and Anarcho-Syndicalism*, p. 39.

23. Jeremy Jennings, *Syndicalism in France: A Study of Ideas* (New York: St Martin's Press, 1990), p. 23.

24. Benjamin Martin, *The Agony of Modernization: Labor and Industrialization in Spain* (Ithaca, N.Y.: Cornell University Press, 1990), p. 198.

25. Dan Georgakas, "*The Wobblies,* The Making of a Documentary: An Interview with Stewart Bird and Deborah Shaffer," *Cineaste* 10, no. 2 (Spring 1980): 15.

26. See Noel King, "Recent 'Political' Documentary: Notes on *Union Maids and Harlan County USA,*" *Screen* 22, no. 2 (1981): pp. 7–18. King seems to prefer neo-Brechtian documentaries such as *The Nightcleaners,* which appealed mainly to other neo-Brechtian intellectuals.

27. In a conversation with the author (May 1987), Dolgoff admitted that many IWW members were far from being anarchists, but related his own efforts to maintain an anarcho-syndicalist position within the organization during the 1930s. See also Dolgoff's autobiography, *Fragments: A Memoir* (Cambridge, U.K.: Refract Publications, 1986), pp. 53–54.

28. These debates are discussed in Dubofsky, *We Shall Be All,* pp. 260–62.

29. For more on the "Paterson Pageant," see Steve Golin, *The Fragile Bridge: Paterson Silk Strike, 1913* (Philadelphia: Temple University Press, 1988).

30. Hakim Bey, "An Esoteric Interpretation of the I.W.W. Preamble," *International Review* 1 (1991): p. 3. For a less charitable view of anarcho-syndicalism and the recent incarnation of the IWW, see Michael William, "The 'Bufe-ooneries' Continue: A Response to Chaz Bufe's 'Primitive Thought' and to the Misery of Anarcho-Syndicalism," *Demolition Derby* 1 (n.d.): 18–29. In a similar vein, P. D. Anthony writes that "syndicalists create for themselves the impossible dilemma of trying to solve the problem of authority by emphasizing the importance of work, which is, in the present day, inseparable from the problem of authority." See Anthony's *The Ideology of Work* (London: Tavistock, 1977), p. 110.

31. *Metello* is adapted from Vasco Pratolini's celebrated novel, and an Italian critic praised the film for emphasizing the protagonist's 'maturity' in rejecting anarchism and embracing mainstream socialism. See Vittorio Cordero Montzemolo, ed., *Talking with Mauro Bolognini* (Milan: Ministry of Italian Foreign Affairs, 1977), pp. 158–63.

32. Josef Chytry, *The Aesthetic State: A Quest in Modern German Thought* (Berkeley and Los Angeles: University of California Press, 1989), p. 84. The relationship between the 'play impulse' and nineteenth-century working-class revolts is examined in Frank Hearn, "Remembrance and Critique: The Uses of the Past for Discrediting the Present and Anticipating the Future," *Politics and Society* 5, no. 2 (n.d.): 201–27. Hearn believes that 'the working-class community . . . supported a kind of integrated experience which synthesized play and work, non-instrumental and instrumental activity, and the past, the present and the future' (p. 212). Although Terry Eagleton recognizes the critique of industrial capitalism embedded in Schiller's play impulse, he also regards it as a theory of bourgeois hegemony. See Terry Eagleton, *The Ideology of the Aesthetic* (Oxford, U.K. and Cambridge, Mass.: Basil Blackwell, 1990), pp. 102–19.

33. Theodor Adorno and Max Horkheimer, *Dialectic of Enlightenment,* trans. John Cumming (New York: Continuum, 1972), p. 142.

34. Clair's remarks are quoted in R. C. Dale, *The Films of René Clair, Volume One: Exposition and Analysis* (Metutchen, N.J. and London: Scarecrow Press, 1986), p. 187.

35. *Plans'* decidedly authoritarian socialism is discussed by Eugen Weber in *The Hollow Years: France in the 1930s* (New York and London: W.W. Norton, 1994), pp. 122–23.

36. The comparison to Tzara is made by Anson Rabinbach in *The Human Motor: Energy, Fatigue and the Origins of Modernity* (New York: Basic Books, 1990), p. 34. For more on Lafargue, see Leslie Derfler, *Paul Lafargue and the Founding of French Marxism: 1842–1882* (Cambridge, Mass. and London: Harvard University Press, 1991).

37. Raoul Vaneigem, *The Revolution of Everyday Life* (Seattle: Left Bank Books, 1983), p. 38. A 1918 Dadaist manifesto urges the 'introduction of progressive unemployment by means of comprehensive mechanization of all activities. Only through unemployment can the individual gain the possibility of discovering for himself the truth of life and at last accustom himself to experiencing it.' See Richard Hulsenbeck, ed., *The Dada Almanac,* English edition by Richard Green (London: Atlas Press, 1993), p. 73.

38. Allen Thiher, *The Cinematic Muse: Critical Studies in the History of French Cinema* (Columbia and London: University of Missouri Press, 1979), p. 72.

39. Kropotkin is quoted in Camillo Berneri's "The Problem of Work," anthologized in Vernon Richards, ed., *Why Work? Arguments for the Leisure Society* (London: Freedom Press, 1983), p. 72.

40. Richard Boston makes a distinction between anarchists such as "Bakunin, Kropotkin, and Tolstoy," and Boudu, who supposedly exemplifies "chaos." While Boudu is certainly not an ideological anarchist, a case could be made that Boston oversimplifies the relationship between certain currents within the anarchist movement, past and present, and Boudu's admittedly pre-political penchant for loafing. See Boston's *Boudu Saved From Drowning* (London: British Film Institute, 1994), p. 43.

41. Marx's comments from *Grundrisse* are quoted in William Leiss, *The Domination of Nature* (New York: George Braziller, 1972), p. 84.

42. Wolfgang Fritz Haug, *Critique of Commodity Aesthetics: Appearance, Sexuality and Advertising in Capitalist Society* (Minneapolis: University of Minnesota Press, 1986), p. 6.

43. Jacques Attali, *Noise: The Political Economy of Music,* trans. Brian Massumi (Minneapolis: University of Minnesota Press, 1985), p. 89.

44. Chanan is quoted in Nicholas Spice, review of *Repeated Takes and Elevator Music, London Review of Books* 17, no. 13 (July 5, 1995): 6.

45. Potamkin's observations on the film are in his essay "René Clair and Film Humor," anthologized in *The Compound Cinema: The Film Writings of Harry Alan Potamkin,* selected, arranged, and introduced by Lewis Jacobs (New York and London: Teacher's College Press, 1977), p. 407.

46. Kerzhentsev's Soviet version of Taylorization and the 'cult of the machine' in Soviet-era art and theater is discussed in Richard Stites, *Revolutionary Dreams, Utopian Vision and Experimental Life in the Russian Revolution* (New York and Oxford: Oxford University Press, 1989), pp. 145–64.

47. Murray Bookchin, *The Ecology of Freedom: The Emergence and Dissolution of Hierarchy* (Palo Alto, Calif.: Chesire Books, 1982), p. 263.

48. Dudley Andrew, *Mists of Regret: Culture and Sensibility in Classic French Film* (Princeton, N.J.: Princeton University Press, 1995), p. 60.

49. Richard Porton and Lee Ellickson, unpublished interview with Jean-Luc Godard, May 1994, New York.

50. As early as 1970, the sociologist Alfred Willener grasped the contradictory nature of Godard's Maoism, since he observed that "some (including himself?) see him as a Maoist, others as a left-wing or right-wing anarchist, or perhaps even as an 'ambidextrous' anarchist—in any case, he cannot easily be labelled." See *The Action-Image of Society: On Cultural Politicization,* trans. A. M. Sheridan Smith (New York: Pantheon Books, 1970), p. 266.

51. For a discussion of the "anarchistic" tendencies within French Maoism, see Belden Fields's "French Maoism," anthologized in Sonya Sayres, Anders Stephanson, Stanley Aronowitz, and Fredric Jameson, eds., *The '60s Without Apology* (Minneapolis: University of Minnesota Press, 1984).

52. See Robert Stam, *Subversive Pleasures: Bakhtin, Cultural Criticism, and Film* (Baltimore: Johns Hopkins University Press), 1989, p. 51.

53. See Silber's review of *Tout va bien,* "Anarchist Outlook Mars Film on Workers," *Guardian,* March 7, 1973.

54. Lou Sin Group, "Lutte des Classes sur le Front Cinematographique en France," *Cahiers du Cinéma,* May–June 1972.

55. *May '68 and Film Culture* (London: British Film Institute, 1978), p. 30.

56. See Christian Braad Thomsen, "Filmmaking and History: An Interview with Jean-Pierre Gorin," *Jump Cut* 3 (September–October 1974).

57. Jan Robert Bloch, "How Can We Understand the Bends in the Upright Gait?" *New German Critique* 45 (Fall 1988): 11. Bloch's ill-informed condemnation of "individualist utopians and anarchy" was one of his least admirable contributions to utopian theory. See his *The Principle of Hope,* Vol. 2, trans. Neville Plaice, Stephen Plaice, and Stephen Knight (Cambridge, Mass.: MIT Press, 1986).

58. Richard Gombin, *The Origins of Modern Leftism,* trans. Michael K. Perl (Harmondsworth, U.K.: Penguin Books, 1975), pp. 88–90.

59. Carl Boggs, for example, maintains that "Pannekoek deduced that the concept of production constitutes the basis of all social existence . . . if the anarchists desired to return to a vanishing society of free and equal artisans, the council communists seemed to want to preserve the imagined social reality of a homogenous . . . and heroic proletariat that was destined to disappear with the onset of bureaucratic state capitalism." See Boggs's review of three books on Pannekoek, *Telos* 42 (Winter 1979–1980): 181.

60. Paul Mattick, *Anti-Bolshevik Communism* (White Plains, N.Y.: M.E. Sharpe, 1978), p. 61. Mattick claims that Trotsky was convinced that "not one serious socialist will begin to deny to the Labor State the right to lay its hands upon the worker who refuses to execute his labor power."

61. See, for example, Cornelius Castoriadis, *Workers' Councils and the Economics of*

a Self-Managed Society (Philadelphia: Wooden Shoe, 1984). For an analogous investigation of the Bolsheviks' success in eradicating post-1917 experiments in workers' control, see Maurice Brinton, *The Bolsheviks and Workers' Control 1917–1921: The State and Counter-Revolution* (Detroit: Black and Red, 1970), pp. 25–50.

62. See, for example, the review of *Coup pour coup* in *Cahiers du Cinéma* 239–240 (May–June 1972): 8. See also Jill Forbes, *The Cinema in France: After the New Wave* (Bloomington and Indianapolis: Indiana University Press, 1992), pp. 20–33.

63. Erwin Piscator, *The Political Theater: A History, 1914–1929* (New York: Avon, 1978), p. 94. For a play entitled *In Spite of Everything* (produced in 1922), Piscator describes the "Praktikabel" stage as being divided into "various acting areas . . . terraces, niches and corridors. . . . In this way the overall structure of the scenes was unified and the play could flow uninterrupted, like a single current sweeping everything along with it." Piscator's aspiration to "show the link between events on the stage and the great forces active in history" preceded Godard and Gorin's film by more than fifty years.

64. Given the fact that experiments in workers' self-management had tended to often deteriorate into bureaucratic showcases in 'liberal' communist countries such as Yugoslavia, anarchists were skeptical of the revolutionary potential of the LIP workers' attempt to organize libertarian socialism in one factory. See, for example, Negation, ed., *Lip and the Self-Managed Counter-Revolution,* translated from *Negation* 3 (Detroit: Black and Red, 1975).

65. Roger Gregoire and Fredy Perlman, *Worker-Student Factory Committees* (Detroit: Black and Red, 1969).

66. Fredy Perlman, *The Reproduction of Daily Life* (Detroit: Black and Red, 1970).

67. René Viénet, *Enragés and the Situationists in the Occupation Movement, France, May '68* (New York: Autonomedia, 1992), pp. 86–87.

68. Ibid., p. 122.

69. Keith A. Reader with Khursheed Wadia, *The May 1968 Events in Prance: Reproductions and Interpretations* (New York: St Martin's Press, 1993), p. 89. The phrase "fictional intensification of symbolic exchange" is found in Pierre Bourdieu and J. C. Passeron, *Les Héritiers* (Paris: Minuit, 1964), p. 53.

70. Mikhail Bakhtin, *Rabelais and His World,* trans. Helene Iswolsky (Cambridge, Mass. and London: MIT Press, 1968), p. 378.

71. Jonathan Leake points out that the May 1968 "general strike" introduced one important term to the French language: *groupuscule*. The term was basically a variation on the concept of the affinity group, emphasizing "small-scale integrity" and self-organization. Using the term loosely, however, the more authoritarian factions are also sometimes referred to as "groupuscules." See Jonathan Leake, "The Group," *Black Eye* 8 (1989): 2–12.

72. P.m., *Bolo' Bolo* (New York: Semiotext(e), 1985). Surprisingly, few films have tackled the skepticism toward technological modernity that European historians such as E. P. Thompson and Peter Laslett chronicle in their work. One of the few exceptions is David Miller's *Lonely are the Brave,* an adaptation by screenwriter Dalton Trumbo of avowed anarchist Edward Abbey's novel *The Brave Cowboy.* This film, a

pet project of its star Kirk Douglas, recounts a crusty cowboy's jailbreak and, above all, his defeat of the authorities' newfangled technology with the assistance merely of a trusty horse. In recent years, Abbey's work has become a major influence on ecological activists in the far West, particularly the group Earth First!, which drew concrete inspiration from his novel *The Monkey Wrench Gang*.

73. G. P. Maximoff, ed., *The Political Philosophy of Bakunin* (New York: Free Press, 1953), p.30.

74. Studs Terkel, *Working: People Talk About What They Do All Day and How They Feel About What They Do* (New York: Ballantine Books, 1972), p. xiii.

75. Moshe Lewin, *The Making of the Soviet System: Essays in the Social History of Interwar Russia* (New York: Pantheon Books, 1985), p. 37. In contradistinction to the heroic image of the Soviet Stakhanovite, Dovzhenko's *Ivan* (1932) mercilessly lambasts an "anarchist idler."

76. Carl Boggs, *Gramsci's Marxism* (London: Pluto Press, 1976), p. 44.

77. Antonio Gramsci, "Americanism and Fordism," anthologized in *Selections from the Prison Notebooks*, ed. and trans. by Quentin Hoare and Geoffrey Nowell Smith (New York: International Publishers, 1971), p. 280. During the 1970s, some Italian anarchists viewed the Gramscian tradition as the forerunner of the "historic compromise" between the Communist Party and Christian Democrats they despised. See, for example, Claudia V, "Al Servizio del compromesso storico," *Revista anarchista* 5, no. 7 (October 1975).

78. Joan Mellen, "*Ombre rosse:* Developing a Radical Critique of the Cinema in Italy," *Cineaste* (Spring 1972): 52.

79. Maurice Brinton, *The Irrational in Politics* (San Francisco: Arcata Press, 1987), p. 27.

80. For an informative analysis of the distinctions between conformist psycho-analysis and the work of political Freudians such as Fenichel, see Russell Jacoby, *The Repression of Psychoanalysis* (New York: Basic Books, 1983).

81. Félix Guattari, *Molecular Revolution: Psychiatry and Politics* (New York and Harmondsworth, U.K.: Penguin Books, 1984), p. 209.

82. Miklós Haraszti, *A Worker in a Worker's State,* trans. Michael Wright (New York: Universe Books, 1978), pp. 112–13. After Haraszti completed the manuscript in 1973, he was arrested and eventually put on trial for the rather vague crime of "grave incitement." In 1974 he was given an eight-month suspended sentence. According to Michael Wright, the court costs he was ordered to pay—9,600 forints—were the equivalent of "nearly four months pay for a skilled worker." Michael Burawoy analyzes Haraszti's toil at piecework as part of "the ideological effects of the labor process" under state socialism in *The Politics of Production: Factory Regimes Under Capitalism and Socialism* (London: Verso, 1985), pp. 156–208.

83. Andrew Ross, *No Respect: Intellectuals and Popular Culture* (New York and London: Routledge, 1989), p. 52. In this context, it might be worthwhile to cite Herbert Schiller's recent critique of certain tendencies within cultural studies: "The power of the Western cultural industries is more concentrated and formidable than ever; their outputs are more voluminous and widely circulated; and the transnational

corporate system is totally dependent upon information flows, yet the prevailing interpretation sees media power as highly overrated and its international impact minimal. Its usefulness to existing power is obvious." Schiller's remarks are quoted in Tom Frank, "Dark Age: Why Johnny Can't Dissent," *Baffler* 6 (1995): 11.

84. Néstor García Canclini, *Hybrid Cultures: Strategies for Entering and Leaving Modernity*, trans. Christopher L. Chiappari and Silvia L. López (Minneapolis and London: University of Minnesota Press, 1995), p. 155.

85. James Roy MacBean, *Film and Revolution* (Bloomington and London: Indiana University Press, 1975), p. 279.

86. Ien Ang, *Living Room Wars: Rethinking Media Audiences for a Postmodern World* (New York and London: Routledge, 1996), p. 113.

87. Edward S. Herman, "Postmodernism Triumphs," *Z Magazine* 9, no. 1 (January 1996): 17.

88. See John Zerzan, *Elements of Refusal* (Seattle: Left Bank Books, 1988), pp. 149–54.

89. For the influence of the Autonomist movement on American libertarian Marxists, see the two issues of the publication *Zerowork* (1975).

90. Boggs, *Gramsci's Marxism*, p. 90. Boggs observes that Gramsci's early work is based in "syndicalist and some anarchist thought."

91. Vernon Richards, ed., *Errico Malatesta: Life and Ideas* (London: Freedom Press, 1980), p. 65.

92. Mario Tronti, "The Strategy of Refusal," *Semiotext(e): Autonomedia—Post-Political Politics* 3, no. 3 (1980): 26–34. Tronti does, however, reject the anarcho-syndicalist notion of the mass strike as "romantic naivety." For an overview on autonomism and other left tendencies that flourished in Italy during the 1960s and 1970s, see Robert Lumley, *States of Emergency: Cultures of Revolt in Italy from 1968 to 1973* (London and New York: Verso, 1990).

93. Refusal of work as a "new form of struggle" was argued by John Zerzan in several articles published in the Detroit-based anarchist journal *Fifth Estate*. Council communist Charles Reeve responded to Zerzan in the French journal *Spartacus* by maintaining that strategies such as sabotage and absenteeism would not hasten the abolition of wage labor and could only lead to "privatistic" rebellions. These debates are collected in Échanges et Mouvement, ed., *The Refusal of Work: Facts and Discussions* (London: Echanges et Mouvement, 1979).

94. See, for example, Martin Sprouse, ed., *Sabotage in the American Workplace: Anecdotes of Dissatisfaction, Mischief and Revenge* (San Francisco: Pressure Drop Press, 1992). This book includes anecdotal evidence of workplace resistance narrated by, among others, waitresses, factory workers, and fast-food employees.

95. "The Myth of the Happy Worker," anthologized in *A Radical's America* (Boston and Toronto: Little, Brown, 1962), pp. 115–16.

96. See, for example, Root and Branch, ed., *Root and Branch: The Rise of the Workers' Movements* (Greenwich, Conn.: Fawcett Publishers, 1975). The volume contains essays by, among others, Anton Pannekoek, Jeremy Brecher, and Stanley Aronowitz that betray the influence of the council communist tradition.

97. Schrader summarized the film as imbued with the "politics of resentment and claustrophobia" in an interview published years after the release of *Blue Collar*. See Kevin Jackson, ed., *Schrader on Schrader* (London and Boston: Faber & Faber, 1990), p. 148. See also Gary Crowdus and Dan Georgakas, "Blue Collar: An Interview with Paul Schrader," *Cineaste* 8, no. 3 (1978): 34–37, 59; Michele Russell et al., "*Blue Collar:* Detroit Moviegoers Have Their Say," *Cineaste* 8, no. 4 (1978): pp. 28–31.

98. Despite its Leninist (and, on occasion, Maoist) rhetoric, the LRBW could reasonably be deemed a retooled version of American syndicalism. For an in-depth analysis of the League's activities (as well as the history of a precursor movement— the Dodge Revolutionary Union Movement or DRUM), see Dan Georgakas and Marvin Surkin, *Detroit: I Do Mind Dying* (New York: St Martin's Press, 1975). For a production history of *Finally Got the News,* see Dan Georgakas, "*Finally Got the News:* The Making of a Radical Film," *Cineaste* 5, no. 4 (1971): 2–6.

99. This is the figure quoted by Jacqueline Jones in *American Work: Four Centuries of Black and White Labor* (New York: W.W. Norton, 1998).

100. Hegel is quoted in Barbara Wright's introduction to Raymond Queneau's novel *The Sunday of Life* (New York: New Directions, 1977), p. vii. Queneau's hero is not a worker, but a heroic simpleton. The book's focus is lightheartedly metaphysical, not political.

101. See C. Wright Mills, "Letter to the New Left," in Perlin, ed., *Contemporary Anarchism,* pp. 53–63.

102. See David Robinson, "Escape from the Working Class," *Times* (London), July 5, 1975.

103. These biographical details are recounted in an interview with Faraldo from *Film* (London, June 1973), p. 10.

104. For a view of Tanner's critique of Swiss democracy, see Philippe Haudiquet, 'Un Enfant du mois de mai,' *L'Avant-Scène du Cinéma* 108 (November 1970): 8.

105. Marianne Enckell, *La Fédération jurassiene: Les Origines de l'anarchisme en Suisse* (Paris: Canevas Éditeur, 1971). In her introduction, Enckell links her rediscovery of the Swiss anarchist legacy to the events of May '68. Harry Braverman's observation that "the destruction of craftsmanship" took place during "the period of the rise of scientific management" is especially apropos in this context. See Braverman, *Labor and Monopoly Capitalism,* p. 135.

106. This is how Jonathan Steinberg summarizes Kropotkin's homage to the anarchist watchmakers in *Why Switzerland?* (Cambridge, U.K.: Cambridge University Press, 1983), p. 133.

107. Jim Leach, *A Possible Cinema: The Films of Alain Tanner* (Metuchen, N.J. and London: Scarecrow Press, 1984), p. 69.

108. See, for example, Henri Lefebvre, *Critique of Everyday Life, Volume One,* trans. John Moore (London and New York: Verso, 1991), esp. pp. 50–60.

109. Richard Linklater, *Slacker* (New York: St. Martin's Press, 1992), p. 18.

110. Bob Black, *The Abolition of Work and Other Essays* (Port Townsend, Wash.: Loompanics, n.d.), p. 50. In the book's final essay, "Anarchism and Other Impedi-

ments to Anarchy," Black claims that even anarchists have become prey to ideological rigidity and argues that "we need anarchists unencumbered by anarchy."

111. Elizabeth Young and Graham Caveney, *Shopping in Space: Essays on America's Blank Generation Fiction* (New York: Atlantic Monthly Press, 1992), p. 34. Young and Caveney are in fact referring to the protagonists of Bret Easton Ellis's *Less than Zero*.

112. Patrick Durfee, "Slackspace: The Politics of Waste," in Graham Brahm Jr. and Mark Driscoll, eds., *Prosthetic Territories: Politics and Hypertechnologies* (Boulder, Colo., San Francisco, and Oxford, U.K.: Westview Press, 1995), p. 21.

113. Zygmunt Bauman, *Modernity and Ambivalence* (Ithaca, N.Y.: Cornell University Press, 1991), p. 186.

114. See Lee Ellickson and Richard Porton, "'I Find the Tragicomic Things in Life': An Interview with Mike Leigh," *Cineaste* 20, no. 3 (1994): 11.

115. Kathi Weeks, *The Problem with Work: Feminism, Marxism, Antiwork Politics, and Postwork Imaginaries* (Durham, N.C. and London: Duke University Press, 2011), p. 26.

116. Mark Fisher, *Capitalist Realism: Is There No Alternative?* (London: Zero Books, 2009), p. 39.

117. Fabien Lemercier, "Benoît Delépine and Gustave Kervern," *Cineuropa*, November 25, 2008. https://cineuropa.org/en/interview/88103/.

118. This is a paraphrase of Rancière's conclusions, taken from Donald Reid's introduction to *The Nights of Labor: The Workers' Dream in Nineteenth-Century France*, trans. John Drury (Philadelphia: Temple University Press, 1981), p. xxxv.

119. Marina A. Sitrin, *Everyday Revolutions: Horizontalism and Autonomy in Argentina* (London: Zed Books, 2012), p. 36.

120. Ibid., p. 148.

Chapter 4. Film and Anarchist Pedagogy

1. See Giroux's critique of the "interactionist ideology" of Rousseau, A. S. Neill, Carl Rogers, and Joel Spring in *Theory and Resistance in Education: A Pedagogy for the Opposition* (New York, Westport, Conn., and London: Greenwood Press, 1983), pp. 218–20. It should be noted that Giroux does not use the appellation "anarchist; among this quartet, only Spring, and possibly Neill, could be properly identified as anarchists.

2. See Julia Simon, *Mass Enlightenment: Critical Studies in Rousseau and Diderot* (Albany: State University of New York Press, 1995), esp. pp. 19–27.

3. Jean-Jacques Rousseau, *Émile, or On Education*, trans. Allan Bloom (New York: Basic Books, 1979), p. 93.

4. Ibid., p. 116.

5. Jean Starobinski, *Jean-Jacques Rousseau: Transparency and Obstruction*, trans. Arthur Goldhammer (Chicago and London: University of Chicago Press), p. 216. Starobinski remarks that it is a mistake to read *Émile* as a "paean to unreflective feeling." He demonstrates how Rousseau builds a "sophisticated trap. . . . Rousseau

posits the necessity of mediation (since a teacher is always necessary) but at the same time rejects it (since the teacher preaches the gospel of immediacy)."

6. Michael P. Smith, *The Libertarians and Education* (London: George Allen & Unwin, 1983), p. 8.

7. Godwin's views on education, culled from his articles in the *Enquirer,* are quoted in George Woodcock, *William Godwin: A Biographical Study* (London: Porcupine Press, 1946), p. 129.

8. Max Stirner, *The False Principle of Our Education, or Humanism or Realism,* trans. Robert H. Beebe, edited by James Martin (Colorado Springs, Colo.: Ralph Myles, 1967), p. 11.

9. Ibid., p. 27.

10. G. P. Maximoff, ed., *The Political Philosophy of Bakunin: Scientific Anarchism* (New York: The Free Press, 1953), pp. 331–37.

11. Bakunin is quoted in Richard B. Saltman, *The Social and Political Thought of Michael Bakunin* (Westport, Conn. and London: Greenwood Press, 1983), p. 41.

12. Stirner, *False Principle,* p. 22.

13. Jonathan Beecher and Richard Bienvenu, *The Utopian Vision of Charles Fourier: Selected Texts on Work Love, and Passionate Attraction* (Columbia: University of Missouri Press, 1983), p. 420.

14. Joan Connelly Ullman, *The Tragic Week: A Study of Anticlericalism in Spain, 1875–1912* (Cambridge, Mass.: Harvard University Press, 1968), p. 3.

15. Francisco Ferrer, *The Origins and Ideas of the Modern School,* trans. Joseph McCabe (New York and London: G.P. Putnam's Sons, 1923), p. 17.

16. Joel Spring, *A Primer of Libertarian Education* (New York: Free Life Editions, 1975).

17. Ivan Illich, *Deschooling Society* (New York and Evanston, Ill.: Harper & Row, 1970), p. 11.

18. Ibid., p. 26.

19. Smith, *Libertarians and Education,* pp. 27–42.

20. Raymond Allan Morrow and Carlos Alberto Torres, *Social Theory and Education: A Critique of Theories of Social and Cultural Reproduction* (Albany: State University of New York Press, 1995), p. 226.

21. Proust is quoted in Roger Shattuck, "Teaching the Unreachable: Nietzsche, Proust, Kipling and Co.," *Salmagundi* 108 (Fall 1995): 9.

22. Philippe Ariès, *Centuries of Childhood: A Social History of Family Life,* trans. Robert Baldick (New York: Vintage Books, 1962). Ariès is cited by, among others, Smith and Spring. For a critique of Aries, see Leonard Pollock, *Forgotten Children: Parent–Child Relations from 1500 to 1900* (Cambridge, U.K.: Cambridge University Press, 1983).

23. Peter Coveney, *The Image of Childhood: The Individual and Society: A Study of the Theme in English Literature* (Baltimore: Penguin Books, 1967), p. 33. Subsequently (p. 92), Coveney remarks that "for the great Romantics . . . the child was an active image, an expression of human potency in face of human experience." He distinguishes this from the "debased-romantic, Victorian concept of innocence"—e.g.,

"the vacuities of *Little Lord Fauntleroy*"—where it decays into "something statically juxtaposed into experience."

24. Hugh Cunningham, *The Children of the Poor: Representations of Childhood Since the Seventeenth Century* (Oxford, U.K.: Basil Blackwell, 1991), pp. 107–8. Cunningham also notes that Thomas Beggs believed that slum children were "predatory hordes of the street" who "seemed 'almost to belong to a separate race.'"

25. Arnold is quoted in Ian Hunter, *Culture and Government* (London: Macmillan, 1988), p. 115.

26. Paul Avrich, *The Modern School Movement: Anarchism and Education in the United States* (Princeton, N.J.: Princeton University Press, 1980), p. 13.

27. See also Michael Holquist, *Dialogism: Bakhtin and his World* (London and New York: Routledge, 1990), pp. 107–48. For a specific application of Bakhtin's concept to film, see Robert Stam's observation that the "chronotope . . . historicizes space and time," in Robert Stam, *Subversive Pleasures: Bakhtin, Cultural Criticism, and Film* (Baltimore: Johns Hopkins University Press, 1989), p. 41.

28. For more on the BBC production, see George Ford's "Dickens's *Hard Times* on Television: Problems of Adaptation," in George Ford and Sylvère Monod, ed., *Hard Times: An Authoritative Text—Backgrounds, Sources and Contemporary Reactions, Criticism* (New York: W.W. Norton, 1990), pp. 401–11.

29. For an interesting comparison of *The Blackboard Jungle* and some more recent classroom films, see Gilles Gony, "Le Prof et la horde: sur *Blackboard Jungle, Mery per Sempre et Train of Dreams,*" *Cahiers de la Cinématheque*, December 1990, 67–73.

30. Barry K. Grant, *Voyages of Discovery: The Cinema of Frederick Wiseman* (Urbana and Chicago: University of Illinois Press, 1992), p. 57.

31. Edward A. Krug, *The Shaping of the American High School* (Cambridge, Mass.: Harvard University Press, 1964).

32. Michael Katz, *The Irony of Early School Reform* (Cambridge, Mass.: Harvard University Press, 1968).

33. Paul Rabinow, ed., *The Foucault Reader* (New York: Pantheon Books, 1984), pp. 183–86.

34. Raymond Williams, "Introduction," in Charles Dickens, *Hard Times* (New York: Fawcett, 1966), p. 7.

35. See Basil Bernstein, *Class, Codes, and Control* (St Albans, U.K.: Paladin, 1973).

36. This view contrasts with the generous view of Dewey's liberalism outlined by Robert B. Westbrook in *John Dewey and American Democracy* (Ithaca, N.Y. and London: Cornell University Press, 1991).

37. This is Wiseman's own description of Central Park East. See Cynthia Lucia, "*Revisiting High School:* An Interview with Frederick Wiseman," *Cineaste* 20, no. 4 (1994): 6. For an account of the school's educational policy, see Deborah Meier, *The Power of their Ideas: Lessons for America from a Small School in Harlem* (Boston: Beacon Press, 1995).

38. Carl R. Rogers, *Freedom to Learn* (Columbus, Ohio: Charles E. Merrill, 1969), p. 162.

39. Ramon Menendez's *Stand and Deliver* (1987) includes a more cynical Hol-

lywood version of this approach to standardized testing. An Advanced Placement examination in mathematics is used as a gimmick to reinforce the traditional American ideology of upward mobility.

40. This passage from Dewey's *Democracy and Education* is quoted in Andrew Delbanco, "John Dewey's America," *Partisan Review* 63, no. 3 (1996): 516.

41. De Fontenay is quoted in P. N. Furbank, *Diderot: A Critical Biography* (New York: Alfred A. Knopf, 1992), p. 68.

42. See, for example, Julia Kristeva, *Revolution in Poetic Language,* trans. Margaret Waller (New York: Columbia University Press, 1984).

43. Justin Chang, "The Class," *Variety,* May 23, 2008, https://variety.com/2008/film/awards/the-class-3-1200522111/.

44. Pierre Bourdieu, *Political Interventions: Social Science and Political Action,* trans. David Fernbach (London and New York: Verso Books, 2008), p. 52.

45. Ibid., p. 56.

46. Simon, *Mass Enlightenment,* p. 58.

47. Peter Kropotkin, *Fields Factories, and Workshops,* edited by Colin Ward (London: Allen & Unwin, 1974), p. 26.

48. See Fernand Braudel, *On History,* trans. Sarah Matthews (Chicago: University of Chicago Press, 1983).

49. Alan Pinch, introduction to Alan Pinch and Michael Armstrong, eds., *Tolstoy on Education: Tolstoy's Educational Writings 1861–1862* (Rutherford, Madison, and Teaneck, N.J.: Farleigh Dickinson University Press, 1982), p. 35. Caryl Emerson provocatively claims that although Tolstoy might "advocate abolition of hierarchy . . . the fact that Count Tolstoy is now at the feet of the peasants is not significant. The axis has not changed. It is still the omnipresent monologic *kto kogo* ('who does what to whom') . . . still cast in what Bakhtin would call a 'pedagogical dialogue': 'Someone who knows and possesses the truth instructs someone who is ignorant of it and in error.'" Although there is undoubtedly some truth in Emerson's critique, she seems to conflate Tolstoy's pedagogy with his aesthetic agenda as a novelist. See Emerson's essay "The Tolstoy Connection in Bakhtin," in Gary Saul Morson and Caryl Emerson, eds., *Rethinking Bakhtin: Extensions and Challenges* (Evanston, Ill.: Northwestern University Press, 1989), p. 152.

50. Susan Buck-Morss, *The Dialectics of Seeing: Walter Benjamin and the Arcades Project* (Cambridge, Mass. and London: MIT Press, 1989), p. 55.

51. Ibid., p. 279.

52. Jeffrey Mehlman, *Walter Benjamin, for Children: An Essay on His Radio Years* (Chicago and London: University of Chicago Press, 1993), p. 25.

53. Roland Barthes, *The Grain of the Voice: Interviews 1962–1980* (New York: Hill & Wang, 1985), p. 242.

54. Marie Fleming, *The Anarchist Way to Socialism* (Totowa, N.J.: Roman & Littlefield, 1979), p. 195.

55. Ratgeb (Raoul Vaneigem), *Contributions to the Revolutionary Struggle Intended to be Discussed, Corrected and Principally Put into Practice Without Delay,* trans. Paul Sharkey (London: Elephant Editions, 1990), p. 14. "Ratgeb" observes, however, that

"individual re-appropriation of goods stolen by the State and the employer class merely feeds the commodity process, unless it becomes a collective action and leads to a total liquidation of the system."

56. Alex Swerdling, *Orwell and the Left* (New Haven, Conn. and London: Yale University Press, 1974), p. 20.

57. Harold Hart ed., *Summerhill: For and Against* (New York: Hart, 1970), pp. 24, 153.

58. See Jonathan Kozol, *Death at an Early Age: The Destruction of the Hearts and Minds of Negro Children in the Boston Public Schools* (New York: Houghton Mifflin Harcourt, 1967), and Jonathan Kozol, *Free Schools* (New York: Houghton Mifflin Harcourt, 1972).

59. Paul Avrich, *The Modern School Movement: Anarchism and Education in the United States* (Princeton, N.J.: Princeton University Press, 1980), p. 352.

60. Wilder continually uses this figure, which is difficult to verify, in interviews and press releases. See, for example, the program note for *Approaching the Elephant* at the International Film Festival, Rotterdam, 2015, https://iffr.com/en/2015/films/approaching-the-elephant.

61. Email from Alexander Khost to the author, January 13, 2016.

62. Matt Zoller Seitz, "Approaching the Elephant," Rogerebert.com, February 20, 2015, https://www.rogerebert.com/reviews/approaching-the-elephant-2014.

63. A. S. Neill, *Summerhill* (Harmondsworth, U.K.: Penguin, 1968), 115.

64. Ibid., p. 62.

65. Joseph Todd, "From Deschooling to Unschooling: Rethinking Anarchopedagogy after Ivan Illich," in Robert Haworth *Anarchist Pedagogies: Collective Theories, Actions, and Critical Reflections on Education* (Oakland, Calif. and Edinburgh: AK Press, 2012), p. 73.

66. Jean Maitron, *Histoire du mouvement anarchists en France (1880–1924)* (Paris: Société Universitaire d'Éditions et de Librairie, 1951), pp. 344–49.

67. Everett Reimer, *School is Dead* (Garden City, N.Y.: Doubleday, 1971), p. 55.

68. See Goodman's essay "Children's Rights," anthologized in Taylor Stoehr, ed., *Decentralizing Power: Paul Goodman's Social Criticism* (Montreal and New York: Black Rose Books, 1994), p. 39. Responding to anarchist-inspired arguments that label childhood an artificial construct, Goodman observes that "historically, treating children like adults meant bringing a six-year-old to court for petty theft and hanging him, and having nine-year-olds pick straw in the factory, not because their labor was useful, but 'to teach them good work habits.'" For more on the children's-rights debate, see Beatrice Gross and Ronald Gross, eds., *The Children's Rights Movement: Overcoming the Oppression of Young People* (Garden City, N.Y.: Anchor Press/Doubleday, 1977).

69. See William G. Simon, *The Films of Jean Vigo* (Ann Arbor, Mich.: UMI Research Press, 1981), pp. 54–95. Brian Mills observes that the film's opening sequence allows us to glimpse for a moment the Fourieresque "lost domain." See his "Jean Vigo, Anarchy, Surrealism and Optimism," *Cinema* 8, (1971): 24.

70. José Lebrero Stals, 'Childhood, Path of Escape,' trans. Adriana Benzaquén, *Public* 12 (1995): 82.

71. This is a quotation from Jacques Fillon's *Programmes and Manifestos on Twentieth Century Architecture,* quoted in Sadie Plant, *The Most Radical Gesture: The Situationist International in a Postmodern Age* (London and New York: Routledge, 1992), pp. 58–59. Plant remarks that the concept of *dérive* "acted as something of a model for the 'playful creation' of all human relationships."

72. Eddie Lee Sausage, "Concerning Psychogeography, Play, and the Bastille of Meaning," *Smile No. 6: Snicker; A Magazine of Multiple Becomings,* p. 14.

73. Joan Ungersma Halperin, *Félix Fénéon: Aesthete and Anarchist in Fin-de-Siècle Paris* (New Haven, Conn. and London: Yale University Press, 1988), p. 24.

74. Allon White, *Carnival, Hysteria, and Writing: Collected Essays and Autobiography* (Oxford, U.K.: Clarendon Press, 1993), pp. 132–33.

75. *The Complete Jean Vigo* (New York: Lorrimer, 1983), p. 58.

76. Herbert Read, *Selected Writings: Poetry and Criticism* (New York: Horizon Press, 1964), p. 370.

77. Simon, *Films of Jean Vigo,* p. 79.

78. Read, *Selected Writings,* p. 365.

79. Alexander Nehamas, *Nietzsche: Life as Literature* (Cambridge, Mass. and London: Harvard University Press, 1985), p. 121.

80. Alan Lovell, *Anarchist Cinema* (London: Peace News, 1962), p. 5.

81. P. E. Salles Gomes, *Jean Vigo* (Berkeley and Los Angeles: University of California Press, 1971), p. 164.

82. Jonathan Rosenbaum speculates that certain motifs in the cabin sequence, as well as Jean's ambivalent relationship with Juliette, point to what might be termed submerged "bisexual" themes. See "Jean Vigo's Secret," in Jonathan Rosenbaum, *Placing Movies* (Berkeley and Los Angeles: University of California Press, 1995), pp. 272–80.

83. Marina Warner, *L'Atalante* (London: British Film Institute, 1993).

84. Denis Diderot, *Jacques the Fatalist,* trans. Michael Henry (Harmondsworth, U.K. and New York: Penguin Books, 1986), p. 202.

85. For a more positive evaluation of *If . . .*'s anarchist aspirations, see Mick Mercer, "Instructions for Taking Up Arms If . . .," *Vague* 16–17 (1988): 5–12.

86. Anderson is quoted in Allison Graham, *Lindsay Anderson* (Boston: Twayne Publishers, 1981), p. 119.

87. Gerald Graff's essay "Arnold, Reason, and Common Culture" is anthologized in Samuel Lipman, ed., *Culture and Anarchy* (New Haven, Conn. and London: Yale University Press, 1994), p. 197.

88. Matthew Arnold, in Lipman, ed., *Culture and Anarchy,* p. 41. Ed Cohen demonstrates that Charles Kingsley's ideal of "muscular Christianity"—the belief that "healthy minds" are products of "healthy bodies"—"became a popular paradigm for the educated middle-class male." Cohen concludes that "the rhetorical exchange between 'mental'" and "muscular" ideals underscores the subtending interest that

unites them: both Kingsley's parodic voice and his narrative persona agree that the essential (male) goal is making money." See Cohen's *Talk on the Wilde Side: Toward a Genealogy of a Discourse on Male Sexualities* (New York and London: Routledge, 1993), pp. 39–40.

89. Robert J. C. Young, *Colonial Desire: Hybridity in Theory, Culture and Race* (New York and London: Routledge, 1995), p. 71.

90. For a critique of *If . . .*'s Brechtian aspirations, see Alan Lovell, "Brecht in Britain—Lindsay Anderson" (on *If . . .* and *O Lucky Man*), *Screen* 16, no. 4 (Winter 1975–1976): 62–70.

91. Elizabeth Sussex, *Lindsay Anderson* (New York: Praeger, 1969), pp. 68–91.

92. Jonathan Gathorne-Hardy, *The Old School Tie: The Phenomenon of the English Public School* (New York: Viking, 1977), p. 309.

93. For an account of Neill's intellectual evolution, see Jonathan Croall, *Neill of Summerhill: The Permanent Rebel* (London, Melbourne, and Henley, U.K.: Ark Paperbacks, 1983).

94. Kingsley Widmer, "Anarchist in Academe: Notes from the Contemporary University," *Social Anarchism: A Journal of Practice and Theory* 14 (1989): 5.

95. See Zygmunt Bauman, *Legislators and Interpreters: On Modernity, Post-Modernity, and Intellectuals* (Ithaca, N.Y.: Cornell University Press, 1987); Antonio Gramsci, *Selections from the Prison Notebooks,* ed. and trans. Quintin Hoare and Geoffrey Nowell Smith (New York: International Publishers, 1971); Russell Jacoby, *The Last Intellectuals: American Culture in the Age of Academe* (New York: Basic Books, 1987); J. P. Nettl, "Ideas, Intellectuals, and Structures of Dissent," in Phillip Rieff, ed., *On Intellectuals: Theoretical Studies/Case Studies* (Garden City, N.Y.: Doubleday, 1969), p. 55; Bruce Robbins, *Secular Vocations: Intellectuals: Professionalism, Culture* (London and New York: Verso, 1993). See also Bruce Robbins, ed., *Intellectuals: Aesthetics, Politics, Academics* (Minneapolis: University of Minnesota Press, 1990); Edward W. Said, *Representations of the Intellectual* (New York: Pantheon Books, 1994).

96. Paul Avrich, *The Russian Anarchists* (Princeton, N.J.: Princeton University Press, 1967), p. 22.

97. Bakunin is quoted in ibid., p. 94.

98. Christopher Frayling, *Things to Come* (London: British Film Institute, 1995), p. 14. As Frayling notes in his monograph, Wells attempted, unsuccessfully, to convince Stalin that his technocratic vision of the future should be emulated by the Soviet regime.

99. Alvin Gouldner, *Against Fragmentation: The Origins of Marxism and the Sociology of Intellectuals* (Oxford, U.K.: Oxford University Press, 1985), p. 158.

100. Carl Davidson, *The New Radicals in the University and Other SDS Writings on Student Syndicalism* (Chicago: Charles H. Kerr, 1990), p. 47. The text was written in 1966–1967, and reprinted as part of Charles H. Kerr's "Sixties' Series. Davidson was vice president and inter-organizational secretary of SDS in the mid-1960s. See also former LA State college professor Jerry Farber's influential, if dubiously titled, manifesto *The Student as Nigger* (New York: Pocket Books, 1969). It is also instructive

to compare Davidson's manifesto with a 1966 pamphlet issued by the Situationist International. The situationists were intrigued by the Berkeley events and express their belief that the students "by revolting against their studies . . . have automatically called that society into question. From the start they have seen their revolt against the university hierarchy as a revolt against *the whole hierarchical system,* the dictatorship of the economy of the State." See Internationale Situationiste and Students of Strasbourg, *On the Poverty of Student Life: Considered in its Economic, Political, Psychological, Sexual, and Particularly Intellectual Aspects, and a Modest Proposal for its Remedy* (London: Dark Star and Rebel Press, 1985; reprint of 1966 pamphlet). For Anglo American counterparts to the situationist position, see Alexander Cockburn and Robin Blackburn, eds., *Student Power: Problems, Diagnosis, Action* (Baltimore: Penguin Books, 1969).

101. This passage from Chomsky's essay, "The Responsibility of Intellectuals" is quoted in Milan Rai, *Chomsky's Politics* (London: Verso, 1995), p. 150.

102. See Paul Mattick Jr, review of *Manufacturing Consent, Cineaste* 20, no. 1 (1993). Achbar and Wintonick's reply is in *Cineaste* 20, no. 3 (1994).

103. Pierre Bourdieu, *Homo Academicus,* trans. Peter Collier (Stanford, Calif.: Stanford University Press, 1988), p. 279. It is amusing that David Lodge, a novelist known for his wry jabs at academics in satirical novels like *Changing Places* and *Small World,* reviewed the English translation of *Homo Academicus.* See "L'Uni Left in a State," *Guardian,* December 9, 1988, p. 15.

104. Anthony Giddens, *Politics, Sociology and Social Theory: Encounters with Classical and Contemporary Social Thought* (Stanford, Calif.: Stanford University Press, 1995), p. 49. Giddens attributes Weber's support of a value-free university realm partially to the fact that "he witnessed the retardation of the careers of some of his friends, notably Michels and Simmel, as a result of strictly non-intellectual considerations—Michels because he was a Social Democrat, and Simmel because he was a Jew." In a study of Weber's theory of intellectuals, Ahmad Sadri rather simplistically asserts that Bakunin's "anti-intellectualism" entails a "conspiracy theory of intellectuals." Appropriately enough, Chomsky's view of the manufacture of consent has also occasionally been labeled a conspiracy theory. See Sadri's *Max Weber's Theory of Intellectuals* (New York and Oxford, U.K.: Oxford University Press, 1992), p. 138.

105. Bourdieu, *Homo Academicus,* p. 176.

106. Noam Chomsky, *Radical Priorities,* edited with an introduction by C. P. Otero (Montreal: Black Rose Books, 1981), p. 25.

107. Bourdieu, *Homo Academicus,* p. 31.

108. The full transcript of the Chomsky–Foucault exchange is anthologized in Fons Elders, ed., *Reflexive Water: The Basic Concerns of Mankind* (London: Souvenir Press, 1974), pp. 135–97. In Jim Merod's view, "when Foucault suggests, as he does in his debate with Chomsky, that justice is a ruling-class concept, he feeds the complacency of the conventional humanist." Yet, oddly enough, Merod bases his critique on neo-Marxist principles, conveniently neglecting the fact that Chomsky has never been a Marxist. See Merod's *The Political Responsibility of the Critic* (Ithaca, N.Y. and London: Cornell University Press, 1987), p. 176. The televised version of

the Foucault-Chomsky exchange is disc one in the Icarus Films DVD release of *Philosophy: Debates and Dialogue: A 4-part series by Fons Elders.*

109. In his biography of Foucault, James Miller writes that although Chomsky "had read *The Order of Things* and knew Foucault's work on eighteenth-century linguistics," he was stunned that the Frenchman was "invoking Mao Tse-tung and denying the need for even the most rudimentary principles of justice! Perhaps he had misunderstood." Miller also observes that "the nonchalant savagery of Foucault's political views in those years startled not only radical humanists like Chomsky, it also dumbfounded some of the philosopher's young Maoist allies who were then in the midst of the debating the scope and meaning of 'popular justice.'" See Miller's *The Passion of Michel Foucault* (New York and London: Simon & Schuster, 1993), pp. 202–3.

110. Foucault's observation is included in an interview conducted by Bernard-Henri Levy. See Levy's *Adventures on the Freedom Road: The French Intellectuals in the 20th Century* (London: Harvill Press, 1995), p. 372.

111. For a brief overview of Paper Tiger's early days, see Dee Halleck, "Paper Tiger Television: Smashing the Myths of the Information Industry Every Week on Public Access Cable," in Douglas Kahn and Diane Neumaier, eds., *Cultures in Contention* (Seattle: Real Comet Press, 1985), pp. 36–41.

112. Alvin Gouldner, *The Dialectic of Ideology and Technology* (New York: Seabury Press, 1976), p. 185.

113. Mark Dery, *Culture Jamming* (Westfield, N.J.: Open Magazine Pamphlet Series, 1993), p. 6.

114. See Paulo Freire, *Education for Critical Consciousness* (New York: Continuum, 1987), p. 19. From a different cultural perspective, Alexander Trocchi's proposal for a "spontaneous university"—an "invisible insurrection of a million minds"—sought to extend education beyond the boundaries of the classroom. See Andrew Murray Scott, ed., *Invisible Insurrection of a Million Minds: A Trocchi Reader* (Edinburgh: Polygon, 1991).

115. Alexander Cockburn, "Sex, Guys, and High Bohemia," *Interview,* September 1989, p. 150.

116. Astra Taylor, "Serfing the Net," *Baffler* 18 (December 2009), https://thebaffler.com/salvos/serfing-the-net.

117. See Louis Marcorelles, *Living Cinema,* trans. Isabel Quigley (London: George Allen & Unwin, 1973).

118. See Deborah Epstein Nord, "The Social Explorer as Anthropologist: Victorian Travelers Among the Urban Poor," anthologized in William Sharpe and Leonard Wallock, eds., *Visions of the Modern City* (New York: Proceedings of the Heyman Center for the Humanities, 1982), pp. 118–30.

119. For information on Garrin's video installations, as well as his own tapes documenting the Tompkins Square events, see Anna Indych, "Paul Garrin," *Poliester* 13 (Fall 1995): 34–37. For a scholarly appraisal of the events in Tompkins Square Park, see Janet L. Abu-Lughod, *From Urban Village to East Village: The Battle for New York's Lower East Side* (Oxford, U.K. and Cambridge, Mass.: Basil Blackwell, 1994).

120. Murray Bookchin makes a distinction (which some may consider overly facile) between a recent current he labels "lifestyle anarchism"—distinguished by "privatism, kicks, introversion, and post-modernist nihilism"—and the tradition of revolutionary anarchism that spans from the nineteenth century to the Spanish Civil War. See Bookchin's *Social Anarchism or Lifestyle Anarchism? An Unbridgeable Chasm* (San Francisco and Edinburgh: AK Press, 1995).

121. Colin Ward, *Housing: An Anarchist Approach* (London: Freedom Press, 1983), p. 31.

122. See Manuel Castells, *The City and the Grassroots* (Berkeley and Los Angeles: University of California Press, 1983).

123. See Bob McGlynn, "From Tompkins Square to Gdansk," *Black Eye* 6 (1988): 14–15.

124. Edward W. Soja, *Postmodern Geographies: The Reassertion of Space in Critical Social Theory* (London and New York: Verso, 1989), p. 235. For an analysis of the economic roots of post-modernity that is intimately aligned with the housing crisis and the politics of spatiality, see David Harvey, *The Condition of Postmodernity* (Oxford, U.K.: Basil Blackwell, 1989).

125. Douglas Kellner, *Media Culture: Cultural Studies, Identity and Politics between the Modern and the Postmodern* (London and New York: Routledge, 1995), p. 335.

126. See the *Shadow* 2 (April 1989).

127. See Hans Magnus Enzensberger, "Constituents of a Theory of Media," in *Critical Essays* (New York: Continuum, 1982), pp. 46–76.

128. See Englander's introduction to Adilkno, *Cracking the Movement: Squatting Beyond the Media,* trans. Laura Martz (Brooklyn, N.Y.: Autonomedia, 1990), p. 9.

129. Reclus is quoted in Kristin Ross, *The Emergence of Social Space* (Minneapolis: University of Minnesota Press, 1988), p. 91.

130. Freddy Buache, *The Cinema of Luis Buñuel,* trans. Peter Graham (New York: A.S. Barnes, 1973), pp. 30–37.

131. Bunn Nagara, "Libertarian or Liberal," *Libertarian Education* 30 (1987): 3–5.

132. Starobinski, *Jean-Jacques Rousseau,* p. 215.

133. For examples and criticisms, see Valerie Walkerdine, *Schoolgirl Fictions* (London and New York: Verso, 1990), James Donald, *Sentimental Education* (London and New York: Verso, 1992), See, for example, Wendy Ayotte, "Self-determination for Children," *Anarchy: A Journal of Desire Armed* 27 (Winter 1990–1991): 18–21, Pierre Bourdieu and Jean-Claude Passeron, *Reproduction in Education, Society and Culture,* trans. Richard Nice (London and Beverly Hills, Calif.: Sage, 1977), Gregory L. Ulmer, *Applied Grammatology: Post(e) Pedagogy from Jacques Derrida to Joseph Beuys* (Baltimore and London: Johns Hopkins University Press, 1985), and Jane Gallop, ed., *Pedagogy: The Question of Performance* (Bloomington and Indianapolis: Indiana University Press, 1995).

134. For an overview of Lettrism, an avant-garde movement considered the precursor of many of the aesthetic tendencies within the subsequent Situationist International, see David Trend, "Letters and Characters," *Afterimage* 13, no. 6 (January 1986): 6–8. At the time of its release, Eric Rohmer wrote a scathing review of *Venom*

and Eternity. See Eric Rohmer, *The Taste for Beauty,* trans. Eric Volk (Cambridge, U.K.: Cambridge University Press, 1989), pp. 53–58.

135. Author's unpublished interview with Tuli Kupferberg, New York, November 1995. For an example of Kupferberg and Topp's magazine anthologies featuring children's contributions, see, for example, *Swing* 4 (Fall 1961). During the 1960s and 1970s, hundreds of "underground" American high-school newspapers intriguingly demonstrated the creativity of students participating in their own self-education. See, for example, John Birmingham, ed., *Our Time is Now: Notes from the High School Underground* (New York, Washington, and London: Praeger Publishers, 1970).

136. Aja Romano, "You may not have understood Vine, but its demise is a huge cultural loss," *Vox* 28 (October 2016), https://www.vox.com/2016/10/28/13439450/vine-shutdown-loss-to-black-culture.

137. Stephen Humphries, *Hooligans or Rebels? An Oral History of Working-Class Childhood and Youth 1889–1939* (Oxford, U.K.: Basil Blackwell, 1981).

138. Gilles Deleuze, *Negotiations 1972–1990,* trans. Martin Joughin (New York: Columbia University Press, 1990), p. 175.

139. See, for example, J. Hoberman's observations on Watkins's film in *Film After Film (Or What Became of 21st Century Cinema?)* (London and Brooklyn: Verso Books, 2012), pp. 50–51.

140. Jacques Rancière, *The Emancipated Spectator,* trans. Gregory Elliott (London and Brooklyn: Verso Books, 2009). p.19.

141. Ruth Levitas, *The Concept of Utopia* (Oxford, U.K.: Peter Lang, 1990), p. 170.

142. Antoine de Baecque, *Camera Historica: The Century in Cinema,* trans. Ninon Vinsonneau and Jonathan Magidoff (New York: Columbia University Press, 2012), p. 199.

143. See *Revolutionary Romanticism: A Drunken Boat Anthology,* ed. Max Blechman (San Francisco: City Lights Publishers, 2001).

144. David Armitage, "The Anarchist Cinema of Peter Watkins," in *Perspectives on History* 51, no. 9 (December 2013), https://www.historians.org/publications-and-directories/perspectives-on-history/december-2013/the-anarchist-cinema-of-peter-watkins.

145. David Walsh, "Five films on historical and political themes," *World Socialist Web Site,* September 27, 2001, https://www.wsws.org/en/articles/2001/09/tff2-s27.html.

146. Mikhail Bakunin, "Preface to Second Instalment (sic) of *L'Empire Knouto-Germanique* (June–July 1871), in Eugene Schulkind ed., *The Paris Commune of 1871: The View from the Left* (New York: Grove Press), 1974).

147. Peter Kropotkin, "From the Commune of Paris," (1880) in ibid., 225.

148. See Edith Thomas, *The Women Incendiaries* (Chicago: Haymarket Books, 2007.)

149. See Edith Thomas, "The Women of the Commune," *Massachusetts Review* 12, no. 3 (Summer 1971): 409–17.

150. Kristin Ross, *Communal Luxury: The Political Imaginary of the Paris Commune* (London and Brooklyn: Verso Books, 2015), p. 27.

151. Ibid., p. 49.

152. Hamish Ford, "Producing revolutionary history on film: Henri Lefebvre's urban space and Peter Watkins's *La Commune (Paris, 1871)*," *Jump Cut* 57 (Fall 2016), https://www.ejumpcut.org/archive/jc57.2016/-FordLaCommune/index.html.

153. Rancière, *Emancipated Spectator,* p. 22.

154. Stuart Edwards, *The Paris Commune, 1871* (Chicago and New York: Quadrangle Books, 1971), p. 277.

155. See John Merriman, *Massacre: The Life and Death of the Paris Commune* (New York, Basic Books, 2014).

156. The quote is from an essay by Watkins that appears on his website: "The Role of the American MAVM, Hollywood and the Monoform." See http://pwatkins.mnsi .net/PW_Statement3.htm.

157. Email from Philip Rizk to the author, February 20, 2017.

158. See Lèopold Lambert, "#NYC Commune Project Introduction," *Funambulist,* January 6, 2013, https://thefunambulist.net/cinema/nyc-commune-introduction.

159. Dorothy Knowles, *Armand Gatti in the Theatre: Wild Duck Against the Wind* (London: Athlone Press, 1989), p. 203.

160. See Chiara Bottici, *Imaginal Politics: Images Beyond Imagination and the Imaginary* (New York, Columbia University Press, 2014).

161. *La Commune* is an acknowledged influence on Robert Greene's *Bisbee '17* (2018), an account of the so-called "Bisbee Deportation" of 1917, in which I.W.W. members, immigrants, and sympathizers were expelled from the town of Bisbee, Arizona, after mine owners feared that a massive strike would paralyze the town. Although the film's slick editing style might not please Watkins, Greene clearly shares the elder filmmaker's pedagogical aspirations. See Richard Porton, "Review of *Bisbee '17*," *Cineaste* (Winter 2018): 48–50.

Chapter 5. The Elusive Anarchist Aesthetic

1. Donald Drew Egbert, *Social Radicalism and the Arts/Western Europe: A Cultural History from the French Revolution to 1968* (New York: Alfred A. Knopf, 1970), p. 45.

2. André Reszler, "Bakunin, Marx and the Aesthetic Heritage of Socialism," *Yearbook of Comparative General Literature* (Bloomington: Indiana University Press, 1973).

3. Peter Bürger, *Theory of the Avant-Garde,* trans. Michael Shaw (Minneapolis: University of Minnesota Press, 1984).

4. Peter Uwe Hohendahl, *Prismatic Thought: Theodor W. Adorno* (Lincoln and London: University of Nebraska Press, 1995), p. 210.

5. M. H. Abrams, *Natural Supernaturalism: Tradition and Revolution in Romantic Literature* (New York and London: W.W. Norton, 1973), p. 350.

6. Michael Henry Scrivener, *Radical Shelley: The Philosophical Anarchism and Utopian Thought of Percy Bysshe Shelley* (Princeton, N.J.: Princeton University Press, 1982).

7. See Richard Kearney, *The Wake of Imagination* (Minneapolis: University of Minnesota Press, 1988), pp. 155–88.

8. To be specific, I am referring to Stewart Home's belief that the avant-garde "cult of the artist . . . reproduces class values by privileging form over content, art over life, distance over participation." See Home's *Neoism, Plagiarism and Praxis* (Edinburgh and San Francisco: AK Press, 1995), p. 34. Home cites philosopher Roger Taylor's book *Art, Enemy of the People* (Hassocks, U.K.: Harvester Press, 1978) as an exemplary theorization of his critique of the institution of art.

9. Bürger, *Theory of the Avant-Garde,* p. 49.

10. See Home, *Neoism, Plagiarism,* p. 49. A neoist manifesto, "Discourse on the Suppression of Reality," proclaims that "today, we are no longer stupid enough to imagine that what we do is new, or even that such an assertion does not imply a progression—and hence a certain amount of 'originality.'" See Stewart Home, *Neoist Manifestos* (Stirling, U.K.: AK Press), p. 33. In Hakim Bey's vision of tentative utopia, "the temporary autonomous zone," art "as commodity will simply become impossible; it will instead be a condition of life." See Bey's *T.A.Z. The Temporary Autonomous Zone: Ontological Anarchy, Poetic Terrorism* (Brooklyn, N.Y.: Autonomedia, 1991), p. 132.

11. See Raymond Williams, *Culture and Society 1780–1950* (New York: Columbia University Press, 1981), pp. 59–60.

12. See J. Hoberman's remarks on *Guns and the Trees* in David E. James, ed., *To Free the Cinema: Jonas Mekas and the New York Underground* (Princeton, N.J.: Princeton University Press, 1992), pp. 113–18.

13. Max Raphael, *Proudhon/Marx/Picasso: Three Studies in the Sociology of Art,* trans. Inge Marcuse, edited, introduced, and with a bibliography by John Tagg (Atlantic Highlands, N.J.: Humanities Press, 1980), p. 25.

14. Meyer Schapiro, *Modern Art, 19th and 20th Centuries: Selected Papers* (New York: George Braziller, 1978), p. 52.

15. James Henry Rubin, *Realism and Social Vision in Courbet and Proudhon* (Princeton, N.J.: Princeton University Press, 1980), p. 98.

16. Proudhon, quoted in T. J. Clark, *Image of the People: Gustave Courbet and the 1848 Revolution* (Greenwich, Conn.: New York Graphic Society, 1973), p. 166.

17. See Jeffrey Kaplow, "The Paris Commune and the Artists," in John Hicks and Robert Tucker, eds., *Revolution and Reaction: The Paris Commune 1871* (Amherst: University of Massachusetts Press, 1973), p. 152.

18. Jerrold Seigel, *Bohemian Paris: Culture, Politics and the Boundaries of Bourgeois Life, 1830–1950* (New York and London: Penguin, 1986), p. 311.

19. Quillard is quoted in ibid., p. 311.

20. A phrase from Tuli Kupferberg's "Notes Towards a Theory of Bohemianism," *Birth* 1 (Autumn 1958): 3. Kupferberg was a poet, cartoonist, and musician (perhaps best known for his participation in the anarchist rock group The Fugs) with strong anarchist sympathies. *Birth* was one of his self-published magazines.

21. Strutfield is quoted in Roslyn Jolly, *Henry James: History, Narrative, Fiction* (Oxford, U.K.: Clarendon Press, 1993), p. 57.

22. This quotation is from an interview with Dolgoff in Paul Avrich, *Anarchist Voices: An Oral History of Anarchism in America* (Princeton, N.J.: Princeton University Press, 1995), p. 425.

23. See Clark, *Image of the People.*

24. Seigel, *Bohemian Paris,* p. 404.

25. Josef Chytry, *The Aesthetic State: A Quest in Modern German Thought* (Berkeley and Los Angeles: University of California Press, 1989), p. 223.

26. Wallace Fowlie, "Rimbaud and the Commune," in Hicks and Tucker, eds., *Revolution and Reaction,* p. 168.

27. Mikhail Bakunin, *God and the State* (New York: Dover Publications, 1970), p. 25.

28. Fredric Jameson concludes that *Un Chien andalou* "is . . . an explosive document of modern anarchism" that finds its "explicit political expression in his next movie, *L'Âge d'or.*" He does not elaborate on this assertion, however. See Fredric Jameson, *The Ideologies of Theory: Essays 1971–1986,* Vol. 1, *Situations of Theory* (Minneapolis: University of Minnesota Press, 1988), p. 129.

29. Buñuel described Acín as "an anarchist from Huesca, a drawing teacher" who "won a hundred pesetas in the lottery: and gave him twenty thousand to make *Las Hurdes.*" See José de la Colina and Tomás Pérez Turrent, *Objects of Desire: Conversations with Luis Buñuel* (New York: Marsilio Publishers, 1992), p. 31.

30. This is what Buñuel told Joel Sucher and Stephen Fischler when they interviewed him in Mexico in the early 1980s (personal communication with Sucher, July 1985).

31. Bakunin, quoted in Reszler, *Bakunin, Marx,* p. 48.

32. André Breton, quoted in Francisco Aranda, *Luis Buñuel: A Critical Biography,* trans. and edited by David Robinson (New York: Da Capo Press, 1976), p. 73.

33. It is also interesting to note in this context that Kropotkin believed that the Roman Empire came to embody the worst excesses for the state—"the domination by the rich who had appropriated the land to themselves and the misery of those who cultivated it." See Kropotkin's "The State: Its Historic Role," in P. A. Kropotkin, *Selected Writings on Anarchism and Revolution,* edited with an introduction by Martin A. Miller (Cambridge, Mass.: MIT Press, 1970).

34. This quotation is from the synposis of the film in Aranda, *Luis Buñuel,* p. 76.

35. Max Stirner, *The Ego and Its Own,* edited by David Leopold (Cambridge, U.K. and New York: Cambridge University Press, 1995), pp. 59–60.

36. The full quotation is "Christianity is precisely the religion *par excellence,* because it exhibits and manifests, to the fullest extent, the very nature and essence of every religious system, which is *the impoverishment, enslavement, and annihilation of humanity for the benefit of divinity.*" See Bakunin, *God and the State,* p. 24.

37. See José Antonio Maravall, *Culture of the Baroque: Analysis of a Historical Structure,* trans. Terry Cochran (Minneapolis: University of Minnesota Press, 1986). See also the discussion of Buñuel's updating of *parodia sacra* in Robert Stam, *Subversive Pleasures: Bakhtin, Cultural Criticism, and Film* (Baltimore: Johns Hopkins University Press, 1989), p. 103.

38. Paul Avrich, introduction to Peter Kropotkin, *The Conquest of Bread* (New York: New York University Press, 1971), p. 7.

39. David Robinson, "'Thank God—I Am Still an Atheist': Luis Buñuel and *Viridi-*

ana," in Joan Mellen, ed., *The World of Luis Buñuel* (Oxford, U.K. and New York: Oxford University Press, 1978), pp. 237–38.

40. Walter Benjamin, *Reflections,* trans. Edward Jephcott (New York: Schocken Books, 1978), p. 189.

41. Ado Kyrou, *Luis Buñuel* (New York: Simon & Schuster, 1963), p. 96.

42. The situationists, however, were often scathing in their assessments of the surrealists. The surrealists, not surprisingly, returned the (dis)favor. Jean Schuster, for example, Breton's so-called "right-hand man," described *Society of the Spectacle* as "the most soporific book" he'd ever read. He also condemned Raoul Vaneigem's work as hopelessly derivative, and the situationists' faith in the French proletariat during 1968 as "cretinism pure and simple." See Paul Hammond, "Specialists in Revolt," *New Statesman,* December 4, 1987. For some remarks on the situationist debt to surrealism (particularly Breton), see Peter Wollen, *Raiding the Icebox* (Bloomington and Indianapolis: Indiana University Press, 1993), pp. 120–21.

43. Kristine Stiles, "Sticks and Stones: The Destruction in Art Symposium," *Arts Magazine,* January 1989, p. 54.

44. For an account of this split, see the introduction to Simon Ford, *The Realization and Suppression of the Situationist International* (Edinburgh and San Francisco: AK Press, 1995), pp. viii–ix.

45. For Debord's account of his differences with the art-oriented situationists such as Asger Jorn, see his essay, "The Situationists and the New Forms of Action in Politics or Art," in Elizabeth Sussman, ed., *on the passage of a few people through a rather brief moment in time: The Situationist International 1957–1972* (Cambridge, Mass. and London: MIT Press, 1989), pp. 148–53.

46. Ford, *Realization and Suppression,* p. vii.

47. Debord, "The Situationists and the New Forms of Action," p. 29.

48. See Thomas Y. Levin, "Dismantling the Spectacle: The Cinema of Guy Debord," in Sussman, ed., *on the passage,* p. 74.

49. Two American video artists, Isaac Cronin and Terrel Seltzer, emulated the situationists' not particularly playful brand of pedagogy in their 1982 tape *Call It Sleep.* For a highly critical view of the Cronin/Seltzer tape, see Home, *Neoism, Plagiarism,* pp. 117–19.

50. Guy Debord, "Détournement as negation and prelude," anthologized in Iwona Blazwick, ed., *an endless passion . . . an endless banquet* (London and New York: Verso and Institute of Contemporary Arts, 1989), p. 29.

51. Guy Debord, *Society of the Spectacle and Other Films* (London: Rebel Press, 1992), p. 71.

52. Richard Dyer, *Stars* (London: British Film Institute, 1979), p. 68.

53. Greil Marcus, *Lipstick Traces: A Secret History of the Twentieth Century* (Cambridge, Mass.: Harvard University Press, 1989); Jon Savage, *England's Dreaming: Anarchy, Sex Pistols, Punk Rock and Beyond* (New York: St Martin's Press, 1991); Neil Nehring, *Flowers in the Dustbin: Culture, Anarchy, and Postwar England* (Ann Arbor: University of Michigan Press, 1993). See also Paul Taylor et al., *Impresario: Malcolm*

McLaren and the British New Wave (New York: New Museum of Contemporary Art, 1988).

54. For an account of the film's production, see Savage, *England's Dreaming,* pp. 498–502.

55. E. P. Thompson, *The Making of the English Working Class* (Harmondsworth, U.K.: Penguin, 1968), p. 78.

56. V. Vale and A. Juno in their introduction to *Pranks! (RE/Search No. 11,* San Francisco), p. 5.

57. *Village Voice* "rockbeat" column included in Negativland, *Fair Use: The Story of the Letter U and the Numeral 2* (Concord, Calif.: Seeland, 1995), p. 2. This book, which reprints many newspaper articles and all of the correspondence between Negativland and their adversaries, presents a comprehensive overview of the controversy.

58. Stewart Home, "Plagiarism," *Edinburgh Review* 78–79 (n.d.): 261. Home differentiates his notion of plagiarism from what he considers postmodernist ideologists' alienated notion of "appropriation."

59. Negativland, "Fair Use," in Ron Sakolsky and Fred Wei-Han Ho, eds., *Sounding Off! Music as Subversion/Resistance/Revolution* (Brooklyn, N.Y.: Autonomedia, 1995), p. 84.

60. See Billboard Liberation Front and Friends, *The Art and Science of Billboard Improvement* (San Francisco: Los Cabrones Press, 1990).

61. See Robert Stam, with Richard Porton and Leo Goldsmith, *Keywords in Subversive Film and Media Aesthetics* (Oxford, U.K. and Malden, Mass.: Wiley Blackwell, 2015), p. 175.

62. McKenzie Wark, *The Spectacle of Disintegration: Situationist Passages out of the Twentieth Century* (London and New York: Verso, 2013), p. 92.

63. Jarrod Shanahan, "Let's Apocalypse! A Discussion with the Anti-Banality Union," *Vice,* March 2, 2013, https://www.vice.com/en_ca/article/wdp99q/lets-apocalypse-a-discussion-with-the-anti-banality-union.

64. Chytry, *Aesthetic State,* p. xii.

65. For an account of the Munich Revolution and Landauer's ties to the city's bohemian avant-garde, see the chapter "Revolution in Bavaria," in Eugene Lunn, *Prophet of Community: The Romantic Socialism of Gustav Landauer* (Berkeley and Los Angeles: University of California Press), pp. 291–342.

66. For a discussion of *The Liberal War,* see David James, "Presence of Discourse/Discourse of Presence: Representing Vietnam," *Wide Angle* 7, no. 4 (1985): 47–48.

67. According to Erika Gottfried, this comment was on a dope sheet for a newsreel featuring an interview with Emma Goldman during her return to North America in the 1930s. This newsreel is included in Sucher and Fischler's *Anarchism in America.*

68. See D.D., "A Night at the Movies," *Resistance* (November–December 1948), pp. 9–11. Jackson Mac Low believes that the piece was written by Daniel De Wees (letter to the author, July 1996).

69. *Resistance* 9, no. 1 (June–July 1950): 5–8.

70. Patrick Brantlinger, *Bread and Circuses: Theories of Mass Culture as Social Decay* (Ithaca, N.Y. and London: Cornell University Press, 1983), p. 23.

71. A welcome exception to this trend is Gregory D. Sumner's study of Macdonald's magazine *politics*. Sumner does not endorse Macdonald's mass culture thesis, but terms it a "creative mistake . . . which prompted him to move beyond conventional boundaries in his search for a new radicalism." Sumner writes that "already in the 1940s he understood that debates about militarism and the bureaucratic state, race and gender relations, and the moral autonomy of the individual were eclipsing the class issues that had preoccupied the Old Left." See Sumner's *Dwight Macdonald and the Politics Circle* (Ithaca, N.Y. and London: Cornell University Press, 1996), pp. 86–87.

72. See, for example, James Naremore, *The Magic World of Orson Welles* (Dallas: Southern Methodist University Press, 1989), revised edition; Michael Denning, *The Cultural Front* (London and New York: Verso, 1996).

73. See Harvey Teres, *Renewing the Left: Politics, Imagination and the New York Intellectuals* (Oxford, U.K. and New York: Oxford University Press, 1996), pp. 62–64.

74. See Paul Gorman, *Left Intellectuals and Popular Culture in Twentieth-Century America* (Chapel Hill and London: University of North Carolina Press, 1994), p. 180.

75. See the appendices "The Main Enemy is in Moscow" and "I Choose the West" in Dwight Macdonald, *The Root is Man* (Brooklyn, N.Y.: Autonomedia, 1995), pp. 157–63.

76. For an account of Macdonald's resurgent radicalism during the 1960s, see Michael Wreszin, *A Rebel in Defense of Tradition: The Life and Politics of Dwight Macdonald* (New York: Basic Books, 1994), pp. 370–86. Wreszin notes that Macdonald "became involved in the defense for the cases of Morton Sobell, who had been tried for espionage with the Rosenbergs, and Junius Scales, who had been sentenced to six years in prison under the Smith Act, which made mere membership in the Communist Party a criminal activity." This alone should disprove simplistic assumptions that Macdonald was some sort of reflexive anticommunist.

77. Dwight Macdonald, *Dwight Macdonald on Movies* (Englewood Cliffs, N.J.: Prentice Hall, 1969).

78. Ibid., p. 367.

79. Umberto Eco, "The Structure of Bad Taste," in *The Open Work,* trans. Anna Cancogni (Cambridge, Mass. and London: Harvard University Press, 1989), p. 193.

80. John Fiske, *Television Culture* (London and New York: Routledge, 1988), p. viii.

81. See José Pierre, ed., *Surrealisme et anarchie* (Paris: Editions Plasma, 1983).

82. Alan Lovell, "The Importance of Criticism," *Peace News,* June 1, 1962, p. 5.

83. In this regard, a 1946 article by Jackson Mac Low anticipates the tenor of Lovell's piece by sixteen years. Mac Low reviles the "ordinary American" settings of Hollywood films, calling them "for the most part . . . sleek spotless jobs by an interior decorator with mildly "modern" ideas." This "pseudo-realism" is then connected to "the falseness that appears in the speeches of Roosevelt and Churchill and in the advertisements for the mass-produced commodities." See Mac Low's "The Movies: A Note on Falsification," *Why? An Anarchist Bulletin* 5, no. 5 (October 1946): 8–9.

84. Lovell confessed to me that he had read little on anarchism when he published *Anarchist Cinema* in 1962. He wrote that he had been influenced mainly by writings on surrealism and some articles he had read by Dwight Macdonald in *politics* (letter from Lovell to the author, September 1987).

85. Alan Lovell, "The Demigods," *Peace News,* January 11, 1963, p. 5.

86. This article is anthologized in Taylor Stoehr, ed., *Format and Anxiety—Paul Goodman Critiques the Media* (Brooklyn, N.Y.: Autonomedia, 1995), pp. 205–8.

87. See ibid., pp. 217–22.

88. Richard Kostelanetz, "Anarchist Art," *The Raven* 33, no. 1 (Spring 1996): 96.

89. Stam, Porton, and Goldsmith, *Keywords,* p. 145.

Afterword

1. See, for example, Jason Blumenfeld, Chiara Bottici, and Simon Critchley eds., *The Anarchist Turn* (London and New York: Pluto Press, 2003) and Duane Rousselle and Sureyyya Everen eds., *Post-Anarchism: A Reader* (London and New York: Pluto Press and Halifax and Winnipeg: Fernwood Press, 2011.)

2. Email from "Heatscore," April 23, 2017.

3. David Graeber, *Possibilities: Essays on Hierarchy, Rebellion, and Desire* (Oakland, Baltimore, and Edinburgh: AK Press, 2007), pp. 302–10.

4. See Iain McKay ed., *Direct Struggle Against Capital: A Peter Kropotkin Anthology* (Oakland, Baltimore, and Edinburgh: AK Press), 2014, p. 8.

5. See Vittorio Frigerio, "Aesthetic Contradictions and Ideological Representations: Anarchist Avant-Garde vs. Swashbuckling Melodrama," *Film-Philosophy* 7, no. 3 (December 2003), http://www.film-philosophy.com/vol7–2003/n53frigerio. See my reply, "Vagaries of Taste: "How 'Popular' is "Popular Culture," http://www.film-philosophy.com/vol7–2003/n57porton.

6. Nicole Brenez and Isabelle Marinone eds., *Cinémas libertaires: au service des forces de transgression et de révolte* (Villeneuve d'ascq, France: Presses Universitaires du Septentrion, 2015).

7. Gilberto Perez, *The Material Ghost* (Baltimore: Johns Hopkins University Press, 1998), p. 277.

8. Chris Ealham, *Living Anarchism; José Peirats and the Spanish Anarcho-Syndicalist Movement* (Oakland, Baltimore, and Edinburgh: AK Press, 2015), 78.

9. Jesse Cohn, *Underground Passages: Anarchist Resistance Culture: 1848–2011* (Oakland, Baltimore, and Edinburgh: AK Press, 2014).

10. Jesse Cohn, "What is Anarchist Cultural Studies? Precursors, Problems, and Prospects," anthologized in Nathan J. Jun and Shane Wahl, eds., *New Perspectives on Anarchism* (Lanham, Md.: Lexington Books, 2010), p. 419.

11. David Weir, *Anarchy & Culture: The Aesthetic Politics of Modernism* (Amherst: University of Massachusetts Press, 1997).

12. Antliff inists that "anarchist modernists did not seek refuge from 'politics' in the realm of 'culture,' as literary historian has recently claimed in *Anarchy and Culture* . . . Emma Goldman's reply to Max Eastman rings as true today as it did in

May 1919: the separation of politics from culture is a Marxist formulation, utterly foreign to anarchism." See Allan Antliff, *Anarchist Modernism: Art, Politics, and the First American Avant-Garde* (Chicago and London: University of Chicago Press, 2001), p. 263.

13. Nathan Jun, "Towards an Anarchist Film Theory: Reflections on the Politics of Cinema." https://theanarchistlibrary.org/library/nathan-jun-toward-an-anarchist-film-theory-reflections-on-the-politics-of-cinema.

14. See Michael Löwy, *Morning Star: Surrealism, Marxism, Anarchism, Situationism, Utopia* (Austin: University of Texas Press, 2009).

15. Matthew S. Adams, "*To Hell With Culture:* Fascism, Rhetoric, and the War for Democracy," *Anarchist Studies* 23, no. 2 (2015): 30. See also Michael Paraskos ed., *Rereading Read: New Views on Herbert Read* (London: Freedom Press, 2007).

16. Robert Stam, with Richard Porton and Leo Goldsmith, *Keywords in Subversive Film/Media Aesthetics* (Oxford, UK and Malden, Mass.: Wiley Blackwell, 2015), pp. 30–31.

17. Joshua Clover, *Riot. Strike: Riot: The New Era of Uprisings* (London and New York: Verso, 2016).

18. See Christopher Robé, *Breaking the Spell: A History of Anarchist Filmmakers, Videotape Guerillas, and Digital Ninjas* (Oakland: PM Press, 2017.)

19. Email from Robé, April 23, 2017.

20. Graeber, *Possibilities,* p. 328

21. Maple Razsa, *Bastards of Utopia: Living Radical Politics After Socialism* (Bloomington and Indianapolis: Indiana University Press, 2015), pp.10–12.

22. Jane Gaines, "Political Mimesis," anthologized in Jane Gaines and Michael Renov eds., *Collecting Visible Evidence* (Minneapolis: University of Minnesota Press, 1999.)

23. Theodor Adorno, "The Essay as Form" *New German Critique* 32 (Spring–Summer 1984): 151–71.

24. William J. Fishman, *East End Jewish Radicals, 1875–1914* (London: Duckworth, 1975), p. 154–55.

25. Ibid., p. 154.

26. See, for example, the discussion of Goldman and Reitman's relationship in Paul Avrich and Karen Avrich, *Sasha and Emma: The Anarchist Odyssey of Alexander Berkman and Emma Goldman* (Cambridge, Mass.: Belknap Press of Harvard University Press, 2012), pp. 197–201.

27. The complexities of Parsons's political trajectory—including her formulation of a "false biography—the story that she was the daughter of Mexican and Native American parents" and her ambiguous relationship to the Communist Party are meticulously examined in Jacqueline Jones, *Goddess of Anarchy: The Life and Times of Lucy Parsons, American Radical* (New York: Basic Books, 2017).

28. See Fredy Perlman, *Birth of a Revolutionary Movement,* a 1969 pamphlet available at https://libcom.org/history/birth-revolutionary-movement-yugoslavia.

29. Ćućrić's essay, "For an Idea, Against the Status Quo" is, from a dossier on Žilnik available online at https://www.zilnikzelimir.net/index.php/essays.

30. During a Skype conversation in July 2017, I asked Stajanovic what he meant by identifying himself as a "communist without a party." He replied that, among other things—and with respect to the legacy of the Yugoslav revolutionary project in particular—it meant that even though he agreed with the critique of socialist self-management, he strongly adhered to the concept of "social property" formulated by the Yugoslav communists.

31. Davide Turcato, *Making Sense of Anarchism: Errico Malatesta's Experiments With Revolution, 1889–1900* (Oakland, Baltimore, and Edinburgh: AK Press, 2015), p.77.

32. It is also worth noting that Lazar Stojanovic's *Plastic Jesus* (1972), an experimental film that, according to the filmmaker, reflects an "anarcho-individualist stance," was banned for eighteen years in the former Yugoslavia. Its assault on Titoist ideology was considered subversive by this ostensibly "liberal" state socialist regime.

33. Mark Bray, *Translating Anarchy: The Anarchism of Occupy Wall Street* (Winchester, UK and Washington, D.C.: Zero Books, 2013), p. 156. See also, Aragorn!, ed., *Occupy Everything: Anarchists in the Occupy Movement: 2009–2011* (Berkeley, Calif.: LBC Books; Creative Commons, 2012).

34. See Ramon Glazov, "Adbusted," *Jacobin,* October 28, 2013, https://www.jacobin mag.com/2013/10/adbusted/.

35. Email from Livingston, July 4, 2017.

36. Andréa Picard, "Film/Art: Disappearances After the Revolution: On Alberto Grifi and Massimo's Sarchielli's Anna," *Cinema Scope* 50, http://cinema-scope.com/columns/filmart-disappearances-after-the-revolution/.

37. The indebtedness of certain anarchist writers to the precepts of Athenian democracy is most evident in the work of writers such as Murray Bookchin and Cornelius Castoriadis. More recently, former SDS member James Miller has expressed skepticism concerning his youthful fealty to the concept of "participatory democracy" in *Can Democracy Work?: A Short History of a Radical Idea, From Ancient Athens to Our World* (New York: Farrar, Straus, and Giroux, 2018), pp. 228–29.

38. Email from Astra Taylor to the author, November 11, 2018.

39. See Ashanti Alston, "Beyond Nationalism, But Not Without It," https://libcom .org/library/beyond-nationalism-not-without-it.

40. See, Peter Kropotkin, "Are Prisons Necessary?" https://www.panarchy.org/kropotkin/prisons.html.

41. Hinton is quoted Timothy Shenk, "Booked: The Origins of the Carceral State," *Dissent,* August 20, 2016, https://www.dissentmagazine.org/blog/booked-origins -carceral-state-elizabeth-hinton.

42. Phillip Conklin and Mark Jay, "Opportunity Detroit," https://www.jacobinmag .com/2018/01/detroit-revival-inequality-dan-gilbert-hudsons.

43. Astra Taylor, "Prisons without Crime: Brett Story on Her Genre-Subverting Doc on Mass Incarceration, "The Prison in Twelve Landscapes," *Filmmaker,* April 14, 2016, https://filmmakermagazine.com/98021-prisons-without-crime-brett-story -on-genre-subverting-doc-on-mass-incarceration-the-prison-in-twelve-landscapes/.

44. See, for example, the anonymous statement, "Why Incarcerated Lives Matter

to the Black Lives Matter Movement: https://supportprisonerresistance.noblogs.org/post/2016/08/03/power-on-the-inside-why-incarcerated-lives-matter-to-the-black-lives-matter-movement/.

45. Keenaga-Yamahtta Taylor, *From #Black LivesMatter to Black Liberation* (Chicago, Haymarket Books, 2016), p. 219.

46. David Judd, "Police Crimes Too Big to Hide," *Socialist Worker,* June 21, 2016, https://socialistworker.org/2016/06/21/police-crimes-too-big-to-hide.

47. Kristian Williams, *Our Enemies in Blue: Police and Power in America* (Cambridge, Mass.: South End Press, 2007.)

48. Patrisse Khan-Cullors and Asha Bandele*, When They Call You a Terrorist: A Black Lives Matter Memoir* (New York: St. Martin's Press, 2018), p. 187.

49. Jay Kuehner, "Welcome to Calais: Sylvain George and the Aesthetics of Resistance, *Cinema Scope* 47, http://cinema-scope.com/cinema-scope-magazine/interviews-welcome-to-calais-sylvain-george-and-the-aesthetics-of-resistance/.

50. Howard Eiland and Michael W. Jennings, *Walter Benjamin: A Critical Life* (Cambridge, Mass. and London: Belknap Press of Harvard University Press, 2014), pp. 131–33.

51. See Uri Gordon and Ohal Grietzer, eds., *Anarchists Against the Wall: Direct Action and Solidarity With the Palestinian Popular Struggle* (Oakland: AK Press, 2013).

52. Email correspondence with Adam Khalil, March 2018; See Audra Simpson, *Mohawk Interruptus: Political Life Against the Borders of Settler States* (Durham, N.C.: Duke University Press, 2014).

53. See Aragorn!, "Locating An Indigenous Anarchism." https://theanarchist library.org/library/aragorn-locating-an-indigenous-anarchism.

54. James Miller, "What *does* Democracy Look Like," *Literary Hub* (September 21, 2018) https://lithub.com/what-does-democracy-look-like/.

55. For an account of the occupation of the Thala police station, see (Anonymous Author), "In the Heart of Tunisia: The Occupied Police Station: https://libcom.org/library/heart-tunisia-thala-occupied-police-station.

Index

RICHARD PORTON is an editor at *Cineaste* and has taught film studies at the College of Staten Island, Hunter College, Rutgers University, and New York University.

The University of Illinois Press
is a founding member of the
Association of University Presses.

―――――――――――――――――――――――

Composed in 10.75/13.5 Adobe Minion Pro
with Avenir display
by Jim Proefrock
at the University of Illinois Press
Cover designed by Jim Proefrock
Cover illustration: Cover image:
Film frames photo ©iStock.com/STILLFX
Manufactured by Sheridan Books, Inc.

University of Illinois Press
1325 South Oak Street
Champaign, IL 61820-6903
www.press.uillinois.edu